ASPECTS OF BRITISH POLITICAL HISTORY 1914–1995

Aspects of British Political History 1914–1995 examines all the major themes, personalities and issues of twentieth-century political history in a clear and digestible form.

- introduces fresh angles to long-studied topics
- consolidates a great body of recent research
- analyses views of different historians
- offers an interpretive rather than narrative approach
- gives concise treatment to complex issues ,
- directly relevant to student questions and courses
- carefully organised to reflect the way teachers tackle these courses
- Stephen Lee is an experienced textbook author
- illustrated with helpful maps, charts, illustrations and photographs

Stephen J. Lee is Head of History at Bromsgrove School. His many publications include *Aspects of British Political History 1815–1914*, *Aspects of European History* (in two volumes), *The European Dictatorships, 1918–1945*, *The Thirty Years' War* and *Peter the Great*.

Aspects of History is a series of text conceived and written by Stephen J. Lee specifically for the A-Level and first-year undergraduate history student. It introduces the reader to a wide range of interpretations, ideas and research and includes volumes covering Britain and Europe.

ASPECTS OF HISTORY
Stephen J. Lee

Already published

ASPECTS OF BRITISH POLITICAL HISTORY 1815–1914

ASPECTS OF EUROPEAN HISTORY 1494–1789

ASPECTS OF EUROPEAN HISTORY 1789–1980

In preparation

ASPECTS OF ENGLISH HISTORY 1450–1603

ASPECTS OF ENGLISH HISTORY 1603–1714

ASPECTS OF ENGLISH HISTORY 1714–1815

ASPECTS OF BRITISH POLITICAL HISTORY 1914–1995

Stephen J. Lee

London and New York

First published 1996
by Routledge
11 New Fetter Lane, London EC4P 4EE

Simultaneously published in the USA and Canada
by Routledge
29 West 35th Street, New York, NY 10001

Routledge is an International Thomson Publishing company

© 1996 Stephen J. Lee

Typeset in Garamond by Keystroke,
Jacaranda Lodge, Wolverhampton
Printed and bound in Great Britain by
TJ Press (Padstow) Ltd, Padstow, Cornwall

British Library Cataloguing in Publication Data
A catalogue record for this book is available from the British Library

Library of Congress Cataloging in Publication Data
A catalogue record for this book has been requested

ISBN 0–415–13102–2
0–415–13103–0 (pbk)

For Max and Joan

CONTENTS

List of illustrations   ix

1 Introduction to British political history 1914–95   1

2 The First World War and its impact   21

3 The decline of the Liberal party 1914–40   38

4 The 1924 Labour government   54

5 Baldwin and the Conservative ascendancy between the wars   68

6 The General Strike   82

7 The first crisis of Labour 1929–39   97

8 The economy, unemployment and government policy
  between the wars   109

9 Versailles, foreign policy and collective security 1918–33   129

10 Foreign policy and appeasement 1933–9   144

11 The Second World War and its impact   166

12 The Labour government 1945–51   179

13 The Conservative decade: domestic policies 1951–64   195

14 Years of reform and crisis 1964–79   211

15 Thatcherism and after, 1979–95   229

16 The second crisis of Labour 1979–92   247

17 Foreign policy and defence 1945–70   261

18 Foreign policy and defence 1970–95   276

19 Britain and Europe since 1945   286

20 The British Empire and Commonwealth in the twentieth
    century   304

21 The Irish issue 1914–96   320

22 Equal opportunities and women's rights in twentieth-century
    Britain   338

23 Immigration, race relations and the plural society   350

24 Primary sources for British political history 1914–95   360

    Notes   393
    Select Bibliography   410
    Index   415

ILLUSTRATIONS

FIGURES

1	Prime Ministers 1908–95	3
2	Europe in the First World War	23
3	General elections 1906–10	40
4	General election of 1918	48
5	General elections 1922–29	56
6	General elections 1931–35	101
7	Unemployment between the wars	112
8	Europe between the wars	132
9	General elections 1945–51	180
10	General elections 1955–64	196
11	General elections 1966–74	212
12	General elections 1979–92	230
13	Britain and the Cold War	265
14	Britain and the European Community	288
15	The Commonwealth in 1995	317
16	Ireland in the twentieth century	321
17	The master chemist	372
18	The splendid sword	373
19	Careless talk costs lives	374
20	Very well, alone	375
21	All behind you, Winston	376
22	Under which flag?	377
23	Under which flag?	378
24	Still hope	379
25	A great mediator	380
26	The Welfare State	381
27	Wife, child and welfare state to support	382
28	Socialists!	383

PLATES

1	Henry Herbert Asquith	44
2	David Lloyd George	45
3	James Ramsay MacDonald	59
4	Stanley Baldwin	71
5	Neville Chamberlain	149
6	Winston Churchill	170
7	Clement Attlee	184
8	Harold Macmillan and Anthony Eden	198
9	Alec Douglas Home	204
10	Harold Wilson	213
11	Edward Heath	217
12	James Callaghan	219
13	Margaret Thatcher and John Major	243

1

INTRODUCTION TO BRITISH POLITICAL HISTORY 1914–95

Like its predecessor, *Aspects of British Political History 1815–1914*, this book is intended to introduce the reader to a range of interpretations on modern Britain. It is designed to act as a basic text for the sixth-form student and to introduce the undergraduate to the increasingly wide range of ideas and research. I hope it will also capture the imagination of the general reader who likes to go beyond narrative into the realm of debate.

Why *political* history? And what does it mean? During the 1970s and 1980s there was an outpouring of books specifically on social and economic history, a departure from the older type of text, which aimed to cover all areas but within the broad context of political history. To some extent the focus on social and economic history is part of a process of establishing a new balance. In the words of G.R. Elton, the reaction against political history, 'although often ill-informed and sometimes silly, has its virtues. These arise less from the benefits conferred upon other ways of looking at the past, than from the stimulus given to political history to improve itself.'[1]

Political history now seems to be making a determined comeback, although in a more eclectic form, covering a wider spectrum and drawing from social and economic issues. It is also based more on controversy and debate and less on straight narrative.

Political history may be defined as 'the study of the organisation and operation of power in past societies'.[2] It focuses on people in positions of authority; on the impact of their power on the various levels of society; on the response of the people in authority to pressures from below; and on relationships with power bases in other countries. The study of political history fulfils three functions. One is the specific analysis of the acquisition, use and loss of power by individuals, groups, parties and institutions. A second is more generally to provide a meeting point for all other components: social, economic, intellectual and religious – these can all be brought into the arena of political history. But above all, political history offers the greatest potential for controversy and debate. As Hutton maintains, 'More than any other species of history, it involves the destruction of myths, often carefully conceived and propagated. No other variety of historian experiences to such a constant, and awesome, extent, the responsibility of doing justice to the dead'.[3]

The rest of this chapter will outline the main political issues covered in this book before considering two general themes which run through the twentieth century as a whole.

THE MAIN POLITICAL ISSUES 1914–1995

The period opens with the First World War (Chapter 2), in which Britain played a crucial military role: she increased her land-based commitment on the Western Front to equal that of France and did more than any other power to bring about the defeat of the Ottoman Empire in a war on the periphery. The surprising development of the war was that there were few major naval engagements, but British seapower ultimately proved crucial in the blockade against Germany in 1918. Overall, Britain played a more pivotal and varied military role in the First World War than in the Second. The impact of the war on Britain was considerable, expanding the scope of Government power and authority. There also occurred an upheaval in party politics resulting in the split in the Liberal party between Asquith and Lloyd George and the emergence of a coalition under the latter in 1916. The war provided Lloyd George with a launch into peacetime political ascendancy up to 1922, although ultimately he fell because of the lack of a party-political base. Chapter 2 also deals with the paradoxical impact of the war on each of the political parties, ultimately so different from what seemed most likely at the outset. It looks at the complex impact on the economy and society. In some ways the war acted as a radicalising force, while in others it accelerated, or reversed, pre-war trends. Such a traumatic experience was bound to have a wide range of contradictory results.

Chapter 3 examines the fortunes of the Liberal party. One of the great institutions of the nineteenth century, this had evolved out of the Whigs during the 1860s. The Liberals had alternated in power with the Conservatives, then experienced a bleak twenty-year period after 1885 before winning a landslide in 1906. A major theme of the period

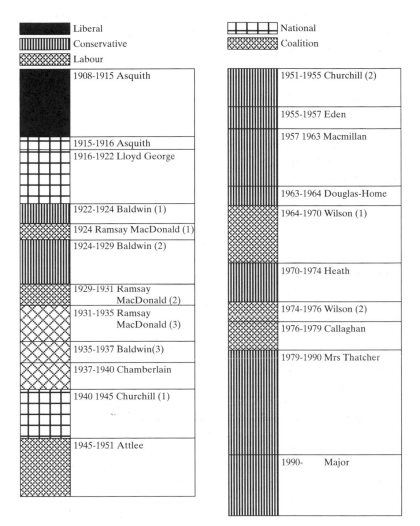

Liberal		National
Conservative		Coalition
Labour		

Figure 1 Prime Ministers 1908–95

1914–39 was the Liberals' decline as one of the two major political parties. Explanations for, and the implications of, this decline are considered. Was it already apparent before 1914? Was it the direct consequence of the First World War? And was it continuous – or were there periods of intermittent recovery?

The counterpart to Liberal decline was the rise of the Labour party.

This was relatively slow between 1900 and 1914, when it averaged 30 to 42 seats in Parliament. The First World War saw Labour make the necessary electoral breakthrough as a result of the 1918 Representation of the People Act and the decline of the Liberals. Labour was able to form its first government in 1924 because of a unique set of circumstances, dealt with in Chapter 4. As a minority government, dependent on Liberal support, it was inherently vulnerable. Its record in office was one of constraint and cautious achievement, but this was interrupted by a series of crises which brought about an early general election and a Conservative landslide.

The real beneficiaries of the upheaval of the First World War were the Conservatives, who dominated the political scene for two decades (Chapter 5). They were in power from 1922 to 1923 and between 1924 and 1929, while they also controlled the National Governments between 1931 and 1940. Above all, they scored huge election victories in 1924, 1931 and 1935. Part of their appeal was their claim to be the party of moderation and consensus, a role which Baldwin played convincingly and with skill. In large measure, however, the success of the Conservatives during this period was also due to the problems facing the Liberals and Labour. Baldwin also appeared to score a major victory in his handling of the 1926 general strike. This had roots which went deep into the crisis of the coal industry as well as the overall economic problems experienced by Britain between the wars. Chapter 6 analyses these long-term causes and the more immediate factors which turned a dispute within the coal industry into a general strike. There were clearly two sides in the conflict and battle-lines were carefully drawn between the Government and the Trades Union Congress (TUC). The population at large tended to polarise into support and opposition, and these poles often related to social class and occupation. It is, however, important to avoid too stereotypical an analysis. The eventual failure and long-term effects of the General Strike are also considered, allowing for variations in interpretation.

The General Strike did not, however, damage Labour too fundamentally because MacDonald was back in power in 1929 (Chapter 7), this time with Labour as the largest single party in the House of Commons, although lacking an overall majority. The first eighteen months of this government were relatively promising and MacDonald's achievements were more substantial than they had been in 1924. He was, however, affected by an economic disaster which was initially beyond his control. To the inexorable increase in unemployment before 1929 was added the impact of the Wall Street Crash on Britain's finances. MacDonald's response to the apparent threats to the stability of the Bank of England was to appoint the May Committee in 1931 and to act upon its recommendations for heavy cuts in public expenditure. This split the Labour party, the majority withholding its support for its leader. MacDonald therefore formed a National Government, consisting primarily of Conservatives, but also with a few Labour and Liberal ministers. Chapter 7 considers three key issues related to these events. Was MacDonald misguided in his acceptance of the May Report? Did he subsequently betray the Labour party in establishing a National Government? And did the 1931 crisis have any serious long-term effect on the Labour party?

Although it was Labour which was unfortunate enough to be caught out by the 1931 crisis, all three political parties were bemused by Britain's economic problems. In retrospect, this is not really surprising, since the inter-war economy was in a state of upheaval (Chapter 8). One feature was the decline of the traditional, or staple, industries, especially iron and steel, shipbuilding, coal and textiles. Another was the rise of several new industries, including motor vehicles, chemicals and electricity supply and manufacturing industries. The changing regional bases of industrial growth and decline were so extensive that they profoundly affected the patterns of unemployment, which reached a peak during the 1930s. This eventually fell back by 1938, although the extent of government responsibility for this is debatable. Ironically, this was also a period of growing prosperity for a large part of the population, which casts a large question mark over whether the thirties was really the 'Devil's decade'.

Meanwhile, British foreign policy had to deal with two major powers which were affected in very different ways by the First World War – Germany and Russia (Chapter 9). The former was the subject of the Treaty of Versailles, in which Britain played a vital – and controversial – role. This was followed by an attempt to shore up the post-war settlement in the form of collective security which, however, contained a significant number of defects. These included a huge gap in the arrangements to contain Germany: unlike France, Britain confined its policy of containment to western Europe and expressed a total unwillingness to become involved in the east. This was largely because of a persistent suspicion of Soviet Russia which cancelled out the more positive relations developed with and around Germany.

Collective security was therefore inherently vulnerable. During the 1930s it was replaced by appeasement as Britain's response to European problems and threats (Chapter 10). To a certain extent, however, it had always been one of the strands of collective security and was therefore in part a logical consequence of it. The practical results were that Britain put pressure on France to cut her security connections with eastern Europe and to accept without serious objection Hitler's re-militarisation of the Rhineland in 1936, his Anschluss (1938), and the annexation of the Sudetenland to Germany in 1938. Chamberlain's record at the Munich Conference in September 1938 has attracted more controversy than any other action in foreign policy over the whole century. The theories behind this are therefore considered at length, as are those for the reversal of appeasement in 1939 and the guarantee to Poland which eventually led to Britain's declaration of war on Germany on 2 September 1939.

For the second time in a quarter of a century, therefore, Britain was involved in total war (Chapter 11). Unlike the First World War, Britain's military role was largely on the periphery – in North Africa and Italy, at sea, and in the air. Britain was the combatant which kept the war going long enough for the Soviet Union and the United States to become involved and finish Germany off. During the whole process, Winston Churchill provided highly effective leadership, although his precise role has been subject to some reinterpretation. In political terms, Britain established an authoritarian government much more quickly in the Second World War than in the First, although full democracy returned rapidly in 1945. There is no doubt that the war benefited Labour much more than the Conservatives, healing their rift of the 1930s, while it all but finished off the Liberals. Economically, the war continued the process of British decline, while socially there were more consequences than after the First World War. This was canalised in the Beveridge Report of 1942, which provided the theoretical foundations of the modern welfare state and especially the National Health Service. The precise extent to which such changes were due to the war, is, however, debatable.

Even before the end of the Second World War a general election was held in Britain which swept Churchill out of office and gave Labour a huge overall majority – its first ever (Chapter 12). At the time this result came as a major shock, but most historians argue that it should not have done – that it was the result of Britain being radicalised by the experience of war and by the increased expectations of social reform, which Labour was considered most likely to deliver. The changes made by the 1945–51 Labour government were fundamental. They included the welfare state, with its integral national health service, and the nationalisation of a number of key industries and enterprises.

These have been considered a radical break with the past and the introduction of a new type of state with more centralised governmental controls. But was this true? It could also be argued that the changes which emerged after 1945 had their roots very much in the periods 1905–14, 1914–18 and 1918–39, as well as in the second experience of total war.

After establishing the welfare state, Labour gave way to the Conservatives (Chapter 13), who won three general elections in a row in 1951, 1955 and 1959. The Conservatives retained most of the reforms which had been introduced by the Attlee government, deciding only to renationalise the steel industry. The length of their tenure of office was due partly to the effectiveness of ministers like Butler, Maudling, Macleod, Macmillan and Heath and partly to a series of favourable objective factors. These included a period of economic growth which the Conservatives claimed as their doing, an assertion which is examined. They also benefited from Labour's internal divisions between the left, who wanted to press on with the destruction of the capitalist system and the abandonment of nuclear weapons, and the right, led by Gaitskell. The decline of the Conservatives was due to the reversal of the earlier factors which had operated in their favour. After 1960 the economy took a downturn and had serious political effects with which Macmillan could not cope. The Conservatives also faced a series of scandals, to which most ailing governments seem to be prone. Meanwhile, Labour had recovered its unity with the reconciliation of the left and right under the pragmatic leadership of Harold Wilson. This enabled him to win a narrow majority in the 1964 general election, which he substantially increased the following year.

The period 1964–79 saw a full return to two-party politics: Labour under Wilson dominated the period 1964–70, the Conservatives under Heath were in power between 1970 and 1974, and Labour returned between 1974 and 1979, initially under Wilson, who was succeeded by Callaghan. It was a period of crisis and reforms (Chapter 14). The latter saw an attempt to deal with a wide range of issues which had been shelved by the Conservatives between 1951 and 1964. Reforms affected the civil service and other areas of the administration, local government, moves towards devolution for Scotland and Wales, changes in the House of Commons committee system, attempts to modernise the House of Lords, enlargement of the electorate by reducing the voting age to 18, and a wide range of bills covering social issues including the death penalty, sexual offences, divorce, race relations, sex discrimination, industrial relations. Crisis affected mainly the economy, with balance of payments deficits, inflation and industrial disruption on a scale unknown since the 1920s. This accelerated during the 1970s. Heath attempted to move towards government de-control, but failed. The crisis in industrial relations had a profound political impact, helping more than anything else to bring down Heath in February 1974 and Callaghan in 1979.

The election of 1979 was to prove one of the most significant of the twentieth century. It brought to power a prime minister who was determined to reverse the previous consensus that had existed between Labour and the Conservatives about the broad stream of economic and social policy (Chapter 15). She was committed to reducing the role of government, although ironically this meant the actual extension of its powers. She based her economic policies upon the principles of monetarism, she introduced the notion of privatisation and restructured central and local government. She was able to do all this as a result of three successive election victories in 1979, 1983 and 1987. In these she was assisted partly by external factors, such as the Falklands War of 1982 which diverted public opinion from the unpopularity of her earlier policies, and partly because of the divisions within Labour. Overall, some observers have advanced the claim that there was a 'Thatcher revolution', although it could be asked whether her policies were primarily ideological or opportunist.

Meanwhile, the Conservatives were given an extended lease on power by the second crisis to have affected the Labour party (Chapter 16). Following their defeat in the 1979 general election, Labour experienced a substantial swing to the left, which gave the leadership to Michael Foot and caused the withdrawal of the right to form the new Social Democratic Party (SDP). Labour's policies also moved leftwards, including a commitment to unilateral nuclear disarmament. The party was, however, severely embarrassed by the activities of its far-left Trotskyist fringe and by the massive erosion of support from the sectors of the population who traditionally supported it. The loss of four consecutive general elections forced a review of both the organisation and policy of the Labour party. This was undertaken by Kinnock, Smith and Blair, who moved the party steadily back towards the centre ground and adopted a more pragmatic approach in the tradition of Gaitskell and Wilson. Although Labour lost the 1992 general election, their recovery was well under way and by 1995 they seemed well placed to win the next election.

Returning to 1945, another strand in Britain's post-war history was her foreign policy (Chapter 17). Britain emerged from the Second

World War convinced that she could continue her role as one of the superpowers. This was largely because of her role, along with the United States and the Soviet Union, in defeating Nazi Germany. During the 1940s Britain took the leading role in the Cold War, often having to prod the United States into securing Europe against perceived Soviet aggression. This goes against the more traditional view that Britain was a moderating force in the Cold War. By the beginning of the 1950s it became clear that Britain was overstretching herself in her foreign commitments and measures were already being considered to reduce these. It was, however, the 1956 Suez Crisis which confirmed and accelerated the trend, although there is an historical debate on the extent to which Suez damaged British interests in the Middle East. A major factor in the changes in British defence policy after 1956 was the need to modernise Britain's defences without increasing expenditure: this was to remain the most important theme for the next forty years. The turning point was the 1957 Sandys White Paper, which combined a streamlining of conventional forces with the adoption of nuclear weapons within a special relationship with the United States. A further acknowledgement of a declining world role came with the reduction and ending of imperial commitments in the early 1960s, which in turn meant that it made more sense for Britain to consider a closer defence relationship with Europe – a theme pursued by Conservative and Labour governments. The clinching argument was the economic crisis which seemed constantly to affect Britain after 1965.

After 1970 foreign policy took some strange twists (Chapter 18). At first a Conservative government under Heath tried to increase Britain's defence role, only to be defeated by economic problems and the impact of the situation in the Middle East. Heath also gave priority to membership of the EEC. Wilson initially cut back on defence after returning to power in 1974, only for Callaghan to increase Britain's commitment to European defence – largely because of the declining role of US defence as a result of Carter's presidency. Mrs Thatcher sought to honour previous commitments for increased expenditure and brought policy back to 1957. At the same time, she decided to upgrade nuclear weapons from Polaris to Trident. Since this accompanied increased expenditure on defence in Europe, the result had to be cuts in the navy. The South Atlantic therefore became the vulnerable area, which was exploited by General Galtieri in Argentina's invasion of the Falklands in 1982. The war which followed briefly revived Britain's military prestige and allowed Mrs Thatcher to claim that Britain had recovered some of her world standing as well. She cultivated a new friendship with the United States and emphasised the importance of Britain's role in the Cold War. In reality, little had changed. Further defence cuts followed during the 1990s and the end of the Cold War seemed to reduce the need for Britain's commitments in Europe. Future 'rationalisation' – or contraction – seemed likely by the end of the century.

The counterbalance for decline as a world power was the search for a more distinctively regional role (Chapter 19). This inevitably meant closer involvement with Europe. But Britain sought this very much on her terms and consistently tried to avoid the integrationist pattern preferred by the continental states. Hence, during the 1940s Britain steered the first attempt at co-operation into a loose economic structure and a traditional style of military alliance, the North Atlantic Treaty Organisation (NATO). When, during the 1950s, the European Communities were formed by France, West Germany, Italy, Belgium, the Netherlands and Luxembourg, Britain sought to develop a looser free trade area. During the 1960s and 1970s, however, Britain became convinced of the need to join the EEC, which was finally accomplished in 1973. Even then, Britain showed anti-integrationist tendencies and there was some debate, analysed in Chapter 19, as to whether Britain actually gained on balance from membership.

The transition to a European state overlapped Britain's decline as an imperial power (Chapter 20). Although the British Empire reached its greatest extent immediately after the First World War, a number of decisions had to be taken in the 1920s and 1930s about its future. The most successful of these was the confirmation and refinement of dominion status in the 1931 Statute of Westminster. Attempts to deal with other problems, such as the status of India and Palestine, were interrupted by the Second World War. After 1945 the European imperial powers experienced a wave of anti-colonial pressure. Britain reacted more positively than France or the Netherlands and the process of her decolonisation was therefore more orderly. It was also accompanied by the emergence of the Commonwealth, an organisation which was sufficiently loose and amorphous to adapt successfully to a post-colonial role.

Chapters 17 to 20 placed the focus on Britain's external role. There is one further dimension to examine – an issue which was once internal but had become externalised. Ireland (Chapter 21) has consistently been the most complex regional problem faced by the United Kingdom. United with Britain by the 1800 Act of Union it seemed on course for Home Rule, when this was disrupted by the outbreak of war in 1914. The First World War radicalised the whole situation, bringing about the decline of the moderate Irish Nationalists and boosting the more extreme republicanism of Sinn Fein and, in strong opposition, the Ulster Unionists of the North. The result in 1922 was partition rather than Home Rule. Thereafter, the experience of the two parts of Ireland was very different. The South managed to overcome its extreme republicanism, to marginalise Sinn Fein, and to evolve into a moderate bipartisan system. The North, by contrast, remained dominated by inflexible Unionism until the outbreak of disturbances in 1968. Following the imposition of direct rule from Westminster in 1972, the British Government tried a variety of policies to resolve the problem, eventually arriving at an all-Irish solution, involving a complex relationship with the Irish Republic.

The two final chapters cover the political, social and economic changes experienced by women and by immigrants. The paradox here is that the actual majority of the population were treated over much of the twentieth century as minority groups. Between them these constituted over 60 per cent of the population. In each case there was a long haul to the achievement of equality and integration. In the case of women (Chapter 22), the political franchise, extended in 1918 and 1928, preceded the concession of other rights. Full social equality was achieved only during the 1960s and 1970s with a series of measures designed to remove direct or indirect discrimination in the workplace. By 1995 it still appeared that women's opportunities, although much more broadly based, tapered very narrowly at the highest levels of industry, the professions and, despite Britain having a woman prime minister, in politics. Finally, Britain has always been a multi-cultural society, consisting as it has done of four home nations and a number of regional entities. But, as the centre of a worldwide empire, it attracted large numbers of immigrants from overseas (Chapter 23), paradoxically mainly after the process of decolonisation had started. Measures taken by the British government covered two separate – but related – issues: immigration and integration. Immigration controls were relaxed immediately after the Second World War in an effort to fill vacant posts with certain sectors, only to be tightened up from 1962 onwards. At the same time, legislation was introduced on race relations to ensure that discrimination was squeezed out. There was, however, a backlash, with pressure from minority groups for the repatriation of Commonwealth immigrants, and far right wing movements threatening and committing acts of violence against the black communities.

TWO KEY ISSUES IN THE TWENTIETH CENTURY

Issue 1: British decline?

It is a common assertion that Britain reached the peak of her economic strength between 1850 and 1875, before being gradually overhauled by a newly united Germany and a newly healed United States. During the forty years before the First World War, the main manifestations of British power were imperial and maritime: Britain had a worldwide commitment, while Germany came increasingly to dominate the Continent.

The First World War is often seen as the beginning of the long process of British decline (Chapter 1). If so, we should distinguish between economic decline, which was inexorable, and continuing political and military influence. In some respects, as Chapter 9 shows, Britain had never been better off by comparison with her rivals. Germany had been crushed, France was depleted, Russia had been through revolution and civil war, the United States was withdrawing into isolation. The British Empire was larger than it had ever been and the navy was as yet still larger than that of the United States. Yet, in many ways, this was all comparative. British strength existed because of German weakness: this did not last much beyond the beginning of the 1930s.

Meanwhile, British economic decline was an important factor between the wars (Chapter 8). Again, this was relative: the staple industries were fundamentally affected by the contraction of overseas markets, while the new industries began to take part of their place, but it was clear that Britain was slipping further behind the United States and Germany in the long-term economic perspective which goes back into the period before 1914.

All the same, the general balance was that between the wars Britain was still one of the world's great powers. Could the same be said of the period after 1945? Here great-power status was a delusion. Because Britain had been one of the victorious Big Three during the Second World War, successive governments tried to join in the superpower stakes. Chapter 17 shows how Britain actually forced the pace of American foreign policy after 1945 and sought to maintain her imperial role. In the process, Britain chose not to become part of a regional grouping with other European states, thereby missing out on the earlier stages of European integration which were to prove such an important part in the recovery of Italy, France and Germany (Chapter 19).

12

Again, however, the economic base had contracted, this time to the point where Britain was forced to cut back on her overseas commitments. The process was already under way before the 1956 Suez crisis, but the latter confirmed that Britain's role was in the process of fundamental change (Chapter 17). Documents like the 1957 Sandys White Paper called this rationalisation. The rest of the world saw it as decline. Decolonisation was another part of the process (Chapter 20); Dean Acheson's much publicised view that Britain had lost an Empire but not yet found a role was characteristic of this.

Several developments followed the acknowledgement of decline. One was the adoption of nuclear weapons: Britain became a nuclear power because she acknowledged her decline on the world scene, not because she wished to prolong the pretence that she was a superpower (Chapter 17). Nuclear weapons placed the emphasis on defence, not active involvement. Unlike the United States and the Soviet Union, Britain did not after 1956 seek to increase her conventional forces as well. It was the latter which ensured continuing status as a major power, since only conventional weapons can be used in maintaining influence throughout the world. Thus it is significant that, as Britain adopted Polaris nuclear weapons systems in the 1960s, she also withdrew from east of Suez; as she upgraded Polaris to Trident in the 1980s, she also withdrew her presence from the South Atlantic (Chapter 18). Meanwhile, Britain sought to perpetuate her importance in a 'special relationship' with the United States. But this was also a manifestation of decline. Macmillan succeeded in persuading Eisenhower to accept this relationship in 1957, even though it had been rejected in 1947, precisely because Britain *was* in decline and no longer a challenge to American hegemony.

There were occasional attempts to revive Britain's perceived importance. One example was Eden's attempt in 1956 to reassert Britain's primacy in the Middle East and frustrate the designs of Gamal Nasser (Chapter 17). Another was Mrs Thatcher's use of a highly opportune victory over Argentina in the 1982 Falklands War to revive British prestige (Chapter 18). On the other hand, any revival was illusory and it would be too much to say that Britain's role subsequently expanded. Instead, regional commitments continued to be the main target. Even though Mrs Thatcher revived Britain's status as junior partner of the United States and backed President Reagan's tough stance in the Cold War, Britain played comparatively little part in the collapse of the Soviet Union. She was also unable to resist the inexorable cutting of defence expenditure to make way for other priorities.

These were the result of the more constant and insidious form of decline – economic. This was always there below the surface in the 1950s (Chapters 11 and 13), as the infrastructure of Britain's world economic role had been severely damaged during the Second World War. The 1950s had disguised the decline, but a series of economic problems hit Britain almost continuously after the early 1960s (Chapter 14). In these circumstances active involvement on the world scene became an irrelevance, especially since, by the 1970s, Britain had, in terms of gross domestic product (GDP) fallen behind France and Italy as well as the United States, Japan and Germany.

A comparison between Britain in 1914 and Britain in 1995 therefore shows that Britain had slipped from the position of a world power to that of regional influence on the outer fringes of Europe, while 'the British Empire' had been replaced by 'the Commonwealth of Nations' (Chapter 20). Decline is a descriptive term and clearly applies to Britain's twentieth-century experience. Yet it is also highly loaded and politically charged. The right of the political spectrum tends to focus on the manifestations of decline as reduced involvement on the world scene, contracting armed forces and lower economic influence on the open and competitive market. The left, by contrast, would see 'decline' in these terms in a more positive light. It could be argued that decline has really meant the changing of priorities. For example, the cost of the welfare state was the contraction of British military prestige worldwide (Chapters 12 and 17); the recognition of Third World rights and nationalism was paid for by the quite deliberate process of decolonisation (Chapter 20) which, it should be remembered, was far smoother and less painful than that experienced by the French, the Dutch and the Belgians.

Decline can therefore be understood in the positive sense of maturing and moderating. These are gains which offset the losses of prestige which were once so important. The one factor which is constant to both, however, is the economic performance. Ultimately this is what caused the choices to be made which reflected Britain's decline. It also cast positive light or negative shadows upon it.

Issue 2: British consensus?

One of the key concepts offered by modern political analysts is the operation of consensus in British politics and society, both between the two world wars and since 1945. In particular instances this is open to different interpretations and the details will be discussed in virtually every chapter. For the time being, a general statement of the argument may be advanced as follows.

Political consensus implies a general acceptance of certain broad principles by the major political parties within the electoral arena. It does not, however, mean agreement on all issues and there will be attempts made by each party to exploit certain differences for the sake of its own political identity. In particular, the traditional confrontational politics of the British parliamentary system has to be maintained. Consensus can therefore still be associated with conflict. At the same time, it prevents violent swings between government policies; instead there is an underlying continuity in the way in which governments dealt with the key areas such as the economy, industry, welfare, foreign policy and defence. There have been several distinct periods during the twentieth century when political consensus seems to have operated.

The first example was the First World War, during which a national emergency brought a suspension of party rivalries and the emergence of a coalition government under Lloyd George in 1916 (see Chapter 2). This continued well into peacetime, the Conservatives continuing to co-operate with the Lloyd George Liberals until 1922. There was thus a huge majority in Parliament for government policies. The ending of the coalition brought a different type of consensus, based upon a return to normal party politics. There were widespread fears that the rise of Labour would radicalise British politics and widen the gulf between left and right, but in fact the reverse occurred. The 1920s were generally a period of moderation and continuity. Baldwin, Prime Minister in 1923 and from 1924 to 1929, moved the ideas and policies of the Conservatives quite deliberately towards the central ground (Chapter 5). Labour moved towards the centre from the left when Ramsay MacDonald was in Downing Street in 1924 (Chapter 4) and between 1929 and 1931 (Chapter 7). It is true that there were instances of direct ideological confrontation, especially over the Zinoviev Letter in 1924 (Chapter 4) and the General Strike in 1926 (Chapter 6). But, by and large, the two main parties either pursued moderation to enhance their electoral support at the expense of the declining Liberal party (Chapter 3) or they had moderation forced upon them by the serious nature of the inter-war economic problems (Chapter 8). Indeed, the 1931 financial crisis imposed such political pressures that consensus was re-cast into something resembling the earlier coalition. The National Governments between 1931 and 1939 were based upon a broad electoral agreement between the Conservatives, most of the Liberals and a few Labour MPs; MacDonald won a huge majority in the general election of 1931 and Baldwin another in 1935. The National Government was eventually subsumed during the Second World War in Churchill's coalition government. Based again on the needs of the moment, this was more widely based than the National Government, since it included representatives from the Labour party as a whole (Chapter 11).

The period after 1945 saw the return of the bipartisan system in which Labour and the Conservatives contested power against each other, with the Liberals ceasing for a while to have much impact. This did not, however, end the experience of consensus which had developed earlier; instead, consensus was redefined within an informal mode rather than as a National or coalition government. During the war there had been a broad measure of agreement about the need for future reforms and both the major parties accepted in broad terms the neo-Keynesian line of state intervention in economic and social issues. Attlee's Labour government of 1945–51 did much to put into operation the basic measures of the welfare state and the National Health Service (Chapter 12). The Conservatives, it is true, resisted certain specific measures and fought especially hard against the nationalisation of the steel industry. But, when they resumed power in 1951, the Conservatives retained most of the reforms Labour had introduced (Chapter 13). It has been said that politics operated rather like a ratchet. Because undoing the Labour programme would have been so difficult, the Conservatives were forced to move their whole position leftwards. Some Conservative ministers, like Butler, MacLeod, and Macmillan, fitted well into this new consensus. The Labour leader, Gaitskell, in turn, resisted pressures to take the Labour party through to the radical left (Chapter 13). So strong was the overlap between Butler and Gaitskell that the phrase 'Butskellism' was coined. Party conflicts continued as normal, but the most serious disagreements were over external issues like the 1956 Suez Crisis.

Between 1964 and 1979, however, consensus wobbled badly without, as yet, being overturned. Faced with mounting economic problems, both Labour and the Conservatives sought initially to apply more radical measures, before being forced to move back towards the centre (Chapter 14). Wilson moved his 1964–70 administration further in the direction of government control, only to return to more traditional expedients. Heath (1970–4) at first tried to cut taxes and curb trade union powers but was forced to abandon these measures by the rise in oil prices and industrial unrest. Wilson attempted another shift to the left between 1974 and 1976, only for Callaghan (1976–9) to have to apply the sort of measures to try to bring about economic recovery which were considered almost right-wing. Consensus therefore re-imposed itself despite attempts to break free from it. Beneath the surface, however, two important trends were occurring. One was the capture of the soul of the Conservative party by Mrs Thatcher, who won its leadership contest in 1975. Her ideas were based on monetarism rather than neo-Keynesianism, upon minimal rather than sustained government intervention to deal with key economic issues such as unemployment. The other was the swing of much of the Labour party to the left, preparing the way in the future for a major split within Labour's ranks.

The 1979 general election brought to power a leader determined to replace consensus with 'conviction politics'. Her three Conservative administrations, which lasted from 1979 to 1990, made monetarism and privatisation the key components of her economic policies (Chapter 15), while Labour resisted fiercely and, under Michael Foot (1981–4), moved strongly to the left (Chapter 16). Never at any point since 1918 had the ideologies of the two parties been so far apart and it seemed that the overlap between Baldwin and MacDonald, or between Butler and Gaitskell, had gone forever. Or had it? By 1991 it seemed that consensus was beginning to make a comeback – but for tactical rather than ideological reasons. The first move was made by Labour, as Kinnock expelled the far left. Smith and Blair continued the move back to the centre by accepting that at least some of Mrs Thatcher's measures could not be undone in the future (Chapter 16). In effect, they were acknowledging the move of the ratchet to the right, just as the Conservatives in the 1950s had not been able to undo the ratchet to the left. The process was further assisted by the challenge to Mrs Thatcher's position in 1990 and her replacement as Conservative leader and Prime Minister by the more moderate John Major (Chapter 15). The ideological and policy gap between the parties had narrowed by 1995, even though the polemics and personal attacks were as strong as ever. The question – still to be answered – was this: had consensus actually returned, or was it merely a political regrouping for a future migration from the central ground? An answer is attempted in Chapter 16.

The extent of consensus was, therefore, considerable in domestic policy, with the exception of the period between 1979 and about 1993. Did the same apply to foreign policy and defence? By and large it did. Labour strongly pressed Britain's status as a great power during the 1940s (Chapter 17), with the Conservatives in full agreement. There was similar consensus over Britain's involvement in the Korean War (1950–3). The Suez Crisis of 1956, it is true, attracted unanimous Labour criticism, but there were also misgivings within the Conservative party, resulting in the premature retirement of Eden in 1957. Labour could find little objection to the subsequent rationalisation of Britain's military role which meant, in effect, the reduction of her conventional forces (Chapter 17). There was some controversy over Britain's increase in nuclear weapons, but this was within the Labour party, not between the official policies of the government and the opposition. Indeed, the decision that Britain should be a nuclear power was originally taken by Attlee's Labour administration and eventually seen through by Macmillan and the Conservatives, with the support of the leadership of the Labour opposition under Gaitskell. Labour and the Conservatives followed broadly similar policies on conventional defence forces between 1964 and 1979 (Chapters 17 and 18); Heath aimed to expand Britain's role slightly, but it was Labour under Callaghan which proposed an increase in the expenditure to give Britain a more credible European role.

All this seems to indicate that foreign and defence policies were pursued with some continuity between 1945 and 1979. But what about the period after 1979, when domestic consensus so obviously came apart? There are examples of the same thing happening in foreign policy (Chapter 18). The Labour party, under Foot, abandoned the traditionally accepted policy of nuclear deterrence, making defence for the first time one of the key issues of contention between the parties. On the other hand, consensus re-established itself in this area more quickly than over domestic issues. Kinnock realised that Labour's defeat in the 1987 general election was due partly to Labour's feeble defence policy: acceptance of the nuclear deterrent therefore made a tactical return. Meanwhile, the Conservatives recognised that the state of the economy required further cuts in conventional defence expenditure – with which Labour could hardly quibble. A common factor in this new consensus was that defence was peripheral to the real battleground – domestic policies.

Consensus came more slowly over the issue of Britain's involvement in the European Economic Community (Chapter 19). This was initially pressed most strongly by the Liberals and then adopted by Macmillan as official Conservative policy from 1960. Labour became converted after 1964; Heath's Conservative government finally gained admission in the early 1970s; and Wilson's second Labour administration renegotiated the terms in Britain's favour in 1975. Britain's move to Europe can therefore be seen as an inter-party issue, with opposition coming within parties – mainly from the Conservative right wing and the Labour left. After 1979 the Labour party as a whole projected a much stronger anti-European stance, especially between 1981 and 1987. But, as with defence, Kinnock saw the need to accept the current situation. This meant that the leadership of both the main parties, along with the Liberal Democrats, followed a policy which was pro-European, if suspicious of further integration. Again, the real conflict came within the parties, the anti-European element of the Conservatives doing much to embarrass Major's administration in 1994.

In two areas there has been almost complete consensus throughout the period since 1945. One is Ireland, both parties condemning the policies of the IRA and favouring the progressive movement to the all-Ireland solution examined in Chapter 21. Another is the decision to decolonise and convert the British Empire into the Commonwealth of Nations (Chapter 20). Although there were factions within the two main parties which considered the pace to be too fast, or too slow, there was no fundamental disagreement between the parties themselves. Independence was given by Labour and the Conservatives in more or less equal measure.

Has there been social consensus, relating to social class, to gender and to ethnic origin? At first sight, such an idea might seem paradoxical, yet this is an area in which the debate is just as constructive as in politics and decision-making.

On the one hand, social class might seem a very unpromising area for consensus, since it has remained more strongly based in Britain than in almost any other western state. On the other hand, it has been progressively reduced by the democratising effect of two world wars (Chapters 2 and 11) and by the political consensus on the need to redistribute wealth and establish the welfare state (Chapters 12 and 13). It would also be wrong to see social classes as a fixed entity. Instead, the boundaries between them are always changing and even the social categories of A, B, C1 and C2 are open to considerable re-interpretation. The way in which social classes relate to political parties can also be misleading. The stereotypes of the Liberals and Conservatives as middle-class parties and Labour as the party of the working class will not do. The Conservatives have always had a substantial working-class base, while Labour has aimed to detach as many middle-class voters as possible. Public opinion polls indicate substantial shifts of voting behaviour at various stages. Labour attracted a large part of the middle-class vote in the 1940s and again in 1965, while polls in 1994 and 1995 seemed to indicate that this trend was returning. The Conservatives won a large proportion of the working-class vote in the 1980s, amounting to an overall majority in 1983 (Chapter 15).

As controversial as social class is the issue of gender (Chapter 22). At the beginning of the century there was a broad disagreement between the parties on the issue of women's suffrage. The Liberals opposed, Labour pressed their cause, while the Conservatives enjoyed the political discomfiture suffered by both. Enfranchisement was supported by all parties at the end of the First World War, but the subsequent development of social equality meant different things to different parties until a broad consensus emerged during the 1960s and 1970s with the pursuit of legislation on equal opportunities. Differences remained, but these were to be found within rather than between parties. Gender issues were not a fundamental question with most of the population, indicating that there was generally a consensus perhaps qualified by an underlying feeling that women were expected to carry an inequitable share of domestic work. At the fringes, however, were two influences which periodically moved towards the central ground and reduced the consensus. One was the influence of feminism, the other the pressure for the return of women to domestic and child-caring roles.

Potentially the most volatile issue is immigration and race relations (Chapter 23). Almost every country of mixed ethnic composition has seen periods of racial tension. Britain has been no exception, with periodic race riots, with the activities of the British Union of Fascists in the 1930s and the National Front in the 1970s, and the inner-city violence of the 1980s. On the other hand, these have been exceptional. The norm has been for steady integration and the absorption of the skills of ethnic communities within the economy. It could be argued that a consensus has developed about the rights of communities. Whether this actually means that integration has been achieved is, of course, another issue. As in all the cases referred to, Britain by 1995 was poised at a particular stage in her evolution where certain trends might be predictable in outline, but where variable and unknown external factors made alternative courses and patterns possible.

2

THE FIRST WORLD WAR
AND ITS IMPACT

The official reason given for Britain's declaration of war on 4 August 1914 was the German invasion of Belgium, which was intended to deliver a rapid knock-out blow against France. Britain had undertaken by the Treaty of London (1839) to guarantee Belgian neutrality. To a large extent, however, Belgium was the pretext to enable the Prime Minister, H. H. Asquith, and the Foreign Secretary, Sir Edward Grey, to persuade wavering members of the Cabinet to honour Britain's commitments to France.[1] The strange truth is that, although the British Government had no formal alliance with France, it considered that it was honour-bound to go to war on her behalf. This was the result of the gradual tightening up of relations between the two countries ever since the 1904 Anglo-French *Entente*. The scope of the agreement had initially been confined to resolving their disputes in Egypt and Morocco but this was gradually extended to a diplomatic undertaking to protect each other's interests; hence Britain had sided with France against Germany at the 1906 Algeciras Conference and over the Agadir Crisis in 1911. Britain had also geared her defensive response to an ever-increasing German threat by undertaking military and naval co-operation with France. By 1914 Britain was committed to defend the French coastline in the event of a German attack, in return for a French promise to defend the Mediterranean. Britain had also made preparations to despatch a British Expeditionary Force (BEF) to assist the French armies to repel a German attack. By 1914, therefore, a *de facto* alliance existed between Britain and France, although the precise nature of Britain's military obligations was to be defined more precisely after the actual outbreak of war.

This chapter will examine Britain's military role in the war, together with the political, social and economic impact of the war on Britain in the future. These themes will tie in with all the other chapters on the inter-war period.

THE CONDUCT OF THE WAR

Britain's role in the defeat of the Central Powers divides naturally into one which was land-based, or continental, one which was peripheral, and one which was within her longstanding naval traditions. How crucial were these?

The initial contributions to the land-based war were influenced by the perception that Britain was primarily a sea-power. The British Expeditionary Force, under Sir John French, comprised only four divisions in August 1914, compared with the French power of seventy divisions and the German of seventy-two. In the early stages, therefore, the British played a supporting role; they can be seen as the top edge of the blade, but the French provided the blade itself. The BEF slowed down the German advance at Mons in August, but it was the French who bore the full brunt of the German attack at the Marne in September, thereby destroying the Schlieffen Plan. The BEF was more crucial in its own right at the first Battle of Ypres between October and November 1914 and von Kluck, the German commander, observed that the BEF had been the main factor in preventing the German capture of Paris. In the process, over half the British contingent had been killed or wounded. At this point Britain's military contribution was steadily upgraded. The first attempt to do this was through Lord Kitchener's scheme of voluntary recruitment which produced, by early 1915, over 1 million British troops, with further additions from Canada, Australia, New Zealand, South Africa and India. These played a vital role at Neuve Chapelle, Loos and the second Battle of Ypres. The final stage was the introduction of conscription in May 1916, which placed Britain on an equal footing with France in bearing the brunt of German strength. While the French defended Verdun, the British attacked the Germans on the Somme. Casualties mounted rapidly to about 420,000 (compared with 194,000 French and 465,000 German).[2] Despite the futility of this offensive, for which the High Command under Haig was strongly criticised, it has been argued that the Somme and Verdun between them broke the back of the German armies. British troops were also involved in the third Battle of Ypres, or Passchendaele, in which they suffered 324,000 casualties. In the same year, there was a major British initiative at Cambrai, with the first use of tanks to break through German lines. Overall, the British military contribution to the war in France was unsurpassed by any other power – and was to be considerably more important to the eventual defeat of Germany than Britain's campaigns on the western front during the Second World War.

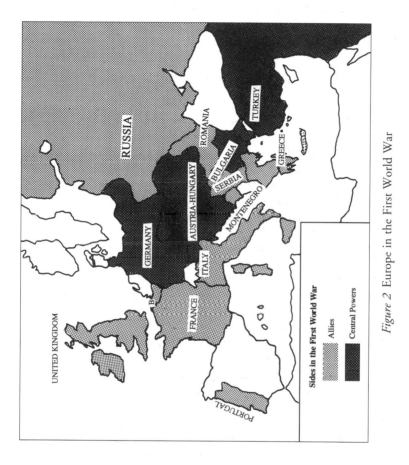

Figure 2 Europe in the First World War

Britain had on many previous occasions used a peripheral strategy of attacking a continental enemy from different directions. During the First World War, in the Dardanelles campaign of 1915, an attempt was made to assist Russia against the Turks, the reverse of what had happened in the Crimean War (1854–6). The aim was to develop supply lines to Russia to enable the latter to increase its war effort against Germany and thereby relieve the pressure of the Germans on the Western Front. There would be the added advantage of enticing Greece and Romania into the war which would, in turn, increase the pressure on Austria-Hungary. But the whole campaign was a failure and the British and Empire landings at Gallipoli could not be sustained. Much more successful were the British military campaigns in Iraq and Palestine. British forces captured Baghdad in 1917 and an extensive Arab revolt against the Turks was organised by T.E. Lawrence. British troops drove the Turks back and Allenby captured Jerusalem in 1917 and Damascus in 1918. Britain therefore did more than any other power to eliminate Turkey, which signed an armistice on 30 October.

Before the outbreak of war it had always been taken for granted, first, that British seapower was fundamental and, second, that this would be asserted by victories in battle. After all, the last naval engagement on classical lines had been as recent as 1905 – the Japanese victory over the Russian fleet at Tsushima. The first assumption was correct, but not the second. During the First World War there were no spectacular engagements, largely because both sides avoided risking their fleets. This applied as much to Admiral Jellicoe as it did to the Germans. Neither of the war's two major engagements, the Falklands (December 1914) and Jutland (May 1916) can be compared with Tsushima nor, for that matter, with Trafalgar. The importance of Jutland was not that it produced a decisive victory: indeed, Britain lost 14 ships to Germany's 11. Rather, it induced the Germans to avoid any further risks to their surface fleet by confining it to port for the rest of the war.

This meant that the real struggle at sea was one of attrition, with Britain as the main target and ultimate victor. German strategy was to use unrestricted submarine warfare against merchant shipping supplying the British Isles and France, in an attempt to starve the Allies into submission. This resulted in heavy losses of merchant shipping (430 ships in April 1917 alone) and several notorious incidents such as the sinking of the *Lusitania* in April 1915. However, the German attempt led to the entry of the United States into the war, which finally finished off the campaign on the Western Front. Also, the effectiveness of the submarine warfare was greatly reduced when Lloyd George introduced the convoy system to protect merchant shipping in 1917. From this time onwards fewer than 1 per cent of convoyed ships were lost. British attrition depended less on submarine warfare than on a surface blockade of German ports. This, too, was an attempt to prevent essential food supplies and raw materials reaching Germany. It was based very much on traditional principles already well tried and tested a hundred years earlier in the Napoleonic Wars. This eventually did to the Central Powers what the German submarine war failed to do to the Allies: it brought Germany close to starvation and incited mutiny in the fleet at Kiel and Hamburg and also among soldiers at Cologne.

Overall, Britain's contribution in the First World War might be seen as the most varied and most complete of all the Allied powers. Against the recent trend of her history, she upgraded her forces to play a mainstream military role. This was combined with a peripheral role against the Turks, initially unsuccessful but eventually resulting in Turkey's defeat. Britain also maintained a crucial naval role, not so much in destroying the German fleet – this had to be left to the Treaty of Versailles – as in containing it and imposing a blockade which undermined from within a war effort which was being worn down from without. All this presents some important contrasts with Britain's performance in the Second World War. Then, Britain could not play an initial continental role because of the early defeat of France. Hence the peripheral role was to prove more important. Britain also maximised her use of the new dimension of aerial warfare which, between 1914 and 1918, was still in its infancy. Above all, Britain's key role between 1940 and 1941 was to keep the war going until other stronger adversaries – the Soviet Union and the United States – entered it to destroy Germany. Britain's role in the First World War was therefore more complete than it had been in any other conflict in her history.

THE POLITICAL IMPACT

It would have been surprising if a military effort on this scale had not led to substantial political changes. Some were apparent in the short term; others were longer-term trends for which the war had acted as a catalyst; and one was a political revolution which would, in all probability, not have occurred without the war.

In the shorter term, Britain's first experience of total war inevitably meant the widening of government powers. This, however, was a gradual process, in contrast to the Second World War, when the transition was immediate (see Chapter 11). In the first instance powers were precautionary, and the country was left largely to continue as normal. The Defence of the Realm Act (DORA) of August 1914 enabled the government to impose censorship and to nationalise those industries considered vital to the war effort. As the demands of the front grew, government powers were correspondingly extended. Conscription was introduced for all men under 41 in May 1916, while tough measures were taken against conscientious objectors. Meanwhile, there had been growing government interference in the lives of the British people through a series of smaller measures designed to condition the population to being at war. A number of Licensing Acts reduced the opening hours of public houses and increased the tax on alcohol; a minimum wage was introduced in munitions factories; the import of luxury goods was controlled by the McKenna Duties; strikes were banned by the Munitions of War Act; summer time was introduced to save fuel; and food rationing was introduced throughout the country in 1918. Underlying all these changes was an unprecedented increase in government-sponsored information. This took the form especially of atrocity propaganda, designed to induce a ferocious hatred of the enemy. It was done in the form of posters, cartoons and lurid descriptions of alleged brutality on women and children. Particularly sensational was the coverage of the shooting of nurse Edith Cavell by the Germans in 1915 for helping the escape of Allied soldiers. At first propaganda was co-ordinated by Charles Masterman from the National Health Insurance Commission. Eventually in 1916 Lloyd George set up a Department of Information and also a National War Aims Committee. Finally he elevated the Department to a Ministry in 1918 and placed it under Lord Beaverbrook.

Along with extended governmental powers came an experiment in coalition politics. This went through four distinct phases.

At first there was little change. There had been no real precedent for a war of this scale and intensity; it was therefore assumed that it could be pursued by the normal process of party government. After all, one of Asquith's main concerns in August 1914 had been to prevent any split in his Liberal administration which might lead to a more broadly based one. It soon became apparent, however, that Asquith was essentially a peacetime Prime Minister, preferring to leave the conduct of the war to the military. Increasingly, however, he came under heavy criticism. This led to the second stage, in which Asquith conceded that he would have to extend the range of his administration.

The immediate reason was the shells scandal of 1915, occasioned by the inadequacy of munitions production. According to *The Times*: 'British soldiers are dying in vain because more shells are needed. The government, who have so severely failed to organise adequately our national resources, must bear their share of the grave responsibility'.[3] Asquith was made to see the limitations of the Liberal government and set up a coalition in May 1915. This comprised several Conservatives, and Arthur Henderson as the sole Labour member, as well as Liberals. The specific cause of the crisis was dealt with by placing Lloyd George in charge of the Ministry of Munitions – but this was to be the political base from which more damaging attacks were to be made upon Asquith in the future.

The third stage was the creation of a more genuine coalition, under a new Prime Minister. It was Asquith's misfortune that there was in the background a rival willing to take on the burdens of wartime leadership; the same applied to Neville Chamberlain in 1940. Lloyd George made two recommendations for the more effective conduct of the struggle against Germany. One was the introduction of conscription, which Asquith did reluctantly concede. The other demand was that the political and military leadership of the war should be more closely integrated in the form of a smaller war cabinet. Since this would be alien to Asquith's style of government, Lloyd George advanced himself as an alternative leader and received large-scale support both at Westminster and from the press. His pressure succeeded and Asquith was forced to give way to Lloyd George in December 1916. Under the latter's leadership, the new coalition saw Britain through to victory by November 1918.

By this time, Lloyd George had been able to convert his wartime leadership into a peacetime equivalent, thus carrying coalition politics into a fourth phase. He received his mandate in the general election of December 1918 in which the 'coupon' agreement, drawn up between the Conservatives and a large part of the Liberal Party, produced a landslide victory. The supporters of the Coalition won 478 seats, 335 of which went to the Conservatives, 133 to the Liberals and 10 to Labour. The opposition included 23 non-Coalition Conservatives, 28 Asquithian Liberals and 63 Labour MPs, while the 73 Sinn Fein members refused to take up their seats at Westminster. The new peacetime coalition therefore had a working majority of 332. Lloyd George had the clearest possible peacetime mandate. He exercised it abroad as a statesman of international renown, playing the linchpin role at the Paris peace-conference. At home, he lost some of the powers he had held under the Defence of the Realm Act but nevertheless retained his quasi-presidential image, aloof from the party-political struggle which afflicted lesser premiers with smaller majorities. At least, this was the case until 1922, when his luck, reputation and support all ran out. At their inner sanctum, the Carlton Club, the Conservative party decided on 29 October that the time for coalitions and mercurial statesmen had run out. Party politics should now be resumed, even if it meant the accession of Andrew Bonar Law, whose best-known comment on authority had been: 'I must follow them; I am their leader!'

Why was Lloyd George able to maintain an unchallenged ascendancy for six years? The early impetus was provided by the special circumstances of World War I. These placed a premium on the sort of characteristics which in peacetime would be associated with a political maverick: boldness, a capacity to take swift decisions with minimal consultation and a capacity for charismatic and inspirational leadership. Much the same applied to the opportunity given to Churchill by World War II. In the circumstances, who else was there? Asquith had already had his chance – and had shown his limitations. Andrew Bonar Law was probably the least striking leader the Conservatives had ever had, while his rival within the party, Lord Curzon, was deeply unpopular for his arrogant style. Once installed in December 1916, Lloyd George made his position impregnable by fundamentally rearranging the structure of his administration. He established an Imperial War Cabinet, comprising selected politicians and military leaders and served by a streamlined secretariat under Sir Maurice Hankey. This was ideally suited to the authoritarian style which Lloyd George preferred. He was also fortunate in that the Conservatives were prepared to concede him this power. They were genuinely convinced that he was preferable to Asquith and for them he had the additional recommendation of polarising the Liberals into two mutually hostile factions. The latter point encouraged the Conservatives to keep him in power after the war as well. As a powerful leader without a party base, he was for a while acceptable to a powerful party which lacked an effective leader. Bonar Law was the first to recognise his own shortcomings, although he conceded rather more to Lloyd George than the rest of the Conservative party would have wished: 'He can be Prime Minister for life if he likes.'

In fact, Lloyd George survived another four years and failed to reach another general election. Once the immediate requirements of the war had ended, his administration became more and more vulnerable. The rot set in with its inappropriate economic measures; it has, for example, been argued that he brought the post-war boom to a premature end by an unnecessarily severe policy of deflation which actually precipitated the collapse it was supposed to prevent. In addition, the Geddes Axe of 1922 removed at a blow the credibility of his promises to build 'homes fit for heroes' and to implement the measures in the 1918 Education Act. There was also a general malaise in industrial relations, which was not helped when Lloyd George decided to implement the 1919 Sankey Report by returning coal mines to private ownership. This provided the catalyst for a series of miners' strikes which eventually culminated in the General Strike of 1926 (see Chapter 6). Lloyd George's reputation was further tarnished by allegations of corruption at home through the sale of political honours in return for contributions to a political fund under his control. In fact, this was a manifestation of his greatest weakness – the lack of a party base. He had become acutely conscious of this by 1920, when he had tried, unsuccessfully, to form a 'national party' which would have merged his own Liberal supporters with the majority of the Conservatives. By 1922, therefore, it was apparent that one of the most powerful prime ministers in British history had also become the most vulnerable to sudden desertion. The occasion for this was his mishandling of the Chanak crisis in the Ottoman Empire, which the Conservatives used as an opportunity to withdraw their support. The case for doing this was strongly put by Stanley Baldwin at the 1922 Carlton Club meeting. Lloyd George, he argued, had become as much a danger to the Conservatives as to the Liberals. The very remoteness of his presidential position, once beneficial, was now an impediment to political progress.

> He is a dynamic force, and it is from that very fact that our troubles, in my opinion, arise. A dynamic force is a very terrible thing; it may crush you but it is not necessarily right. It is owing to that dynamic force, and that remarkable personality, that the Liberal party, to which he formerly belonged, has been smashed to pieces; and it is my firm conviction that, in time, the same thing will happen to our party.[4]

The extraordinary career of Lloyd George can be seen as an immediate political effect of the First World War. There were, however, longer-term results, related largely to party politics. In each case there was an apparent contradiction: the eventual effects on each of the parties seemed diametrically opposed to their initial fortunes on the outbreak of war. This apparent contradiction would seem to indicate the importance of the war in *transforming* those fortunes.

Before the beginning of the war the Liberals were experiencing great difficulties. They had clung to power in the election of December 1910 only through the support of the Irish Nationalists, and it seemed that they would lose the next general election which would be held in 1915 at the latest. Liberal Governments had also come up against problems with militant trade unionism, demands for women's suffrage, a crisis with the House of Lords, and a reactivated problem with Ireland. The outbreak of war seemed to offer salvation: it swept away the other problems, froze party politics, put off the next general election and gave the Liberals a chance to revive their political fortunes by showing effective management of a national emergency. Yet, in the longer term, the promises held out in 1914 did not materialise. Indeed, the Liberals slid into permanent decline, coming nowhere near to winning a general election in the future. The reasons for this are examined in Chapter 3. One is the major split between Asquith and Lloyd George from 1915 onwards. When the latter established himself in power in 1916 he proved that the war could be run by effective leadership without a party base. Hence the Coalition Government, combined with the personal appeal and effectiveness of Lloyd George, cancelled out the advantages which war seemed to hold out to the Liberals in 1914.

Labour were also in a difficult position on the outbreak of war. Although they had managed to secure a solid base of seats in the House of Commons (30 in 1906, 40 in January 1910 and 42 in December 1910), they were not even close to achieving a breakthrough. The outbreak of war seemed only to exacerbate matters. The Labour party argued strongly that the war was fundamentally wrong and that the duty of the government was to restore peace and promote co-operation between the workforces of Europe. A leading socialist and Labour campaigner, G.D.H. Cole, warned of the possible effect of war on industrial relations.

> If Labour continues throughout the war to allow gains won by industrial warfare in time of international peace to be filched from it, it is laying up a store of misery and hardship in the future. All the old battles will have to be fought over again, and instead of being further on the road to emancipation, Labour will have lost ground.[5]

This was certainly the position of the Labour leader, James Ramsay MacDonald, who additionally opposed the war from more fundamental principles of pacifism. On the other hand, many members of the party were as strongly motivated by patriotic sentiments which were channelled into the Coalition Government by Arthur Henderson. It seemed, therefore, that Labour were likely to be split, and permanently damaged, by the war. The reverse happened, as is shown in Chapter 4. The extension of government controls, especially in the economic sector, set a precedent for the sort of policy which Labour hoped to achieve on a more permanent basis. The war also had a levelling effect on society; even though this was temporary, again it provided an indication that the reduction of class differences could be accomplished without the corollary of a revolution. Finally, the 1918 Representation of the People Act greatly swelled the ranks of Labour voters since it enfranchised men from the lower levels of the working class. This enabled Labour to achieve the breakthrough which had eluded it before 1914.

The outbreak of war seemed to come at a bad time for the Conservatives. By 1914 they had fought their way back from their disastrous performance in the 1906 general election, when they had secured only 133 seats to the Liberals' 400. In the second general election of 1910 they came close to taking power from the Liberals and, given the latter's problems from 1911, they would have stood an excellent chance of scoring a Conservative landslide in 1915. The war put a stop to all that. Lord Curzon found this intensely frustrating. He said in the House of Lords in January 1915:

> We, as an Opposition, are in a rather peculiar position in this war. We have no share either in official responsibility or in executive authority in connection with the war. Many of us – myself, for instance – know little more about it than the man in the street.[6]

Curzon, in fact, offered his services several times as part of a coalition government, but he was never taken up on this. The emergence of Lloyd George appeared to be another factor preventing the Conservatives from breaking back into government, for which they had to wait until 1922, a full 17 years since they had last held power: this was the longest continuous period without a Conservative prime minister in two centuries of British history. And yet the period which followed was dominated by the Conservatives to a quite unprecedented degree. It is clear that the First World War paid a long-term dividend to the Conservative Party. The suspension of general elections allowed the Liberals to disintegrate into factions rather than regroup as an opposition to a possible Conservative government in 1915. The personal ascendancy of Lloyd George enabled the Conservatives to gain experience within a coalition government while, at the same time, disguising their own weakness of leadership. 1914–22 was therefore a period of waiting – until Baldwin lit his pipe on the political scene. In the meantime, the Conservatives steadily built up their popular base as a result of the 1918 Representation of the People Act. This probably resulted in as many votes being gained in the future by the Conservatives as by Labour, largely because disillusioned ex-Liberals voted Conservative to counter the growing popularity of Labour on the left.

When dealing with the overall political effects of the First World War, it is always pointed out that those powers which lost experienced a revolution. In Russia the Tsarist regime was swept away in March 1917 and the Provisional Government in October; Austria-Hungary experienced a series of revolutions as it fell apart into its ethnic constituents; and Germany was transformed from the second Empire into the Weimar Republic. But two of the victorious Allies also experienced a revolution. Italy, for example, saw the delayed impact of war in the rise of a fascist regime under Mussolini by 1922. And Britain underwent a radical political change in its relationship with Ireland.

The First World War completely distorted the trend that Irish history appeared to be taking up to 1914. Asquith's Liberal Government had introduced the third Home Rule Bill in 1912, with the full support of the 84 Irish Nationalist MPs. Due to come into effect in 1914, this would have provided Ireland with a form of devolution: control over her internal affairs and dual representation at Westminster and Dublin. The settlement was, however, suspended when the First World War intervened. During the next four years the more extreme republican movement took the initiative in the form of Sinn Fein and the IRA; these organised the 1916 Easter Rebellion against British rule and demanded complete independence for Ireland. The republicans also gained considerable popular support as a result of the attempts of the British Government to extend conscription to Ireland. By the time of the 1918 general election the whole situation in Ireland had been transformed, the moderate Irish Nationalists having been displaced by Sinn Fein in the South and the Ulster Unionists in the North. Attempts to revive Home Rule collapsed and the 1922 settlement was based on the partition of Ireland. This particular legacy of the First World War, which could well be the longest lasting, is examined in greater detail in Chapter 2.

THE ECONOMIC AND SOCIAL IMPACT

The dislocation caused by the First World War has never seriously been questioned. It would be pointless to attempt to do so. Britain had after all lost 750,000 men, or about 9 per cent of men under 45[7] and the shortage of houses was estimated at some 800,000, none having been built during the war years. For many the conflict had been a shattering experience and readjustment to normal life proved highly complex. The economic trends which operated before, during and after the war are, however, open to debate. We may, for example, ask whether the war exerted a cataclysmic effect on a healthy economy, reducing it within a period of four years to only a shadow of its former strength? Or did it merely accelerate a trend which was already taking place? Alternatively, did it exert a temporary change, only for the economy to revert to its previous condition once the war had ended? Or did it provide a permanent but selective uplift for certain parts of the economy, perhaps at the expense of others? It will be shown that all of these processes occurred. Although they appear incompatible and contradictory, this is only to be expected. After all, the economy of any advanced industrial state is highly complex, consisting of different components at differing stages of development and working at differing speeds.

The experience of industry was especially complex. During the First World War some of the staple industries – iron and steel, coal and ship-building – experienced a resurgence, followed by rapid contraction with the arrival of peace. Did this mean that the war had brought about the decline, or would it have happened anyway?

On the one hand, there was evidence of a pre-1914 decline in the staple industries by comparison with the performance of those of Germany and the United States, Britain's main rivals. One explanation is therefore that Britain's industrial performance after 1918 was simply a continuation of pre-1914 trends and that the war had temporarily stimulated the staple industries, thereby disguising the underlying trend of decline. The real reasons for this decline were structural. British staple industries had been the first in the field and, although they had established an initial lead, they had failed to modernise or to organise into effective units. On the other hand, the war played an important part in interrupting the pre-1914 channels of commerce upon which Britain's industrial production had depended so heavily. In 1919 the total volume of British overseas trade stood at only 65 per cent of the volume of trade in 1913, the last complete year before the outbreak of war. Three examples were particularly significant. One was the loss of

33

the Indian market for textiles, upon which a substantial part of the early industrial revolution had been based; this was due to the Indian production of cotton and increasing competition from Japan. Another was the loss of two-thirds of the British market in South America which had been won by the United States during the upheaval of the war. A third was the end of British coal and steel exports to Europe as the continental countries built up their own capacity after 1919. From this perspective it would seem that the war interacted with an earlier trend and made it worse. The war was also highly misleading. In the short term it inflated the staple industries through a sudden increase in demand for warships, armaments and military equipment. This expanded capacity then had to cope with the sudden collapse in demand after the war and with the huge gaps where Britain's overseas markets had once been.

All this applied essentially to the traditional industries. The newer industries, especially those based on electricity and motor manufacturing, generally benefited from developments during the First World War. Before 1914 these had been very slow, comparing unfavourably with their German and American rivals. It is true that the consumer-based demand for motor vehicles declined for a while from 1914 but, during the 1920s and 1930s, all aspects of the new industries flourished as never before; indeed their prosperity partly compensated for the crisis in the staple industries (see Chapter 8). Specific wartime benefits had been the development of new methods and materials, encouraged by the Department of Scientific and Industrial Research, set up by the Coalition Government in 1916. Production processes were rationalised and engineering components standardised – both setting the new industries up for the future use of assembly-line methods.

Integrating these points gives the following overall perspective. In the short term, the First World War reversed the trends in both the staple and the new industries. The former were temporarily boosted by the extraordinary demands of war; but once these demands were removed, the original deficiencies became the more obvious and the decline was accelerated by the artificial nature of the boost. The new industries were making slow advances which were stopped by the war in a consumer sense. But the developments in research and management during the war gave them a powerful advantage when they were able to return to normal production, providing the impetus which had been lacking before the war.

The impact of the war on finance and trade was more direct than on industry. Before 1914 Britain had been a large-scale creditor, with a massive input into her annual balance of payments from invisible earnings in the form of overseas investments and services such as insurance and shipping. These were not immediately affected. At first the government took measures to prevent any collapse in confidence by providing backing for certain commercial bills which would not otherwise have been paid in the special circumstances of war. In 1914 there was also an overall increase in the gold reserves held at the Bank of England. It did not, however, take long for massive changes to occur. According to A. S. Milward, the pre-war framework was 'violently disrupted by the First World War'.[8] The main reason for this was that Britain rapidly used up her reserves and investments in her quest for victory. By 1917 costs had risen sharply and Britain had become increasingly dependent on loans from the United States; by 1918 her war debts stood at over £850 million. This changed the whole basis of Britain's international role. Before 1914 she had been a net creditor on a massive scale, which had helped offset her industrial decline relative to Germany and the United States. After the war Britain's invisible earnings operated on a much tighter line and there were more and more occasions in the 1930s when she experienced what would once have been inconceivable: a balance of payments deficit. To make matters worse, Britain experienced difficulties during the 1920s within the new international financial system. She had once found security in relating sterling to the gold standard. Her return to this in 1925 created enormous problems and she had to withdraw again in 1931. From being the world's international financial power, Britain sank into the shadow of the United States, a process completed by the Second World War.

Society and social issues were affected by the war in two ways. The first was direct, based on government involvement through a process which can be seen as largely political. The second was indirect, largely through the operation of economic forces which were often beyond the government's control. In both cases there were different trends, reflecting the complexity of Britain's social systems.

As with the economy, there was no single pattern of social problem and government solution. In some ways the war interrupted social policy about to be undertaken by the government. For example, the Liberal President of the Board of Education, Pease, said that a new education bill would be introduced into Parliament in 1914. This, however, was suspended for four years and, when it resurfaced in 1918, education had to take its place on the queue of social priorities. The Fisher Education Act was therefore much more restricted than Pease's earlier proposals. In complete contrast to education, there were some ways in which the war seemed likely to act as a progressive influence by revealing the necessity for further social action; unfortunately, the government could not fully deliver. This was the case especially with health. The treatment of the war-wounded placed massive strains on existing services, while large-scale recruitment had revealed the poor health experienced as a matter of course by many thousands of men. The main administrative change was the establishment of the Ministry of Health immediately after the war, but there could, as yet, be no attempts to extend the basic health provisions provided by the Liberals before 1914. The National Health Service was the product more of the Second World War than of the First. Similar problems existed with housing and unemployment insurance: on demobilisation these became major political priorities. But Addison's Housing Act (1919) scarcely scratched the surface because its subsidies tended to promote building at the upper end of the price-range, while the Unemployment Insurance Act of 1920 was overtaken by the rapid increase in the numbers of men out of work following the collapse of the post-war boom. Finally, there were instances of the government managing during the war to overcome problems that had plagued it earlier only to rediscover them with the arrival of peace. This applied to industrial relations. The war had brought increased co-operation between the government and trade unions. This had followed a period of unprecedented conflict before 1914. After 1918 there was a return to confrontation, but in specific areas, the main pressure point being the coal industry.

There were also several changes which might be described as *informal*, in that they were either beyond government control or had to be dealt with in a way which went against earlier government policies. In some ways the war exerted a profound social impact through its operation as a catalyst for economic change. This applied especially to the increase in unemployment, which created a massive political problem that was to reach its peak during the early 1930s. Alternatively, the war seemed to divert attention from a fundamental issue which had been a source of contention beforehand, only to give a good reason for resolving it afterwards. This applied especially to the movement for women's suffrage. The militant campaigns of the Women's Social and Political Union (WSPU), firmly resisted by Asquith's pre-war government, had been suspended in 1914. But the very threat of their revival in 1918 was probably a powerful factor in the enfranchisement of women at the end of the war (see Chapter 22). On the other hand, the war in some instances acted as a temporary impetus for change, only for this to be cancelled subsequently by another, more permanent influence of the war. For example, the First World War contributed directly to the expansion of the female workforce, itself an indication of a social revolution. Yet, on the return to peace, the underlying problems of demobilisation and the inexorable increase in unemployment led to a period between the wars when women actually faced increased discrimination from employers.

Overall, the impact of the First World War was complex and contradictory. It is therefore essential to allow for a variety of cross-interpretations and to accept that contradictions and paradoxes can be as important as resolved theories to historical understanding.

3

THE DECLINE OF THE
LIBERAL PARTY 1914–40

The decline of the Liberal party is one of the great changes in the political history of the twentieth century. The facts and figures are dramatic.

The high point of Liberal success was reached in the landslide of 1906 when, after two decades spent in political exile, they won 377 seats. Although they remained in power until after the outbreak of the First World War, some of their support bled away in the two general elections of 1910, when they won 275 and 270 seats in January and December respectively. The real change, however, occurred in the general election of 1918 when, for the first time in their history, they became, with 163 seats, the third largest party in the Commons. In 1922 the situation deteriorated even further as they shrank to 115 seats. A temporary recovery occurred in 1923 when the Liberals secured 158 seats but they slumped in 1924 to 40. They never again succeeded in reaching three figures, winning 59 seats in 1929, 37 in 1931 and 21 in 1935. Another collapse took place in 1945, the year of the Labour landslide, when the Liberals won only 12 seats. This chapter will examine and explain the way in which this process occurred.

WERE THE LIBERALS IN DECLINE
BEFORE 1914?

Searching for the roots of Liberal decline has caused considerable controversy.

One argument is that the Liberal party had been exhausted by the array of problems which confronted it before 1914. This is put especially strongly by George Dangerfield in his influential work *The Strange Death of Liberal England*. Between 1910 and 1914 the Liberal governments faced a series of debilitating crises involving conflicts with the House of Lords, militant trade unions and the suffragettes. These battered the whole array of Edwardian Liberalism into submission so that 'by the end of 1913 Liberal England was reduced to ashes'. Indeed, these problems 'slowly undermined England's parliamentary structure until, but for the providential intervention of a world war, it would have certainly collapsed.'[1]

Thus the decline of the Liberal party was in part due to the revolt against Liberalism from a variety of quarters, with the psychological impact this had. Particularly dangerous was the revival of the old Irish problem, now given additional dangers by the development of opposition within Ulster to the Liberal policy of Home Rule.

One effect of this crisis was the beginning of electoral decline, already apparent before 1914. The Liberals had even lost their overall majority by December 1910, depending for their power on the good-will of Labour and the Irish Nationalists. Further losses were incurred in by-election results. Between 1911 and 1914, the Liberals surrendered Cheltenham, Oldham, South Somerset, North Ayrshire, Manchester South, Crewe, Manchester North West, Midlothian, Newmarket, Reading, South Lanarkshire, Bethnal Green, Leith and Ipswich.

Part of the problem was the growth of Labour. In a sense, the policy of allowing Labour close proximity to the Liberals was a deadly mistake. The Liberals first of all enabled the movement to grow up within the party by means of the Lib-Lab arrangements before 1900. Then, when Labour separated from the Liberals the latter agreed in 1903 to an electoral pact which gave the Labour party a block of 30 seats in the House of Commons. This was a short-sighted policy; thinking only of the short-term advantages they might achieve against the Conservatives, the Liberals entirely ignored the longer-term threat posed by Labour. Indeed, it had become clear by 1914 that the electoral pact had already broken down. The Labour party was intending to put 150 or more candidates in the field in the next general election; these would almost certainly have proved a serious threat to the Liberals and the Conservatives would have picked up a consider-able number of seats as a result of the split vote of the left. Such a threat would have made it virtually impossible for the Liberals to stage anything like a respectable recovery in the future.

The relations with Labour also had serious internal effects on the Liberal party. Liberals on the radical wing were in favour of main-taining the relationship with Labour, whereas the other wing, comprising business and industry, were deeply suspicious of any attempts to adulterate liberalism with socialism. The introduction of Labour

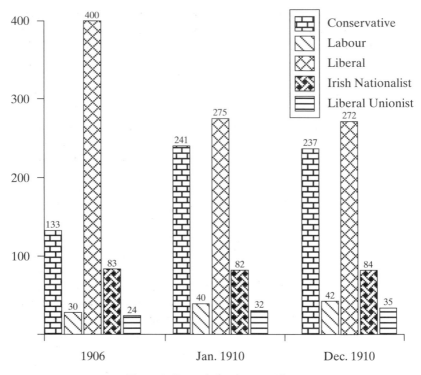

Figure 3 General elections 1906–10

candidates in by-elections also caused a rift among the Liberals as to what reaction should be taken. Increasingly many Liberals saw the main enemy as Labour, which in some cases was enabling the Conservatives to take the seat. Much the same thing was happening in local elections: the Conservatives were winning wards because of Labour's decision to contest Liberal seats. Again, it was only a matter of time before the whole electoral map was transformed.

Such is the case for the inevitability of Liberal decline. There are, of course, arguments against it. It is one thing to talk of exhaustion. Governments do periodically reach the end of the road, appearing to run out of policies and even the will to govern. This may even be confirmed by electoral defeat at the next polls. But the result is generally a spell in opposition, not permanent political decline. The Liberals may well have lost the next general election, due before the end of 1915. But to assume that this would have led to their permanent demise says too much at this stage about the strength of Labour as a viable alternative. The threat of Labour to the Liberals has been greatly exaggerated. It did not yet have the national organisation to take over from the Liberals as the main party of the left; after all, its main strength was, at this stage, in local government rather than in parliamentary politics. Where they challenged the Liberals they generally did badly. Labour candidates finished third in all twelve by-elections between 1910 and 1914 and there was a complete lack of evidence that Labour was anywhere near the point of electoral breakthrough; according to Cook, 'If the Liberals were in difficulties prior to 1914 neither MacDonald nor the Labour Party was facing the future with any great confidence.'[2]

Nor can the troubles piling up against the Liberals before 1914 be seen as catastrophic. In fact, it is often argued that the Liberals were coping rather well. Adelman, for example, believes that 'it cannot be said that the government's record was wholly unsuccessful or, from a party point of view, demoralising.'[3] The House of Lords, after all, was defeated on a fundamental constitutional issue and the Liberals faced nothing in their continued opposition that they had not experienced before. The suffragettes were prevented from achieving their objectives and the wave of industrial unrest was contained 'reasonably successfully'.[4] It might be argued that Ireland was more of a difficulty but Asquith's government was far better placed than Gladstone's had been. The Liberals were broadly agreed on Home Rule, whereas twenty years earlier they had been divided; they were hampered in the implementation of the Home Rule Act by a delay by the House of Lords, whereas in 1894 this had been an absolute veto. And the party was not moving towards disintegration as a result of concentrating on Ireland above all other issues. If ever the Liberal party looked like collapsing over Ireland it was in the 1880s and 1890s, not in 1914.

Electoral changes between 1906 and 1914 were disappointing to the Liberals, but not catastrophic. There are other examples of similar losses within the same timespan, without a party being permanently affected: Labour's substantial majority of 146 in 1945 was to be reduced in 1950 to 5. In any case, the loss of Liberal seats was not paralleled by an equivalent reduction of public support (43.2 per cent in January 1910 compared with 49 per cent in 1906). And, even allowing for the haemorrhaging of seats between 1906 and 1910, the Liberals were still far stronger in 1914 than they had been at any time between 1886 and 1905. They were experiencing all the problems of a government which had dominated the scene for some years, and which had dealt with a number of controversial issues. A substantial leakage of support is quite normal in such a case and becomes a major crisis only if there is internal disunity. The Liberal party was, however, reasonably cohesive by 1914. Asquith lost surprisingly few ministers through resignation, and Grey maintained:

'There is one great abiding cause of satisfaction in having been in this cabinet – we have been in it 7½ years and I believe it can be said with truth that the personal relations of all of us have not only stood the long strain but have gained in attachment.'[5]

This is hardly compatible with Dangerfield's view that the Liberals were facing imminent extinction as a major political force.

THE IMPACT OF THE FIRST WORLD WAR 1914–1918

The argument that the Liberal demise was inevitable by 1914 is, therefore, suspect. There is, however, a well-established alternative. This is that the transformation in the British electoral system, which made possible the rise of Labour at the expense of the Liberals, was brought about by the First World War – and that it was not necessarily related to what had happened before the war. This case has been put most vividly by T. Wilson:

The Liberal party can be compared to an individual who, after a period of robust health and great exertion, experienced symptoms of illness (Ireland, Labour unrest, the suffragettes). Before a thorough diagnosis could be made, he was involved in an encounter with a rampant omnibus (the First World War), which mounted the pavement and ran him over. After lingering painfully, he expired.[6]

There is much to be said for this approach. War invariably acts as a catalyst for political change. As an extraordinary occurrence, it transforms conventional political procedures and reverses normal priorities and it would be surprising if this had no impact on at least one of the parties in the political system. It so happened that the war resulted in the suspension of party politics. This, in turn, ended the period of Liberal domination and boosted the chances of the Conservatives and, more significantly for the long term, of Labour.

The First World War significantly weakened the Liberals in several ways. First, the conduct of the war did to the party within two years what eight years of contentious peacetime policy had not: it split the

Liberals down the middle. A major crisis developed in 1915 over the 'shell scandal', involving a serious shortage of munitions. The Liberal government was broadened into a coalition, probably as an alternative to fighting – and losing – a general election. Unfortunately, this was not the end of the Liberal party's problems. Doubt was cast on Asquith's leadership; according to A.J.P. Taylor, he was 'as solid as a rock, but like a rock, incapable of movement'.[7] Asquith came under direct attack not only from the Conservatives but more seriously from the Lloyd George faction within the Liberals. Lloyd George accused Asquith of being unable to provide effective control over the generals and to lead the War Committee. There were also major disagreements over key issues such as the introduction of conscription, which Asquith opposed. The strength of feeling was such that Asquith was forced in 1916 to resign. His replacement by Lloyd George did not, however, restore harmony to the Liberal party. Asquith retained a large following outside the government, so that Lloyd George had to staff his War Cabinet mainly with Conservatives such as Bonar Law, Milner and Curzon. Asquith remained Liberal leader and, as such, retained control of the party machinery. Lloyd George, however, refused to accept Asquith's primacy and appointed a chief whip over his own supporters. The Liberals were now in effect two parties. This was not without precedent in peace-time. But when, in time of war, had British politics presented such a spectacle? The antipathy between the two factions was at times very bitter; even though Asquith generally refrained from rocking the boat too violently, other members of his group attacked Lloyd George's policy on the franchise and on conscription in Ireland.

The second contribution to the weakening of the Liberals was the role of Lloyd George during and immediately after the war. His perception of what Britain needed was essentially non-partisan. He was undoubtedly a national rather than party leader and was convinced that he could most effectively lead Britain through the war into peace and reconstruction within the context of a coalition government rather than with the resumption of party politics. It is easy to understand why he was anxious to maintain the coalition. If he attempted to reunite the Liberal party he would encounter opposition from the Conservatives, with the effect that Bonar Law would become prime minister and introduce policies with which Lloyd George disagreed. He clearly hoped to use the wartime coalition to bring about reconstruction after the end of the war, before returning to the problem of restoring the credibility of the Liberal party as an electoral force. Hence the Lloyd George Liberals formed an electoral agreement with the Conservatives

Plate 1 Henry Herbert Asquith, 1916.
Reproduced by permission of 'PA' News.

Plate 2 David Lloyd George.
Reproduced by permission of 'PA' News.

known as the 'coupon', by which candidates supporting the coalition from either party were given a clear run. Asquith and his supporters found this unacceptable and therefore campaigned separately. The result was that the Liberals entered the 1918 general election, their first since 1910, as two parties. This served only to perpetuate the party division, showing that it was not confined to wartime.

Third, the environment of war created a crisis within Liberal ideology. To some, Liberalism involved the principle of pacifism. There were certainly elements within the Liberal party which opposed the involvement of Britain in the war. These became members of the Union of Democratic Control and opposed both Asquith and Lloyd George. To others, Liberalism meant defeating the autocracies of the Central Powers. Thus, in the words of M. Swartz:

> Firm Liberal supporters of the war followed Lloyd George's migration towards the Conservatives. Strong opponents of war policies were driven beyond the pale of the Liberal party and into the political wilderness, often seeking refuge in the Union of Democratic Control before struggling into the Labour camp.[8]

Even the less contentious elements of Liberalism were suddenly challenged; policies required in wartime were very much out of keeping with Liberal principles. This applied especially to legislation restricting individual liberty, especially in the form of censorship and the Defence of the Realm Act. There had never been a total war before to act as a gauge or to provide reassurance that, in the longer term, Liberal principles might be safely restored.

The Conservatives had no such crisis of conscience; indeed, they benefited enormously from the changed circumstances between 1914 and 1918. The war was not of their making so that they were not immediately implicated with the policy decisions taken before 1914. On the other hand, they had no qualms about the justness of the cause and were able to project even more strongly their traditional role as the party of patriotism. They were even given the opportunity of sharing power for the first time since 1905. It is true that they had no equivalent of Lloyd George within their ranks and that they were, in effect, a party without a leader. On the other hand, Lloyd George was essentially a leader without a party. In his frustration he was forced to give Bonar Law the ministerial experience he would otherwise have lacked, thus easing the way of this rather unprepossessing politician to future premiership in 1922.

The war also had a positive impact on the Labour party. First, it led to the defection of many disillusioned Liberals, via the Union of Democratic Control, into the Labour movement. Some of these were radical thinkers and, according to Swartz, 'the Liberal party lost, while Labour gained, young politicians whose allegiance was vital to the success of a party of the left'.[9] This also improved the chances of Labour being able to transcend its existing base and to project an appeal to the middle as well as the working classes.

Second, and more fundamentally, Labour benefited in electoral terms. Their position before 1914 had been immensely frustrating: they had developed a permanent claim to a block of seats within Parliament but lacked the impetus to break through into the position of a major party. Such a transformation has, in fact, happened only twice in the politics of the United Kingdom – both in the First World War. One example was the considerable increase in Labour's popular vote in 1918; the other was the transformation of Irish politics by the sudden eclipse of the moderate Irish Nationalists and the rise of the more extreme Sinn Fein. War often acts as a major catalyst for change. For the losers it can mean revolution, as in Germany and Russia, or even territorial disintegration, as in Austria-Hungary. For the winners change is likely to be within the existing constitutional framework, but it can be radical none the less. Some of the constraints which just about manage to prevent radicalisation in peacetime are swept away in time of war, with the result that social, economic and political transformation is greatly accelerated. The First World War therefore meant that Labour could break through, sooner rather than later; it provided Labour with the impetus which carried it to even greater electoral achievements in the 1920s.

Specifically, the war provided a more egalitarian climate; it brought a sharper focus on the vital contribution of the working man – and woman. It cleared Labour of the sort of charges to which it had been vulnerable – that it was unpatriotic and anarchistic. Membership of Lloyd George's coalition government gave Labour a taste of responsibility without associating it with the sort of acrimonious exchanges which were tearing the Liberals apart. The war also moderated the stance of trade unions and the end of industrial unrest helped in virtually doubling their membership between 1914 and 1918. The affiliation of many trade unions to Labour was vitally important in providing a link between the workforce and the party so that, when the opportunity arose for them to vote, they knew exactly what to do.

This opportunity came in 1918. Some historians maintain that the key factor in the decline of the Liberals was the 1918 Representation of

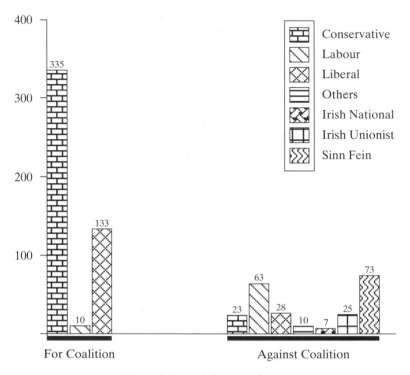

Figure 4 General election of 1918

the People Act rather than the split between Asquith and Lloyd George or the social changes brought about by the war. After all, this argument runs, parties have divided both before and since, without falling inevitably into decline. What made the real difference was the threefold expansion of the electorate, with its inevitable pay-off for the Labour party. In 1918 the Labour vote expanded to 2.4 million votes, compared with a much lower level of 0.5 million in January 1910, their pre-war peak. In the same period the Liberals won 2.7 million, compared with 2.9 million in January 1910. The Conservatives moved from just under 3 million to 3.5 million. It seems quite clear that the large majority of the newly enfranchised voters supported Labour and that there was a small leakage from the Liberals to the Conservatives. The impact on the seats in 1918 was spectacular, the Conservatives winning 335, the Liberals 161 and Labour 73. What happened was that Labour contested far more seats than ever before and, while not actually winning many more at this stage, split the vote which had previously gone to the

Liberals so as to hand seats to the Conservatives. In other words, the 1918 election saw the reversal of the electoral pact of 1903 which, throughout the period before 1910, prevented such a split and gave the Liberals a clear run against the Conservatives.

By 1918, therefore, the Liberal party had shrunk alarmingly. Even so, it could have done a great deal worse. It had still won 161 seats to the Conservatives' 335. This was not too different from the result in 1895 when the Liberals had won 177 to the Conservatives' 340. On the other hand the third party differed considerably between the two years. In 1895 there were 71 Liberal Unionists – who had split with the party over Ireland but remained Liberals in other respects and might conceivably re-unite with the main party in the future. In 1918, however, the 73 Labour members were entirely independent from the Liberal party and were certainly not considering a merger with them. Furthermore, they had 2.4 million votes to the Liberals' 2.7 million. Any further expansion in their popular vote might have devastating results on the number of Liberal seats in the future.

CONTINUING DECLINE 1918–1939

The First World War had therefore provided the conditions necessary for Labour to break through into a major share of the popular vote. The 1918 Act had prevented the Liberals from holding their own in a redefined political contest. The real damage was momentarily hidden by the fact that the great Liberal statesman, Lloyd George, was still prime minister. The question now arising was whether or not Labour could translate its increase in the popular vote into a sufficient increase in their seats to make the Liberal decline permanent.

Decline is rarely a continuous process and can be highly misleading. It can be seen in two ways. First, it might resemble a tide which can, of course, change; in this sense, decline is followed by recovery. Second, it may be compared with a current, with an underlying momentum in one direction; at the same time, there may well be cross-currents which, although weaker, temporarily hide the main flow. The problem for the contemporary observer is that there can be no certainty as to whether a process is acting as a tide or a current. Is a recovery therefore a reversal of earlier decline or only a brief exception to a long-term process? This is something that only the historian, with the advantage of hindsight, can resolve. During the 1920s there were times when the Liberals were optimistic that the tide was turning and that they would be able to recover at least some of their former influence. What they were seeing, however, were the complex cross-currents of the political system. Then, during the 1930s, the cross-currents became weaker and the process of decline was inexorable as the underlying current became more and more apparent.

There were several positive – and therefore misleading – developments in the 1920s. One was the reunification of the Liberal party. In 1923 it was given, quite gratuitously, an issue upon which to fight. The Conservative leader, Bonar Law, who succeeded Lloyd George as prime minister in 1922, argued strongly for the reintroduction of protection. On Law's retirement through ill health in 1923, Baldwin decided to put the issue to the electorate. Both branches of the Liberals were determined to resist any such inroads into the policy of free trade, and formally announced their reunion to fight Baldwin's proposal. The electoral signs were also favourable, as the Liberals secured an increase from 17.5 per cent of the popular vote in 1922 to 29.6 per cent in 1923.[10] This compares with Labour's performance of 29.5 per cent and 30.5 per cent respectively. It is easy to see how contemporaries might have interpreted this as the beginning of recovery, brought about perhaps by the end of a damaging split between two prominent personalities. It seemed that Labour's rate of increase was slowing and that the Liberals were winning back many of their erstwhile supporters.

The Liberals were also in a position where they could influence politics and government. In 1924, and again in 1929, they held the balance of power. This meant that Labour could form an administration only with their open – or tacit – support. Similarly, the Liberal party could also blow the whistle on either government whenever it chose to do so. Asquith clearly saw this as a means of turning round the fortunes of the Liberals. He reasoned that giving Labour a chance to govern in 1924 would demonstrate to the electorate their inability to do so. He therefore expected the tide to turn against Labour, in the process sweeping the Liberals back to power.

The 1920s were also a period of remarkable progress in Liberal ideas. These were contained in a series of published policy statements. One was the *Green Book* of 1925, or *The Land and the Nation*, in which Lloyd George argued for state intervention to ensure agricultural reforms which would guarantee agricultural improvements. Another was the 1928 *Yellow Book*, or *Britain's Industrial Future*, which suggested the establishment of a National Investment Board to expand the industrial economy and initiate a public works scheme. Liberal ideas on the economy were also publicised through a series of 'Summer Schools', and Lloyd George's ideas on industrial reconstruction (although not those on agriculture) received the open backing of the leading economist of the day, J.M. Keynes. The most important Liberal contribution to the economic debate was, however, the pamphlet *We Can Conquer Unemployment*. Published in 1929, this argued that a programme for building houses and roads could add 600,000 men to the workforce. Lloyd George entered the 1929 general election confident that the Liberals would benefit from such initiatives and pull back a significant proportion of the votes which had, since 1918, gone to Labour.

In retrospect, we can see that these positive trends were misleading. The 1923 election results were an aberration going against the under-lying current, which reasserted itself in the election of 1924. Then the Liberals lost to Labour 46 seats they had won in 1923 without Labour opposition. More characteristic of the real state of the Liberal party were the 1922 and 1924 elections. In 1922 the Lloyd George (or National) Liberals won a total of 62 seats, compared with 136 in 1918, losing 39 to Labour. The Independent Liberals of Asquith increased their tally from 28 in 1918 to 54 in 1922 but also lost seats to Labour. Both groups, therefore, were unable to fend off the advance from this direction. The 1923 election result, which saw a Liberal recovery, was not a true indication of the long-term trend, since the additional Liberal seats were gained from the Conservatives. This was at a time when the Conservatives had undermined their own position by com-mitting themselves to an unpopular policy of protectionism, thereby giving the Liberals the opportunity to reunite around a specific policy of free trade.

The election of 1924 showed the real extent of the Liberal calamity, which had been partially concealed in 1923. This election was fought on the record of Labour's first government and, in particular, on the 'red scare' surrounding the so-called Zinoviev Letter. Logically, therefore, it should have reflected badly on Labour. But Labour actually gained popular support, increasing its share of the vote from 30.5 per cent in 1923 to 33 per cent in 1924, even though the number of Labour-held seats declined from 191 to 151. The Liberal share of the vote and seats both collapsed dramatically between 1923 and 1924, the former from 29.6 per cent to 17.6 per cent, the latter from 159 to 40. What happened was confusing at the time but clear enough in retrospect. Labour held the gains it had made from the Liberals while losing a number of seats to the Conservatives. The latter had entirely recovered from the dip in popularity caused by their attempt to introduce protection in 1922 and were now riding high on a crest of anti-socialist feeling from that part of the electorate which would never be expected to vote Labour. This included a significant number of Liberals who were now transferring their allegiance to the Conservatives for two reasons. One was that they disliked Asquith's decision to give Labour a chance in 1924 – and were therefore punishing him at the polls. The other was that their fear of Labour and socialism was stronger than their commitment to Liberalism and drove them permanently into the refuge of the Conservative camp. All that was needed to complete the Liberal collapse was for those Conservatives who had voted Liberal in 1923 – because of their feelings on the issue of protection – to revert to their usual loyalty now that this issue had been removed. Thus 68 seats won by the Liberals in 1923 went straight back to the Conservatives in 1924 and to these were added a further 37. The 'red scare' and the failures of the 1924 administration were therefore visited indirectly on the Liberals rather than directly on Labour.

This trend was confirmed by the 1929 election. The Liberal disaster of 1924 was not reversed, only slightly modified. They increased their proportion of the vote from 17.6 per cent to 23.4 per cent and their seats from 40 to 59. But this was extremely disappointing. They had been better prepared for this election than for any other since 1918 and their few gains were at the expense of the Conservatives – to be expected after the latter's problems in power between 1924 and 1929. The real beneficiaries were Labour, who increased their vote from 33.1 per cent to 37.1 per cent and their seats from 151 to 288. This was largely because of the underlying failure of the Baldwin administration to tackle the growing problems of unemployment and industrial relations; it was obvious to the working classes that the real alternative to Baldwin had to be MacDonald rather than Lloyd George. In any case, Labour had by this stage had more recent experience of government than the Liberals. In addition, the electoral system was now clearly working in their favour. As Adelman maintains, 'The 1929 general election therefore represents the end of the road for the Liberal party as far as their attempt to re-emerge as a potential party of government is concerned.'[11]

From the beginning of the 1930s onwards the current flowed more strongly against the Liberals and there were fewer prospects of recovery. The party split three ways in the 1931 election. There were 4 supporters of Lloyd George, 37 National Liberals under John Simon and 31 Official Liberals following Herbert Samuel. This played havoc with the party's organisation, especially since Lloyd George had pulled out of supporting the rest of the party financially. It also destroyed any notion of their standing as a viable alternative to Labour and the Conservatives; the Simonites were pro-Conservative and anti-Labour, Lloyd George's supporters pro-Labour and anti-Conservative, and only the Samuelites anti-Conservative and anti-Labour. The two elections of the 1930s offered very little hope of revival. It is true that the number of Liberal seats increased in 1931 from 59 to 68 but, more significantly, the popular vote fell from 23.4 per cent to 10.2 per cent. This again points to the peculiarities of an electoral system which, in 1931, gave Labour 52 seats from 30.6 per cent of the vote.

Even the imaginative policies put forward in the 1920s in the Green and Yellow Books now faded, appearing distinctly colourless. The Summer School has been described as an 'uninspired meeting of speech-makers, almost devoid of controversy and debate, a place where party stalwarts could go for a week's rest and listen politely to addresses from the podium'.[12] Instead, the majority of the Liberals moved towards the policies of retrenchment conditioned by the arrival of the Great Depression. This served only to submerge any claim to a unique identity within the political spectrum. Lloyd George had once hoped to push back the Conservative right and Labour left with an expansion of the Liberal centre. This aspiration was, however, killed off during the 1930s; according to Thorpe, the Liberals were 'squeezed out by the moderation of the National Governments and the growing realism of Labour'.[13]

The real measure of the changing fortunes of the Liberal party is the number of ministers it contributed to coalition governments in times of national emergency. During the First World War the Liberals had dominated the government and provided the prime minister. During the Second World War the Liberals were not represented at all in the cabinet. Instead, this was led by an ex-Liberal who, having lost his seat in the election of 1918, decided that his political future would be better served by returning to the party of his origin, the Conservatives.

4

THE 1924 LABOUR GOVERNMENT

Labour emerged as an independent political party with the formation of the Labour Representation Committee (LRC) in 1900 and proceeded to win two seats in Parliament.[1] Following an electoral pact organised by James Ramsay MacDonald, secretary of the LRC, and Herbert Gladstone of the Liberal party, Labour secured 30 seats in 1906, the year of the Liberal landslide. These were increased in January 1910 to 40 and in December to 42. The breakthrough, however, came in the First World War, for reasons given in Chapter 3. In 1918 Labour increased their tally to 63 seats and the support of 22.2 per cent of a greatly enlarged electorate; by 1922 this had become 142 (29.5 per cent). The bulk of these votes came from trade union members recently enfranchised and newly affiliated to the Labour party (4.32 million by 1920).[2] Between 1918 and 1922 the party also won 14 by-elections and augmented its parliamentary experience and performance. Following the election called in 1923 by the Conservative prime minister Baldwin, Labour found itself with 191 seats and an unexpected opportunity of political power.

This chapter looks at four main issues relating to a young party's first experience of government. First, it examines the circumstances in which Labour was able to take office and the degree to which it was prepared for it. It then considers Labour's achievements at home and abroad, explaining why Labour's measures were less radical than many expected. Third, it reviews the party's internal deficiencies which, together with external pressures and intrusions, help explain why Labour's first experience of power was so short-lived. Finally, it considers the significance of this experience and of the sweeping electoral impact of the 1924 general election.

LABOUR IN OFFICE

To a large extent Labour's opportunity in 1924 was the result of a uniquely favourable set of circumstances which prevented either of the other two parties from forming a government.

In the first place, the man who had dominated British politics since 1916 had been removed from contention. Lloyd George, discredited by the Chanak crisis and by the allegation that he had connived at the sale of honours, had been displaced by a Conservative government in 1922. This, however, struggled to offer a clear and sustained alternative to the coalition government, even though it secured an overall majority in the 1922 election (345 seats out of 615). For one thing it was poorly led: Andrew Bonar Law proved the most insignificant premier since the Earl of Aberdeen. His successor, Stanley Baldwin, was made of more promising stuff, but was confronted immediately by a bitter internal split over the issue of tariff reform. Debates on protection and free trade had proved highly dangerous for the Conservatives on two previous occasions. Peel's determination to repeal the Corn Laws in 1846 had split the Conservative party, while Chamberlain's attempt to restore protection divided the Conservatives so badly in 1905 that the Liberals won a landslide election in 1906, ending over twenty years of Conservative political predominance. In 1923 the issue of tariffs once again showed its power as a catalyst for political change: although the Conservatives secured the largest number of seats, the electorate left them 50 short of an overall majority.

With the Conservatives in temporary disarray, the initiative, surely, should have rested with the Liberals. In a way it did: the two wings of the party had reunited and their combined tally of seats had risen to 159. On the other hand, the nature of this initiative was not to form a government themselves but, rather, to decide who else should do so. Lloyd George and his supporters would have preferred to join a coalition government with the Conservatives – but this was not on offer from Baldwin. Alternatively, the Liberals might have allowed the Conservatives to form a minority government with their tacit support. Asquith, however, reasoned that this would look like a 'bourgeois coalition' to keep socialism out and that the Liberals would later be punished at the polls for such a strategy. It would be far better, he considered, to give Labour a chance. In this way, Labour would soon show its deficiencies and inexperience. Since the Liberals could bring Labour down at any time, there was no long-term risk to the country. In the meantime, the electorate would be given a taste of unpalatable

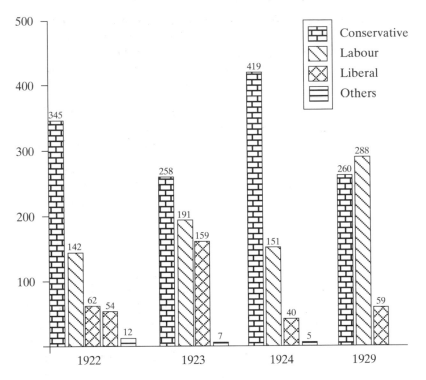

Figure 5 General elections 1922–29

radical policies which would soon persuade substantial numbers of disillusioned Labour supporters to switch their support to the Liberals at the next election. The Conservatives were also prepared to follow this strategy, Neville Chamberlain believing that Labour 'would be too weak to do much harm but not too weak to get discredited'.[3]

Labour was therefore put into power by political enemies who supposed that it would proceed to destroy itself. The Conservatives expected uncontested power next time, while the Liberals hoped to replace Labour as their main rivals. There can rarely have been a more cynical reason for giving a new party a chance of forming its first administration.

Was the Labour party capable of meeting this challenge and of snatching something positive out of such pessimism? Responsibility certainly came much sooner than expected. J.R. Clynes recalled:

As we stood waiting for His Majesty amid the gold and crimson of the Palace, I could not help marvelling at the strange turn of Fortune's wheel, which had brought MacDonald the starveling clerk, Thomas the engine-driver, Henderson the foundry labourer, and Clynes the mill-hand, to this pinnacle.[4]

There is, however, no doubting their determination to make full use of the opportunity and to avoid being dependent on any other party. The National Executive of the Labour party had already stated that

should the necessity for forming a Labour Government arise, the Parliamentary party should at once accept full responsibility for the government of the country without compromising itself with any form of coalition.[5]

As a calculated gamble, this was a strong response to the Liberal stratagem. Clearly a minority Labour government would be to some extent dependent upon the goodwill of the Liberal party in the Commons and could be outvoted at any time if the latter were to withdraw their support. On the other hand, a close relationship with the Liberals would ultimately be more beneficial to the latter, enabling them to continue the recovery already apparent in 1923. This might well mean a subsequent decline in Labour's vote, since the two parties were contesting the support of very much the same parts of the electorate. Neither could hope to squeeze any further the Conservatives, who had hit their electoral bedrock in 1923. It therefore made sense for Labour to show a healthy degree of independence, and to pursue policies which were distinctively its own – while at the same time avoiding open provocation. Above all, it had to prevent the Liberals gaining experience of government and to deny them any share in the credit for reforming legislation.

The weakness of the new cabinet was its lack of political experience. Only two of its members had held high office before: Viscount Haldane, now Lord Chancellor, had served Asquith's Liberal government before 1914, and the new Home Secretary, Arthur Henderson, had been the token Labour member of Lloyd George's wartime coalition government. On the other hand, the 1924 cabinet was, in the words of Beloff, 'a not undistinguished administration'.[6] Great care was taken to include moderates, such as Lord Parmoor as Lord President, J.R. Clynes as Lord Privy Seal, Philip Snowden as Chancellor of the Exchequer and C.P. Trevelyan as President of the Board of Education. The only radical was the Minister of Health, J. Wheatley, and no attempt was made to represent the left wing of the Labour party, including the Democratic Labour party and the Social Democratic Federation. This course, it was reasoned, would be more likely to prolong the experiment with government and less likely to scare off the electorate at the end of it.

Labour's major asset was undoubtedly the leadership of James Ramsay MacDonald, the most impressive parliamentary and public speaker of the inter-war period. He had the looks, elegance and personal assurance which helped stamp Labour on the imagination of a large part of the working class and to impress an increasing proportion of the middle class. He was seen, almost immediately, as 'the Gladstone of the Labour party', and A.J.P. Taylor's retrospective view is that MacDonald was quite simply 'the greatest leader Labour has had'.[7] The question in February 1924 was whether he would have long enough in power to pursue a distinctive and successful programme of reform.

LABOUR'S ACHIEVEMENTS AT HOME IN 1924

As events turned out, Labour was allowed only nine months. Historians are divided as to whether much was achieved in this time. H.A. Clegg considers the measures introduced were 'a creditable record',[8] showing, in the view of C.F. Brand, 'that Labour could govern responsibly'.[9] Mowatt, however, maintains that, 'even to its more moderate supporters, the first Labour government was largely a disappointment'.[10] What should we make of these views?

There was certainly one major achievement. The administration's chief reform was Wheatley's Housing Act, which showed a determination to treat housing as a recurrent difficulty and to make up for the failures of the Coalition government to tackle the shortage. Wheatley improved Chamberlain's earlier measure by increasing the subsidy from £6 to £9 and the length of time over which it was payable from 20 to 40 years. This did much to relieve the longstanding housing shortage through a combination of government action and initiative within the building industry. The result was the construction of 521,700 houses within the next nine years, the main beneficiaries being the large cities, especially Birmingham. On the negative side, the Act failed to deal with the problem of low-quality housing. Slum-clearance was not promoted and conditions remained dreadful for large numbers of the impoverished and unemployed. The Act did nothing to provide effective rent controls, the problems being highlighted by rent strikes in London and Glasgow.

In one case, a major measure was set in motion – but the benefits

Plate 3 James Ramsay MacDonald, 1935.
Reproduced by permission of 'PA' News.

were not felt until 20 years later. Labour placed more importance than either the Conservatives or the Liberals on state education and Charles Trevelyan, minister of education, aimed to reduce the impact of the Geddes Axe (see Chapter 8) by restoring state scholarships. He also set up the Hadow Committee, which eventually reported in 1926, some time after the fall of the Labour government. This proposed that the school leaving age be raised to 15 and that primary schooling be separated at the age of 11 from secondary schooling, to which everyone had an entitlement. These recommendations have been seen as the direct continuation of reform in line with earlier landmarks like Forster's Education Act of 1870 and Balfour's Act of 1902, and were eventually to be incorporated into Butler's 1944 Act.

In some areas, Labour showed a remarkable degree of continuity with previous governments. In its economic policy, for example, Labour exposed itself to the charge of its more radical supporters that it had lost sight of its real priorities. As chancellor of the exchequer, Snowden had much in common with Gladstone; his 1924 budget cut government expenditure, reduced taxation, repealed the McKenna Duties, and partially removed duties on tea, sugar, cocoa, coffee and dried fruit. At the same time, the government was unwilling to undertake more adventurous policies to deal with the problem of unemployment; socialist measures advocated while in opposition were one thing, but coming to terms with the realities of the situation whilst in power was another. Snowden and MacDonald came increasingly to accept the economic orthodoxy that the level of unemployment depended on the level of economic and commercial activity, and that there was little immediate scope for direct government intervention. Hence Labour had virtually no immediate impact on the levels of unemployment. The underlying rate did fall, between December 1923 and June 1924, from 10.6 per cent to 9.3 per cent, but this was no more than a 'normal seasonal adjustment' and the rate had returned to 10.6 per cent by September 1924.[11] The government could only hope to soften the blow by adjusting unemployment benefits. Hence the minister for labour, Shaw, introduced two Unemployment Insurance Acts. One ended the necessity of waiting three weeks between periods when benefits were claimed, during which time help had been sought from the Poor Law. By the second act, benefits for men increased from 75p per week to 90p, for women from 60p to 75p and for children from 5p to 10p.

Several reforms were introduced but had to be given up because of constraints imposed by the absence of a parliamentary majority or simply by lack of time. One example was an unsuccessful attempt to end the means test for old age pensions. Another concerned the regulation of working hours. Despite government sponsorship, a private member's bill concerning the working hours of shop assistants was squeezed out, while an attempt to secure a maximum 48-hour working week failed to make it beyond the drafting stage by the time the government fell.

Two issues showed an actual change of mind by the government. While in opposition, the Labour party had strongly supported the principles of nationalised industries and military disarmament. MacDonald's ministry soon made it clear that it had no intention of implementing these in 1924. The MPs representing mining constituencies complained about this apparent change of heart and introduced their own measure; lacking the support of the government and encountering opposition from the Liberals and Conservatives, this was, however, heavily defeated. MacDonald also swallowed some of his preferences by following a traditional defence policy. This was signalled in advance by the appointment of Lord Haldane to the Committee of Imperial Defence, a role he had held in Asquith's pre-1914 Liberal government.

It is hardly surprising that disappointment should have been the reaction most commonly felt about Labour's measures in 1924. The Liberals and Conservatives were disappointed that Labour had actually proved itself capable of moderate reform, while much of the rank and file were disappointed by the absence of more radical measures. But MacDonald refused to be pushed into radicalism and, for a Labour government, took surprisingly strong measures against the large number of strikes in 1924. Following the dockers' strike, organised by Ernest Bevin of the Transport and General Workers' Union (TGWU), and the strike of the London Transport workers, MacDonald declared a state of emergency and made it quite clear that it was prepared to use the Emergency Powers Act.

Throughout 1924 MacDonald was determined to project a moderate image – and this is the key to understanding his domestic policies. He was aware of widespread public misgivings, even panic, on his appointment in January. He knew that there were predictions of a Bolshevik revolution in Britain, along with the end of marriage and the confiscation of private wealth. MacDonald was clearly unsettled by this reaction and invested his first term as prime minister in showing that Labour was a force for 'step by step' reform,[12] not for revolution. In a letter to Lord Parmoor, he stated that he wanted above all to 'gain the confidence of the country'.[13] The results were a series of cautious changes which had firmly in mind the prospect of future power. Most historians now agree on this. According to Marquand, 'MacDonald had not become prime minister to devise a new economic policy, but to prove that Labour could form a presentable government and to drive the Liberals out of the middle ground of politics'.[14] This view is echoed by G. Phillips: 'Labour wished to establish its reputation for financial responsibility, and to see a complete return to prosperity, before it attempted anything more adventurous in the way of social reconstruction.'[15] In one respect, MacDonald found that being in a minority government was an advantage since he had a strong reason for avoiding the socialist policies preferred by the left wing of the party but which he himself opposed. He was able, quite openly, to squeeze the left. According to Beatrice Webb, 'MacDonald wants 8 million voters behind him and means to get them even if this entails shedding the I.L.P., the idealistically revolutionary section who pushed him into power'.[16]

Whether or not he succeeded in this strategy depends on an analysis of Labour's performance in the election of November 1924.

LABOUR'S ACHIEVEMENTS ABROAD IN 1924

MacDonald made his largest impact on international diplomacy. This was strange for a statesman who had gained the reputation of being a pacifist and who might therefore be seen as a 'soft' negotiator. The European situation in 1924, however, was ideally suited to MacDonald's style; Rhodes James goes so far as to say that Labour was 'lucky'.[17] The tough gestures had all been made in 1923, with the German government's determination to evade reparations payments and the French invasion of the Ruhr. The time was now ripe for a compromise between France and Germany – and MacDonald proved an effective mediator. On this occasion, Britain had no particular interests beyond the maintenance of European peace, and so MacDonald could legitimately say that Britain 'supported both sides'.[18] The result was the Dawes Plan, which followed the careful and patient diplomacy carried out by MacDonald at Chequers and the London Conference.

The Dawes Plan made possible the withdrawal of French troops from the Ruhr, in return for Germany's undertaking to pay reparations in accordance with an annual 'index of prosperity'. It was accompanied by a series of loans to provide much needed stability for the German economy. This was unquestionably the major success of MacDonald's ministry. He had dealt with the most difficult issue in European affairs since 1919 and could claim, with some justice, that he had achieved 'the first really negotiated agreement since the War'.[19] At the same time, he was exceptionally fortunate in not having to deal with the hardline prime minister, Poincaré, who had just been replaced in France by Herriot, the more pacific Radical leader. He was also assisted by the more rational approach being conducted in Germany by the new foreign minister Stresemann. According to W.N. Medlicott,

> It was only after the decisive victory of the Left in the French elections in May 1924, and the accession to office of the Radical-Socialist Edouard Herriot on 2 June, that MacDonald's achievement as a peacemaker became possible.[20]

This should not, however, detract from an achievement described more generously by Mowatt:

> For MacDonald, it was something of a personal triumph. He had presided with great skill, and in looks and manner perfectly fitted the part of the magnanimous international statesman, and in private gatherings was able to pour oil on troubled waters with benign effect.[21]

MacDonald intended to go further. According to its 1923 election manifesto, Labour stood for 'a policy of International Co-operation through a strengthened and enlarged League of Nations; the settlement of disputes by conciliation and judicial arbitration.'[22] MacDonald was not in favour of making it compulsory for the League of Nations to intervene against aggression; hence he declined support for the draft Treaty of Mutual Assistance. He opted for the alternative course of making it mandatory to refer disputes to international arbitration, giving his support instead to the Geneva Protocol. He preferred, in other words, arbitration to intervention. He did not, however, have time to complete the process. Baldwin's Conservative government refused to ratify the Geneva Protocol and opted in 1925 for the Locarno Treaties (see Chapter 9). Even so, it could hardly be said that this was a reversal of Labour's policy, merely a slight change in emphasis. There was nothing to suggest that Labour had been pursuing policies which the Conservatives regarded as unacceptable. Indeed, much of the later success of Austen Chamberlain was due to foundations laid by MacDonald.

By far the most problematic area of Labour's foreign policy was Britain's relations with Bolshevik Russia. The Soviet regime was recognised in February, with a commercial treaty following in August 1924. Then, in return for Soviet compensation to British bondholders for investments confiscated by the Bolsheviks, the Labour government undertook to provide a loan. This was bound to antagonise the other two parties and to give them the opportunity to accuse Labour of being soft on Communism. Lloyd George, who had previously suggested a trade agreement himself, now called Labour's measure 'a fake' and 'a thoroughly grotesque agreement'.[23] The Labour party itself attached unwarranted importance to the treaty; many saw it as a means of opening up the Russian market to British goods and of solving the underlying problem of unemployment, whereas in practice it had virtually no effect.

Thus it seemed that relations with Germany and France represented the positive pole of Labour policy; relations with Russia the negative. The latter was already attracting extensive opposition before the domestic crises which broke on Labour in the second half of 1924. The combination of the two brought an early election and the fall of MacDonald's government.

WHY WAS THE 1924 GOVERNMENT SO SHORT-LIVED?

Any minority government lives on borrowed time and is particularly vulnerable to changes in views by other parties. The events which led to the fall of the 1924 Labour government were, however, particularly traumatic.

Following constant sniping from the Liberals and Conservatives over Labour's unemployment policies and relations with the Soviet Union, MacDonald began to look increasingly vulnerable. He was soon to be plagued by a series of mishaps. In the first place, he was called upon to explain why he had received 30,000 £1 shares in McVitie and Price from Sir Alexander Grant, who was subsequently given a baronetcy. MacDonald did succeed in clearing himself of the allegation of bribery and impropriety, since Grant's name had been put forward for the award some time before the payment. Worse, however, was to follow with the Campbell case. Charges were brought, under the Incitement to Mutiny Act, against J.R. Campbell, the editor of a Communist paper, who had published an appeal to soldiers not to fire on workers in a state of emergency. When the Attorney General decided not to proceed with the charge, the Conservatives accused the government of shirking its responsibility and introduced a vote of censure. The Liberals proposed, as an alternative, the establishment of a select committee to investigate the matter. MacDonald refused to go along with this and took the subsequent vote as a confidence motion. When he was defeated by 364 votes to 191, he asked the King for a dissolution and the latter reluctantly agreed.

Had MacDonald miscalculated? It could be argued that he had chosen the worst possible issue on which to make a stand: the one thing which could be expected to rouse the middle classes against Labour was the fear of Communist influences. The atmosphere created by the Campbell Case greatly helped the Conservatives in the subsequent general election, particularly since it was to be followed by their tactical use of the Zinoviev Letter (see p. 66). On the other hand, MacDonald was holding out on an important, if in this case contentious, matter of principle – that the government had the right to deal with alleged criminal conspiracy without being pressurised by other parties. There were also two possible advantages to be gained by the Labour party. In the first place, MacDonald's stand would help restore the confidence of the left and the trade unions, which had been alienated by his use of emergency powers during industrial disputes. And second, the time had come to punish the Liberals for joining the vote of censure and to replace them permanently as the main rivals to the Conservatives.

The result of the election, held in November 1924, was an apparent landslide for the Conservatives, who won 419 seats to Labour's 151 and the Liberals' 40. It is likely that MacDonald had expected defeat, but not accompanied by such a large increase in the Conservative vote compared with their showing in 1923. How can we explain this outcome?

There were two deficiencies within the Labour party itself. One was a longstanding problem with its image. Labour was not, at this stage, able to project itself as a national party which transcended class interest; instead, it appeared very much 'the political arm of a sectional interest'.[24] It depended too obviously on the trade union movement for its finances and for the vast majority of its membership, which made it difficult to break into the non-unionised middle classes. The second difficulty was the specific handling of the 1924 election campaign. MacDonald was late off the mark and failed to match the brilliant use made of radio by the Conservatives. Baldwin was entirely in his element on the airwaves and maximised his use of the new medium. MacDonald's special gift was speaking at public meetings, but this was not to become as important as the use of radio until it could be projected into the living room by means of television. Labour's campaign appeared tired and defensive, and contrasted all too clearly with the ebullience of the reunited and rejuvenated Conservatives.

The election campaign is, however, best remembered for the intrusion of a 'red scare'. Four days before the election, the *Daily Mail* published the transcript of a letter allegedly from Zinoviev, a member of the Soviet triumvirate, to the British Communist party. This contained instructions on how to 'paralyse all the military preparations of the bourgeoisie and make a start in turning an imperialist war into a class war'.[25] The authenticity of the letter appeared to be established by a formal complaint from a senior official at the Foreign Office to the Russian chargé d'affaires in London. There has been a longstanding debate as to whether it was genuine; it seems, however, that the case is still an open one and that the forgery thesis has not been conclusively proved.[26] What was particularly important about the Zinoviev Letter was that it was used by the Conservatives to attack Labour's recent policy towards the Soviet Union as ill-conceived and dangerous. What MacDonald had done, they argued, was to increase the likelihood of Soviet agitation within Britain through the agency of the British Communist party and, quite possibly, through the left wing of Labour itself.

Was the Zinoviev Letter, and the use made of it, the major factor in Labour's election defeat? At the time, Philip Snowden argued that it 'whipped up a large number of indifferent electors to vote for Conservative candidates.'[27] There is much in this, since the emphasis on the 'red' peril squeezed the middle-class vote away from the Liberals towards the Conservatives. It has also been argued that the Red Letter put Labour at a fundamental disadvantage by forcing it on to the defensive. This, also, is convincing. Labour had, after all, been in power on sufferance and now needed to put to the electorate a positive statement of its achievements and potential for the future. It also needed to project the image of a party which could be trusted not to depart in any way from the constitutional conventions of the day. Any indication of radicalism below the surface would destroy any prospects of continuing the experiment. This is precisely what the Conservatives wanted to establish, and their chance of doing so came with the Zinoviev Letter. The issue in the 1924 election was not, therefore, the future of moderate reform as Labour had wanted, but the lurking dangers of fringe radicalism. It has, on the other hand, been said that the Zinoviev Letter made comparatively little difference. According to R. Lyman, 'it seems clear that it did no more than sharpen the outlines of the election results; the Conservatives would have won a clear majority, and the Liberals would have suffered catastrophe even without it.'[28] Similarly, Beloff argues that the Zinoviev Letter affected 'a campaign already faltering'.[29]

How badly was Labour affected by the outcome of the election? The reduction in Labour seats from 191 to 151 was clearly disappointing, but this concealed a more significant development: an actual growth in popular support. Labour increased its total number of votes from 4.4 million in 1923 to 5.5 million and its share from 30.5 per cent to 33 per cent. This contrasted with a stunning collapse of the Liberal vote from 4.3 million to 2.9 million which meant a reduction in Liberal seats from 159 to 40. It is tempting to match the two and to assume that Labour increased its support by detaching left-wing Liberal voters, much as MacDonald had hoped would happen. What appears to have occurred, however, is that substantial numbers of right-wing Liberals voted Conservative, a key factor in the increase in the total Conservative vote from 5.5 million to 8 million which swelled their seats from 258 to 419. Labour's extra support probably came from a more or less even split between them and the Conservatives of the 2.1 million additional voters in 1924.

At all events, this was not so much a defeat for Labour as a triumph for the Conservatives and a catastrophe for the Liberals. It ended the brief period in which three parties had just about managed to fit into an electoral system designed for two. The Liberals had been squeezed out of the reckoning and Labour had taken their place – not a bad legacy for nine months in government. By the time of the next election, in 1929, Labour had reduced the electoral imbalance of 1924 by winning 288 seats to the Conservatives' 260. This gave it a second, and more promising, chance of power.

5

BALDWIN AND THE CONSERVATIVE ASCENDANCY BETWEEN THE WARS

In theory Britain has a bipartisan political system. There have, however, been times when one party has exerted a long-term domination for several successive governments. The Conservatives had, for example, been on top between 1885 and 1905, when they had won four out of the five general elections. The pattern was broken at the beginning of the twentieth century when, in 1906, the Conservatives won only 133 seats to the Liberals' 400. But this proved to be the Liberal party's Indian summer and the Conservatives were already on the road to recovery before 1914. In the general elections of January and December 1910 they won 241 and 237 seats respectively, just over 30 short of a greatly reduced Liberal tally.

Between the two world wars the Conservative party reached summits not previously or subsequently achieved. As a result of the 1918 general election they were by far the largest party, with 335 seats, although they continued to serve under Lloyd George in the Coalition Government until 1922. The Conservative tally increased to 345 in 1922, but dropped back to 258 in 1923: although the largest single party, the Conservatives lacked an overall majority and Labour were put into power in 1924 with Liberal support. Following the collapse of this government at the end of the same year, the Conservatives won a land-slide in 1924, securing 419 seats out of 615. In 1929 the Conservatives secured only 260, the only time between the wars that they came second in the number of seats; on this occasion Labour won 288 and formed a second government until 1931. During the 1930s the Conservative identity was, to some extent, merged with the National Government, but the party won two colossal victories in this period. In 1931 it secured 473 seats, followed by 432 in 1935, the largest numbers ever achieved by any party.

There is something paradoxical in all this. The Conservative revival followed the First World War, which is usually seen as a radicalising force. The war brought social changes and greatly enhanced the expectations of the new voters added to the electorate by the 1918 Representation of the People Act. The Conservatives were hardly the party best suited to fulfil this radicalism. Indeed, the next time a world war broke into the pattern of British politics, the radicalising experience swept Labour into power (see Chapter 12). This chapter seeks to explain the paradox by considering two main issues. What reasons can be given for the Conservative dominance during the inter-war period? And did the Conservatives' domestic record justify the faith placed in them by the electorate?

WHY DID THE CONSERVATIVES DOMINATE THE INTER-WAR PERIOD?

The main reason for the Conservative ascendancy was that Britain was in a period of transition which was, as yet, incomplete. Changes brought by the First World War were balanced by elements of continuity with the pre-war world. The Conservatives benefited as much as anyone from the *change*, while making the *continuity* their special preserve. They were the only party with a foot on each side of the 1914–18 divide.

It is usually argued that the political change brought about during the First World War primarily benefited the Labour party. The 1918 Representation of the People Act extended the suffrage to men in the lower levels of the working class, who might have been expected to use their vote to ensure a future Labour government that was committed to social change. It is certainly true that by 1918 the Labour party had been able to break through the constraints of the British electoral system in a way which had not been possible before 1914 (see Chapter 3). On the other hand, the Conservatives benefited even more. In the first place, the First World War saw a revolution within the United Kingdom which eventually resulted in the secession of Ireland (see Chapter 21). The effect was that the Conservatives no longer had to contend with a large group of Irish MPs allied more or less permanently to one of the other major parties. In the elections of 1885, 1886, 1892, 1895, 1900, 1906, January 1910 and December 1910, the Irish Nationalists had provided a remarkably consistent block of between 80 and 85 MPs who nearly always backed the Liberals. In the 1917 election, the Irish Nationalists were down to 7, and the 73 new Sinn Fein MPs refused to take up their seats. A thirty-year-old constraint on the Conservatives was therefore suddenly removed. The Conservatives also benefited greatly from the fracturing of the British left. As a result of this, many anti-Conservative votes were transferred from the Liberals to Labour without building up Labour sufficiently to become a real rival to the Conservatives. Hence the right was strengthened in relative terms. The distorting effect of the British electoral system transformed this into an absolute superiority. In the 1922 general election, for example, the united right (the Conservatives) won 56 per cent of the seats in the House of Commons with just 38 per cent of the total vote, while the split left (Labour and the Liberals) won 42 per cent of the seats with 59 per cent of the vote.

The Conservatives therefore had a unique opportunity to benefit from change. But they also presented themselves as the party of continuity. Unlike Labour, they had reassuringly deep roots in the past; unlike the Liberals, they had strong prospects for the future. The policies pursued by the Conservatives guaranteed this connection. Moderation was the underlying principle: this was instinctive to the nature of the party in the 1920s and, at the same time, strongly pragmatic. The Conservative movement towards the centre of British politics was a successful strategy, since it increased the pressure on the fractured left. Had the Conservatives moved to the right, the Liberals might have occupied the ground vacated and thus found an escape from the advance of Labour from the left. The result might have been a three-way split. As it was, the Conservatives squeezed the Liberal party even more severely than did Labour, as was shown in the 1924 general election, when many former Liberals became Conservative voters. The policies of moderation meant emphasising traditional values along with a recognition of the need for cautious reform. The former included renewed emphasis on the importance of property, which alone could ensure that the right to vote would now be accompanied by enhanced economic status. The Conservatives stressed that the alternative approach was socialism, which would activate class conflict and extremism. At the same time, they made it clear that they did not propose to repeal as a matter of principle whatever measures might be introduced by another government. The Conservative supporter could therefore expect short-term as well as long-term continuity.

To some extent the image of moderate Conservatism was due to Stanley Baldwin, who led the party between 1923 and 1937 – for all but seven years of the inter-war period. He had entered Parliament in 1908 and, between 1916 and 1922, was Financial Secretary to the Treasury, eventually becoming President of the Board of Trade. He became Chancellor of the Exchequer in 1922 and, after the retirement of Bonar

Plate 4 Stanley Baldwin, 1930?
Reproduced by permission of 'PA' News.

Law through ill-health, Prime Minister between 1922 and 1923. His second and longest ministry (1924–9) followed a brief interlude of Labour in power. In 1929 he was again replaced by Labour and agreed to serve under Ramsay MacDonald when the latter converted his ministry into the National Government in 1931. Baldwin acted as Lord President of the Council between 1932 and 1935 before resuming his role as Prime Minister, at the head of the National Government, between 1935 and 1937.

He was probably the major asset that the Conservatives had. In the first place, 'he symbolised the victory of honesty and principle over the cynical opportunism which they associated with Lloyd George and his circle.'[1] He was a rare phenomenon – a politician who did not resort in election campaigns to mud-slinging. He was tough when he had to be and flexible the rest of the time. Most important of all, however, was his image as a moderate. More than any other politician he was able to reconcile and conciliate, except during the brief period of industrial conflict over the General Strike. He was widely perceived as a straightforward and honest man, contrasting favourably with the mercurial Lloyd George. He was also the one Conservative who was most likely to maintain the allegiance of the 30 or so per cent of the working-class vote upon which the Conservative ascendancy rested. He was even liked and trusted by politicians within the Labour party; Attlee, for example, maintained that 'he always seemed more at home with our people, particularly the older trade union people, than with his own lot.'[2] Baldwin himself once said: 'I sometimes think, if I were not leader of the Conservative Party I should like to be the leader of the people who do not belong to any party. At any rate I should like to feel I had got them behind me.'[3] *The Times* neatly encapsulated his special strength when it said in 1930: 'he cultivates the character of an amateur in politics to a point which is maddening to ardent politicians.'[4]

Behind this uncomplicated facade was a complex character with a variety of political skills. Harold Macmillan, who was one of the ablest of the younger Conservatives in the 1920s, remarked later that he was 'a supreme Parliamentarian' with 'a unique hold on all sections of the his party and the House as a whole'.[5] He had the ability to sway the House with speeches which appealed to the emotions without being platitudinous. In 1922, for example, he declared to the Commons:

> Four words of one syllable each are words which contain salvation for this country and for the whole world. They are 'Faith', 'Hope', 'Love', and 'Work'. No Government in this country today which

has not faith in the people, hope in the future, love for its fellow men, and which will not work and work and work, will ever bring this country through into better days and better times.[6]

He was also highly adept at the art of party politics. According to Lloyd George, he was 'the most formidable antagonist whom I ever encountered'.[7] 'Churchill felt that he was 'the greatest party manager the Conservatives ever had',[8] a view endorsed by L.C.B. Seaman:

> in his quiet way he was a much better manager of men than Lloyd George, because he always saw others as persons whereas Lloyd George saw them only as props to be used, or not used, in his lifelong political conjuring act.[9]

A typical example was his decision to bring Winston Churchill into his cabinet after winning the 1924 general election. In offering a post to a potential rebel he set a political precedent, to be followed frequently by future prime ministers, of neutralising future attacks on governments from strong backbenchers.

Baldwin was, of course, highly fortunate to preside over the most widely supported and effectively organised of the national parties. Indeed, it could be argued that the Conservatives, in a class sense, were now the only party which genuinely had a nationwide appeal. They had much more support from the upper and upper-middle classes than had the other two parties put together, together with most of the lower-middle class and a good third of the vote of the working class. The last of these categories included significant numbers of non-unionised workers and those who took pride in Empire or showed qualities of self-reliance. The party's organisation was vitally important in mobilising this support. Funds poured in from private and corporate donations. These were put to effective use in extending the network of party agents and workers who provided essential support for the constituency associations. The Conservatives had always been in the lead in developing local organisations, whether in the days of F.R. Bonham in the 1830s or J.E. Gorst in the 1870s. Conservative candidates had ready access to effective speakers, to pamphlets and leaflets, and to voluntary workers and canvassers, many of whom were women. Such attributes were essential to the Conservatives' electoral success. Their huge victories in 1924, 1931 and 1933 were built on the detachment of marginal seats from Labour and the Liberals: winning these required a special effort, as did retaining them once they had become Conservative marginals.

Finally, the Conservatives had more than their share of a commodity essential to politicians – luck. They were given an immense boost through the troubles of others. The left had divided between the Liberals and Labour, and each of these, in turn, experienced damaging splits which either prevented or delayed recovery. The Conservatives had no more than a peripheral influence on these developments. Nor could they have known that of all the general elections of the twentieth century, that of 1929 was the best one to lose. The financial crisis which hit Britain in 1931 destroyed for a decade the equilibrium and unity of the Labour party while leaving the Conservatives entirely intact to impose their control on the 1930s.

HOW EFFECTIVE WERE CONSERVATIVE GOVERNMENTS BETWEEN THE WARS?

There is no doubting the extent of Conservative domination between the wars. There is, however, some question as to what the Conservatives actually did to earn their large majorities or how effectively they used them once they had attained them. Some historians have argued that Baldwin's governments were short on actual achievements and that caution did on occasions lead to indolence. Is this a fair assessment, or was there evidence of sustained activity and reform?

There is little to praise about the Conservative governments between the fall of Lloyd George in 1922 and MacDonald's first ministry in 1924. Two views can be considered widely representative. Mowat considers that 'Baldwin's government, like Bonar Law's, had little positive achievement to its credit',[10] A.J.P. Taylor refers to 'this dull government'.[11] The only piece of legislation of any real significance was Chamberlain's Housing Act of 1923, the purpose of which was to stimulate the building industry and, at the same time, to develop private enterprise. But even this had a limited impact, promoting building in the higher price-range in middle-class areas, but with few benefits for housing programmes for the working class. Baldwin's first government was, in any case, brought to an end later in the same year by a decision to hold a general election on the issue of tariff reform. How sensible was this? It could be argued that the whole thing was badly bungled. Baldwin was forcing the Conservatives to confront an issue which had already divided them twice in the past – over the Corn Laws in the 1840s and over Chamberlain's proposals for tariff reform after 1900. Was it really necessary to go through the process again and, in doing so, to lose 88 seats? On the other hand, calling the 1923 election on the issue of protection had its advantages. Baldwin must have suspected that the Conservatives might have to give up power after the election: he certainly made no effort to cling on to it, with or without Liberal support. But by giving up power in 1923, the Conservatives could be said to have exorcised the protection issue at the expense of a brief spell in opposition. In any case, it was only a matter of time before the Conservatives returned with a greatly increased majority as a result of the 1924 landslide. On that occasion Baldwin's campaign was highly effective, and he made full use of the radio and of the propaganda opportunity offered by the Zinoviev Letter crisis.

Baldwin returned to power in December 1924 with a strong cabinet which included Austen Chamberlain as Foreign Secretary, Neville Chamberlain as Minister of Health, Winston Churchill as Chancellor of the Exchequer, and Sir William Joynson-Hicks as Home Secretary. The main task undertaken by this ministry was the defeat of the General Strike in 1926. This was undoubtedly a major success, compared with which the other activities of the government must have appeared humdrum. Indeed, the amount of legislation was relatively limited for a five-year government with a huge majority.

One of the earliest measures was the return to the gold standard, announced by Churchill in 1925. Although this had been demanded by many financiers, it was regarded as unwise by economists such as J.M. Keynes, who argued that Britain would suffer severely because of the differential of 10 per cent between British and American prices. This did indeed hamper British exports and made Britain much more vulnerable to economic and financial developments in the United States. The impact of the American crisis after 1929, especially in 1931, was much more severe as a result of the return to the gold standard which, in any case, eventually had to be reversed. Less controversial was the Electricity Supply Act of 1926. The national grid system and the establishment of the Central Electricity Supply Board were undoubtedly a major advance on the previous system whereby local authorities had been responsible for providing electrical power. On the other hand, this change took a considerable time to implement and was still incomplete at the outbreak of the Second World War. Also in 1926, the Government set up the British Broadcasting Company, to be financed by a licence fee and under the control of a board of governors presided over by the Director General. This was significant in two ways. It provided Baldwin with a highly effective medium through which to display his powers of public speaking. It also established a pattern for the public corporation of the future, and was to be used extensively by the 1945–51 Labour governments.

Baldwin's government provided the finishing touches to the extension of the suffrage through the Representation of the People Act of 1928. But the circumstances in which it was introduced were hardly edifying: it slipped through as a result of an indiscretion by the Home Secretary, Joynson-Hicks. Without consulting his colleagues, he stated in a speech that the government was committed to enfranchising women on the same basis as men. The Prime Minister could hardly go back on such an undertaking and the Act gave the vote to all women over the age of 21. There is also an element of self-interest: it was assumed that the majority of women would vote Conservative, especially since they on the whole lacked connections with trade unionism and Labour. This, however, backfired in the 1929 general election, in which the Conservatives actually received only 10 per cent of the extra votes created by the Act. Part of the reason for this was the Trade Disputes Act (1927). As a follow-up to the General Strike, this banned general and sympathetic strikes and also made the political levy to the Labour party subject to written permission by trade unionists, a process of contracting in rather than the earlier one of contracting out. This was widely seen as a vindictive act which alienated moderate trade-union support and was in part responsible for the size of the anti-Conservative vote in the 1929 general election. The period just before the election also produced an embarrassment when the government failed in 1929 to secure its proposed revisions of the Prayer Book. Although accepted by the House of Lords, these were rejected by the House of Commons as a result of a Conservative split. To some extent, this was a fuss about nothing, drawing attention away from more positive issues; A.J.P. Taylor describes the outcry as 'the echo of dead themes'.[12]

It would be a mistake to assume that Baldwin's government lacked any dynamism. The most active influence was Neville Chamberlain, who was responsible for putting twenty-one bills through Parliament between 1924 and 1929. Four were of particular importance. One was the Pensions Act 1925, which extended the scope and provisions of the Old Age Pensions Act introduced by the Liberals in 1908. More influential was the Widows, Orphans and Old Age Contributory Pensions Act (1925). Everyone previously covered by National Health Insurance was now forced to be insured for widows' pensions as well as for sickness and unemployment. Allowances were introduced for children and orphans of insured workers; a pension of 50p per week was available at 65 and a full state pension at 70. According to L.C.B. Seaman, this was 'a milestone in the history of social security legislation'.[13] Was he right? It might be argued that it was an important consolidating measure, extending further the provisions introduced by the pre-war Liberal governments. On the other hand, it was an extension rather than an innovation – and did not significantly expand the role of the welfare state. All it did was to prevent the welfare state from slipping backwards during a time of growing unemployment difficulties. Rather than being progressive, therefore, it might be considered anti-regressive. Much the same could be said of the Unemployment Insurance Act of 1927, which reduced the benefits available, even though the contributions payable were increased; to balance this, the previously limited period of cover was now extended indefinitely.

More worthy of praise was the 1929 Local Government Act, which Seaman sees as 'one of the century's major administrative statutes before 1945'.[14] On the positive side, this did much to reduce the inflexibility of the areas of local government and also the extent to which functions overlapped. It provided for the review of local government boundaries every ten years, abolished the traditional Boards of Guardians and transferred their powers and functions to the counties and county boroughs. It also introduced a set formula for the provision of central government grants. On the other hand, there were still two regressive influences within the local government system. The opportunity was not taken to abolish rates as the main form of local government financing or to find a more progressive alternative. Similarly, the abolition of the Boards of Guardians did not mean the end of some of the harsh assumptions about poverty which characterised the nineteenth century. The administrative reforms did not, in other words, have much overlap with more progressive attitudes towards the welfare state.

Despite the accusation that the government had ducked many issues and had not introduced a particularly effective record of domestic reform, Baldwin went into the 1929 election with the slogan of 'Safety First', perhaps the least inspiring campaign slogan ever devised. This was acutely felt by some of the younger Conservatives, who were unhappy with the limited measures and with the inability to deal effectively with the rising problem of unemployment. Such critics included Robert Boothby, Oliver Stanley and Harold Macmillan. The last, in particular, wanted to see a new form of conservatism which would enhance the power of the state and appeal to the working man by state aid to industry and the involvement of workers on management boards. If ever there was a missed political opportunity this was it. The Conservative government could have made whatever changes it had wanted. It had a huge majority, a weak and divided opposition, and relative unity within its own ranks before 1929. The measures proposed by Macmillan were hardly revolutionary, or even radical; they would have been a logical extension of Disraeli's conservatism in the 1860s and 1870s. But they were ignored. The foundations of the welfare state, laid by the Liberals before 1914, received virtually no additions from the Conservatives, despite the intervention of the First World War and a changed economic climate.

A certain disappointment was reflected by the results of the 1929 general election, which was actually a serious blow to the Conservatives. The electorate had increased, as a result of population growth and the 1928 Representation of the People Act, by almost 6 million. Of these, only 600,000 extra votes went to the Conservatives; Labour, by contrast, received an extra 2.9 million. It is true that a strange quirk in the electoral system gave Labour more seats than the Conservatives (288 to the Conservatives' 260), even though they had fewer votes (8.4 million to 8.7 million). Even so, this was an election which the Conservatives did not deserve to win and, considering the problems faced by the subsequent Labour government, one that the Conservatives must have been glad not to have won.

Between 1931 and 1940 Britain was ruled by a series of national governments. The Conservatives dominated these in terms of parliamentary support and the number of ministers within the cabinet. Between 1931 and 1935, however, Baldwin played a supporting role to MacDonald, before taking over the premiership between 1935 and 1937. The last three years, under Chamberlain, saw the conversion of the National Government into what was, for all intents and purposes, a Conservative administration.

Baldwin's decision to play the supporting role between 1931 and 1935 has been questioned by some historians. It is, however, understandable for several reasons. In the first place, he genuinely believed in what Ramsay MacDonald was doing. He said in 1932: 'our aims must be national and not party.'[15] The National Government also provided Baldwin with the ideal opportunity to apply his preferred policy of moderation: Conservative policies now had to be moderate to be acceptable to the other parties. Finally, there was a more pragmatic motive: he wanted to divert attention for a while from the question of the party's leadership. Baldwin's position had come under challenge after 1929. Various Conservatives criticised his policies, whether for being too cautious in the domestic sphere or for the India Bill, which was the main grounds of Churchill's complaint. One of the more obvious successors was Neville Chamberlain, who had built up a formidable reputation as the man who got things done. But Baldwin was determined to maintain his leadership, since he felt that his vision of reconciliation, which he regarded as the key contribution the Conservative party had to make, was not yet complete. Submerging the Conservatives' identity within the National Government provided a means of silencing his critics and of deferring the leadership debate to a more appropriate time. Hence it made sense for Baldwin to continue to lead the party but, for the time being, not the country.

What was achieved between 1931 and 1935? Neville Chamberlain, now Chancellor of the Exchequer, was by far the most important influence in MacDonald's government. He continued the line which had already been started by Snowden, who had introduced pay cuts in his 1931 budget and taken Britain off the gold standard in September of the same year (see Chapter 7). Chamberlain maintained the pressure by reducing interest rates from 6 per cent to 2 per cent by 1932 in order to promote economic recovery through 'cheap money'. In 1932 he also introduced the Import Duties Bill which imposed a duty of 10 per cent on goods entering Britain except from the Empire. The intention was to go further still; a free trade area was therefore proposed for the Empire at the Ottawa Conference in 1932, but instead of a multilateral agreement only a series of bilateral agreements was reached. Meanwhile, the problems of the depressed areas were covered by the Special Areas Act in 1934, which allocated a total of £12 million. Unemployment was dealt with by the Unemployment Act of 1934, which restricted unemployment benefit to an upper limit of 26 weeks.

Were such measures sufficient? On the one hand, Britain did pull out of the Depression more quickly than the United States, or France, or Germany. It has been argued that the economic crisis of the 1930s has been exaggerated and that the decade has been given an undeserved reputation (see Chapter 8). On the other hand, it is open to question as to how much this recovery owed to the policy of the government in general or the Conservatives in particular. Indeed, several direct criticisms can be advanced. First, the policy put forward at the Ottawa Conference was little more than a throwback to the arguments of Joseph Chamberlain before 1906 – and it invited the same response. The more advanced economies in the Empire, especially Canada and Australia, feared that an imperial tariff barrier would damage their industries. Second, plans to assist depressed areas could not expect to have any real effect on the structural problems of heavy industry. Much more significant was the gradual and long-term development of the new industries. Chamberlain refused to adopt Keynesian policies to reduce the levels of unemployment or to consider imitating the policy of the New Deal being implemented in the United States. His 1934 Unemployment Act was even unsuccessful in trying to depoliticise the dole by setting up the Unemployment Assistance Board to set the rates of payment. There were many demonstrations during the following years against the levels set and the government had to intervene.

Foreign policy, meanwhile, was sinking into a morass. Collective security, the main achievement of the 1920s, was under serious threat with the rise of Hitler to power and the expanding ambitions of Mussolini. MacDonald had no answer to the new Europe which was now emerging. He had been in his element while promoting reconciliation in 1924 and had shown the way to Locarno in 1925. He had also played an important role in the Geneva Disarmament Conference during his 1929–31 ministry. But this had failed and the need for his pacific talents had ended. 'It would have been far better', maintains R. Rhodes James, 'if MacDonald had been quietly shunted into retirement in 1932 or 1933 and Baldwin had taken his place.'[16] Against this is the point that the Conservatives had themselves developed no clear basis for foreign policy, except for what amounted to an almost abject non-interventionism.

In the 1935 general election the National Government, which was still composed mainly of Conservatives, won 432 seats and 53.7 per cent of the vote, only slightly down on its performance in 1931. This seemed to indicate that the majority of the population considered that the expectations which they had had of the National Government had to some extent been fulfilled and that, with the retirement of MacDonald, Baldwin could be entrusted with a third term of office. By this time, however, Baldwin seemed to have lost many of his former powers and, like MacDonald before him, began to look tired and politically jaded. He did, however, rise to one occasion. Indeed, perhaps he was the only politician of the day capable of handling the delicate situation in 1936 concerning Edward VIII's proposed marriage to Mrs Simpson, an American divorcee. He managed to impress upon the monarch that it would be impossible to break an essential code within both the monarchy and the Church of England and, at the same time, remain head of state. There was a real threat that the crown would be discredited and that the link which it provided between Britain and the Dominions would be broken. Baldwin's tactful but firm pressure brought the desired result, and the abdication crisis was followed by the coronation of George VI in 1937, the first to be broadcast on television. But, like MacDonald, Baldwin outlasted his political and diplomatic skills; again, this became clear in an unsuccessful record in foreign policy. He was, for example, contaminated by the unpopular Hoare–Laval Pact of 1935 and, when that collapsed in ignominy, by the unsuccessful application of sanctions against Mussolini. He was also slow to respond to the needs for British rearmament and was widely blamed after the event for the poor state of Britain's defences by 1938 and 1939.

When Baldwin retired in 1937, there appeared to be an opportunity for a change of direction and pace. Chamberlain, the earlier dynamo of the party, now seemed set to revive its flagging momentum. He was certainly seen as a stronger prime minister than Baldwin and one who could bring new ideas to domestic and foreign issues. His legislation was certainly more impressive than any introduced during Baldwin's third ministry, including the 1937 Factory Act, the 1938 Coal Mines Act and the establishment of the British Overseas Airways Corporation (BOAC) in 1939. Once again, however, foreign policy proved the undoing of a strongly based administration. Chamberlain's reputation was severely compromised by his involvement with the policy of appeasement and, following his declaration of war on Germany in September 1939, his inadequate performance as a wartime leader. These issues are further covered in Chapters 10 and 11.

CONCLUSION

Conservative moderation between the wars was based on policies which were generally uncontroversial, or which would at least be acceptable to a significant number of people who would normally have supported other parties. Finding the consensus was what Baldwin, above all, aimed to do – and he did it with remarkable success. Having a low profile between the wars and pursuing a policy of moderation may well have been appropriate for the period and unique circumstances after World War I. There was, however, an eventual backlash after World War II. The very qualities which had made the Conservatives popular and reassuring from 1918 made them suspect in 1945. The electorate judged in 1945 that the Conservative record between the wars meant that they could not be trusted with the task of social transformation which now attracted a higher premium than moderation and 'safety first'. It therefore switched to Labour, thus ending the Conservative domination and introducing a more obviously bipartisan period.

6

THE GENERAL STRIKE

The General Strike of 1926 was the only occasion in British history when most of the nation's workforce stopped work in support of the cause of one particular union.

In outline, British miners were in dispute with the mineowners who, in 1925, proposed to increase working hours and reduce wages to make the coal industry more competitive. Baldwin's Conservative government tried to prevent a conflict by providing a nine-month subsidy to maintain the existing level of wages; at the same time it appointed the Samuel Commission to propose a longer-term solution. In March 1926 the Commission recommended the ending of the subsidy, along with the introduction of temporary wage cuts until the owners could reorganise the mines more effectively. This was rejected by the owners, who announced a unilateral reduction of wages in April 1926. The miners resisted and appealed to the Trades Union Congress (TUC) for support. The TUC negotiated with the government to try to avert a general strike, which it was prepared to call, if necessary, to back the miners' cause. When these negotiations broke down between 2 and 3 May, the TUC General Council called out transport and railway workers, printers, gas and electricity workers, and those employed in heavy industry. The remaining workers were to follow in due course. The government, in the meantime, had taken special precautions to combat the effects of the strike. These proved so effective that on 12 May the TUC decided to end the General Strike and accept the Samuel Memorandum. This was, however, rejected by the miners, who were left to fight alone until the end of the year, when the threat of starvation forced them back to work.

This chapter deals with three main issues related to the events of 1925–6. Why did Britain fall over the brink into a general strike in the first place? What was the range of views within the country concerning the strike and the strikers? And what was the significance of the General Strike in the short and longer terms?

THE REASONS FOR THE GENERAL STRIKE

Four separate strands have to be disentangled before a full perspective can emerge on the reasons for the General Strike. One is the underlying state of the economy with the contraction of the basic industries and the consequent growth of unemployment and social hardship. The second is the specific impact of such conditions on the coal industry, which suffered more severely than any other. The third is the crisis which developed within the coal industry as the two sides – pit owners and miners – pursued aims which proved irreconcilable. The fourth, and most critical, is the policy pursued by the government to deal with this confrontation.

The General Strike occurred during a period of painful economic adjustment. This was due partly to the shrinking of the staple industries such as coal, steel, textiles and heavy engineering which, before the First World War, had accounted for over 50 per cent of Britain's industrial output and 70 per cent of her exports. These continued after 1919 to take up most of Britain's resources and investment, even though they were becoming increasingly inefficient. Little was done to improve or modernise production techniques, in the way that was taking place in the United States and Germany, and the need for urgent readjustment was clouded by the illusion of security created by being on the winning side in the First World War. The problem was compounded by Britain's return to the gold standard in 1925, which inflated the price of exports by about 10 per cent, and by the growing pressure exerted within Britain by the growth of newer and more efficient industries like electricity and gas. As heavy industry became less and less competitive there was a strong tendency to blame lack of productivity on the level of wages, making industrial conflict more and more likely.

These problems were at their most intense in the coalmining industry – although their seriousness was not immediately apparent. Coal had originally powered the Industrial Revolution and, right up to 1913, Britain had been the world's largest exporter, secure in the annual increase in the world demand by 4 per cent. During the war the demand still exceeded supply and favourable external factors meant that the problems of adjusting to peace were less apparent than in other industries; British coal was given a reprieve from the competition of the United States, which experienced a miners' strike in 1922, and of the Ruhr in Germany, which was invaded by the French in 1923. But from 1918 onwards British coal had become increasingly vulnerable. Its domestic market was shrinking with the decline of the staple industries and with the switch of key forms of transport to oil and electricity. Markets abroad had shrunk considerably and British exports had to face competition from Polish coal and from the dramatic increase in German supplies after the Dawes Plan ended the French occupation of the Ruhr in 1924. Suddenly, British production had become uneconomic. The main factor was the organisation of the privately owned collieries; here coal mining was less mechanised even than in Poland, and about 80 per cent continued to be extracted by hand-pick. There were few prospects for the improvement of working conditions or for increased productivity.

All the ingredients therefore existed for confrontation between employers and employees. Indeed, antipathy between the two sides was more extreme in the coal industry than in any other. In the manufacturing industries many employers had been entrepreneurs, who had invested much of their own money, time and effort. This had meant a not infrequent common interest between employers and employees. The same tradition did not, however, exist in the mining industry. Mineowners rarely reinvested their profits for development and had allowed other countries to overtake Britain in mining techniques and infrastructure. Their response to growing competition from abroad was to demand a reduction in wages and the lengthening of the working day, thus passing the problem downwards to the workforce. This accorded with the view of some of the orthodox economists, who argued that the market should be allowed to find its own level of wages. To the miners, by contrast, the problem was caused not by increasing wage costs, but a lack of proper investment, which could best be provided by full government control. From 1919, therefore, the miners' demands usually included a working day of six hours, a pay increase of 30 per cent, and the nationalisation of the mines.

Such arguments produced a series of conflicts between the mine owners and the miners. In 1921, for example, the owners attempted to reduce wages, a strategy repeated in 1925. On the first occasion, the miners had received no support from workers in other industries. By 1925, however, the TUC had come to see its involvement as essential. It was, after all, the ultimate representative of the miners against the owners. In this conflict the contrast between the sides was particularly clear and seemed symbolic of the crisis within British industry as a whole. Moreover, if the miners lost their case, workers in other sectors would soon be similarly squeezed. At the same time, the TUC had to be careful not to precipitate conflict by seeming to give unconditional support to the miners, thereby reducing the latter's inclination to negotiate.

The dispute, originally one between miners and owners, had therefore reached a new level. On one side were the representatives of the whole labour movement. On the other was the government, the attitude of which was crucial.

What, precisely, was its position? The government had temporarily controlled the mines during the First World War, but had ended this in 1921, ignoring the recommendations of the 1919 Sankey Report for 'the principle of State ownership'.[1] At first the government maintained that the dispute between owners and miners was not its direct concern – until pressure was applied by the TUC in 1925. Then, for a while, its response was cautious and defensive. On 'Red Friday', for example, Baldwin conceded a subsidy, which would last until the Samuel Commission had had time to report. At the same time, however, he began to make preparations to deal with a general strike if and when it occurred. This was done under the 1920 Emergency Powers Act, which enabled the government to take emergency measures to counteract threats to 'the supply and distribution of food, water, fuel or light, or with the means of locomotion'.[2] The government was clearly playing a waiting game until its own preparations were complete.

Baldwin's handling of the drift towards industrial conflict has been criticised on two grounds. The first charge is that he failed to take the opportunity offered by the Samuel Report to find a solution to the impending conflict. Despite the urgings of a number of moderate businessmen, Baldwin made no attempt to enforce it, thus accelerating the move towards a miners' strike. On the other hand, it is difficult to see how the implementation of the Report would have helped in any way. The mineowners had rejected that part which placed upon them the onus for improvements and rationalisation, while the miners had refused to take a temporary cut in wages; their official response had been 'Not a minute on the day, not a penny off the pay'. Baldwin would merely have diverted the wrath of the miners from the owners to the government. The only thing which would have prevented a strike was the restoration of the subsidy. But the Report had specifically advised against this and any move in that direction would have been interpreted as a major climbdown by the government. According to Clegg:

it is almost inconceivable that they [the government] could have renewed the subsidy so as to allow further negotiations unless they had first been given a firm commitment to accept wage cuts. . . . They also had to consider their followers, especially those in parliament, many of whom had been unhappy over Red Friday, and would not have tolerated what they would have seen as an abject and wholly unnecessary surrender.[3]

Baldwin cannot, therefore, be held responsible for the owners' announcement of a unilateral wage cut on 30 April, nor for the subsequent lockout and beginning of the miners' strike.

More serious is the second charge, that Baldwin did less than he could have done to negotiate a settlement with the TUC to avert the General Strike announced by Ernest Bevin for 3 May. The TUC was less militant than the miners, and clearly wanted a negotiated settlement which would avoid a general strike and the implications that would have for the millions of other workers the TUC also represented. Baldwin's answer was peremptory. In response to industrial action taken by printers at the *Daily Mail*, he refused to see a delegation from the General Council in the early hours of 3 May and clearly signalled the end of talks. According to L.C.B. Seaman:

> Baldwin's cessation of talks was the most provocative action taken by any participant in the sequence of events up to that moment; and the readiness of the T.U.C. to go on negotiating even after it, indicates that the General Strike took place because Baldwin forced their hand.[4]

By this analysis, Baldwin was more concerned about maintaining the recently re-established unity of the Conservative party than about averting industrial conflict. Any instincts for conciliation he might originally have possessed were clearly subordinated to a desire not to provoke cabinet hardliners like Winston Churchill, Neville Chamberlain and Joynson-Hicks. To have done otherwise would, in the view of Phillips,

> have required an intellectual capacity to grapple with complex industrial issues, an imagination to take the long rather than the short view, and the courage to meet illinformed criticism.[5]

An alternative view is that Ramsay MacDonald was trapped by events. According to McDonald:

> the General Strike was the accidental by-product of an unsuccessful attempt at high level co-operation between the government and the T.U.C. to avert a coal stoppage. Neither the government

nor the T.U.C. had consciously planned to have a massive confrontation.[6]

There is something in this. Well intentioned and moderate though it was, it was very unlikely that the TUC would be able to persuade the miners to accept a pay cut. Without it, the government could not hope to implement the Samuel Report. Any renewal of the subsidy would involve a major climbdown, so what was there to negotiate about when the TUC delegates came to Downing Street on 3 May? The strike of the printers at the *Daily Mail* was, admittedly, an excuse for the government's hardline response, but would the extension of the negotiating period have done anything except discredit Baldwin with his own cabinet?

Whatever his motive, Baldwin did not come well out of the movement of the TUC towards a general strike. He appeared tired and jaded and was pushed into a corner by his cabinet. There was even an element of hopelessness: 'everything I care for is being smashed to bits at this moment.'[7] Ironically, however, his reputation was to be salvaged and transformed over the next nine days.

CONTEMPORARY VIEWS OF THE GENERAL STRIKE

The General Strike is often portrayed as a bitter, if peaceful, enactment of class war within the United Kingdom. This approach is simplistic and hides a considerable degree of variation between the views of each sector of society. The stereotypes – TUC, trade unionists, Conservatives, and others – therefore need to be re-examined for the range of individual attitudes which most of them contained.

The TUC had a wide spectrum. The General Council included moderates like Arthur Pugh, General Secretary since 1925, and Ernest Bevin, formally General Secretary of the TGWU. They aimed to find support, from within local government and the church, to persuade the government to negotiate an early end to the strike. Some members were right wingers who favoured ending the action as quickly as possible; one example was W.M. Citrine, who had once been on the left of the trade union movement. By contrast, F. Bramley, who had preceded Pugh, had been a right-winger and had moved to the left. There was a surprising degree of hostility expressed against the General Council by ordinary trade union members. George Hodgkinson, a shop steward, believed that

The TUC structure made it impossible for it to handle a national dispute. Having been given the power, it didn't know how to delegate the responsibility.[8]

R.E. Scouller of the National Union of Clerks, Glasgow, complained that 'We did the donkey work, while the General Council sat round issuing edicts.'[9]

At local level there were also differences of opinion. Some leaders of individual trade unions were moderates. J.H. Thomas, General Secretary of the NUR, worked hard to achieve a compromise. He had also served in MacDonald's 1924 government as Colonial Secretary and was therefore conversant with the need to prevent the strike from damaging Labour politically. He was, however, distrusted by the radicals, many of whom were, not surprisingly, to be found in the miners' union. Most of the miners were fully behind the statement of their leader, A.J. Cook, that: 'We are going to be slaves no longer and our men will starve before they accept any reductions in wages.'[10] Some were prepared to take this literally, while others were forced by the end of the year to concede that their families had first call on their loyalty and that they had no option but to return to work.

Ranged against the TUC and the individual unions were the members of the government, who presented to the nation the impression of unanimity. In reality, however, there were as many shades within the cabinet as on the General Council. Some ministers remained moderate throughout the period of the strike. Sir Arthur Steel Maitland, minister for labour, had wanted to avoid the strike in the first place and supported the unofficial negotiations between Samuel and the TUC during the course of the strike. Others, like Lord Birkenhead, started as moderates but swung firmly behind the government once the strike had come to be considered a threat to the constitution. Others, again, remained hardliners throughout. A typical example was Sir William Joynson-Hicks, who emphasised the 'Communist threat'. Another was Winston Churchill, Chancellor of the Exchequer. On the eve of the strike Churchill said:

> Now the country faces the terrible blasting devastating menace of a general strike . . . a general strike will inevitably lead to some Soviet of Trade Unions with real control of the country and the effectual subversion of the state.[11]

Conservative backbenchers all supported the government, although with varying degrees of enthusiasm. To many the 'red peril' was reasserting itself. Others regarded themselves as fairminded but beleaguered by the action of the TUC. Sir Philip Gibbs, for example, said that

> My sympathies have always been on the side of the underdogs and the underpaid, but they were not in favour of this general strike, which was an attempt by the T.U.C. to coerce the Government of the country and take over its power.[12]

Younger and more progressive Conservatives, such as Harold Macmillan, MP for Stockton, placed the blame less on the miners than on the mineowners, whom they saw as implacable and irresponsible. These views could not, however, be articulated while the strike was in progress.

What of the parliamentary opposition? Labour MPs were almost entirely behind the TUC – partly because of the traditional ideological and organisational connection, and partly because most of the strikers would normally be expected to vote Labour. How Labour were perceived to behave in these circumstances would be vitally important for their future credibility with the electorate. There were, however, shades of support, the counterpart to the shades of opposition shown by the Conservatives. The Labour leader, MacDonald, wanted the earliest possible negotiated settlement, fearing that the Conservative government would use the strike to discredit the Labour party; it was important, therefore, to prevent the more radical Labour backbenchers from doing or saying anything which might be construed as an attack on the constitution.

Unlike the other two parties, the Liberals were openly split. Lloyd George consistently opposed the government's stance against the miners and the TUC, hoping instead to 'coordinate and consolidate all the progressive forces'.[13] At the other extreme, Simon argued that the strikers were involved in illegal action. Other leading Liberals like Asquith and Runciman started by supporting the government but eventually shifted their position and urged the government not to fight to the finish.

The Christian churches also reflected a range of opinions. The leadership tried, where possible, to promote conciliation between the two sides. On 7 May, for example, the Archbishops of Canterbury and York, together with three Bishops and several nonconformists, considered at Lambeth a means of ending the strike and came up with a three-point strategy. The TUC should call off the strike, the owners should allow work to resume on the basis of the conditions before the strike, and the government should restore the subsidy – all until a more lasting solution could be found. In the process, however, harsh things were said to the strikers. The Archbishop of Canterbury believed that the strike was 'so intolerable that every effort is needed . . . which the Government may make to bring that condition of things speedily to an end.' At the same time, he warned Baldwin against becoming intransigent and succumbing to the views of 'the truculent and fighting attitude' of some of his colleagues.[14] The official Catholic view was more uncompromising. Cardinal Bourne maintained in a sermon on 9 May that:

> It is a direct challenge to a lawfully constituted authority, and inflicts without adequate reason, immense discomfort and injury on millions of our fellow-countrymen. It is therefore a sin against the obedience which we owe to God, who is the source of that authority.

A greater degree of social compassion was shown by a parish vicar, who wrote in a letter on 4 May:

> as to the miners I am all with anyone who will fight for the maintenance of their wages. . . . They simply cannot afford to live on less. . . . I wish you Good Luck in the name of the Lord.[15]

Many Protestants opposed the government's position; this was especially the case with the Presbyterian Central Assembly, which strongly upheld the right of the workers to a decent living wage.

The legal profession came up with diverse interpretations of the General Strike. The prominent barrister and Liberal MP, Sir John Simon, argued that the whole action was illegal, that working contracts had been broken and that those who took part in the strike were personally accountable. 'Every Trade Union leader who has advised and promoted that course of action is liable in damages to the uttermost farthing of his personal possessions.'[16] Similar views were expressed by Mr Justice Astbury who ruled, in the Chancery Division of the High Court, that the General Strike was against the Trade Disputes Act of 1906 since there could be no trade dispute between the TUC and 'the Government and the nation'.[17] On the other hand, this interpretation was later challenged by legal experts like A.L. Goodhart, who argued that the General Strike was a 'sympathetic' strike and therefore not against the 1906 Trade Disputes Act as Simon and Astbury had claimed.[18]

The media normally acts as a cross-section of public opinion. The General Strike, however, saw the polarisation of viewpoints so that, in this one instance at least, the stereotypes prevailed. This was because the entire daily press was knocked out by the printers joining the first wave. Those papers which did publish were set up specifically for the purpose and were therefore bound to reflect the extremes. The government case was put by the *British Gazette*, which was organised by Churchill as an official propaganda channel. Hence it articulated views like: 'there can be no question of compromise of any kind. Either the country will break the General Strike, or the General Strike will break the country.'[19] Broadcasting was less directly affected than the press by strike action and Sir John Reith, the general manager, tried to steer a moderate course, fearing that the BBC – at this stage still a private company – would be taken over by the government at Churchill's instigation. It did, however, come under heavy government pressure and air time was given to the prime minister but denied to the Archbishop of Canterbury. The TUC could legitimately claim that the majority of the population was not properly informed about the circumstances relating to the strike; it would have done better not to have called out the printers in the first place, since this would have ensured a more balanced news coverage.

REASONS FOR THE DEFEAT OF THE GENERAL STRIKE

Two key factors were involved in the failure of the General Strike. One was the relative weakness of the TUC leadership and the tactical errors it committed. The other was the government's comprehensive planning and the effective way in which Baldwin handled the crisis.

Historians have generally argued that the TUC played its hand badly. According to C.L. Mowat: 'For the rank and file it was a triumph; for most of its national leaders a humiliation.'[20] S. Pollard maintains that 'The strike brought forth much capacity for organization, enthusiasm and solidarity of ordinary membership, but these were wholly nullified by the attitude of its leaders.'[21] How, precisely, were these limitations shown?

In the first place, the TUC was overawed by the enormity of the step it had taken. Most members of the General Council disliked the term 'general strike', some preferring the strategy of a series of local strikes. They eventually settled for what they hoped would be a swift 'national' strike that would be called off as soon as a settlement had been negotiated with the government to end the coal dispute. There was never any intention of taking on the government at a political level. This placed the TUC at a considerable disadvantage. Far from acknowledging the moderation of the TUC's approach, the government proceeded to accuse it of launching a political offensive against the constitution itself. In addition, the TUC had no means of forcing the government to negotiate on the coal dispute and, once it had become clear that Baldwin was determined to hold out on this issue, the TUC felt that it had no option but to back down and call off the General Strike. There was also the fear that the longer the struggle continued the more likely it was that it would be taken over by radicals and converted into a more extreme display of force. In this event, it would certainly become politicised, possibly even revolutionary.

The General Council's understandable caution affected the quality of its leadership. Numerous trade union branches complained about indecision at the centre. The response to the callout on 4 May of railway, transport, iron, steel and printing workers, was excellent. But the engineers and shipyard workers, unleashed on 11 May, were given no clear instructions and were then told to return to work on the following day. Throughout the period of the strike it was clear that the TUC had entirely underestimated the determination of the government to see the crisis through. Nor had it used the period of grace offered by the Samuel Commission to prepare in detail for an extended conflict. Instead, organisation was based on strike committees which were improvised and established by local trades councils. The TUC had even deprived the strikers of any chance of favourable press coverage, as a result of its defective decision to call out the printers as part of the first wave. At the same time, it became increasingly concerned about the future of its strike funds; within the nine days of the strike, some £4 million had been used up out of their total of £12.5 million. Unless the general strike were ended swiftly, it was felt, there would be no prospects of financing action by individual unions on a smaller scale in the future.

Overall, the TUC miscalculated. It assumed that a show of collective trade union strength would be sufficient. It was not. It also expected the government to confine its response to the industrial sector. It did not. Two different wars were therefore being fought out at the same time; for the TUC it was partial, for the government total.

The government had been preparing for the confrontation during the nine months between the granting of the subsidy and the eventual report of the Samuel Commission. During this period it had taken a series of essential measures. These included the consolidation of coal stocks and a systematic preparation of an emergency structure. The country was subdivided into ten areas, each under a civil commissioner. There would also be an emergency committee for supply and transport, together with an organisation for the maintenance of supplies, the main intention of which would be to co-ordinate the activities of strike-breakers. These measures were crucial, showing Baldwin's determination to go far beyond the rudimentary outlines of emergency organisation that had existed the previous year. When the General Strike occurred, the government made immediate use of the Emergency Powers Act, submitting Orders in Council to Parliament to requisition essential land, buildings, vehicles and fuel. Such preparations enabled the government to maintain essential services during the period of the strike. Food supplies were kept flowing, although prices increased to cover the extra costs of haulage. According to Phillips the government's planning for road haulage 'appeared afterwards to be the most vital . . . aspect of the success of the emergency administration'.[22]

Effective organisation was reinforced by a highly successful propaganda campaign. Baldwin associated the strike directly with an attack on constitutional government, which meant that the government was seen as something much higher than one of the parties in an industrial dispute. His views were regularly repeated in the *British Gazette*. On 5 May the public read that 'The general strike is . . . a direct challenge to ordered government . . . an effort to force upon some 42,000,000 British citizens the will of less than 4,000,000 others'.[23] The following day Baldwin declared that 'The general strike is a challenge to Parliament, and is the road to anarchy and ruin.'[24] He continued:

> Constitutional Government is being attacked. . . . Stand behind the Government. . . . The laws are in your keeping. You have made Parliament their guardian.[25]

The same message was repeated on the BBC on 8 May: 'I am a man of peace. But I will not surrender the safety and the security of the British Constitution'.[26] In this way the government was able to project itself as a force for moderation, while the strikers were portrayed as the authors of aggression.

Historians agree that such measures were crucial. According to McDonald, 'the government's policies and actions had, in effect, defeated the General Strike'. Its supply and transport organisation had 'neutralised the T.U.C.'s strike policy and destroyed the hopes of a quick victory', while its insistence on unconditional surrender 'dealt a blow to the T.U.C. hopes of forcing the cabinet to resume negotiations'.[27]

THE EFFECTS OF THE GENERAL STRIKE

The immediate results were negative. The miners, whose case against wage reductions had been the main factor involved in the General Strike, were now isolated and abandoned. Their prospects were worse than ever before. There was no chance that the government, which had seen off a national threat, would now heed the action of a single union, and any further chance of support from workers in other industries had gone for good. Despite the hopelessness of their position, the miners struggled on until the end of 1926 before being forced back to work on lower pay scales. Of all the sectors of the working class, they became the most embittered and potentially the most radical. The collieries remained unchanged and the owners, who had been reprieved by a victory which they had not won, were unrepentant. The coal industry was severely affected through the fall in production: the amount of coal mined in 1926 was under a half of that produced in the previous year; 28 million tons were lost for export, and huge quantities were imported from Germany and Poland. There were also knock-on effects on other industries, as altogether 500,000 men were made redundant and some £270 million were lost in wages. Of course, these figures reflected the damage done by the miners' strike rather than by the General Strike. It is, however, arguable that the defeat of the General Strike destroyed any chance of much needed reorganisation in the coal industry and put the clock back several decades.

Moving beyond the specific impact on mining, the General Strike can be seen as something of a turning point in industrial relations. Indeed, H.A. Clegg argues that 'The general strike was the most important episode in the history of British trade unionism.'[28] This can be supported in three ways.

After 1926 there were obvious curbs on the power of trade unionism in Britain. In part, these were imposed by Baldwin's government in the immediate aftermath of the General Strike. The Trade Disputes Act of 1927 declared illegal any sympathetic strike and made it necessary for trade union members to authorise personally any political levy made on their behalf. Changes were occurring simultaneously within the trade union movement. Membership, for example, fell by the end of 1926 from 5.5 million to under 5 million. There were also fewer strikes from 1927 onwards as trade union leaders tried to avoid further bruising conflicts not only with the government but also with employers. This process was directly influenced by a swing to the right and the predominance of moderates like Ernest Bevin.

This may give the impression that trade unionism was severely weakened. But industrial relations also improved in a more positive sense as trade union leaders and employers looked increasingly for grounds for collaboration and compromise. Sir Alfred Mond, head of Imperial Chemicals, had the full support of the TUC when he said 'We realise that industrial reconstruction can be undertaken only in conjunction with and with the co-operation of those entitled to speak for organised Labour'. The TUC, meanwhile, told the 1928 Congress that 'the unions can use their power to promote and guide the scientific reorganisation of industry.' Employers became more aware of the need for a degree of conciliation and, paradoxically, the General Strike had helped reduce class antagonisms. The middle classes had become more aware of the meaning of manual occupations when they had carried out voluntary duties during the course of May 1926. The position has been aptly summarised by A.J.P. Taylor: 'The General Strike, apparently the clearest display of the class war in British history, marked the moment when class war ceased to shape the pattern of British industrial relations'.[29]

The General Strike also had a major impact on political developments between 1926 and 1929. This took a surprising turn. Although the government had apparently scored a major victory over organised labour, any positive effect was shortlived. This was due partly to its own mistakes after 1926 and partly to the more positive strategy of the Labour Party.

Baldwin's government pursued a series of policies which seemed calculated to irritate and alienate, rather than reconcile. The Trade Disputes Act consolidated working-class support behind Labour, who contested it bitterly as it went through Parliament; it was, however, just about understandable in a government which wanted to avoid any further possibility of a general strike in the future. But other measures seem unnecessary. These included the reduction of unemployment benefit and the adoption of the principle that eligibility for benefit must be accompanied by a genuine search for work. Above all, the Conservative party seemed to become more and more disunited, with a growing rift between the hardliners, like Churchill, and the younger moderates, with Baldwin scarcely managing to hold the centre. In the circumstances, it is hardly surprising that, only three years after his fighting performance during the General Strike, he should have resorted to 'safety first' as the Conservative election slogan.

The Labour party, in the meantime, was able to prove that the defeat of the General Strike did not mean the decline of Labour as a political movement. Here the wisdom of MacDonald's aloofness during 1926, which had so infuriated some of the radicals, becomes apparent. The truth was that Labour had outgrown its dependence on the trade unions and was now appealing to a wider constituency; 1926 had actually helped MacDonald project this more extended appeal. 'I am an outsider. I stand apart. I am not a member of a trade union'.[30] This did not, however, mean that Labour lost the trade unionists. Quite the reverse. Those workers who had placed their faith in industrial action now became disillusioned with the TUC and opted instead for political action through the Labour party. This showed in the vastly increased support for Labour in the 1929 election. For the first time in its history Labour became, with 288 seats, the largest party in Parliament, due mainly to the predominance of moderates like Ernest Bevin.

This serves to refocus attention from the events of 1926 to those of 1931, the subject of the next chapter. Those who argue that the General Strike was in some ways a turning point for Labour go on to say that many of the gains were subsequently cancelled out by the crisis confronting Labour between 1929 and 1931. The revised view, however, sees the General Strike as part of a continuum of events from 1918 to 1931 which did little either to weaken the trade union movement or to enhance the political prospects of Labour. Rather than reversing the positive effects of the General Strike, therefore, the crisis of 1931 merely subsumed the whole continuum.

7

THE FIRST CRISIS OF
LABOUR 1929–39

After a brief spell in office in 1924, Labour returned to power in 1929. Ramsay MacDonald's second ministry was based on a firmer electoral base than his first: in the 1929 general election Labour had, with 288 seats, become the largest party in the Commons, although it was still dependent on Liberal support. MacDonald now had the opportunity to prove that Labour could do more than merely survive. He could continue the foreign and domestic policies of 1924 and demonstrate that, in future, Labour could be entrusted with an overall majority as a mandate for extensive reform.

In fact, the second Labour government of 1929–31 had a very mixed record. There were certainly achievements, although these were mostly apparent in foreign policy, which continued to be MacDonald's main interest. He had already contributed much to the settlement of the German question in 1924; in 1929 he and Henderson, the new Foreign Secretary, helped resolve the two remaining problems of reparations and the occupation of the Rhineland. The 1929 Young Plan reduced by over two-thirds the amount of reparations payable by Germany and rescheduled the repayments over the next 59 years, while in 1930 the last remaining troops of occupation were pulled out of Germany. Mac-Donald was also determined to give practical application to his pacifist principles by securing arms reductions and planning for a general disarmament conference under the auspices of the League of Nations. His most specific achievement here was the London Conference of 1930, in which it was agreed that the ratio of warship building between Britain, the United States and Japan should be restricted to 5:5:3. At the same time, he also promoted negotiations on trade issues, especially on the vexed question of tariffs.

This was a positive set of achievements which exceeded those of

1924. But all MacDonald's measures proved only temporary. Hopes of improved prospects with Germany were soon to be dashed by the rise of Hitler, which also had a knock-on effect against the disarmament proposals advanced by MacDonald. He was also to find that the Japanese would soon be exceeding the limits placed by the London Conference on their shipbuilding. Above all, any attempts to secure international trading agreements were to be wrecked by the impact of the great slump.

MacDonald's domestic achievements have been more extensively criticised by historians. Adelman, for example, considers that 'the Government's record was uninspiring'[1], and Pelling that they were 'singularly unsuccessful'.[2] These views are perhaps a little harsh, considering the range of reforms introduced and attempted. Arthur Greenwood's Housing Act of 1930 extended the subsidy for housebuilding and introduced a scheme of slum clearance. The Land-Utilisation Act and the Agricultural Marketing Act established a series of marketing boards. And the Coal Mines Act of 1930 reduced the hours worked by miners from 8 to 7½ hours a day. The government also attempted a series of other measures which might have earned it the reputation of a major reforming ministry had they succeeded. These included an education bill to raise the school-leaving age to 15, a bill to introduce a maximum working week of 48 hours, and an attempt to repeal the Trade Union Act of 1927. But the major problem was that Labour had to deal with unpredictable Liberal support in the House of Commons and constant Conservative opposition in the Lords which frustrated the government's reforming programme.

All of this was, of course, familiar to Labour. Its experience of government in 1924 had been constantly fettered by the obstructive attitudes of the other parties. MacDonald's approach was to ease this pressure on Labour partly by showing that his policies were not so different to those of the other two and partly by appealing for a consensus which would transcend party politics. He said in the first debate in the 1929 Parliament: 'I wonder how far it is possible, without in any way abandoning any of our party positions . . . to consider ourselves more as a Council of State and less as arrayed regiments facing each other in battle'.[3]

These two objectives seemed in 1929 to make perfect sense. By 1931, however, the situation had so changed that their practical implementation threw Labour into the worst crisis the party had ever experienced. The catalysts for this change were the increase in unemployment and the 1931 slump.

MACDONALD'S HANDLING OF UNEMPLOYMENT AND THE 1931 CRISIS

The Labour government of 1929–31 was affected by highly unfavourable circumstances, the origins of which were entirely beyond its control. MacDonald had returned to power hoping that the more prosperous times which seemed to beckon in 1929 would enable him to deal with the problem of unemployment; indeed, this had been his main promise to the electorate in the 1929 election. Against his expectations, the situation deteriorated rapidly. The total of 1.2 million unemployed in 1929 increased in 1930 to 1.9 million and, by 1931, had more than doubled to 2.6 million. The reasons for this trend are examined in Chapter 8; they are a combination of long-term structural decline in the staple industries and the more immediate impact of the 1929 Wall Street crash in the United States, which accelerated the shrinking of world trade. The implications for the government were extremely serious since increased unemployment meant an inevitable increase in public expenditure to maintain unemployment benefit which, in turn, threatened to result in an unbalanced budget.

The government therefore faced a dilemma: what should the priority be? On the one hand, Labour was supposed to be the party of the working man; on the other it had to project the image of a responsible government and the ultimate test of such responsibility was the safety of the nation's finances in its hands. MacDonald, it has to be said, was so over-awed by the latter that he took remarkably few measures to tackle unemployment. Although the government was quick to identify industrial backwardness as a major cause of unemployment in the staple industries, its intervention was relatively mild. Enquiries were established to investigate options, but the only action taken was to rationalise working hours and production quotas in the mining industry and to unite the London passenger transport network. Instead, MacDonald sought solutions to unemployment in his foreign policy, trying to promote international co-operation to revive international trade which would, in turn, boost production within the staple industries. To much of the party, however, this approach was too circuitous.

The fact of the matter was that MacDonald's government had very little idea as to how to tackle the unemployment problem. For one thing, it lacked any real economic knowledge. To try to offset this, MacDonald set up in 1930 the Economic Advisory Council; including industrialists and economists, this was intended to provide advice for the government. Usually, however, the Chancellor of the Exchequer paid more attention to the advice of Treasury officials since the members of Council were rarely able to agree among themselves. MacDonald was genuinely nonplussed and the more adventurous ideas for tackling unemployment came from outside the government. J.M. Keynes argued consistently for government management of the economy, while Lloyd George and part of the Liberal party drew up a plan for public works consisting mainly of the construction of roads and town planning. The only new ideas within the cabinet came from Oswald Mosley, who argued strongly for a public works scheme before leaving the Labour party to devote himself to fringe politics on the radical right. Throughout 1930 and 1931 the cabinet was concerned primarily with being seen to be financially orthodox. It deliberately avoided new ideas, believing that solutions to unemployment would be found in retrenchment rather than in experimentation.

As well as being the response to the long-term problem of unemployment, this was also the reaction to the emergency of the financial crisis of 1931. The impact of the Wall Street crash hit Europe in May 1931, resulting in the collapse of Credit Anstalt, the Austrian banking network. The crisis spread rapidly to Germany and Britain, with a run on gold in the Bank of England itself. The Conservatives unjustly accused the Labour government of precipitating the crisis in Britain through heavy public expenditure and the Liberals proposed the formation of a committee to consider what economies might be made. The government fell into line by appointing the May Committee, headed by a leading financier. The Committee's report, published in July 1931, made sensational reading. It estimated a budget deficit of £132 million for 1932 and recommended pay cuts for all employees in the public sector, together with a reduction in unemployment benefit by 20 per cent. This greatly exacerbated the crisis by drawing the financial world's attention to the alleged deficit and making it impossible for the government to bridge the gap temporarily with loans.

MacDonald signalled in the clearest possible way his intention of implementing the recommendations of the report. The TUC and a large part of the Labour party tried to put across alternative proposals, which might include a more graduated tax on profits and income. These were, however, rejected by MacDonald and the Chancellor of the Exchequer, Philip Snowden, who pressed for cuts in unemployment benefit. Since most of his cabinet resisted, MacDonald transformed his administration from a Labour into a 'National' government, comprising – under his leadership – four Conservatives, four Labour ministers and two Liberals. A month later, in September, Snowden introduced an

100

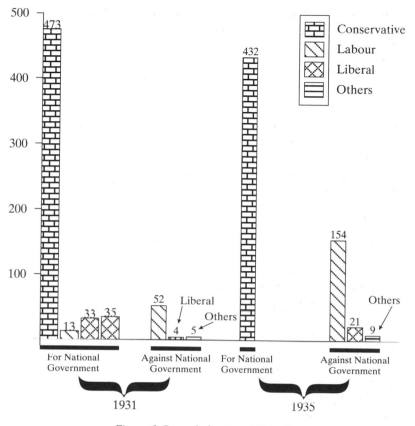

Figure 6 General elections 1931–35

emergency budget, which raised income tax, and cut unemployment benefit by 10 per cent and public sector pay by up to 15 per cent. MacDonald then sought a mandate for further changes in the future under the National Government by calling a general election in October 1931. The results appeared catastrophic for the Labour party, which had now expelled MacDonald from its ranks: they declined from 288 seats to a mere 52. MacDonald's National Government was given a massive vote of confidence by the electorate, but of the 521 MPs who supported it, no fewer than 473 were Conservatives – clearly the real beneficiaries of the 1931 crisis.

This strange turn of events has been the subject of considerable controversy and speculation, which we will now examine.

COMMENTS ON MACDONALD'S HANDLING OF THE 1931 CRISIS

MacDonald's actions in 1931 may be analysed in two main stages: the first, his formation of the May Committee and acceptance of its recommendations; the second, his decisions to establish a National Government and fight a general election.

Most historians argue that it was unnecessary to appoint the May Committee at all. MacDonald had already received advice from the Economic Advisory Council and there were plenty of ideas in circulation from the Liberal party. But the government was economically inexperienced and, lacking any coherent policy, succumbed to the harsh reality of the slump. The action which followed showed, in the words of Cole and Postgate, that the government were

> guilty of the lunacy – or worse – of appointing a committee of their political opponents – to pronounce judgement on their financial policy. This folly was, indeed, largely responsible for their fall; for the financial interests seized their opportunity.[4]

In effect, the May Committee precipitated the crisis and caused the run on the pound which brought about the split in the government and the party. Its advice was badly misplaced. J.M. Keynes referred to the May report as 'the most foolish document I have ever had the misfortune to read',[5] a view reinforced by Ashworth:

> The report presented an overdrawn picture of the existing financial position; its diagnosis of the causes underlying it was inaccurate; and many of its proposals . . . were not only harsh but were likely to make the economic situation worse, not better.[6]

Was the formation of the National Government a necessary consequence of the 1931 crisis? MacDonald clearly thought it was, placing what was, in his view, the national interest, above any loyalty to party. He wrote on 1 September that the rank and file did not have 'the same duty as the leaders' and that he was not 'a machine-made politician'.[7] Neville Chamberlain, who met MacDonald on 22 August, graphically described the latter's position.

> He had founded, nursed, cherished, built up, the Socialist Party. It was painful enough to leave an old party. What must it be for him to contemplate killing his own child.[8]

MacDonald's priority, as he explained it to the cabinet on 24 August, was 'a Government of Persons, not of Parties'.[9] For this, MacDonald received the tribute of King George V, who admired 'the courage with which you have put aside all personal and party interests in order to stand by the country in this grave national crisis'.[10] MacDonald probably hoped to return to his party base after having achieved his national objective but, in the meantime, he was convinced that circumstances warranted his being the first prime minister to suspend the party system in peacetime.[11]

Naturally, the Labour party had a very different perspective on the crisis. Most MPs, constituency associations and trade union officials came to the conclusion that MacDonald had committed a major act of betrayal. He had rejected their advice on alternative financial measures – such as devaluation or a revenue tariff – and, instead, had heeded the May Committee, the leaders of the other parties, and the king. Although some Labour MPs conceded that a certain degree of austerity might be necessary in the short term, why should MacDonald be the person to introduce measures which were essentially Conservative? The honourable course would have been to resign and let the Conservatives implement any cuts. Instead, he aligned himself with the Conservatives and spared Baldwin the odium which such measures would inevitably involve. This was enough of a crime, but worse was to follow. Mac Donald fought an election alongside the Conservatives and saw the massive reduction of Labour seats in the Commons. Arguably, this need not have happened. Had he led Labour into an election in 1931, the scale of the defeat would almost certainly have been far less; the size of the Conservative vote was considerably enhanced by its connection with MacDonald's appeal for 'National' support. MacDonald, in other words, flung open the door to the Conservatives, in the process trapping Labour behind it.

It is hardly surprising that the Labour party should have expelled MacDonald from its ranks for 'his open flouting of Party discipline in joining an anti-Socialist government formed for the purpose of forcing through Parliament anti-working class legislation'.[12] From that moment he was loathed as a traitor by the rest of his party. His reputation has never really recovered. Little attempt has been made to rehabilitate his image since 1931 as all subsequent Labour leaders and post-war prime ministers have hastened to distance themselves from his name.

Some historians see a strong residual sense of futility in MacDonald's gesture; they maintain that the upheaval he brought about was all for nothing. When the new National Government tried to secure credits from France and the United States these were refused and it had to resort to bringing Britain off the gold standard. As Morgan points out:

Thus, devaluation, which Keynes had recommended and the Labour government had gone over the brink to prevent, came four weeks after the formation of the National government. MacDonald's determination had been for nothing. The advice of the Bank of England, which had been taken as absolute gospel, was proved to be worthless.[13]

Furthermore, MacDonald rapidly became disillusioned with his association with the Conservative party and, if his motive had been to lessen the effect of Conservative-style policies which would have been applied even if he had stepped down, he signally failed.

The criticism which has been heaped upon MacDonald might give the impression that what he did in 1931 was unique in British political history. This would be quite false. There are at least two precedents of a prime minister causing a split within his party through holding out for what he considered a vital national interest; in each case, this followed a period of major contributions to the internal development of that party. Sir Robert Peel, who presided over the transformation of the Tories into the Conservatives, brought about a major rupture in 1846 when he forced through the repeal of the Corn Laws with the support of the Whigs but against the views of two-thirds of his own party. The political impact was immense, the Conservatives managing to govern for only five years out of the next thirty-three. W.E. Gladstone, who did more than anyone else to convert the Whigs into Liberals, inflicted similar damage to his own party in the 1880s and 1890s by focusing on the policy of Home Rule for Ireland. The subsequent defection of a block of Liberal 'unionists' to the Conservatives ensured the latter's political pre-eminence for twenty years after 1885. MacDonald might be seen as following in the footsteps of Peel and Gladstone; despite contributing more than anyone else to the early development of his party he condemned it to political exile for the next decade.

There is a particularly close parallel between the strategies used by MacDonald and Peel. MacDonald chose not to resign and hand over the reins of government to Baldwin, allowing the Conservatives to implement the May report. A similar situation had arisen in 1846. Faced with the opposition of most of his Conservative party to the repeal of the Corn Laws, Peel might have gone to the country and lost narrowly to the Whigs – who favoured the measure. The Corn Laws would almost certainly have been repealed and the Conservative party would have avoided a major split. Both Peel and MacDonald were convinced that they alone could see the country through its crisis. In each case there was a sense of national destiny which transcended the more mundane level of party leadership. The price paid for this was the enormous enhancement of the other party. In 1846 the Whigs saw the measure they wanted passed while, at the same time, the Conservatives were thrown into disarray. In 1931 the Conservatives were content to see the financial measures which profoundly affected the working class, knowing at the same time that they were being formulated by a socialist prime minister.

If there are historical precedents to MacDonald's policy, then history seems to be playing a strange trick. Why, in retrospect, should Peel and Gladstone be numbered among the icons of their parties, while MacDonald continues to be vilified by his? There are two possible reasons for this.

One lies in the nature of the splits within the three parties. Peel carried sufficient conviction to take one-third of the Conservatives with him, while Gladstone retained the support of the large majority of the Liberals. MacDonald was supported by only twenty-five MPs, a number which halved after the 1931 general election. It could be said, therefore, that MacDonald did not command enough backing to split the party and the fact that he was thrown out diminishes his claim to be considered alongside Peel and Gladstone as a statesman harried by shortsighted party politicians. Second, MacDonald's stand seemed far less worthwhile than Peel's or Gladstone's. The repeal of the Corn Laws in 1846 marked an economic turning point, even if it did split the Conservative party. Gladstone's Home Rule may have failed during his third and fourth ministries, but it was to be seen as a viable solution to the Irish question which was tried again before the First World War. Compared with these, MacDonald's policies seemed transient, even futile. Hence, for all his contributions to the growth of the Labour party, MacDonald 'remains a prisoner of one date – 1931.'[14]

THE IMPACT OF THE CRISIS ON LABOUR AFTER 1931

On the surface, Labour experienced in 1931 the worst crisis in its entire history. The decline in the general election from 288 seats to 46 was seen by many as a massacre. Many prominent MPs lost to Conservative candidates backing MacDonald and, of the former Labour ministers now opposing the National Government, only George Lansbury was returned.

The collapse was nationwide: Labour's representation shrank in Scotland from 37 to 7, in the Midlands from 47 to 7 and in the North East from 22 to 2.[15] To make matters worse, a large part of the working class voted against Labour. This was due partly to the moderate image projected by Baldwin's Conservative party, and partly to the vision of Macdonald in forming a national government of reconciliation. There is also the point that some of the working class had been depoliticised by the slump – and were more concerned about the future of their jobs than about political militancy. In the atmosphere of depression, they were as inclined to accept the prospects offered by a new national government as the promises of a party abandoned by its leader. Labour now drew its only real strength from the areas where the depression had already done the most damage rather than from those which still had some hope of an early recovery.

Labour also experienced financial problems as the party went rapidly into deficit and officials at Transport House, the party's headquarters, had to face a salary cut of 5 per cent. Lack of funds meant that Labour had difficulty in contesting by-elections and had to duck at least five in 1932 alone. Meanwhile, divisions were widening on policy. The main catalyst for this was no longer unemployment, but foreign affairs. Some within the party wanted to persevere with the principles of peace and rearmament while others, like Dalton, preferred tougher measures and felt that 'The party won't face up to realities'.[16] The opposition of Cripps and Lansbury to sanctions against Italy provoked a strong attack at the 1935 party conference, after which Lansbury was forced to resign as Labour leader. The subsequent crises involving Hitler perpetuated the conflict between those who supported and those who opposed re-armament. It was not until 1937 that the Labour party were able to arrive at something resembling a consensus.

All this might seem to indicate a party in terminal decline. But what happened from the mid 1930s was a steady recovery which indicated that Labour's disarray had been superficial rather than fundamental. The 1931 low-water mark was brought about in abnormal and artificial circumstances. Labour were bound to do badly in the election following MacDonald's decision to form the National Government. Three leading cabinet ministers had called for a national government and had secured the support of the other parties. This meant the formation of a coalition which could hardly fail to win a landslide, as Lloyd George's coalition had done in 1918. In these circumstances, Labour did well to mount a campaign at all.

In terms of the party's future, what really mattered was not so much the number of seats won; the British single non-transferable electoral system often distorted the correlation between seats and votes. Rather, it was the proportion of the popular vote which determined whether a party was set into long-term decline, as was the case with the Liberals, or whether, like Labour, it was experiencing short-term – if alarming – fluctuations. In fact, there was a surprising degree of continuity in popular support. In 1929 Labour's 288 seats had been based on the support of 37.1 per cent of the electorate; the 46 seats still represented 30.7 per cent and each one had been fought against tough opposition. The Liberals supporting the National Government had, by contrast, won 35 seats with only 3.7 per cent of popular support, largely because of electoral deals with the Conservatives. The 1931 performance was therefore Labour's bedrock and the situation could only improve. In 1935 Labour secured 37 per cent of the vote – higher even than its share in 1929 – although the artificial circumstances of the National Government translated this into only 154 seats.

Long before the Second World War, therefore, Labour's electoral revival was well under way. The same story could be seen in those by-elections which Labour could afford to contest. In 1932 Labour won Wakefield from the Conservatives and secured Wednesbury. In 1933 Labour regained seats lost in 1931 at Rotherham and East Fulham and also achieved high swings in middle-class seats such as Hitchin. In 1934 Labour recaptured North Hammersmith and Upton, with North Lambeth and Swindon following shortly afterwards. There was also a remarkable recovery in local government elections, following a series of disastrous results in 1931. Of the 836 candidates put forward by Labour in 1932, 458 were elected; this compared with 218 of the Conservatives' 490,[17] and there was an overall swing to Labour which peaked at 14 per cent in Salford and Gateshead. The situation improved further in 1933 as Labour gained control of Swansea, Norwich, Barnsley, Bootle and Sheffield and seven other councils for the first time. Overall in 1933 Labour gained 181 and lost 5, while the Conservatives gained 6 and lost 112, the Liberals gained 5 and lost 33.

Recovery also took the form of internal consolidation which ultimately prepared Labour the more effectively for political responsibility. Changes were made to the party's constitution and the National Executive was reformed. At the same time, programmes were developed for the future, such as 'For Socialism and Peace' (1934) and Labour's 'Immediate Programme' (1937). These contrasted with the absence of a longer-term view in MacDonald's governments and lay behind at least part of the reforms carried out by Attlee's Labour government after 1945.

In this respect, Labour's enforced absence from government had one positive result. Another was the shedding of the more radical left with the decision of the Independent Labour Party (ILP) to disaffiliate from the Labour Party in 1932 after showing persistent opposition to the latter's policy of gradual reform. There was also increased vigilance against penetration by Communists. Above all, Labour benefited from a period of steady, unspectacular and safe leadership. Lansbury took over in 1932, with Attlee as the deputy leader. Attlee assumed the leadership temporarily in 1935, a position subsequently confirmed. Unlike MacDonald, Attlee had a reputation for trustworthiness with every section of the Labour party and did much to heal the rift left by the 1931 crisis. He also presided over improved relations between the Parliamentary party and the TUC; in 1937 Dalton referred to 'harmonised working between the industrial and the political sides of our movement, which has been a happy feature of the post-MacDonald era'.[18]

In the final analysis, the impact of the 1931 crisis on Labour appeared at the time to be devastating but proved, in the longer term, to be superficial. Phillips argues that the Labour split of 1931 was less serious than that of the Conservatives over the repeal of the Corn Laws in 1846, or of the Liberals over Home Rule.[19] The key point here is that MacDonald took only three ministers with him, while the rest of the party remained united. There was no equivalent to the schism within the Liberal party, which produced rival allegiances to Asquith and Lloyd George. The Labour party was therefore able, without tearing itself apart, to vilify the man who had contributed so much to its early development. Indeed, the legend of MacDonald's treachery became an integral part of Labour's recovery.

8

THE ECONOMY, UNEMPLOYMENT AND GOVERNMENT POLICY BETWEEN THE WARS

Between the two world wars the British economy experienced unprecedented trauma, over which interpretations are still divided. The purpose of this chapter is to look at some of the explanations which have been provided. The first section will provide the initial perspective by outlining and explaining the main changes which occurred in the economy between the wars. The second will concentrate on the economic infrastructure, especially industry, transport and trade. The third will cover the social impact of changes within the economic infrastructure, particularly the growth, distribution and implications of unemployment in the 1920s and 1930s. The fourth will deal with the efforts made by governments to tackle the problems which arose and, in the process, look at the economic theories which they accepted and rejected. The 1930s have acquired a thoroughly negative reputation, to the extent of being known as 'the Devil's decade'; the final section will consider whether or not this description is deserved.

ECONOMIC CHANGES IN PERSPECTIVE 1919–39

The twenty-year record of uplift and downturn within the British economy began in 1919 with a post-war boom, considered by D.H. Aldcroft to have been both 'violent and speculative'.[1] In retrospect, it is not really surprising that it should have occurred. The arrival of peace suddenly released those productive sectors of the economy which had been pinned down by the First World War. The end of economic controls interacted with the revived demand for consumer goods and the resumption of pre-war trade patterns to boost industrial production by 20 per cent between 1919 and 1921[2] and to keep unemployment down to 2.6 per cent. Two other factors helped to generate this boom. One was the need to repair wartime damage, which provided a stimulus to heavy industries like shipbuilding; another, according to S.N. Broadberry, was that Britain entered this boom 'before her competitors found their feet.'[3] But in 1921 the boom ended as the conditions which had brought it into existence either faded away or went into reverse. The bubble had been inflated by a speculation of investment which ended during the course of 1921 with the saturation of the markets as well as of consumer needs. Industrial production suddenly fell to below its 1918 level and unemployment was up to 22 per cent in 1921.[4]

Was this decline permanent? Or did a recovery take place between 1923 and 1929? The answer to this question depends on the perspective adopted. On the one hand, there were some positive indications of economic performance which suggested a sustained recovery from the low point of the 1921 slump. The rate of industrial production increased by 2.8 per cent per annum on average, which was actually higher than in the first decade of the twentieth century.[5] This growth was stimulated especially by a series of new industries being developed during the 1920s, including chemicals, motor vehicles and electricity. Until 1926 the building industry added to the momentum, while exports increased between 1926 and 1929, even though they did not attain pre-war figures. On the other hand, the end of the boom removed the cushion which had temporarily softened the impact of the First World War on the British economy. After 1921 the losses incurred became more apparent. These included the reduction of overseas export markets and the increasing amount spent on imports: the consequent gap in the balance of payments was barely covered by invisible earnings from shipping and insurance, since these had also contracted during the war. Meanwhile, Britain had lost her place as the world's financial centre and sterling had been overtaken by the dollar as the world's dominant currency. The infrastructure was heavily damaged by the decline of the traditional or staple industries, especially shipping, textiles and coal. These bore the brunt of the unemployment which steadily increased to 1.4 million in 1925 and then 1.5 million in 1927. Such problems were probably exacerbated by government policies. In 1925, for example, Chancellor of the Exchequer Winston Churchill returned Britain to the gold standard at the pre-war rate of $4.86 to the pound. This made British industry even less competitive by increasing the price of goods and materials. Employers' pressure for wage cuts, especially in the coal industry, led to a deterioration in industrial relations which culminated in the 1926 General Strike (see Chapter 6). Overall, Britain's economic development between 1923 and 1929 lacked the pace shown in other western industrial countries.

The situation deteriorated rapidly after 1929 with the arrival of the Great Depression. This was precipitated by the Wall Street Crash in New York and was communicated through the European banking system by the collapse of Credit Anstalt in 1931. The political impact on Britain was spectacular – the collapse of Ramsay MacDonald's second Labour ministry and the formation of the National Government (see Chapter 7). The economic effect was more insidious as the Depression accelerated the decline of the staple industries that had already occurred in the 1920s. Exports, too, were badly affected, declining by over 33 per cent. The combination of these two factors led to an increase in unemployment from 1.4 million in 1929 to 2.9 million in 1931, equivalent to about 23 per cent of the insured work force (see Figure 7).

Thereafter, however, it declined steadily to 2.7 million in 1932, 2.5 million in 1933, 2.2 million in 1934, 2.0 million in 1935, 1.6 million in 1936 and 1.5 million in 1937. An increase to 1.9 million in 1938 was followed by a fallback to 1.5 million by 1939. Britain's recovery from the Depression was more rapid and complete than that of her industrial rivals. This was partly because of her relatively poor economic performance in the 1920s; the rate of economic growth in that period had not outstripped Britain's industrial and economic strength. Or to put it another way, the British economy was still nearer to its bedrock than were the economies of its rivals, which therefore had further to fall. Britain also escaped the intense speculation on the stock market which had made 1929–31 such a traumatic experience in the United States and Germany.

In many ways it was surprising how strongly the British economy rallied during the 1930s. The revival was essentially domestic-based. One component was an increase in production after the nadir of 1931, when the level had been 84 per cent of that of 1929. This had increased to 93 per cent by 1933 and thereafter it climbed steadily. By 1934 it exceeded the 1929 level by 4 per cent, in 1935 by 10 per cent and in 1937 by 24 per cent.[6] One reason for this was the rapid development of new industries to offset the decline of the staple industries. Another was the housing boom of the 1930s, facilitated by cheaper raw materials and by the low cost of purchase – averaging £450 for a semi-detached house. The varied requirements of house-building helped fuel recovery in other industries. The external manifestation of recovery was a rise in exports, assisted partly by a government policy of tariff

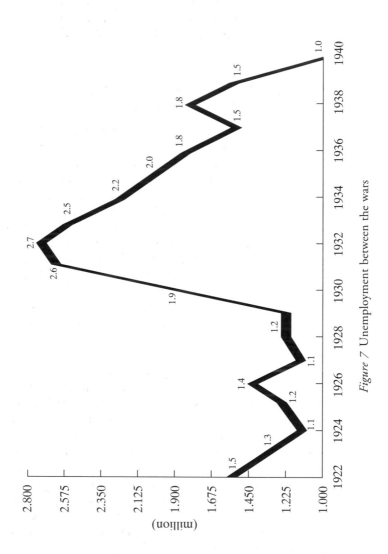

Figure 7 Unemployment between the wars

protection and partly by a general increase in worldwide trade levels. The final factor pulling Britain out of depression – or preventing her from sliding back into it in 1938 – was the rapid pace of rearmament. Ironically, the British economy was at its strongest precisely at the point that it was plunged into another war – which brought with it a new range of problems.

CHANGES TO THE ECONOMIC INFRASTRUCTURE

The British economy had been shaped by the first Industrial Revolution. Between 1750 and 1850 British prosperity and commercial supremacy had come to depend upon four basic, or staple, industries: coal, iron and steel, textiles and shipbuilding. They had provided both the goods for distribution at home and abroad and the means of distributing them; industry and commerce had therefore become closely interconnected. Between the world wars, however, these industries experienced a crisis which manifested itself in the unprecedented rise of unemployment. A more detailed survey of the interwar economy must therefore begin with an analysis of Britain's changing industrial infrastructure during this period.

There were several common factors in the decline of the staple industries. All had been vital in the early stages of the industrial revolution but all declined by comparison with their pre-1914 figure, never managing to reach that peak again. Although they had been temporarily stimulated by the First World War, all experienced a slump after 1921. They suffered under growing competition from other industrial states, including the United States and Germany, by contrast with which they were chronically inefficient. This was partly because they were all overmanned and labour-intensive, lacking the more modern equipment used by their main competitors. They were also affected by the over-valuation of the pound as a result of the return to the gold standard in 1926. Above all, they all suffered as a direct result of shrinking British participation in the world markets. This left them with declining export figures and an industrial capacity which, for the first time, was not being fully used. Hence there were massive redundancies which greatly accelerated the increase in unemployment. Overall, according to D.H. Aldcroft, 'The decline in output of the staple trades conforms to the theory that industries have an s-shaped long-run growth curve. Most maturing industries reach a stage when diminishing returns set in and rates of growth decline or become negative.'[7]

Coal-mining was the most severely affected of all the staple industries. Output peaked in 1913 with 287 million tons, compared with 210 million in 1933 and 237 million tons in 1938. This was a decline in real terms, since world production increased over the same period by 0.7 per cent. There was obviously a reduced demand for British coal, due partly to growing competition from Germany and Poland in the export markets and partly to falling consumption at home in both domestic and industrial use. Sales both abroad and at home had been affected by the increased use of alternative fuels. By 1939, for example, over 50 per cent of the world's shipping was powered by oil, while the domestic user was turning more and more to electricity. The vulnerability of the British coal industry became fully apparent with the recovery of German coal production after the French evacuated the Ruhr in 1924. British coal lacked the ability to compete effectively because of the lack of proper investment in mining techniques, which meant that the coal industry fell increasingly behind its continental counterparts. All the mineowners could suggest to increase competitiveness was a reduction of wages, which inevitably fuelled industrial unrest.

Equally dramatic was the collapse of the cotton textiles industry. By 1938 production had declined by 50 per cent compared with 1913. The vital factor was the collapse of export markets. In 1913 some 80 per cent of Britain's cotton goods had been exported, accounting for 25 per cent of Britain's total exports. By the end of the 1930s textiles counted for only 12 per cent of British exports, while Britain's share of the world market dropped from 65 per cent to 26 per cent.[8] Chief among the lost markets were India and the Far East, which ended the 1930s importing 91 per cent less than in 1913. This was partly because India increased its own production enormously and partly because of the rapid growth in Japanese exports. Britain also suffered from the disadvantage of having been the first in the field as a massive producer. Much of her equipment and technology had become obsolete by the 1920s and Britain's main rivals had the advantage of equipping selectively in accordance with the experience of British firms and of using a larger pool of cheap labour. Meanwhile, Britain was discouraged from sinking investment into modernisation by the fact of the shrinking overseas market. A Committee on the Cotton Industry therefore reported in 1930 that 'we are satisfied, from the evidence laid before us, that the British cotton industry has failed to adapt its organisation and methods to changed conditions and so has failed, and is failing, to secure that cheapness of production and efficiency in marketing which alone sells goods in the East today.'[9]

Shipbuilding also suffered severely, by 1933 collapsing to a mere 7 per cent (133,000 tons) of the 1913 level of 1.93 million tons. By 1938 it was still only just over 1 million tons or slightly over 50 per cent of 1913's production. A large part of the problem was the saturation of shipping needs worldwide; the pre-war carrying capacity was more than enough for inter-war needs.[10] It is true that there had been losses between 1914 and 1918, but these had been made up by a sudden spate of production between 1919 and 1921. From 1921 there was ferocious competition for a much reduced market as British shipbuilding suffered against new rivals who were supported by government subsidies. Britain was also slow to adapt to oil-powered ships, still preferring to build steamships. The overall situation was compounded during the 1930s by the contraction of world trade as a result of the Great Depression.

The experience of the steel industry was mixed. In some respects its decline was as devastating as that of any of the staple industries. Iron exports declined from 1.2 million tons in 1913 to 0.1 million tons in 1938, and British steel production as a proportion of the world's output contracted from 10.2 per cent in 1913 to 8.1 per cent in 1929. This was partly because British firms were much smaller and more inefficient than competitors like the United States Steel Corporation and the German *Vereinigte Stahlwerke*. There were also problems with British equipment: 'Our plant is not, as a whole, so up-to-date as that of Germany'.[11] According to the Chairman of Vickers it was common knowledge that there was 'a very large percentage of steel and engineering businesses which for one reason or another are ill-adapted for modern production.'[12] On the other hand, the steel industry showed more capacity for recovery than the other staple industries. Production rose steadily during the 1930s, against the trend experienced by coal, textiles and shipbuilding. This was certainly not due to any revival in the export markets; instead, two internal developments were responsible. The first was the development of consumer and electrical goods that required steel in growing quantities; the second the acceleration of an official policy of rearmament from 1937 onwards.

Even allowing for the partial recovery of steel production, the overall experience of the staple industries between the wars was decidedly gloomy. At the same time, however, the economic infrastructure was gradually being transformed by the emergence of a series of newer industries like motor manufacturing, electricity, chemicals, aircraft and rayon. Their combined contribution to total industrial output increased from 12.5 per cent in 1924 to nearly 25 per cent by 1939.

The new industries differed from the staple industries in several ways. Structurally they were likely to exist in larger and more efficient units; they employed newer techniques and higher levels of scientific expertise; and, because they depended on sales at home, they did not have to fight for the collapsing export markets. They were also located in different areas. The staple industries had been developed in the nineteenth century on the coalfields and in areas such as Teesside, Tyneside, Merseyside, parts of the Midlands, South Wales, Scotland, West and South Yorkshire, Lancashire and West Cumberland. By contrast, the newer industries were located in London, the South East and the West Midlands. This was largely because they were light industries which needed smaller amounts of power. Electricity was much more suitable than coal for their purposes and this could be supplied across a national grid. New industries could therefore be dispersed to new centres with large populations and consumer spending power. They were not tied to the traditional rail routes, making more use of the rapidly growing road network. Overall, the new industries attracted more capital.

> This is to be expected because the industries which at any point of time offer the most favourable prospects naturally attract the new capital and the inventive and managerial skill, upon which advances in productivity depend, to a much greater extent than industries in decay.[13]

The best examples of this are to be seen in the motor manufacturing and electrical industries.

According to D.H. Aldcroft, 'The motor manufacturing industry was without doubt one of the key sectors in the modernization of British industry during this period.'[14] This was concentrated in Cowley, near Oxford, and the West Midlands, especially Wolverhampton, Birmingham and Coventry. Production increased from 75,000 cars in 1922 to 500,000 in 1937, making Britain the second largest producer in the world. The initial impetus came from the home market as the greater affluence experienced by many people increased their desire to own a car for social and personal reasons. Growth was also stimulated by the building industry since the spread of suburban residence promoted new forms of transport. Conversely, of course, the greater independence offered by the car promoted suburban sprawl. Meanwhile, motoring became a more attractive proposition with the decline of petrol costs: petrol was 2d. a gallon cheaper than it had been in 1914 and during the 1930s the overall cost of motoring fell by something like one-third. Vehicles had also become safer and more reliable, with improvements like pneumatic tyres, improved brakes, windscreen wipers and electric starters. Above all, the motor industry was effectively organised by Morris and Austin and, more than any other manufacturing process, made full use of assembly-line techniques.

S. Pollard implies that there was another sector which was even more successful in adapting to the new conditions of the 1920s and 1930s.

> One of the most critically important of the new industries was electrical engineering, together with the supply of electricity. It could be taken as the symbol of the industrial Britain, freeing other industries from dependence on the coalfields of the north and west, and setting in motion a vast migration to the Midlands and south-east.[15]

This was clearly a new development, since before the First World War Britain had lagged behind Germany and the United States. Most of her industrial equipment was more suited to traditional forms of power, while housing and urban lighting had initially been adapted to gas. During the 1930s, however, the consumption of electricity increased rapidly. The new industries all used it in preference to coal, benefiting from its reduced costs and more efficient plant layout. A further boost was received from domestic appliances: there was a rapid increase in the demand for cookers, irons, vacuum cleaners, washing machines and wirelesses. The expansion in the supply of, and demand for, electricity in turn boosted the electrical manufacturing industry, which benefited greatly from the transmission of power across a national grid. British engineering skills were well suited to the production of heavy plant, which required the construction of large pieces of equipment to individual specification and design. The light section of the electrical manufacturing industry was based on the mass-production of batteries, lamps and domestic appliances. This was so successful that, by 1939, 97 per cent of the vacuum cleaners sold in Britain had been domestically made.

Overall, the new industries were strikingly more successful than the staple industries in adapting to the economic conditions of the 1930s. They made the most of the affluence which undoubtedly existed in sectors of the population by producing primarily for the home market. The collapse of world trade, which had so badly affected the old industries, therefore had little impact on the new. Nor did the new industries have a damaging effect on the staple industries. They did not, for example, compete directly with them for existing customers and markets, since they created their own demand. In some ways they actually benefited specific areas of heavy industry: car manufacturing stimulated a revival of steel production in the 1930s, while electricity helped streamline textile plants. In more general terms it could even be said that the new industries were gradually transforming the whole economic infrastructure. The remaining question, however, is the extent to which they were able to alleviate unemployment.

UNEMPLOYMENT BETWEEN THE WARS

The overall unemployment rate increased from an average of 4.8 per cent between 1881 and 1913 to 14 per cent between 1921 and 1939 or, more specifically, 15.4 per cent between 1929 and 1939 (see Figure 7).

The usual explanation given for this pattern is that unemployment was partly cyclical, relating to world conditions, and partly structural, relating to the particular problems of the staple industries examined in the previous section. D.H. Aldcroft puts a strong case for the structural base of unemployment:

> Prior to 1939 the chief problem of the northern regions and Wales was their heavy dependence on a small group of staple industries, the markets for whose products virtually collapsed largely, though not entirely, as a result of the severe deterioration in the export trade. . . . The main difficulty lay in the excessive reliance on a narrow industrial basis.[16]

There is certainly statistical support for this view. Between 1920 and 1938 the employment within the staple industries fell by over 1 million. The number of coalminers was reduced from 1.08 million to 0.68 million; the corresponding figures for iron and steel were 0.53 million and 0.34 million, while shipbuilding declined from 0.29 million to 0.13 million and textiles from 0.53 million to 0.30 million. Overall, it has been estimated, 50 per cent of Britain's unemployed had been made redundant by the staple industries; by 1932, 35 per cent of miners were unemployed, as were 31 per cent of textile workers, 48 per cent of steel-workers and 62 per cent shipbuilding workers.[17] Average rates were highest where the staple industries had been most dominant within the local economy. Between 1929 and 1936 they averaged 20 per cent in the North East, North West and Scotland, and over 30 per cent in South Wales; during the same period they were 8 per cent or less in the South East and London.[18]

There is, however, an alternative view: that much of the unemployment was not so much structural as self-inflicted. Benjamin and Kochan argue that jobs *were* available but that the difference between the pay and the dole was too small to attract workers to them. Unemployment benefits were 'on a more generous scale than ever before or since',[19] which meant that the unemployed could afford to be choosy in their search for jobs. The argument is based on figures which show that the ratio of benefit to wages was 0.49 on average during the 1930s and 0.57 in 1936. These estimates have, however, been challenged by Hatton, who thereby unpicks the logic of the whole explanation. A more likely proportion of benefit to average wages was 0.36, rising to a maximum of 0.41 in 1936. Taking into account that women and younger people would have been eligible only to lower rates, the proportion for some would have been as low as 0.24. These figures could hardly have been an incentive not to accept whatever work was available. In any case, they are substantially lower than the rates of unemployment benefit payable in the 1950s. If, in the latter decade, unemployment was virtually non-existent, where is the logic of assuming that people in the 1930s would have been demotivated by a lower rate of benefit from seeking work?[20] It would seem, therefore, that the structural explanation for unemployment is still the most convincing one.

To what extent did the growth of the new industries alleviate the problem? They did help offset the *total* unemployment figures: the car industry, for example, increased its workforce from 0.23 million to 0.5 million, and electrical engineering from 0.17 million to 0.33 million. Unfortunately the effect was largely regional, because the new industries affected different areas to those hit by the problem of declining staple industries. Employment opportunities increased most rapidly in Greater London and its environs and the West Midlands, whereas jobs were lost largely in the North East, especially Teesside and Tyneside, in the North West, especially Merseyside and Barrow, in Scotland and in South Wales. It is true that there was some population migration from the depressed areas to take advantage of the new job opportunities. But several factors tended to limit this. That part of the population most affected by unemployment was also likely to be the least mobile: it could not, therefore, be expected to move wholesale to areas where the opportunities lay. Thus, although the population of London and the West Midlands did increase, that of the North West dropped by only 1 per cent. In any case, the new industries were more efficient in terms of manpower and, although jobs were available, they were nothing like sufficient for the needs of the mass of unemployed from the staple industries, even supposing that the latter had been able to move to take them up.

GOVERNMENT POLICY TOWARDS THE ECONOMY AND UNEMPLOYMENT

To what extent did inter-war governments respond to the problems analysed in the previous sections? How deliberate were their efforts to promote recovery – and did these actually work?

Governments were under pressure from two broad economic strategies. One was the Treasury view. Dominated by the theory of supply and demand, this maintained that the market would control the productive forces and the needs for labour. The whole concept was based on equilibrium – whether between import and exports, production and consumption, or borrowing and lending. This could be achieved through a combination of free trade, balanced budgets, low levels of public expenditure and taxation, and the maintenance of the value of sterling through fixed exchange rates and through relating sterling to the gold standard. Against this was the Keynesian view, which argued for increased government expenditure and investment. Industrial and economic growth had to be *stimulated* by the government, which was therefore expected to play a much more direct part in preparing the environment for recovery. Keynes strongly attacked the various implications of the Treasury view. He believed that market forces should not be relied upon and that economic growth was not a self-regulating process. In particular, the government should undertake massive schemes of investment in order to revive industry and cut unemployment. This, he considered would be much more constructive than seeking to maintain the level of the pound, especially when this meant overvaluing it against the dollar.

Clearly, these were very different approaches to the problems of depression and unemployment and proved difficult to reconcile. Overall, it seems that governments by and large preferred the Treasury view, even to the extent of being 'trapped within an economic orthodoxy that originated before the First World War.'[21] Their policies were generally orthodox, linked to budgetary controls and avoiding massive investment. On the other hand, governments did seek increasingly to create a more favourable climate for recovery. During the 1930s they introduced a wide range of measures which shifted slightly from the full constraints of the Treasury view without, however, accepting the full implications of Keynesianism. This partial and unbalanced compromise can be seen in the governments' financial, industrial and unemployment policies.

During the 1920s government financial policies were entirely in accord with the Treasury view. There were some unfortunate consequences. For one thing, Lloyd George unintentionally and prematurely ended the post-war boom in 1921 by bringing in tighter budgetary controls – ostensibly to prevent the boom getting out of hand. For another, the decision by Baldwin's government in 1926 to return to the gold standard actually made exporting more difficult by raising the value of the pound. It also exacerbated industrial conflict and was a key factor in the descent into the General Strike of 1926. The high value of the pound necessitated steep interest rates to prevent the pound from being undermined by speculation. This in turn prevented the borrowing of money for modernisation, which might have made industries more competitive. Such policies were undoubtedly deflationary and probably contributed to the relatively low levels of British industrial performance in the 1920s; certainly they did nothing to raise those levels. According to B.W.E. Alford: 'A dominant feature of the 1920s . . . was the strong determination to get back to the pre-war situation, even though in terms of sound policy it was the reverse of what was required'.[22] The response of MacDonald and Snowden to the 1931 crisis was also in line with the Treasury view. The 1931 budget was not, however, a success; it was followed by the Invergordon Mutiny which, in turn, led to a run on the pound. Different measures were clearly needed and thereafter the National Government diluted orthodox theory with a measure of pragmatism. Coming off the gold standard in 1931 effectively devalued the pound by about 30 per cent and made possible a reduction of interest rates from 6 per cent to 2 per cent. This meant that financial policies were no longer having a deadening effect on the economy. At the same time, there was no large-scale movement towards Keynesianism. Neville Chamberlain, Chancellor of the Exchequer between 1931 and 1937, failed to relate 'easier money' to easier spending and therefore easier production. The government retained the Treasury fear that there might be an artificial boom and can therefore take only a small part of the credit for any recovery that did occur.

The government's attitude to the problems experienced by industries showed a few concessions to Keynesianism while remaining primarily open to Treasury influences. It might, alternatively, be said that the Treasury view itself was becoming less rigid and that the government shifted with it towards an economic central ground. Industrial policies were actually quite varied, showing several different types of response according to perceived needs.

One was the return to protection. The 1932 Import Duties Act established a general tariff of 10 per cent on goods coming into Britain from outside the Empire, although attempts to follow this up at the

Ottawa Conference with an Imperial Tariff did not work (see Chapter 8). It is, in any case doubtful that these measures had any real impact on the levels of British trade and their contribution to any economic recovery was therefore minimal; at the most they reduced the forces threatening to pull this recovery back into recession. More innovative were government measures to create a more favourable environment for industry – clearly a step away from the orthodox Treasury preference for self-regulation. The Special Areas Act (1934) provided £2 million in aid for Scotland, Tyneside, West Cumberland and South Wales, while the Special Areas (Amendment) Act of 1937 introduced concessions on rates, income tax and rents to encourage companies to set up in business in these locations. The impact was disappointing and comparatively few extra jobs were created. Pearce argues that they were essentially 'cosmetic changes' and that 'they were designed to do no more'.[23] Such measures did, however, lead to the establishment of a number of government-financed trading estates from 1935; these, according to Loebl, 'marked the precise point in time when reliance exclusively on market forces to correct local structural problems was reluctantly abandoned.'[24]

The National Governments recognised the connection between the depression and the structural problems of the staple industries; they therefore introduced a series of measures which were intended to streamline and rationalise – again, with limited success. The 1930 Coal Mines Act attempted to increase efficiency by bringing production and prices under the influence of a cartel. But this did not work: according to Aldcroft 'the law became a device by which the available business was spread among all concerns regardless of their relative efficiency.'[25] A slightly more ambitious enterprise was the formation of the British Iron and Steel Federation in 1934 which fixed prices and negotiated quotas with foreign cartels. In the following year the British Shipping (Assistance) Act provided government loans for shipbuilding on condition that the scrapping of existing tonnage exceeded the building of new tonnage by a ratio of 2:1. This did not, however, have the desired effect and many British shipowners placed orders with foreign shipyards. Finally, the Cotton Industry (Reorganisation) Acts of 1936 and 1939 sought to reduce production and to fix minimum prices – to the extent of setting up a Spindles Board to buy and eliminate as many spindles as possible. Such measures had an air of desperation. In complete contrast was the Electricity Supply Act of 1926, which was projective rather than reactive and did more than any other piece of legislation between the wars to provide effective industrial structures. The result was the establishment of the Central Electricity Board, which concentrated production on a few efficient stations, set up transmission lines and interconnected these to form a national grid. But even here there were shortcomings: the electricity industry still lacked standardised frequencies and voltages and there were local variations until well after the Second World War.

The greatest scope for Keynesian solutions was in the handling of unemployment. Inter-war governments, however, seemed to move cautiously between two sets of guidelines, neither of which owed much to Keynes. One was the rudimentary welfare system established by the Liberal governments before the First World War, especially in the 1911 National Insurance Act. The other was the Treasury view, which saw unemployment as a temporary distortion of an organic economy and requiring minimal government intervention. The overall result was little more than a refinement of pre-1914 legislation, with carefully defined financial restrictions. This synthesis can be seen in almost all the measures dealing with unemployment during the 1920s and 1930s. In 1927, for example, Chamberlain's Unemployment Insurance Act reduced benefit payments but, at the same time, extended them from 15 weeks to an indefinite period. Labour's Unemployment Insurance Act of 1930 allowed transitional benefits for those who had never been able to make contributions – but MacDonald's National Government then proceeded to cut benefits by 10 per cent at the end of 1931. In the same year a means test was introduced which made the declaration of all family income compulsory; various sources of income would now affect the levels at which benefit was paid, a change much resented by the unemployed. The 1934 Unemployment Act brought together the various strands of previous legislation, establishing the National Unemployment Assistance Board which paid benefit after the expiry of the period covered by insurance. Although the amount was restored to that payable before the 1931 cut, the means test continued to be applied, further evidence that concessions were always accompanied by restrictions.

Overall we can see that government policy was marginal rather than crucial for economic growth and unemployment during the 1930s. More important were economic factors like the fall in prices which, because it was more rapid than the fall in wages, led to an overall increase in buying power. This, in turn, boosted domestic consumption and led to an expansion of the new industries. This, however, raises the question as to whether the adoption of Keynesian policies would have made any difference to the process. Historians remain divided on this; some, including Aldcroft, maintain that recovery would not have been significantly affected by the application of Keynes's ideas while others, including Youngson and Hatton, believed that it would definitely have added to the pace.[26] Pearce argues that the effects of a Keynesian solution would have been unpredictable:

> The 'Hungry Thirties' might never have existed. On the other hand, there might have been collapse and disaster. . . . No one can really be sure what the results would have been had different policies been pursued.[27]

Alternatively, perhaps a synthesis was beginning to emerge between the various economic strategies. According to Loebl, the Treasury view was modified from 1935 onwards.[28] A. Booth maintains that Keynesianism, too, gradually changed, enabling components of it to become more acceptable to the Treasury.[29] The full synthesis did not, of course, occur until the period immediately after 1945, with the development of the Welfare State. But its roots were to be seen in the 1930s as well as in Britain's second experience of total war.

This brings us to a final question. Did the economy *actually* recover during the 1930s? There are two levels of analysis here. By the first, the economy experienced a serious crisis but recovered by adjusting painfully to new conditions. We have already seen that the decline of the staple industries was to some extent compensated by the rise of the newer industries and that the whole economy was given a kick start by the decision to rearm. A second – and more complex – level of explanation is advanced by B.W.E. Alford, who considers that the recovery was not fundamental but cyclical.

> There were thus periods of cyclical depression and recovery, but the statistical evidence does not support the view that within these phases the economy moved on to a higher growth plane. In the growth sense, therefore, it is difficult to see how one can speak of 'recovery' in the inter-war years. There was not recovery in the sense that there was a return in the 1930s to the previously high levels of growth, since growth was fairly constant over the whole period; there was not recovery in the sense that the health of the economy improved so much over the 1930s as to make it unrecognisable from its previous state.[30]

This self-acknowledged 'pessimistic view' of Britain's economic performance between 1918 and 1939 appears to be backed by figures for the growth of gross domestic product (GDP) between 1913 and 1938. Britain's was 1.1 per cent; ahead of this were Germany (1.6 per cent), Italy (1.7 per cent), Sweden (1.8 per cent) Denmark (1.9 per cent) and the United States (2.0 per cent). Thus the concepts of decline and recovery are relative. The economy during the 1930s did not go into absolute decline and did recover to previous levels. It was not, however, followed by the higher levels of growth experienced after the Second World War by some of Britain's major competitors.[31] This can be seen as the root of some of the problems examined in Chapters 11 and 12.

THE DEVIL'S DECADE?

Perceptions of the 1930s have been influenced by the negative rather than the positive developments of that decade. This was understandable during the period immediately after 1945, when the objective was to extend the range of welfare services, or during the 1950s when there was virtually full employment: by comparison with both, the 1930s appeared very bleak. The visual image of dole queues and hunger marches was overwhelmingly powerful, while contemporary novels and social commentaries provided pathetic written testimony. Most historians, however, have challenged the stereotype. A.J.P. Taylor wrote during the 1960s:

> The nineteen-thirties have been called the black years, the devil's decade. Its popular image can be expressed in two phrases: mass unemployment and 'appeasement'. No set of political leaders have been judged so contemptuously since the days of Lord North. Yet, at the same time, most English people were enjoying a richer life than any previously known in the history of the world: longer holidays, shorter hours, higher real wages. They had motor cars, cinemas, radio sets, electrical appliances. The two sides of life did not join up.[32]

It might be added that never had the 'two nations', once referred to by Disraeli, been so clearly in evidence and, to make matters worse, to each other.

The gap between the haves and have-nots was enormous. The majority experienced unprecedented affluence because the 1930s was a period of economic growth in the domestic sector, once the initial impact of the depression had worn off. The economy, it is true, varied regionally, but it did expand nationally. The development of the new industries was fuelled by consumer prosperity, which was much stronger during the 1930s than is commonly believed. The disposable income of the average family with a member fully employed was at least twice that in 1914, and was, in turn, accentuated by the fall in consumer prices. Families also decreased in size to an average of 2.1 children during the 1930s compared with 3.0 before. The main motive for this was a better standard of living; the method was the contraceptive measures publicised by Dr Marie Stopes.

For most people there was therefore a massive increase in spending power. They used it to enhance their lifestyles in a variety of ways. The standard of diet generally improved with increased consumption of dairy products and meat. With the widespread installation of electricity, home comforts increased, while labour-saving devices like vacuum cleaners and washing machines were sold in ever-increasing numbers, reaching 400,000 per annum by 1938. Entertainment was focused on the film industry and about 1,000 million visits were made each year during the 1930s, many people going twice or three times per week. Motor vehicles, the ultimate sign of affluence, numbered 3 million by 1939. Finally, housing improved more rapidly in this decade than at any other time in Britain's history. The number of houses built was 2.5 million, compared with 1.5 million during the 1920s, and the cost of a semi-detached residence was as little as £400, or two years' wages for many people. It has also been shown that the number of mortgages taken out with building societies increased from 0.55 million in 1928 to 1.39 million in 1937, while the number of owner occupiers increased between 1914 and 1939 from 10 per cent to 31 per cent.[33]

Life on the dole could hardly have been a greater contrast. According to Walter Greenwood unemployment 'got you slowly, with the slippered stealth of an unsuspected, malignant disease'. It induced slouching, shabbiness, furtiveness, suspicion. 'Nothing to do with time; nothing to spend; nothing to do tomorrow nor the day after; nothing to wear; can't get married. A living corpse; a unit of the spectral army of three million lost men.'[34] The effects on Jarrow were vividly described by J.B. Priestley:

> Wherever we went there were men hanging about, not scores of them but hundreds and thousands of them. The whole town looked as if it had entered a perpetual penniless bleak Sabbath. The men wore the drawn masks of prisoners of war.[35]

Other works which helped shape the image of the thirties were George Orwell's *The Road to Wigan Pier* and Allen Hutt's *The Condition of the Working Class*.

There were many stark facts behind these descriptions. The severe reduction in family income meant the spread of poverty, especially in depressed areas like Liverpool, Jarrow and Barrow-in-Furness. There were over 600,000 slum dwellings, most of which lacked baths or their own lavatory. Disease remained rife within the deprived minority of the population, especially tuberculosis. The basic problem was that health care had not yet been provided by the state and families on low incomes could not therefore afford the sort of provision which most people were by now able to take for granted. Even starvation was not unknown. An unemployed man's wife died of pneumonia in January 1933, aged 37. The pathologist said: 'I have no doubt that had she had sufficient food this attack would not have proved fatal. It appears that she deliberately stinted herself and gave such food as came into the house to the children, and so sacrificed her life.'[36] The impact on mental health was widespread. The Pilgrim Trust provided the example of a married man of 50 with a family, who was of 'normal health until unemployed' but who then 'developed constant aches and pains in the head and became a chronic neurasthenic'.[37] There was also an underlying feeling of helplessness. The Bishop of Guildford, for example, was told: 'I feel like an animal in a cage. I can't get out of it.'[38] Other responses, however, included outrage and activism. These manifested themselves, through the National Unemployed Workers Movement (NUWM), in the hunger marches, of which the Jarrow Crusade was the most significant. In terms of publicity these were a massive success and retrospective views of the decade are associated with these more than with anything else.

A similar dichotomy exists in the political system in the 1930s. On the one hand, there was an unprecedented amount of organised violence. Much of it was stirred up by the British Union of Fascists (BUF), set up by Sir Oswald Mosley. Reaching a membership of 20,000 by 1934, this was blatantly anti-semitic and shocked contemporaries with its methods. A Conservative MP, Geoffrey Lloyd, described the Olympia meeting:

> I was appalled by the brutal conduct of the Fascists. . . . I saw with my own eyes case after case of single interrupters being attacked by ten to twenty Fascists. Again and again, as five or six Blackshirts carried out an interrupter by arms and legs, several other Blackshirts were engaged in kicking and hitting his helpless body. . . . It was a deeply shocking scene for an Englishman to see in London.[39]

If democracy was threatened by thuggery, some also saw it as being more generally in peril. The Labour opposition especially argued that the National Government was an artificial contrivance which had swallowed up all the normal processes of British democracy: how could the suspension of party politics lead to anything else but a one-party state and, in turn, allow alternative strategies for economic recovery to be totally ignored? In retrospect, many people came to see the 1930s as a period of lost opportunities and initiatives and it has been argued that this particular devil was not cast out until Labour swept back to power in the 1945 landslide (see Chapter 12).

On the other hand, it must be said that the political response to economic depression was incomparably milder in Britain than anywhere else in Europe. Politicians like MacDonald and Baldwin were above all moderates who saw themselves very much as part of the centre ground with a mission to bring the people together in some form of political consensus. The 1930s was actually one of very few periods in modern British history when the governments in power were supported by 50 per cent or more of the electorate. It is true that the opposition of the 1930s found itself in a more frustrating position than usual. It could also be said that a more genuine consensus emerged after the Second World War when the three parties adopted a more or less common approach which allowed moderation to function within the traditional structure of party politics. But although these are significant within the British context, they are details when compared with the European situation. The essential point is that the forces of moderation in Britain squeezed the radical fringe into the margins, while in most of Europe the radical fringe took over; Hitler accomplished this by a series of draconian measures such as the Enabling Act and the banning of opposition parties (1933), along with the paraphernalia of terror operating the Gestapo, SS and SD. It is surely significant that the only emergency measure introduced into Britain during the whole of the 1930s was the 1937 Public Order Act which gave police forces discretionary powers to ban para-military marches or the wearing of provocative uniforms. If the devil was present in Britain in the 1930s it took surprisingly little to warn him off.

9

VERSAILLES, FOREIGN POLICY AND COLLECTIVE SECURITY 1918–33

Lloyd George, who had led Britain through the latter half of the First World War, was also the main inspiration behind Britain's policy over the peace settlement which was put together between 1919 and 1920. Thereafter, British foreign policy was under the direction of Lord Curzon (Foreign Secretary 1919–24), Ramsay MacDonald (Prime Minister and Foreign Secretary 1924), Austen Chamberlain (Foreign Secretary 1924–9), and Henderson (Foreign Secretary 1929–31).

This chapter focuses on three main themes. How effective was Britain's contribution to the Treaty of Versailles – and to what extent was this settlement fundamentally flawed? How powerful was Britain during the immediate post-war period, and what was her role in developing the policy of collective security after the construction of the peace settlement? Finally, where do Britain's relations with Soviet Russia fit into British foreign policy generally? Were they, as many textbooks seem to imply, peripheral to the mainstream: or did they play a vital role in directing the mainstream?

BRITAIN AND THE TREATY OF VERSAILLES

Even though Britain's participation in the peace negotiations was more carefully discussed and prepared than her entry into the First World War, there was still a bewildering array of cross-currents affecting the British delegation at Paris during the course of 1918 and 1919.

It has been shown by A.J.P. Taylor, M.L. Dockrill and J.D. Gould that Lloyd George was under considerable pressure to come to a just settlement with Germany. This was due partly to the liberal influences exerted by the United States delegation and partly to the need to show something positive for three to four years of slaughter. Hence, in a speech on 5 January 1918, Lloyd George stressed that any settlement must be based on 'reason and justice' and on 'government with the consent of the governed.'[1] At the same time, wrong had been done and 'there must be reparation for injuries done in violation of international law'.[2] By the end of the year, however, other forces had emerged which were less in the interests of a just settlement. The most important of these was the general election campaign of November and early December 1918, which highlighted the whole issue. In the pent-up feelings of an election enmity towards Germany was bound to increase and a number of MPs deliberately played on the 'make Germany pay' and 'hang the Kaiser' themes.

Britain also found herself positioned between two powers with more radical ideas and objectives. The American position, strongly underpinned by the beliefs of President Wilson, was more theoretical, while the French objectives, set forward by Prime Minister Clemenceau, were more punitive and demanding. The British contingent was increasingly divided as to which of these powers was the less objectionable. Politicians, like Bonar Law and Lloyd George, found the French more trying because they were more persistent on matters of detail; according to Law, the French demands were 'a series of pinpricks, involving every calculated humiliation.'[3] Senior civil servants were divided between those, like Sir Eyre Crowe, who preferred to deal with France, and those, like Headlam Morley, who had more sympathy initially with the idealism of President Wilson. When, however, Wilson stuck to his principles to the point of obsession, Headlam Morley, along with the diplomat, Harold Nicolson, and the economist, J.M. Keynes, became thoroughly disillusioned with the American camp without being won over to the French.

Given these difficulties, how successfully did the British delegation shape the Treaty of Versailles? The view of M.D. Dockrill and J.D. Gould is that

> it is scarcely surprising that the British were often overwhelmed by the sheer magnitude of their task. The European settlement, as a result, was a patchwork of compromises between the policies of the United States and of France. . . . Britain's attempts to play a mediating role between her two major associates in European questions was largely unsuccessful.[4]

By contrast, E. Goldstein argues: 'The British delegation at Paris had a well defined set of goals, and was more successful in achieving them than any of its allies.'[5] Furthermore, 'At Paris the British Empire Delegation attained the maximum possible in the circumstances.'[6]

There is, not surprisingly, some evidence to support both views, but the overall balance seems to favour Goldstein. There are several important examples of Britain winning the day against more entrenched positions, in the process showing that mediation *could* succeed. The Rhineland was a case in point. Originally, the French demanded its separation from the rest of Germany, while the American delegation were doubtful that anything needed to be done at all. The British delegation ended the deadlock by substituting the principle of de-militarisation. It is true that part of this package was a guarantee to the security of France by Britain and the United States and that, when the United States Senate failed to ratify the Treaty of Versailles, this might have left Britain in an embarrassing position. Fortunately, Lloyd George had shown some foresight in insisting that the British guarantee would be dependent on the ratification of the American one. A similar compromise was reached on the Saar region of Germany. The French wanted outright annexation but the British delegation pressed Headlam Morley's proposal that France should have use of the coalfields. The area would be administered by the League of Nations for 15 years, after which there would be a plebiscite, in the best traditions of Wilsonian national self-determination. Lloyd George also intervened successfully to prevent the excessive enlargement of Poland at Germany's expense. France wanted a savage cutting back of Germany's eastern frontiers to weaken German power and strengthen a possible French ally. Wilson was sympathetic to the idea since this would provide greater economic viability to Poland as well as the other new state, Czechoslovakia. In this instance, however, Lloyd George succeeded in making both the United States and France accept a compromise. The port of Danzig was to be a 'Free City', administered by the League of Nations and there was to be a plebiscite in Upper Silesia in 1921. He also won over the question of German disarmament. The French proposed that the German army should comprise 200,000 conscripts, to be selected annually by lot; they argued that a volunteer army, which was the alternative, would provide a professional core for future military expansion. Lloyd George, how-ever, felt that a volunteer army was more likely to act as a moderating and restraining force and he eventually won the French delegation over to this view by proposing a limit of 100,000.

Britain was therefore successful in achieving some significant compromises. This might imply a certain softness in Lloyd George's policy. It would, however, be a mistake to imagine so. It was not until the 1930s that Lloyd George became soft, or rather soft-headed, and then mainly in his adulation of Hitler. Between 1918 and 1920 he was

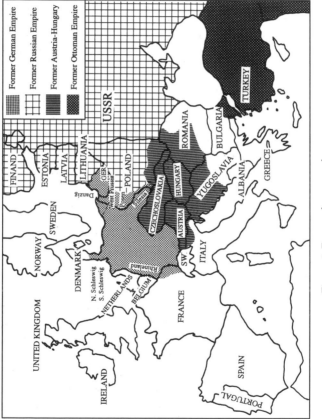

Figure 8 Europe between the wars

capable of being just as tough as Clemenceau where he considered that British interests demanded this. The best example of this is the issue of reparations. Lloyd George's role was not a moderating one here: he was determined that the Germans should pay for the extensive war damage. The Imperial War Cabinet established a committee to suggest a sum. At first it proposed to lay on Germany the entire cost of the war (estimated at £24,000 million), payable in instalments. With this Lloyd George seemed content, partly because it was likely to be popular with the electorate. It has been argued that Lloyd George subsequently doubted the wisdom of imposing high reparations on Germany, which meant that he appeared in the Fontainebleau Memorandum to change his mind. According to Dockrill and Gould,

> British policy at Paris was inconsistent. For example, where reparations were concerned her approach seemed to depend on the vindictive and mercurial behaviour of her public opinion. . . . The Prime Minister was seeking to extract as much as possible for Britain from reparations and yet at the same time was concerned about the likely effects of this on Germany's recovery and on Europe's economic reconstruction.[7]

This sort of interpretation is contradicted by M. Trachtenberg, who credits Lloyd George with greater consistency – and ruthlessness. 'Throughout the period of the peace conference, Great Britain was to pursue a reparation policy more demanding and more intransigent than the policy of any other allied power.'[8] Trachtenberg denies that Lloyd George instinctively favoured moderation but was pushed in a more radical direction. Instead, Lloyd George believed that 'Germany had committed a great crime and it is necessary to make it impossible that anyone should be tempted to repeat that offence.'[9] By this analysis, Lloyd George fought consistently for a high figure, and got it: in 1921 the Reparations Commission fixed the total reparations payment at 136,000 million gold marks, equivalent to £6,600 million.

There is, therefore, a strong case for Lloyd George having succeeded in fulfilling British objectives at Versailles. But this did not mean that his policies met with universal approval within the British delegation. Indeed, there were strong arguments against what Lloyd George, along with the other leaders, had done to Germany. The diplomat, Harold Nicolson, believed that 'The historian, with every justification, will come to the conclusion that we were very stupid men. I think we were.'[10] He referred also to 'moral and intellectual deterioration'.[11] Furthermore:

We came to Paris confident that the new order was about to be established; we left it convinced that the new order had merely fouled the old. We arrived as fervent apprentices in the school of President Wilson: we left as renegades. . . . We arrived determined that a Peace of justice and wisdom should be negotiated: we left it, conscious that the Treaties imposed upon our enemies were neither just nor wise.[12]

Sir James Headlam Morley, a senior civil servant, was no less damning:

I can only say that I have not found one single person here who approves of it as a whole. While in most cases particular clauses can be defended, the total effect is, I am sure, quite indefensible and in fact is, I think, quite unworkable.[13]

The main problem was the delay in addressing the issues, caused partly by the diversion of the 1918 general election and partly by the late arrival of the American delegation. There were also delays in allowing food into Germany after the blockade and starvation resulted. Hence Morley said, 'I am not in the least surprised that this has left a feeling of intense bitterness. It is I think an action, or rather an inaction, as indefensible as anything I have ever heard of.'[14] He also maintained that the Armistice had 'specifically determined the nature and extent of the reparation to be paid by Germany; this is categorically violated in the reparation clauses.'[15]

J.M. Keynes condemned the Treaty above all for being totally unacceptable. He argued that the Treaty aimed to destroy Germany's very means of subsistence. The coal and iron provisions were 'inexpedient and disastrous'. Germany would be left with a capacity to produce only 60 million tons per annum, whereas in 1913 she had consumed 110 million tons. The situation was aggravated by the damage done to German commerce by the restrictions imposed on ship-building and by the new system of tariffs against German exports. Even more serious was that the reparations under consideration were well beyond Germany's means to pay. It was clear to Keynes, who resigned his position in the British delegation in protest, that the real dangers for the future lay not so much in boundary questions as in 'questions of food, coal and commerce'. He was convinced that 'The Treaty, by overstepping the limits of the possible, has in practice settled nothing.'[16]

Such opposition within the British camp helps to explain many of the attacks of conscience which were to affect British foreign policy in the later 1920s and the 1930s. Lloyd George and others came eventually to accept that perhaps there was a moral dimension to the diplomatic situation in 1919 that they had overlooked. The implications of this will be examined in the next section and the next chapter. For the moment, to what extent do the political and historical analyses of Versailles overlap?

The historical interpretations of the Treaty of Versailles have varied in their overall trend. Western historians were initially asked to prepare evidence to prove that the responsibility for the outbreak of the First World War lay with Germany. Their report was presented to the Preliminary Peace Conference in 1919 and was used to justify the insertion of Article 231, the 'war guilt clause'. After the Treaty had been finalised, criticisms by historians soon followed those already made by diplomats. W.H. Dawson, for example, maintained that the boundaries had been harshly redrawn. Germany's frontiers 'are literally bleeding. From them oozes out the life-blood, physical, spiritual and material of large populations'.[17] Later historians, like W. Carr,[18] J. Néré,[19] and S. Marks,[20] considered that these views were lopsided and that Germany must take some of the blame. This approach was strongly reinforced by the work of German historians on the outbreak of the First World War, from F. Fischer in the 1960s to P. von Strandmann in the 1980s;[21] this pointed to the aggressive nature of German foreign policy before 1914 and the extent to which Germany would have imposed its domination over Europe had it won the First World War. M. Trachtenberg and W.A. McDougall, meanwhile, completely rehabilitated the French role, although retaining the criticism of British intransigence over the size of the reparations bill.[22] Some historians, however, have not been tempted by the revisionist trend. A. Lentin, in particular, maintains the more traditional view that the very harshness of Germany's treatment at Versailles was the root cause for subsequent complications in British foreign policy.[23]

THE BRITISH POSITION AND COLLECTIVE SECURITY

It is often assumed that the 1920s represented an important stage in Britain's long decline as a world power. Yet in many respects Britain was more favourably placed by comparison with the other European powers than at any other time in her history.

Britain had emerged from the First World War if not unscathed, at least intact. She had suffered less damage than France and was undefeated, unlike Germany and Russia. In military terms, Britain was remarkably secure during the 1920s. Her navy was still the largest in the world and was not seriously challenged numerically by the United States until 1930, while only France had a larger airforce. The army, it is true, was small, but the threat of Germany had been removed by the military clauses of the Treaty of Versailles. The British government also maintained as high an expenditure on the armed forces as did any of its rivals and, according to the research of J.R. Ferris, 'somewhat exceeded the British norm since 1815'.[24] Ferris makes two further points. First, Britain's regional position had strengthened even if her global one had not. 'During the 1920s, compared to the period between 1893 and 1914, Britain was slightly more powerful in relation to every other European state, while somewhat weaker in relation to Japan and particularly the United States.'[25] Second, and more important, this strength could have continued into the 1930s had British governments shown the necessary determination. 'Even by 1933, in material as against psychological terms, Great Britain was better placed for rearmament than Germany, Italy or Japan. The notorious weakness of her armed forces by the late 1930s was the product of decisions made after 1929.'[26] Britain had also done comparatively well out of the Versailles Treaty, expanding her Empire through the acquisition of German colonies and gaining oil-rich areas in the Middle East as mandates. Several contemporaries were in no doubt about the overall strength of Britain's position. Hitler, for example, wrote in *Mein Kampf* that Britain was 'the greatest power on earth'.[27] Overall, European nations held Britain in higher esteem than at any other time since Palmerston.

This political ascendancy was, however, deeply flawed. For one thing, it lacked a secure economic base. The First World War had inflicted lasting damage to Britain's staple industries and overseas markets so that she could no longer hope to compete effectively with the United States (see Chapter 8). She was also highly vulnerable to the possibility of the recovery of her European rivals; this was especially serious, since Britain's strength was relative, not absolute, deriving from the temporary weakness of others. Above all, the Treaty of Versailles and its aftermath created as many problems as it solved. The most important of these were the enormous resentment its terms had generated within Germany and the absence of any defensive mechanism to prevent future attempts to revise them. Originally, Clemenceau had been prepared to accept the terms of Versailles only because Britain and the United States had been prepared to offer an alliance with France. But when the United States Senate refused to ratify the Treaty, British enthusiasm dwindled and the alliance did not materialise. France therefore made her own arrangements by establishing a diplomatic network involving those countries of eastern Europe who stood to lose a great deal from any German or Hungarian revisionism: Poland, Czechoslovakia and Yugoslavia. Successive British governments found two methods of dealing with this problem. While the revisionist powers were relatively weak, it could be done through containment, a process normally associated with Austen Chamberlain. When the revisionist powers grew stronger and more confident, the process shifted to appeasement, the most advanced form of which was put into practice by Neville Chamberlain.

Collective security had three main purposes. One was to try to contain the possibility of German revisionism and to uphold at least some of the boundaries laid down by the Treaty of Versailles; this can be seen as the defensive element and was of particular concern to the French. The second was to rehabilitate Germany to enable her to re-enter the mainstream of European diplomacy. This was due largely to the conciliatory policies of the German Foreign Minister, Gustav Stresemann, who saw Germany as 'the bridge which would bring East and West together in the development of Europe'. The third was to provide a method for the settlement of disputes which would involve the League of Nations; multilateralism was therefore to replace bilateralism and, more particularly, unilateralism. There would, for example, be no repetition of the French invasion of the Ruhr; equally, France and Belgium would be protected from possible incursions by Germany against *their* frontiers.

The main example of collective security was the Locarno Pact, or the Treaty of Mutual Guarantee, drawn up in 1925 between Britain, France, Germany, Belgium and Italy. This guaranteed the frontiers between Belgium and Germany and between France and Germany. Any disputes would be settled by 'peaceful means' and, if necessary, submitted to a Conciliation Commission or the Council of the League of Nations (Article 2). If authorised by the League Council, the signatory powers would 'come immediately to the assistance of the Power against whom the act complained of is directed' (Article 4).[28] Britain, like Italy, had no direct stake in the boundary question and clearly saw the Locarno Pact as a means of regularising the channels for diplomatic pressure should anything untoward happen in the defined area. The following year Britain was greatly impressed by the willingness of Stresemann to lead Germany into full membership of the League of Nations. Stresemann emphasised that this was a direct follow-up to the Locarno Pact, completing Germany's rehabilitation:

The German Government is resolved to persevere unswervingly in this line of policy and is glad to see that these ideas, which at first met with lively opposition in Germany, are now becoming more and more deeply rooted in the conscience of the German people.[29]

Collective security reached an idealist peak in 1928 with the Kellogg-Briand Pact or the Pact of Paris, by which the 65 signatory states condemned 'recourse to war for the solution of international controversies' and renounced it 'as an instrument of national policy in their relations with one another.'[30]

In some respects collective security was both positive and beneficial. It revived internationalism by bringing to the surface the conflicts inherent in the Versailles Settlement so that these could be resolved by diplomacy through the medium of the League of Nations, which was thereby given a genuine rather than a symbolic role. Second, it made possible the moves towards disarmament which were officially sponsored by the League in 1932. Third, it provided a way out of a dilemma for Britain: now that the United States had withdrawn from European commitments, Britain was understandably less anxious to undertake any direct bilateral commitments to France. Collective security enabled Britain to take part in a multilateral guarantee of French frontiers, while leaving the ultimate responsibility for action to the decision of the League of Nations. The view at the time was highly favourable. According to Churchill, 'At the end of the second Baldwin administration the state of Europe was tranquil, as it had not been for 20 years, and was not to be for at least another 20'. He added that 'A friendly feeling existed towards Germany following upon our Treaty of Locarno', making possible the withdrawal of allied troops from the Rhineland sooner than had been projected by the Treaty of Versailles. Germany was well ensconced in the League of Nations and 'the disarmament clauses of the Treaty of Versailles were not openly violated'.[31] Austen Chamberlain saw the Locarno Pact as 'the real dividing line between the years of war and the years of peace'.[32]

There is, however, another side. Collective security was deeply flawed and might more appropriately be described as the dividing line between confrontation and appeasement – towards which it slid during the 1930s (see Chapter 10). Several factors worked against its long-term success.

One was the underlying German intention to revise the provisions of the Treaty of Versailles. Stresemann was anxious to project himself as the 'good European', seeking reconciliation between Germany and the other powers through open agreements openly arrived at. On the other hand, Stresemann was also a patriot and was as convinced as anyone that the Treaty of Versailles must be revised. Much of his diplomacy was double-edged. He once observed: 'We must get the stranglehold off our neck. On that account, German policy . . . will have to be one of finesse'.[33] He intended, therefore, to find 'the solution of the Reparations question in a sense tolerable for Germany.' He also aimed at 'the protection of Germans abroad, those 10 to 12 million of our kindred who now live under a foreign yoke in foreign lands.' More ominously, he hoped eventually for 'the readjustment of our eastern frontiers'.[34] The other face of the 'good European' was therefore the 'good German'. The former was compatible with the Locarno spirit. The latter was not.

Collective security was also undermined, albeit unintentionally, by Britain. Among an increasing number of British politicians and diplomats was the nagging feeling that the Treaty of Versailles might have been too harsh, and that future adjustments were not, therefore, out of the question. Two historians pursue this theme vigorously. According to A. Lentin, 'one is drawn back to the residual and fundamental phenomenon of a bad conscience about Versailles and a predisposition to sympathise with German complaints about injustice.'[35] A.J.P. Taylor also maintains that, in Britain's subsequent move towards appeasement, 'guilty conscience was undoubtedly the strongest factor'.[36] During the 1920s German revisionism and British conscience could just about co-exist. After 1933, however, the moderate version of revisionism was radicalised by Hitler but it took British statesmen over five years to realise that Nazi foreign policy was not merely a continuation of that of the Weimar Republic. Britain's response was to seek to accommodate the increase in German demands by an extension of her own recognition of the need for fair play. The combination of the two processes was, of course, lethal to collective security, providing a logical connection between Stresemann and Hitler, and between Austen Chamberlain and Neville Chamberlain.

The most serious deficiency of the Locarno system was the total lack of collective guarantees for the boundaries of eastern Europe. It has been argued that there was little Britain could have done about this, since Stresemann refused to bring within the scope of Locarno the frontiers between Germany, Poland and Czechoslovakia. Instead, Germany insisted on signing separate treaties of mutual guarantee with the two countries concerned. The reason for this must have been suspect: it would, in the future be easier to unpick a bilateral agreement than to defy a multilateral one. France recognised the danger and attempted to build her own security system in eastern Europe based on alliances with Poland and Czechoslovakia (1925) and Yugoslavia (1927). She was also connected with the Little Entente, comprising Poland, Czechoslovakia, Yugoslavia and Romania and intended as a barrier against revisionism, whether from Germany or from Hungary. Britain refused to have anything to do with these arrangements, partly through fear of being drawn into a part of Europe in which she had no direct interests, and partly because of a growing conviction that Poland had probably been treated too generously at Versailles at the expense of Germany and that Hungary's borders had been unjustly sliced back. There was, there-fore, no possibility of an Anglo-French combination in eastern Europe to supplement the Locarno pact in western Europe. The only other possibility was a multilateral system designed, with or without German agreement, to maintain the status quo in eastern Europe. This would have had to involve Soviet Russia which, for reasons we shall now see, Britain refused at any stage to consider.

BRITAIN AND SOVIET RUSSIA

Britain's involvement with Bolshevik Russia is often seen as a peripheral issue, subordinate to her more important role in western Europe. It is true that the west represented Britain's main interest; but Russia intruded at several crucial stages and had a significant effect in shaping Britain's responses during the 1920s to collective security and in the 1930s to appeasement.

The Bolshevik revolution of October 1917 raised three main problems for Britain. In the first place, the ideology of the Bolsheviks alienated much of British society and the establishment, although there was some sympathy from the British labour movement. Second, the peace of Brest Litovsk, made between Russia and Germany in March 1918, released large numbers of German troops for an offensive on the western front, which in turn greatly increased the pressure on Britain and France. Third, the Bolshevik regime nationalised all foreign enterprises and repudiated Tsarist debts to western countries like Britain. For these reasons Lloyd George's government intervened, against the new Bolshevik regime, on the side of the White counter-revolutionary forces. One of the White generals, Deniken, was assisted with arms and equipment in November 1918, and British troops were landed at Murmansk and Archangel to defend arms which had previously been sent to assist the Tsarist regime against the Germans. There were also British forces in the Caucasus and eastern Siberia. Altogether, Britain provided 30,000 men and something like £100 million. By 1920, however, Trotsky's reorganisation of the Red Army had proved sufficient to see off the White threats on all fronts and Lloyd George considered that he had no alternative to withdrawing all British troops from Russia. This sparked off a major row with his War Secretary, Winston Churchill, who argued passionately that British troops should actually be reinforced. Lloyd George, however, had never been entirely convinced about the wisdom of involvement in another country's civil war and felt that Churchill was exaggerating the ideological and military threat posed by the new regime: he maintained that Churchill had 'Bolshevism on the brain'.[37]

During the 1920s Britain followed two divergent policies towards Bolshevik Russia. One was flexible and pragmatic, seeking to end the distrust generated during the Civil War; the other was obdurate and ideological, unable to get beyond that distrust. At first the approach was moderate. There was a strong domestic reason for establishing commercial contacts with Russia since these could help replace markets lost to Britain as a direct result of the First World War. Hence in 1921 the Anglo-Soviet Treaty was drawn up. This was followed by a more moderate diplomatic course. In 1922 a conference was convened at Genoa to consider the question of German and Russian debts. According to Lloyd George, it was 'the greatest gathering of European nations which has ever been assembled'[38] and seemed to be the pinnacle of his diplomatic career. Diplomatic recognition followed in 1924, when Ramsay MacDonald's Labour government also advanced a £30 million loan.

Never far beneath the surface lurked the deepest distrust of the Bolshevik regime and its leaders – Lenin, Trotsky, Kamenev and Zinoviev. It came as a shock to see that this regime could also be pragmatic. The Genoa Conference failed to come to a generally accepted settlement of the debt issue and, instead, the occasion was marked by the Rapallo Agreement between Russia and Germany, the last thing the British and French governments expected or wanted. Ideological fears surfaced in 1924 with the Zinoviev Letter. Alleged to be from the Comintern leader, this purported to give detailed instructions for an uprising by British workers against the capitalist system. The result was a serious embarrassment to the Labour party (see Chapter 4) but, more important in the long term, the alienation of almost the entire Conservative party. Baldwin's government (1924–9) was convinced that the Soviet Union, as Russia was now called, was attempting to subvert the British labour and trade union movement. Following a police raid on the London headquarters of the All-Russian Co-operative Society, diplomatic relations were broken off in 1927. Although these were restored when MacDonald returned to power in 1929, little or no attempt was made by any government in the early 1930s to develop closer contacts with Stalin, who had by this time emerged as the undisputed Soviet leader.

The consequences were considerable. British policy towards Russia contributed directly to the vulnerability of collective security. British suspicions prevented Russia from being brought into the Locarno system either in or after 1925. We have already seen that the weakness of collective security was the absence of Locarno guarantees in eastern Europe, a deficiency which France tried to bridge by her own arrangements with Yugoslavia, Czechoslovakia and Poland. The inclusion of Russia might have removed a huge imponderable. But, left without any sort of links – or ties – with the west, Stalin was able to inflict massive damage upon both the western democratic system and its long-term defences. He did this in two ways.

First, he played an important part in Hitler's rise to power in Germany between 1931 and 1933. Finding himself increasingly isolated after 1929, Stalin began to predict the end of western capitalism in the wake of the Great Depression. Germany appeared most likely to collapse first and he had every confidence that Nazism would be a temporary phenomenon which would eventually give way to Communism and a workers' state. The real enemy to the Soviet Union within Germany was not the extreme right but rather the so-called moderate parties which were trying to save the Weimar Republic. Stalin singled out the Social Democrats (SPD) for his particular displeasure and ordered the German Communists (KPD) not to collaborate with them. It is possible that a broad-based coalition, with the SPD, the Centre and the KPD providing between them a substantial majority in the Reichstag, could have kept Hitler from power. This was the first of Stalin's two monstrous errors, which might have been prevented had he been enticed into a diplomatic connection with the west.

Stalin also played a crucial part in Hitler's eventual move towards the outbreak of the Second World War. Would Russia have done a deal with Germany had Stalin been convinced that Britain and France were prepared to resist Hitler? France had, of course, formed the Franco-Soviet Pact of 1935, but Britain sought to detach her from it in the name of appeasement. Would Neville Chamberlain have been quite so keen to do this had Austen Chamberlain established earlier links between Britain and Russia? With such a network, overlapping some sort of guarantee of the frontiers of eastern Europe, there would have been less scope for Hitler to apply pressure on Czechoslovakia in 1938 and Poland in 1939 – even supposing he had been able to achieve power in the first place. With less pressure exerted by Germany, collective security might well have held up more effectively. During the course of 1939 Stalin held parallel negotiations with Germany and with the western powers, before opting for the Nazi-Soviet Non-Aggression Pact in August. More than anything else this gave Hitler the confidence to invade Poland in 1939 and to convert a policy which had previously been primarily revisionist into one which was based on *Lebensraum*. Again, it needs to be asked whether Stalin would have taken this course had Britain involved Russia in the process of collective security at an earlier stage.

CONCLUSION

The Russian Revolution and the Treaty of Versailles occurred within eighteen months of each other. Both presented unfinished business for British foreign policy. Versailles created the German problem. The Russian Revolution prevented the traditional means of containing it – by involving Britain and France in an eastern as well as a western form of collective security. It was in eastern Europe that collective security proved most vulnerable. It is true that the first serious tests were to be in the west, with the aggression of Italy in Abyssinia in 1935 and the German remilitarisation of the Rhineland in 1936. But the real testing ground was in the east, which is where the policy of appeasement was to be applied as an alternative to collective security. It is highly significant that a key justification for appeasement towards Germany was the continued ideological fear of the Soviet Union. Britain, in other words, had revised her views of Germany since 1919 but not of Russia.

10

FOREIGN POLICY AND APPEASEMENT 1933–9

The politicians most directly associated with appeasement were the three prime ministers of the 1930s: Ramsay MacDonald (1929–35), Stanley Baldwin (1935–7) and Neville Chamberlain (1937–40), along with their Foreign Secretaries: Sir John Simon (1931–5), Sir Samuel Hoare (1935), and Lord Halifax (1938–40).

This chapter will consider the origins of appeasement as deliberate policy and its applications over Italy, Spain and Germany. The main emphasis will be on detailed examination of the controversial policy of Chamberlain between the Munich settlement of September 1938 and the declaration of war on Germany twelve months later.

THE ORIGINS OF APPEASEMENT

It is tempting to think of appeasement as a policy which originated in the 1930s as a response to the military threat posed by the dictatorships, and as a replacement for the earlier 'stand firm' policy embodied in collective security. This end-on chronological view of collective security and appeasement is, however, simplistic. There was, rather, an overlap between the two. Collective security had never, for Britain, been a total commitment and there had always been reservations and loopholes which might be seen as incipient appeasement. These reservations rapidly increased during the 1930s. Appeasement did not, therefore, suddenly appear as an alternative to collective security. It coexisted with collective security, grew out of it and eventually replaced it.

There had always been an undercurrent of appeasement in Britain, stemming from the First World War, during which the Union of Democratic Control (UDC) had been established. Comprising a number of MPs and others from the Labour and Liberal parties, this played some part in preparing the British public to accept the policy of appeasement.

But it had little direct impact on the actual formation of that policy. This was due more to the structural defects of collective security and the lack of total commitment to it by the British government. Collective security was tied to the League of Nations without at the same time giving the League sufficient powers to enforce it. Ramsay MacDonald had tried, through the Geneva Protocol of 1924, to ensure that members were compelled to submit disputes between them to arbitration by the League. Baldwin's government had, however, refused to ratify this and throughout the 1920s and 1930s the League lacked teeth. The agreement most directly associated with collective security, the Locarno Pact, was also flawed; it guaranteed the frontiers of France and Belgium, but not those of Poland and Czechoslovakia. It was the latter which were always most likely to be the target for any revisionist policy by Germany, and even Stresemann, the moderate German Foreign Minister between 1923 and 1929, had suggested that Germany's eastern frontiers should not be seen as final. What would Britain do if this were ever put to the test? The question remained hypothetical during the 1920s, as the illusion of collective security remained intact despite its flaws. Germany was a democratic republic and the policy of Stresemann, although revisionist, was restrained. There was general optimism about gradual disarmament and, in the 1928 Kellogg–Briand Pact, over sixty nations renounced 'recourse to war' in their relations with each other. Again, however, collective security meant collective good-will; the mechanism of restraint was incomplete.

Britain had good reasons for wanting it to remain so. She had interests which extended well beyond Europe; indeed, in terms of her economy, strategic interests and Empire, these were as global after the First World War as they had ever been. This meant that over-commitment in Europe would severely unbalance her role abroad. From the early 1920s onwards, successive British governments made it clear that there was a limit to the extent of their likely involvement and that they looked to other countries to play their part. There was sometimes an open threat of unilateral action (or rather, inaction), which can be seen as one of the main strands of appeasement. In October 1922, for example, Bonar Law had said:

> We cannot act alone as the policeman of the world. The financial and social condition of this country makes that impossible . . . if [our French Allies] are not prepared to support us there, we shall not be able to bear the burden alone but shall have no alternative except to imitate the government of the United States

and to restrict our attention to the safeguarding of our more immediate interests of the Empire.[1]

The attitude to European involvement was also conditioned by the existence of the Empire, which, with the addition of the mandated territories, was greatly expanded after the First World War. Despite their considerable resources, it was difficult to collate the security needs of the various dominions.

Collective security was influenced to a large extent by the need to uphold the Versailles settlement and by the perception of Germany as a possible threat in the future. At the same time, however, there were many in Britain who had misgivings about the justice of that settlement and the wisdom of inflicting such harsh measures. Another root of appeasement, therefore, was a stirring of collective guilt as a counterpart to collective security, influenced as far back as 1919 and 1920 by the writings of J.M. Keynes and Harold Nicolson. This was later taken up in a big way by the weekly press.[2] The Treaties of Versailles and St Germain were seen increasingly as 'the malign progeny of the Great War'.[3] There was a widespread feeling that, since the peace settlement had been inequitable, it would be irrational to expect stable inter-national relations without some revision of its terms. This eventually led, within all political parties, to a willingness to give Germany the benefit of any doubt. The beneficiary of this delayed reaction was Hitler; after his appointment as Chancellor in 1933, the weekly papers carried thousands of articles on Nazi Germany.[4] There was a collective blindness to the policy of racism and an underlying sympathy with the direction of Nazism. The *Week-End Review* argued in July 1933: that Nazism was a revolt 'against years of unemployment' as well as 'inequality in international status' and against 'democratic political machinery which is unsuited to the German people'.[5]

From 1933 onwards the thread of appeasement that had always run through collective security became increasingly apparent. This was because the restraints exercised on it by collective security now rapidly disintegrated.

The catalyst for this change was the Great Depression, which promoted political instability that in turn brought about a less harmo-nious atmosphere in Europe. The ideals and structures of collective security were both fatally weakened. R.A.C. Parker argues that the former had relied upon world opinion 'to prevent a resort to force, or the threat of force, in the pursuit of national ambitions'.[6] MacDonald, especially, had hoped that collective security would be strengthened by progressive disarmament, under the auspices of the League of Nations. This aim was bankrupted by Hitler's decision to withdraw Germany from the League of Nations Disarmament Conference in 1933 in preparation for a programme of German rearmament. The structure of collective security, bound as it was to the League of Nations, was also fatally weakened, as was to be shown by the crises generated by the Japanese invasion of Manchuria (1931), the Italian invasion of Abyssinia (1935) and the Spanish Civil War (1936–9). Sir Eric Phipps warned that 'unless there is some machinery for dealing promptly and effectively with European problems they will be solved ultimately by the sword'.[7]

The British government responded by pursuing a dual approach. One line taken was that of least resistance in its dealings with the powers who appeared to threaten the peace. Another was the decision to rearm, taken in the 1935 White Paper entitled *Statement Relating to Defence* and implemented immediately afterwards. It was clear that British prime ministers and their foreign secretaries found that appeasement gave greater flexibility than had collective security. Abroad it meant that they could end Britain's multilateral obligations under the Locarno Pact and, instead, pursue bilateral expedients as they became necessary. This meant, for example, that Britain felt able, in June 1935, to sign the Anglo-German Naval Agreement, irrespective of the views of France. MacDonald, Baldwin and Chamberlain also aimed to liberate Britain from continental commitments, since these were incompatible with the needs of domestic policy: economic recovery and domestic reform. Without such an emphasis the electoral support for the National Government would have been extremely tenuous, since it was upon these priorities that the National Government had been founded in 1931. There was also a direct connection between domestic and foreign policy in the application of appeasement. Britain's domestic recovery depended upon trying to restore world economic stability after the Wall Street Crash and the Great Depression. This meant a long-term aim to remove tariffs, free international trade and revive the international system of loans and credits. The emphasis had therefore to be on renewed economic and political co-operation, which appeasement offered, without the constraining agreements of collective security.

It is clear that Britain led the field in shaking off collective security. It is often argued that this was partly the fault of France, who had always pursued a hard line with Germany and had always applied the concept of collective security *against* Germany. In the changing circumstances of the early 1930s, Britain was anxious to distance herself from this interpretation. An alternative viewpoint is advanced by R.A.C. Parker, who considers that the responsibility for the transition from collective security to appeasement was almost entirely Britain's. The first crises arose not with Germany but in those areas where Britain had fewest direct concerns – Manchuria and Abyssinia. This was pointed out by one of the sub-committees of the Committee of Imperial Defence in November 1935:

> In 1932–33, and again in 1935, owing to our obligations under the Covenant and the position we occupy as the one great sea power remaining in the League, we had no alternative but to play our part – inevitably a leading part – in disputes in which our national interest was at most quite secondary.[8]

Britain therefore took a conscious decision to move away from the League, concerned that she would be dragged into a conflict and convinced that the League was unable to develop a system to prevent this from happening. According to Parker, 'The League "failed" because the British thought it was more dangerous to British security to use it than not to do so; the "failure" of the League was a consequence rather than a cause of British policy.'[9]

THREE EXAMPLES OF BRITISH APPEASEMENT IN ACTION

The gradual weakening of collective security and the ascendancy of appeasement can be seen in Britain's response during the 1930s to Italy, to the Spanish Civil War, and to Germany. British policy towards Italy seemed initially to revive determination through collective security but eventually gave way to irresolution through appeasement. The Spanish Civil War showed the growing caution of the British government and the triumph of appeasement, which was then to be applied, in its most advanced form, towards Germany.

British policy towards Italy was ambivalent. At first it seemed that MacDonald had recreated collective security when, in 1935, Britain, France and Italy joined together in the Stresa Front. This was clearly aimed at the revival of German power and at reviving the Locarno Pact. Then came a more tangible problem when, in October 1935, Mussolini invaded Abyssinia. The British government was thrown into confusion. Before the invasion it had tried, through a speech by Sir Samuel Hoare at the League of Nations, to warn Italy off a policy of aggression. This clearly failed. Then the Hoare–Laval pact, concluded

Plate 5 Neville Chamberlain, 1938.
Reproduced by permission of 'PA' News.

without the knowledge of the British government, offered Italy a large part of Abyssinia provided the war ceased immediately. The British government was sufficiently embarrassed when the news created public outrage to reverse this policy and to take the lead in the League of Nations in imposing sanctions on Italy. These, however, failed to work properly and caused Chamberlain's government in 1937 and 1938 to have a fundamental rethink. Chamberlain wrote to Mussolini in July, urging an agreement between the British and Italian governments. This might be seen as the clearest possible signal that Britain was prepared to act unilaterally outside the scope of agreed League action – in other words, appeasement in its most direct form. Such a policy had, however, been gaining ground as a direct result of British apprehensions over the Spanish Civil War (1936–9), fought between the Republican government and the Nationalist rebels.

Britain saw several problems in this conflict. One was the ideological threat posed by the war, especially by the alleged Communist influences of the Republic, which Britain feared at this stage more than the fascist inspiration behind the Nationalists. According to Edwards's colourful description,

> While fascism and communism were regarded in the Foreign Office as the 'mumps and measles' of world society, the former was believed to be an urgent but short-term problem; the latter a longer-term one, which in consequence was never quite out of view, and especially in regard to policy towards France or Spain.[10]

Thus the National Government leaned more towards the right in the Spanish Civil War. Even so, there was a strongly pragmatic side to British appeasement, perhaps a touch of ruthlessness. Baldwin is reputed to have said in 1936:

> We English hate fascism but we loathe bolshevism as much. So if there is somewhere where fascists and bolsheviks can kill each other, so much the better.[11]

The British government also had a more immediate fear – that the Spanish Civil War might break its national bounds and overspill into a European war. Already it was being seen as a European civil war fought on Spanish soil and British politicians thought it best to confine it to that quarter. The obvious answer was to persuade the various European powers to desist from supporting either of the Spanish protagonists. Hence the British government was instrumental in establishing the Non-Intervention Committee. In its inception this might be seen almost as a revival of collective security since it aimed at imposing restraint and self-discipline on the major powers. But appeasement soon took over as the key emphasis. This showed itself in two ways.

First, no action was taken to prevent Germany, Italy and Russia from supplying the two sides in the war. Italy's contributions to the Nationalists included over 50,000 ground troops, 950 tanks, 763 aircraft and 91 warships. Germany provided 16,000 military advisers, the latest aircraft and the services of the Condor Legion. The problem was that the fascist dictators used the Non-Intervention Committee to express pacific policies while, at the same time, flouting its detailed provisions. The Committee had no powers apart from those of investigating violations of non-intervention, and even these were circumscribed by a regulation that they could only follow a complaint from one of the member states. This was, in fact, rarely done. What would have been the point?

Second, Britain applied pressure to France to prevent her from assisting the Spanish Republic and cancelling out the support of Italy for Franco. In July 1936 Baldwin warned the French Prime Minister, Blum, that if French involvement in the war provoked a conflict with Italy Britain would not support France. On another occasion, Baldwin said that 'on no account, French or other, must he bring us into the fight on the side of the Russians'.[12] Thus the two elements of appeasement merged. The aim of the British government was not to enter the war, and not to give assistance to the Russian cause. Sir Samuel Hoare, First Lord of the Admiralty, said: 'On no account must we do anything to bolster up Communism in Spain.' There was the additional problem that if Communism prevailed in Spain it would soon spread to Portugal. The impact of the overthrow of Salazar's regime there would have disastrous consequences for Portugal's overseas empire – and then for the British Empire, a part of which was adjacent to every Portuguese colony. Considering what eventually happened in the 1970s to the Portuguese empire after the collapse of the right-wing Portuguese regime of Caetano, this suspicion was not without justification.

There can be little doubt that non-intervention helped destroy the Spanish Republic. It failed to restrain Italy and Germany, but it did prevent France going to the Republic's assistance. Britain played a key role in this. According to Puzzo, 'The conclusion is inescapable that the defeat and destruction of the Spanish Republic must be attributed as much to British diplomacy in the years 1936 to 1939 as to German aircraft and Italian infantry.'[13] The British government was also receptive to the so-called 'lessons' of the war, which enhanced its policy of appeasement, especially towards Germany. Baldwin and Chamberlain were all too aware of how the war had brought Germany and Italy closer together in the Rome–Berlin Axis of 1936, thus reversing the Stresa Front. This made it more difficult for Britain to react positively to the remilitarisation of the Rhineland in 1936, to the Anschluss (1938) and to the Sudeten Crisis (1938). Any one of these crises might have caused war to spread from Spain to Europe, with Germany and Italy as allies. In 1938 Chamberlain also learned from the Spanish Civil War the lesson of what damage could be inflicted by aerial bombing. This profoundly influenced the way in which he dealt with Hitler at Munich in September 1938. In this respect, the war gave appeasement its element of fear, a commodity which should not be underestimated in 1938.

British policy towards Germany was affected largely by the failure of the international system on disarmament. Hitler removed Germany from the Geneva Conference in March 1933 on the grounds that France refused to withdraw the ban on German equality with the other powers enshrined in the military clauses of the Treaty of Versailles. In response to Hitler's unilateral action, Britain initially tried through the Stresa Front to reactivate a form of collective security. But this was soon undermined by direct negotiations with Germany that amounted to a clear sign that a policy of appeasement was preferred. These resulted, in 1935, in the Anglo-German Naval Agreement, which allowed Germany to rebuild her navy to within 35 per cent of Britain's naval strength. This effectively destroyed the Stresa Front and undermined all French hope of upholding the Versailles settlement.

More followed. In 1936 Hitler moved to remilitarise the Rhineland, in open defiance of the Treaty of Versailles. The French were not prepared to take action without British support, which was not forthcoming. The Prime Minister, Baldwin, and the Foreign Secretary, Anthony Eden, judged that public opinion would not support action to prevent the German government taking over what was, after all, German territory. Greatly emboldened by the success of his gamble, Hitler proceeded to annex Austria in the Anschluss of March 1938. Again, the British government, now under Neville Chamberlain, took no counter-action, justifying its passive response on the grounds that Hitler was applying the principles of national self-determination which had proved, in plebiscites held after the take-over, to be enormously popular both in Germany and in Austria.

It was, however, in response to the Sudeten crisis of September 1938 that appeasement reached its climax and any remaining pretence of collective security disappeared. Hitler demanded the transfer of the

Sudetenland, with its 3.5 million Germans, from Czechoslovakia to the Reich. Chamberlain put pressure on the Czech government to accede to the transfer and persuaded the French government not to support any Czech resistance. Altogether, Chamberlain met Hitler on three occasions: at Berchtesgaden, at Godesberg and at Munich, where the Sudetenland was finally signed away to Germany. Chamberlain's handling of the Sudeten crisis has caused more controversy and debate than any other single issue in British foreign policy. As we shall see in the next section, Chamberlain has always had his detractors. Before examining their case we should, however, attempt to see what he was trying to accomplish by appeasing Hitler and what he saw as his immediate priorities.

A DEFENCE OF CHAMBERLAIN'S POLICY AT MUNICH

The strongest defender of Chamberlain's policy is A.J.P. Taylor, who provides plausible reasons for almost all Chamberlain's actions in 1938. These include the argument that Chamberlain had natural justice on his side and that his consideration for the aspirations of the Sudeten Germans was well within the legitimate revisionist trend of the time. According to Taylor, Munich can be seen as 'a triumph for British policy . . . a triumph for all that was best and most enlightened in British life . . . a triumph for those who had courageously denounced the harshness and short-sightedness of Versailles'. Indeed, Taylor continues, 'With skill and persistence, Chamberlain brought first the French, and then the Czechs to follow the moral line.'[14] He also maintains that Chamberlain's policy benefited the Czechs. According to Taylor:

> In 1938 Czechoslovakia was betrayed. In 1939 Poland was saved. Less than one hundred thousand Czechs died during the war. Six and a half million Poles were killed. Which was better – to be a betrayed Czech or a saved Pole?[15]

A less controversial line emphasises Chamberlain's pragmatism rather than his idealism. Throughout his dealings with Hitler and Czechoslovakia, Chamberlain gave absolute priority to Britain's security and defences. It has been suggested that he bought time, giving Britain and France time to rearm and the chance to catch up with Germany: Munich was therefore an essential respite. This is not to say that Munich actually *started* the process of rearmament; in fact, it was already well under way.[16] But, on succeeding Baldwin, Chamberlain had declared his intention to speed up rearmament, with the full co-operation of industry and labour. Some historians have argued that Chamberlain did a great deal more than any of his contemporaries for Britain's security. According to R.P. Shay, for example, 'Had Chamberlain replaced Baldwin in 1936 . . . it is likely that British rearmament would have been considerably more advanced than it actually was in 1939'.[17] Chamberlain was therefore pursuing a carefully considered long-term objective. But it was vitally important that Britain's defences should not be put to the test prematurely. As early as 1936 he had written, 'I am pretty satisfied that, if only we can keep out of war a few years, we shall have an Air Force of such striking power that no one will care to run risks with it.'[18] For Chamberlain, therefore, the crisis over Czechoslovakia came at the worst possible time. He felt impelled to follow his instinct that 1938 was too early to risk war. He was supported by the Committee for Imperial Defence (CID), which argued that 'From a military point of view, time is in our favour, and . . . if war with Germany has to come it would be better to fight her in say 6–12 months' time than to accept the present challenge.' Chamberlain never doubted the wisdom of avoiding conflict in 1938. Shortly after his resignation, he wrote in a private letter on 25 May 1940: 'Whatever the outcome, it is clear as daylight that, if we had had to fight in 1938, the result would have been far worse.'[19]

A quantitative assessment suggests that Chamberlain was right. The production of aircraft, for example, was 240 per month in 1938, increasing to 660 per month in 1939. The number of airborne squadrons increased from 6 squadrons in 1938 to 26 in September 1939. Considering the critical role played by the RAF in the Battle of Britain (1940), this amounted to the most vital consolidation. The army also expanded, to make up for the loss of thirty-six Czech divisions to the French alliance. But this was slower and less systematic than the growth of the airforce. More rapid were precautions against air raids and the development of plans for the evacuation of civilians.

This brings us to a second way in which Chamberlain judged that 1938 was the wrong time for a war with Germany. The people of Britain and of the Empire were simply not ready for one – and certainly not on the issues prevalent in 1938. Britain was very much divided on the prospect of a war with Germany at this stage and the Sudetenland was not a good issue on which to achieve a common policy or a national consensus. The population was far from convinced that a stand needed to be made to uphold an apparently irrational territorial arrangement made nineteen years earlier in the Treaty of St Germain. Much as they might dislike and suspect Hitler's methods, the British public and the Dominions could hardly be expected to identify with the cause of keeping 3.5 million Germans in Czechoslovakia, and Chamberlain could hardly be blamed for not trying to force them to do so.

Even if Britain and the Empire *had* been behind a policy of resisting Germany, Chamberlain doubted that there was any practical way in which such a policy could have been implemented. 'You have only to look at the map to see that nothing that France or we could do could possibly save Czechoslovakia from being overrun by the Germans if they wanted to do it.'[20] This might have been prevented during the 1920s when the German army had been limited to 100,000 and a network of alliances had connected the eastern European states with France. But by 1938 Germany had rearmed and the French alliances had collapsed along with the system to which they had been tied: collective security. There remained, of course, the 1935 treaties between France, Czechoslovakia and the Soviet Union. But France was already wavering about honouring her commitment to Czechoslovakia even before Chamberlain's intervention over the Sudetenland. Opinion in France was divided. One view was put in the Chamber of Deputies on 26 February 1938 by the Foreign Minister, Delbos, that 'France's engagements towards Czechoslovakia would be faithfully fulfilled in case of need.' But there was much support for the view that the end of collective security meant that France could not be expected to act in a vacuum. According to Flandin, 'the collapse of the Treaty of Locarno, to which our last treaty with Czechoslovakia was bound . . . rendered the latter null and void.'[21] The French government, especially Bonnet, also emphasised the practical difficulties in securing Soviet help for Czechoslovakia, since the only access for Soviet troops would have been through Poland or Romania.

Nor was there any real possibility at this stage of reactivating collective security. If the various countries of central and eastern Europe had been involved in a war in 1938, they would probably have cancelled each other out by fighting on different sides. Poland had her own territorial claims against Czechoslovakia, as did Hungary. Neither, therefore, was likely to assist Britain and France. Indeed, Poland had a non-aggression pact with Germany, signed in 1934; clearly her main preoccupation was with Russia. Any war involving Russia would automatically place Poland on the side of Germany, as was eventually to happen with Finland in 1940. Romania's position was extremely doubtful, since its right-wing dictatorship had come increasingly under the diplomatic and financial influence of Germany. To make matters worse, it seemed likely that if war were to break out, Italy and Japan would join Germany. If this happened, the Chiefs of Staff pointed out to Chamberlain, there was a strong possibility that Britain and France would be defeated. Chamberlain was acutely aware of this wider European perspective and knew that for Britain and France war was not a realistic proposition. His actions over the Sudetenland were therefore designed to prevent this. He reasoned, quite logically, that the greatest risk was that war might arise out of accident or a misunderstanding, that Britain and France might convey the wrong message to a leader who was volatile and unpredictable. Every effort, therefore, was made to win Hitler's confidence.

This does not mean, as Churchill alleged, that Chamberlain was duped by Hitler. The reverse is arguable – Chamberlain actually had a restraining influence and managed to deprive Hitler of the war he wanted by standing firm on the concessions he was prepared to allow. At Berchtesgaden, Chamberlain and Hitler agreed on the incorporation of the Sudetenland. Chamberlain subsequently got the agreement of the Czech government for this. Then, at Bad Godesberg, Hitler went further, demanding immediate military occupation by Germany. This time, however, Chamberlain proved more obdurate, which suggests that he was a firm negotiator when on ground he considered appropriate. At Munich, Hitler was obliged to adopt the Berchtesgaden agreement. Over the entire period of negotiation over the Sudetenland it was, therefore, Hitler, not Chamberlain, who moved his position. It may seem that Chamberlain was too willing to trust Hitler's word which, as events turned out, counted for nothing. But Chamberlain had never experienced Hitler breaking his word before – Hitler had always been consistently opposed to the Versailles settlement and there was some logic to Chamberlain's belief that Hitler was pursuing a course which would enable Germany to adapt to a new pattern of international relations. In any case, there were precedents in British foreign policy for trusting dictators. Had not Austen Chamberlain said in the 1920s of Mussolini: 'I trust his word when given' and had not Churchill endorsed the government's approval of Mussolini by referring to him as 'Roman genius in person'? If Chamberlain erred in his judgement, then he was in good company.

A CRITICISM OF CHAMBERLAIN'S POLICY
AT MUNICH

The original – and strongest – critic of Chamberlain was his successor, Winston Churchill, who always maintained that earlier resistance to Hitler could have prevented the outbreak of the Second World War. He described Chamberlain as 'the narrowest, most ignorant, most un-generous of men',[22] claimed that Chamberlain had a 'limited outlook and inexperience of the European scene'[23] and argued that Munich was a 'disaster of the first magnitude'.[24] Historians, too, point to the errors committed in 1938. Telford Taylor's damning indictment is that:

> it was Chamberlain who decided that Czechoslovakia could not and therefore should not be protected against the German threat, and who undermined the Czechs' will to resist, shattered the Czech-Franco-Russian defensive alliances, rang down the curtain on the Europe of Versailles, and gave effect to his chosen policy of appeasement.[25]

The starting point to any criticism of Chamberlain's policy is that he presided over a settlement which was inherently dishonourable. Czechoslovakia was the only country in central and eastern Europe to have resisted the internal drift to dictatorship which had, in the 1920s and early 1930s, overtaken the likes of Poland, the Baltic States, Hungary, Romania, Bulgaria, Yugoslavia and Greece. What is more, Czechoslovakia had taken extensive measures to protect herself against possible aggression by Germany. But all these preparations were nulli-fied by an act of betrayal by the democracies of western Europe, at the instigation of Chamberlain himself. It is specious to argue that, in backing self-determination for the Sudeten Germans, he was acting in accordance with the principles of natural justice and that Czechoslovakia had to be prepared to make concessions. There were, after all, plenty of national minorities in Europe at the time and the people most affected were not the Germans but the Magyars. Chamberlain's willingness to see a revision of the inequities of Versailles was, therefore, too selective to be considered an act of conscience. Rather, it was a negative and purely pragmatic response to external pressure. With a characteristic combination of bluntness and eloquence, Churchill told him: 'You were given the choice between war and dishonour. You chose dishonour and you will have war.'[26]

'War' was perfectly feasible as an alternative to 'dishonour' in 1938. Chamberlain was, however, instrumental in breaking up the remaining links in the alliance system which might at this stage have restrained

Germany. He persuaded the French to abandon the obligation which they had under the 1925 Franco-Czechoslovak Treaty. The French adopted the British stance in bringing pressure to bear on the Czechoslovak government to meet the demands laid down by Hitler at Berchtesgaden. It is true that the French needed little persuading. But the role of Chamberlain was still pivotal: the French might well have acted with British support, but were certain not to run any risks without it. In this situation, the other security arrangements simply fell apart. The Russians had no reason to act without the French – indeed, the 1935 Russo-Czechoslovak Treaty expressly forbade them from doing so. They were, nevertheless, willing to apply diplomatic pressure and the Soviet foreign minister, Litvinov, several times urged collective action with Czechoslovakia and France and 'with other states belonging to the League of Nations or outside it' to look for 'practical measures' to uphold the integrity of Czechoslovakia. Chamberlain turned down this and other proposals as action designed for 'an eventuality that has not yet occurred'.[27] Churchill apparently saw through this, warning 'what a mad lack of foresight on our part, at a time of great danger, to put obstacles on the road of the general association of the huge Russian mass with the resistance to a Nazi act of aggression'.[28] It is hardly surprising that the Russians were denied representation at the Munich Conference, since Chamberlain and Daladier feared that Litvinov would undermine the concessions they were expecting to make. A French diplomat, Coulondre, maintained that the mistake at Munich 'was to go there without Russia and with the "Munich spirit"'.[29]

Although the construction of historical 'might-have-beens' is notoriously difficult, it is tempting to speculate on the possible results of resisting Germany in 1938. Chamberlain greatly underestimated the military power already existing in Europe. With a total force of 100 divisions, the French greatly outnumbered the Germans in the west, while their Maginot Line was far more developed than the German equivalent, the Siegfried Line. In central Europe, Czechoslovakia had another powerful set of defensive fortifications, between 30 and 35 divisions, and up to 1,500 aircraft. Even Hitler realised this, for he later said, 'What we were able to see of the military strength of the Czechoslovaks greatly disturbed us; we had run a serious danger.'[30] In the east, the Soviet Union was fast emerging as a major military power, the result of nearly ten years of heavy expenditure on heavy industry and rearmament through Stalin's five-year plans. The Soviet airforce was almost as large as the Luftwaffe and could probably have established air supremacy over Czechoslovakia. Transit from the Soviet Union to

Czechoslovakia was a problem, but this might have been solved by the growing willingness of the Romanian government to allow an air corridor. Overall, Germany would have faced heavy odds to the west and the south. Although war with Russia might well have brought Poland in on Germany's side, the Polish army still relied heavily on cavalry and would have had some difficulty holding off Soviet tanks. War in 1938 would, by this analysis, have been a very different proposition to the war which actually occurred in 1939 – when Germany and Russia collaborated in the partition of Poland, the Czechoslovak factories supplied the German war machine, and British and French forces sat behind the Maginot Line.

Why did Chamberlain abandon a position of such potential strength? The basic reason is that, throughout the crisis, he was haunted by a vision of the total destruction he felt war would bring to Britain. It would involve the bombing of cities and the slaughter of millions of civilians; in this respect, Chamberlain's notion of war was more futuristic than that of the French government, which seemed to have stuck in the backward-looking mentality known as the Maginot Line complex. Chamberlain was more affected than any of his contemporaries by the Japanese bombing of Chinese cities in the 1930s and, above all, by the German bombing of Guernica in 1938. It was no coincidence that the Sudeten crisis was accompanied by the building of air-raid shelters in the London parks and by the mass distribution of gas masks. Chamberlain was convinced that diplomatic failure at this critical time meant physical annihilation. In fact, he greatly overestimated the capacity of the Luftwaffe to inflict this degree of destruction. It has been pointed out that the number of bombs expected in 1938 was not delivered during the whole of the war,[31] even during the saturation bombing of Germany by Britain and the United States in 1944. Chamberlain deduced too much from too little evidence; the destruction of Guernica was a tragedy which captured the imagination but should not have been allowed to influence an entire diplomatic policy. Telford Taylor argues that Munich was a triumph of German propaganda about the power of the Luftwaffe; indeed, it was the 'only victory of strategic proportions that the Luftwaffe ever won'.[32]

Having lost the initiative in Europe, Britain and France did not even benefit militarily from the year's respite after Munich. It is true that the Royal Air Force increased substantially, but the French air force stagnated, resulting in the loss of the Battle of France to the Germans in June 1940. Both Britain and Germany added to their navies between

September 1938 and September 1939, but Germany slightly narrowed the gap between them. In any case, Germany's grip on central Europe increased her contacts with the Balkans, strengthening her drive for self-sufficiency and reducing the damage the Royal Navy could actually do. The British army was also increased, but insufficiently to compensate for the loss of the Czechoslovak divisions; besides, it was still too small to have much impact in 1939 and had reached only nineteen divisions when Hitler invaded France in 1940. The French increased their tanks from 1,350 in 1938 to 2,250 but these were less manoeuvrable than the German panzer divisions. The Germans had also greatly increased their strength on the western front, equalling the 100 divisions deployed by the French. 'All in all', argues Telford Taylor, 'it is clear that, in terms of strength on the ground, the situation was far more favourable to Britain and France in 1938 than in 1939'.[33]

Finally, Chamberlain made a disastrous miscalculation *after* Munich. He entirely failed to allow for the possibility that Hitler might move on to another objective and neglected to take any measures to contain Germany in the future. According to Parker, his influence was entirely negative.

> Chamberlain led the government in 1938 and 1939, particularly in the months after Munich, into rejecting the option of a close Franco-British alliance, which might have acted as a nucleus round which those states with reason to fear the Third Reich could assemble to resist it.[34]

Furthermore, Chamberlain's dislike of Communism blinded him to the possibilities which might have followed a pact with Russia. Churchill had an equally strong aversion to Soviet ideology, as had been affirmed by his earlier support for foreign intervention against the Bolsheviks. Nevertheless, Churchill considered Stalin a lesser evil than Hitler and, from a purely pragmatic point of view, argued strongly for Anglo-Soviet co-operation. Chamberlain remained entirely unconvinced and accorded relations with the Soviet Union the lowest priority; according to Parker, 'he thought collaboration with the Soviet Union undesirable and unnecessary'.[35] This was not only a lost opportunity but also the signal for a diplomatic revolution by Stalin. Litvinov, who had staked his reputation on an accord with the west, was replaced as foreign minister by Molotov, a ruthless pragmatist who inclined more to an agreement with Germany. The result was the Nazi–Soviet Non-Aggression Pact of August 1939, which set in motion the events leading directly to the outbreak of World War II.

THE IMPLICATIONS OF CHAMBERLAIN'S POLICY AT MUNICH

As we have seen, Chamberlain's version of appeasement has tended to attract polarised views. What are we to make of them? A brief survey of Britain's role in the Second World War suggests an overall perspective incorporating elements of each.

Looked at from a strategic point of view there can be little doubt that Chamberlain's policy at Munich was a disaster. It weakened Britain's position in relation to the Continent. It also led to the loss of any eastern allies and contributed to the eventual collapse of France in June 1940. (These were directly connected since French survival in the First World War had been made possible by Germany's preoccupation with Russia.) Britain was able to play only a minimal role on the Continent in 1940 and British troops had to be evacuated at Dunkirk. Unlike Churchill, Chamberlain seemed to have had no grasp of larger strategic issues and it might be argued that Dunkirk was the logical strategic consequence of the diplomacy of appeasement at Munich. On the other hand, Chamberlain *did* understand defence, even if he exaggerated Britain's relative difficulties in 1938. The Royal Air Force was massively strengthened in the year after September 1938 by the rapid construction of Spitfires and Hurricanes. Munich therefore bought time and Chamberlain deserves at least some credit for the victories in the Battle of Britain in 1940. The steady consolidation of the Royal Navy also ensured British supremacy in the Atlantic and, eventually, in the Mediterranean.

The implication of this is that Britain was able to survive in 1940, but was condemned by Chamberlain's policy to a struggle in isolation. Britain managed to prevent a cross-Channel invasion by Germany, but lacked the power to engage Germany directly on the Continent. Her role was increasingly to concentrate on the periphery of Europe – the Atlantic, the Mediterranean, North Africa. This kept the war with Germany going but without any real prospect of victory, since this could be achieved only on the Continent. Thus Britain was involved in a struggle which was entirely different to what might have occurred in 1938 had Chamberlain resisted Hitler's demands over the Sudetenland. The eventual defeat of Germany by 1945 was the result of the conflict being switched back to the Continent. This occurred after two events in 1941. One was Hitler's invasion of Russia, which opened up an eastern front that bled Germany dry. The other was the Japanese attack on Pearl Harbor, which brought the United States into the war with Germany as well and made possible the invasion of western Europe in 1944. These developments, which were themselves entirely unconnected with Munich, finally neutralised the strategic effects of appeasement.

1939: CHANGE FROM OR CONTINUITY WITH 1938?

A series of dramatic events occurred between March and September 1939. The same government which had given Hitler what he wanted at Munich decided, in March 1939, to extend guarantees to Poland and Romania against threats to their independence and, following Hitler's invasion of Poland on 1 September, declared war on Germany. Did these developments amount to a revolution in British foreign policy and the reversal of appeasement? Or was there an underlying continuity during the period between September 1938 and September 1939?

The traditional interpretation is that Chamberlain came to realise that Hitler had broader objectives than had been apparent at Munich and that appeasement would have to be replaced by a policy of containment. There were two milestones in this change of course. One was the anti-Jewish pogrom in Germany, known as Kristallnacht, on 10 November 1938. This drove home to Chamberlain the real meaning of the Nazi regime in Germany and destroyed any illusions he might have had that Hitler was capable of a restrained and rational policy. The second was the invasion of Bohemia by Hitler in March 1939, which convinced Chamberlain that Hitler would now continue to expand Germany's frontiers in defiance of the Munich agreement. Chamberlain wrote, 'As soon as I had time to think I saw that it was impossible to deal with Hitler after he had thrown all his own assurances to the wind.'[36] This realisation of the true nature of Hitler's regime and militarism gave Chamberlain no option but to extend British guarantees to Poland and Romania. When Hitler refused to take these seriously and invaded Poland, Chamberlain stood by his word and declared war on Germany. This was a turnabout to his pacific policy of exactly a year before.

There is another slant to the argument that appeasement was reversed. British policy before 1939 was constrained by certain weaknesses, including military shortcomings, and by the need for time to convince public opinion and the Dominions. As the process of rearmament accelerated in 1939, Chamberlain was able to take a tougher line with Germany without having to take constant account of the danger of defeat. After the scare of 1938, the British public were more resigned to the possibility of war, and upholding the integrity of Poland was a better rallying point than the Sudeten issue had been. It could be argued, therefore, that Chamberlain's new approach was gradual, based less on events in Germany and Bohemia than on a growing confidence in Britain's military strength.

There is, however, an alternative perspective on Chamberlain's policies in 1938 and 1939. The argument for continuity rests on two premises.

One is that Britain's resistance to Germany began well before March 1939. W.N. Medlicott, for example, argues that Britain was not prepared to countenance any major change in eastern Europe.[37] S. Newman considers that the continuity was based not so much on Britain's weakness as on a certain degree of calculation.

> Britain never intended Germany to have a free hand in eastern Europe at all. Thus the guarantee to Poland should not be interpreted as a revolution in British foreign policy, as has so often been argued, but should be seen as the culmination, or rather the explicit manifestation of a strand of British policy going back to before September 1938 which has until recently been overlooked or ignored – the attempt to stem German expansion in eastern Europe by any means short of war but in the last resort by war itself.[38]

It could certainly be said that, rightly or wrongly, Chamberlain made a distinction in his dealings with Hitler between Czechoslovakia and Poland. The former he saw as an artificial contrivance, a remote country in eastern Europe with a large German minority, while the latter was an historic entity, reconstituted after a century of subservience. Despite its fortifications, Czechoslovakia was too vulnerable to be considered strategically important in Europe: the Anschluss with Austria (1938) had resulted in its being almost surrounded by Germany. Poland and Romania were another matter. They provided a vital barrier in eastern Europe against the expansion of two hegemonist powers – Nazi Germany and Soviet Russia. It was very much in Britain's interest to maintain that cordon.

By this analysis, Chamberlain's whole approach in 1938 and 1939 was essentially pragmatic. Chamberlain did not abandon basic principles in 1938 and suddenly rediscover them in 1939. Instead, Britain was attempting by various means to maintain a balance in Europe. According to Newman, 'The Government's failure to contain Germany by peaceful means resulted in the commitment to go to war to prevent her from reaching full strength.'[39] Chamberlain was therefore acting within a long established tradition in British foreign policy of evading war over trouble spots considered of lesser strategic importance and of intervening over areas held to be vital.

The other argument for continuity of British policy between 1938 and 1939 puts an entirely different case. It was not so much a continuing effort to resist Hitler from 1938; rather, it was a continuing quest to appease him in 1939. There was no underlying change in Chamberlain's method: he still hoped to maintain peace with Germany through appeasement. During the crisis over Poland in August, the British government put pressure on the Poles to meet the Germans halfway and to concede to them the use of a Polish corridor. The American ambassador, Joseph Kennedy, said, 'Frankly he [Chamberlain] is more worried about getting the Poles to be reasonable than the Germans.'[40] Similarly, Henderson told Halifax the same day that the German terms seemed 'moderate to me and are certainly only so in view of the German desire for good relations with Britain'. Even after the German invasion of Poland on 1 September, there was a delay before Britain declared war on Germany. This was because discussions were being held on a possible settlement which would involve the withdrawal of German troops and the convening of a conference on Poland. According to Gilbert and Gott, the British government was pursuing a strange policy which amounted to a 'solution without war once war had begun'.

Why, therefore, *did* Chamberlain declare war on Germany? Gilbert and Gott argue that Chamberlain was confronted by such a force of opposition to continued negotiations with Germany that he had no option. Quite simply, 'Without war, the Government would be overthrown'.[41] The trouble started on 2 September, when Chamberlain announced to the Commons that 'If the German Government should agree to withdraw their forces, then His Majesty's Government would be willing to regard the position as being the same as it was before the German forces crossed the Polish frontier'.[42] This got the worst possible reception. According to Julian Amery, 'The House was aghast. For two whole days the wretched Poles had been bombed and massacred, and we were still considering within what time limit Hitler should be invited to tell us whether he felt like relinquishing his prey!'[43] There was also grave disquiet within the Cabinet. To save his government and his own position, Chamberlain had no option but to send the ultimatum at 9 a.m. on 3 September. When this expired at 11 a.m. he announced to the nation that 'this country is at war with Germany'.

Even then, Chamberlain hoped for a negotiated peace with Germany. In 1940 he wrote about impending 'German realization that they can't win and that it isn't worth their while to go on getting thinner and poorer when they might have instant relief'.[44] The suspicion that Chamberlain was not fully pursuing the war was largely responsible for his being replaced in 1940 by Churchill, who adamantly refused to consider any negotiations with Germany. The language used in Churchill's great wartime speeches also symbolised the end of any remaining links with appeasement.

11

THE SECOND WORLD WAR
AND ITS IMPACT

Between 1939 and 1945 the British people had their second experience of total war. There were certain parallels with the First World War: all the military sinews were stretched to their fullest extent; effective political leadership emerged from unpromising beginnings; and there was an extensive, although varied economic and social impact.

BRITAIN'S MILITARY ROLE IN THE WAR

There is no space in this section for a detailed account of Britain's military involvement. Instead, the theme which will be explored is the weakness of Britain in continental terms, contrasted with her strength on the periphery of Europe, at sea and in the air.

Britain's role during the First World War had, from the outset, been both continental and peripheral. This was because the German invasion in August was contained by the French and British armies, so that the conflict was sustained throughout the war in the trenches of the western front. During the Second World War, the opposite occurred. This time the Germans bypassed the Maginot Line, constructed between the wars for the defence of France, and punched a hole through the supposedly impenetrable Ardennes before racing to the Channel ports. The French armies were rapidly defeated and the British government took the decision to withdraw 325,000 troops – British and French – from Dunkirk. Although there has been an extensive debate on whether this decision was appropriate, R. Lamb sees the withdrawal from Dunkirk as a realistic assessment of what was needed.

> Churchill appreciated correctly how poor the French army was in 1940 compared to its predecessor in 1918, and without hesitation

he made the decision in the nick of time to evacuate from Dunkirk the tiny but vital British regular Army and first-line territorial divisions. Then, despite much soul searching, he refused to waste the few precious RAF fighter squadrons on a despairing France.[1]

To a large extent the chance of successful British involvement in a continental war had been lost in September 1938 when Chamberlain had prevailed upon France not to act in defence of Czechoslovakia and in conjunction with Russia; Chapter 10 shows how the Munich Agreement broke up the alliance system which was most likely to defeat Germany in a continental war.

Britain's decision to withdraw from France had one advantage: it created virtual impregnability across the Channel because Britain had two lines of defence, both taking advantage of her geographical position. The Royal Navy was still substantially larger than the German fleet and the Royal Air Force had greatly increased its fighter strength between September 1938 and July 1940; in the crucial period of the Battle of Britain Britain was producing an average of 563 fighters per month, compared with Germany's 156. British losses were also fewer: between August and October 1940 they amounted to a total of 1,116 aircraft, to Germany's 1,660. The RAF also gained control of the air through the superior training of its pilots, the greater manoeuvrability of British fighters like the Spitfire and the Hurricane, and the early use of radar as a warning system. It has to be said, however, that Britain greatly benefited from the muddled objectives shown by Hitler in carrying out his 'Operation Sealion'. In the first place, he had never regarded Britain as a total enemy. Indeed, in his *Second Book*, he had referred to Britain as 'Germany's natural friend'. Consequently, he was always prepared to seek reconciliation, even 'on the basis of partitioning the world'.[2] His early strategy was based on an attempt to force Britain back into neutrality, an objective which seemed about to be accomplished with the British evacuation from Dunkirk. Hitler made a grave blunder in not committing Germany's total military capacity in 1940 to the invasion of Britain, since Britain's survival was the first step in the eventual decline of Hitler's Reich. Hitler also made tactical errors in his handling of the invasion plan. Goering had promised the destruction of the British air defences within four days and that conditions would be ideal for invasion within four weeks. The *Luftwaffe*, however, was diverted from destroying air bases to bombing cities and industrial targets, with the result that the RAF survived what could have been a sudden and devastating blow.

The Battle of Britain was a turning point in the war in two senses. First, it guaranteed Britain's survival: had Britain lost it, the war would have been over in the west. Second, it forced the Germans to back off, and this enabled Britain to do what she had always been best at – carry on the war at a distance, or on the periphery of Europe. One precedent was the Napoleonic War, where the French Emperor, who dominated the Continent, had been held off by the British in Spain and squeezed by the Royal Navy at sea. In terms of direct continental clashes, the land-based powers had been far more important than Britain in bringing Napoleon down: hence the victory of the Russians, Austrians and Prussians at Leipzig in 1813 had been more devastating than that of the British at Waterloo in 1815, in which the Prussians had also played a significant role. So it proved in World War II. There were no famous British victories in Europe: all the great advances before 1944 were made in eastern Europe by the Russians, while from 1944 the brunt of the action in the west fell to the Americans. This is not to minimise Britain's role, but rather to put it into its true perspective. British successes occurred on the periphery: in the air, at sea, and in North Africa and Italy. The strategy of bombing Germany from 1943 onwards was the one means whereby Britain could strike Germany in the vitals while herself standing off and fighting the war at a distance; the strength of the Royal Navy at sea enabled Britain to win the Battle of the Atlantic and frustrate Hitler's attempts to starve Britain into sub-mission through his U-boat campaign on merchant shipping; and the North African campaign forced Germany to divert essential resources from his targets in the east. The last of these three examples shows a particularly close parallel with the Peninsular War. In each case Britain opened up a suppurating ulcer – in Spain against Napoleon and in North Africa and Italy against Hitler. In each case the enemy was so weakened that he succumbed to the fatal blow – delivered not by Britain, but by Russia.

This brings us to the crucial contribution made by Britain to the eventual defeat of Hitler. Her own survival prolonged the war long enough to ensure that Germany was crushed by other powers with vastly greater industrial strength. Britain kept the war going in the vital period between the fall of France in 1940 and Hitler's invasion of Russia in 1941. From 1943 onwards Britain greatly assisted the war effort of the Soviet Union. Her supremacy at sea meant that Russia could be kept supplied by the North Atlantic route to Murmansk, while the bombing of German factories helped constrain the German war base. Most important of all, Hitler was prevented from applying the full strength of his panzer divisions against Russia by the need to bolster up Rommel's campaign against Montgomery in North Africa. It was therefore no coincidence that the Germans were defeated – at virtually the same time – by the Russians at Stalingrad and by the British at El Alamein. Meanwhile, Britain had also established a base for the United States, on which Hitler declared war in 1942. From 1943 onwards the United States Airforce and the RAF alternated their raids with the effect that 'bombing round the clock' eventually left Germany's cities in ruins. In 1944 a huge invasion force, comprising troops from the United States, Britain and the Empire, was co-ordinated at various collecting points on the south coast of England before being launched against the German 'Atlantic wall' in France. The point made by A.J.P. Taylor about North Africa applies with equal validity to western Europe: 'this moment of victory was also the moment when Great Britain ceased to be an independent power capable of waging a great war from her own resources.'[3]

This approach is based on a rational assessment of the power of Britain by comparison with that of the United States, the real victors in the war. It does not, however, take account of the special place held in the memories of those who lived through the war of the importance of Winston Churchill; he is accredited with the inspiration essential for keeping up morale during Britain's darkest hour and with the decisions necessary for eventual victory. His role has recently come under close scrutiny, but R. Lamb speaks for the consensus: 'Despite many blunders and hasty, impetuous decisions, only one verdict is possible. He was a great wartime leader.'[4]

Shortcomings in Churchill's leadership are not hard to find. He bears direct responsibility for a number of the disasters which affected Britain in the early years of the war. These included the fall of Norway, Greece and Singapore. His orders for the destruction of the French fleet on 3 July 1940 meant that Vichy France hurried into collaboration with the Germans and also with the Japanese in South East Asia. He has also been criticised for delaying so long in opening up a second front in France. Was he correct in concentrating on the Mediterranean and in his view that Italy was the 'soft underbelly' of the Axis – given the difficulty that the Allies had in breaking through in the northern part of the peninsula? The campaign in North Africa and Italy helped Russia more than Stalin was prepared to admit, but did it not give Russia too much control in 1945? Was the subjection of eastern Europe by the Russians the result of the delay in opening up a second front in Europe? Might not the war have been appreciably shortened by an

Plate 6 Winston Churchill, 1950.
Reproduced by permission of 'PA' News.

earlier attack on France rather than in North Africa? Britain would certainly have had the concerted support of the French Resistance, the strength of which Churchill consistently underestimated. There were also occasions on which Churchill was badly affected by events and visibly lost his usual rational perspective. In 1944, for example, he had to be talked out of retaliating against Hitler's V1 and V2 rockets by the use of mustard gas on German cities. Finally, there remains the biggest question mark of all. Was it really necessary to authorise the devastation of German cities from the air, including the specific and systematic destruction of Dresden in 1944?

Set against such deficiencies was a record at least the equal of Britain's two other great wartime prime ministers, the Younger Pitt and Lloyd George. He came to the office of prime minister in 1940 with the advantage of having been entirely uncompromised by earlier Conservative policies of appeasement during the 1930s and with an impeccable record of being anti-Nazi (although not, it has to be said, anti-Fascist). He had an unusual degree of energy and self-confidence; he could also inspire others into action, including members of the Liberal and Labour parties. In this respect, he was a complete contrast to Neville Chamberlain, who was thoroughly disliked by Labour politicians. Churchill was well supported by Attlee as deputy Prime Minister and Ernest Bevin as Minister of Labour. As Chairman of the War Cabinet and also Minister of Defence, Churchill was ultimately responsible for military strategy and had the ability to make quick and realistic – if difficult – decisions, such as the evacuation of Dunkirk in 1940. Unlike Chamberlain, he was also willing to make pragmatic decisions reversing previous enmities. When Hitler invaded Russia in 1941, Churchill immediately conducted a propaganda campaign within Britain to make common cause with Russia. His one constant was his entrenched opposition to Hitler, which meant that he had to come to accept Stalin; Churchill said, 'if Hitler invaded Hell, I would at least make a favourable reference to the Devil in the House of Commons.'[5] It has also been argued that Churchill was a supreme diplomat and contributed to the situation in which the United States entered the war. Realising that American public opinion would prevent Roosevelt from becoming involved except in response to an act of aggression, Churchill persuaded the United States to tighten the oil blockade – which induced the Japanese to attack Pearl Harbor. The extension of the war to the Pacific had the disadvantage of spreading British resources more thinly, but this was more than offset by the involvement of the United States against Germany, the theatre which Roosevelt openly declared to be America's priority. From 1942 onwards Churchill was in many ways the linchpin holding together Britain, the United States and the Soviet Union within the Grand Alliance, even though he represented the weakest of the three countries.

Above all, Churchill's wartime leadership is associated with the unparalleled and unprecedented power of his oratory. R. Lamb points out that 'his magnificent speeches in the Commons and his broadcasts galvanized the nation to fight in an all-out effort and, although there were only flimsy grounds for confidence, his obvious faith in final victory inspired the nation.'[6] He made the most famous of his speeches to the House of Commons on 10 May 1940:

> I have nothing to offer but blood, toil, tears and sweat. . . . You ask, What is our policy? I will say: it is to wage war by sea, land and air, with all our might and with all the strength that God can give us: to wage war against a monstrous tyranny, never surpassed in the dark, lamentable catalogue of human crime. That is our policy.[7]

His broadcasts on the wireless also hit the right note. On the Battle of Britain he observed that 'Never in the field of human conflict was so much owed by so many to so few.'[8] On the trials ahead, he exhorted: 'Let us so bear ourselves that, though the British Empire and its Commonwealth last for a thousand years, men shall still say "This was their finest hour"'.[9] Overall, he brought enthusiasm and conviction where there had been little in the first months of the war. He also made hardship bearable while not underestimating the task ahead, using such memorable phrases as 'not the beginning of the end but perhaps the end of the beginning'.

THE POLITICAL IMPACT OF THE WAR

On the outbreak of war in September 1939 Chamberlain maintained his existing cabinet, with the addition of Churchill and Eden, previously seen as rebels for their stance against appeasement. Discredited by a year of inaction, however, Chamberlain was forced to resign his post on 9 May 1940. He was succeeded by Churchill, who immediately established a coalition government. The cabinet itself comprised four Labour ministers, including Attlee and Greenwood, fifteen Conservatives and one Liberal. Altogether, the departments were headed by 52 Conservatives, 16 Labour and 2 Liberals.

The governments of both Chamberlain and Churchill moved much more quickly into a position of total control over the population than had been the case during the First World War. Conscription was introduced at once, by the National Service Act of September 1939, and by 1942 all men and women between 18 and 60 were liable to be called up for different forms of service. Men under 40 were the main category for military service, while most women who were conscripted went into the labour force, especially munitions. These arrangements could be altered at any time under the extensive powers given to the Minister of Labour by Regulation 58A of the Emergency Powers (Defence) Act. Government regulations also covered the protection of the civilian population as well as its mobilisation. The two main functions here concerned the planning and execution of programmes to evacuate children from the major cities, and a civil defence scheme covering air-raid shelters and blackout procedures. Rationing was also introduced at the outset, as were food subsidies and measures to control prices.

Did such powers make Britain, even temporarily, a totalitarian state? The answer has to be no, although with one or two reservations. Totalitarian structures are intended to destroy democracy; the measures of the British government were designed to mobilise a democratic system to fight totalitarianism as effectively as possible. They were widely accepted as essential to maximise the nation's war effort and to ensure the fairest possible treatment of all its inhabitants. Where opposition did occur, it came from specific groups, for specific reasons; here the government proved remarkably tolerant and was prepared to apply its administrative measures with a flexibility one does not normally associate with a totalitarian regime. The largest of the dissident groups was made up of conscientious objectors, who objected to combat roles as a matter of principle. Neville Chamberlain's response in 1939 set the tone for the rest of the war: 'Where scruples are conscientiously held we desire that they should be conscientiously respected and that there should be no persecution of those who hold them.'[10] Churchill agreed: persecution, he believed, would be 'odious to the British people'.[11] Tribunals were therefore specially constituted to find alternatives to direct combat for those so affected.

Occasionally, however, accusations *were* made that the government was resorting unnecessarily to totalitarian powers. This applied especially to some of the more extreme forms of censorship operated by the Ministry of Information; in January 1941, for example, it closed down the Communist paper the *Daily Worker*. This was opposed by the remainder of the press, especially the *Daily Mirror*, as an attack on freedom of expression. At times government propaganda was heavy-handed and lacking in inspiration, contrasting with the more subtle methods employed in Germany by the Ministry of Propaganda and Enlightenment. One of the least successful propaganda campaigns conducted by the government was the poster sequences on loose talk; these were widely felt to be patronising and insulting. George Orwell, who had a good nose for totalitarian systems, was especially critical of the type of public information issued: 'the Government has done extraordinarily little to preserve morale; it has merely drawn on existing measures of goodwill.'[12] This was, perhaps, overstating the problem. The British government did make mistakes, but this is not unusual for a democracy making unfamiliar use of emergency powers. The lack of subtlety in its propaganda was to some extent reassuring as it indicated complete unfamiliarity with it.

The political effect of the war on the population was therefore transitory and full democracy was restored in 1945. The impact on the political parties was, however, more permanent. Of the three, Labour benefited most. The Second World War ended the bitter divisions of the 1930s provoked by the policies of Ramsay MacDonald in 1931 (see Chapter 7). In this respect, it did the very reverse to the First World War, which had brought on the fatal split within the Liberal party (see Chapter 3). Labour was also given a much more substantial taste of responsibility in the Second World War than in the First, when only Henderson had been included in the war cabinet. The nature of this responsibility was to prove crucial. Churchill as overall leader was responsible primarily for running the war effort, while Labour's triumvirate of Attlee, Bevin and Morrison ran domestic affairs and pushed their ideas through the Reconstruction Committee, under the leadership of Greenwood. This provided the key link with the post-war years. Attlee was fully aware of the importance of these special circumstances. 'I am quite certain that the world that must emerge from this war must be a world attuned to our ideas.'[13] He was right. Social perceptions and expectations were radicalised by the war, to the obvious political benefit of Labour. Some historians maintain that Labour's victory in the 1945 general election was predictable as far back as 1941 (see Chapter 12).

In the short term, the Conservatives benefited most from the inter-party truce on political activity drawn up on 26 September 1939, by which the parties agreed 'Not to nominate Candidates for the Parliamentary vacancies that now exist, or may occur, against the Candidate nominated by the Party holding the seat at the time of the vacancy occurring.'[14] This, in effect, perpetuated the huge majority gained by the Conservatives in 1935 for the longest period between general elections in two centuries of British constitutional history. This was not, however, to their advantage in the longer term since they had no reason to organise to defend their seats – except from the occasional challenge from an independent in a by-election. They therefore completely lost touch with the changes in public opinion, which is why their defeat in the 1945 general election came as such a shock to them. For the Liberals, meanwhile, the Second World War was an unmitigated disaster, completing their transition from a major to a minor party. Contributing to this were many of the factors which had operated during the First World War and which favoured the other two parties at the expense of the Liberals. For example, patriotism in wartime was a feeling with which Conservatives tended to be the most comfortable. State control over a much wider area of the economy and society was more acceptable to Labour. It is true that the architect of the welfare state, William Beveridge, was a Liberal, but the actual implementation was the crucial point. During the war Liberal deficiencies could be concealed within the broad consensus of coalition government. Sooner or later, however, party politics would have to return as the main channel for the social and economic pressures which would eventually have to be released.

THE ECONOMIC AND SOCIAL IMPACT OF THE WAR

The economic effects of the war can be seen in two perspectives. The first is the impact on Britain within the context of the rest of the world. The process started by the First World War was completed by the Second. As a result of the First World War Britain lost its position as the centre of international finance and trade. During the Second World War Britain's position contracted still further. British imports from the Empire grew, while her exports dropped; the gap was made up by the transfer of British investments, especially to India and Canada. Even more significant was the extent of lend-lease from the United States to Britain, totalling $27,000 million. According to A.S Milward,

> The absolute dollar cost of the war to Britain would have financed sixteen years of British imports from the U.S.A. at the 1938 level and at 1938 prices, taking no account of British exports or other dollar earnings.[15]

The immediate post-war problem was heavy dependence on the United States as Attlee's Labour Government was forced to raise a loan to replace the cancelled lend-lease programme (see Chapter 12). Unfortunately, the full extent of the shrinkage of Britain's part in the international economy was not recognised by the post-war governments that tried to revive Britain's role in international finance. This meant restoring the sterling area, despite Britain's greatly reduced economic base. Such misplaced optimism has been given as one of the reasons for the relative slowness of Britain's economic growth by comparison with that of Germany, France and Japan – none of which had such extensive commitments (see Chapter 13).

In the home sector of the economy, the picture was more mixed. The extent of industrial damage was enormous, due partly to the physical destruction caused by bombing and partly to the post-war shortage of capital resources and investment: it has been estimated that the capital surplus of £214 million per annum in 1938 became an annual loss of £1,000 million between 1940 and 1945.[16] The war also changed the structure of the workforce, in the process greatly accelerating a trend which had been obvious during the 1930s. The staple industries, especially coal mining and textiles, continued to decline. The impact of the war was not, however, universally negative. Some industries, like iron and steel, engineering, and chemicals, benefited from advances in science and technology under the direct influence of military need. There were also major advances in agriculture. In 1940 the government introduced a national minimum wage for agricultural workers. In return, farmers received guaranteed prices and regular price reviews which contributed to an overall increase in home-produced food from 42 per cent of total consumption in 1938 to 52 per cent in 1945. A.S. Milward maintains that:

> There can be no doubt that not only did the farming community enormously improve its position in the economy as a result of the world war, but that the improvement has been a long-term one.[17]

The extent of these varied changes made a strong case for greater state intervention, partly in the form of nationalised industries and partly in the widespread adoption of Keynesian economics; these provided the essential infrastructure for the social changes, generated by the war, from the early welfare plans to the eventual establishment of the welfare state.

The war is also associated with numerous social developments. It brought revelations about the disparity in the standards of health care and provision and resulted in free school meals as well as the general provision of orange juice, milk and vitamins. There was, in addition, a considerable increase in maternity care and the Emergency Medical Service (EMS) greatly expanded the number of beds available initially for service casualties and then for the population at large. The social landmark of the Second World War was the Beveridge Report, which was published in December 1942. This identified the five major deficiencies or 'giants' as Want, Disease, Ignorance, Squalor and Idleness. The intention was to substitute for the existing Social Insurance, based on Want, a new Social Security, which was intended to cover all five. There followed a series of formative measures in 1944, including the White Paper on Health, two others on Employment Policy and on Social Insurance, and a new Education Act.

These developments are usually seen as the direct result of the social upheaval caused by the conflict. The scale of mobilisation, for example, was considerable. By 1943 something like 17.1 million people were directly involved in the war effort, either in the armed forces, in the home defences or in the essential industries. This was bound to have a levelling effect on the social consciousness of the population, as did the unexpected impact of the policy of evacuation, which started as an emergency measure and turned into a social issue.[18] As H.G. Wells put it,

> Parasites and skin diseases, vicious habits and insanitary practices have been spread, as if in a passion of equalitarian propaganda, from the slums of such centres as Glasgow, London and Liverpool, throughout the length and breadth of the land.[19]

The public reception of the Beveridge Report was a key factor in accelerating the social change. Sharpened by the experience of privation and by the expectation of better things to come, it exceeded all expectations as 70,000 copies of the Report's first printing sold out on the first day of publication.

Most historians see the Second World War as the accelerator of social change. A. Marwick, for example, argues that in general terms war has three main effects. One is 'destructive' and 'disruptive'. A second is that it 'acts as a test of existing institutions'; it also promotes 'participation', which can result in gains such as the vote for women in 1918. Finally, since it is such 'an enormous psychological experience' it must be *for* something, which is likely to promote the desire for reconstruction after the war has finished.[20] M. Bruce maintains that social reform was integral to the experience of war:

> The decisive event in the evolution of the Welfare State was the Second World War, which, coming as it did after a long period of distress . . . challenged the British people to round off the system of social security. . . . The war speeded changes and left a country markedly different and . . . markedly more humane and civilised than that of 1939.[21]

According to P. Addison, the spearhead for such changes came from those sections of the middle class which had been radicalised by the war,[22] while the implementation of the reforms was due to the emergence of a wartime political consensus that narrowed the range of disagreement between the political parties.[23]

There is much to commend these arguments connecting change with war. War is an exceptional situation. It requires a complete change of momentum, an urgency which is not apparent in peacetime. Change, for its part, is not usually a smooth and continuous process. It is the result of an increase in pressure breaking through accumulated obstacles. Hence there are periods of apparently rapid change and periods when change is minimal. It follows that any external agency helping to clear the blockage will accelerate the change. It will, in the process, allow through a greater degree of change than would otherwise have occurred anyway. The most powerful agency is war. This is not to say that major changes cannot occur without war, but it is reasonable to argue that war cannot but be followed by major changes.

A. Marwick and others take it for granted that the social changes covered were all in Britain's best interests. There are, however, dissenting voices, which attribute more negative effects. C. Barnett believes that the social reform initiated by the war through the Beveridge Report exerted a drag effect on Britain's post-war industrial recovery. It diverted significant amounts of investment from industry in favour of the welfare state and meant that Britain fell behind other countries which recovered more rapidly. Because of the welfare state, Britain missed the opportunity of becoming once again a major economic power.[24] This can, however, be countered by the argument that Britain had been in economic decline over a much longer period and that the reason for her failure to recover as rapidly as other countries was that the government still imposed unrealistic obligations on a shrinking economy based upon past greatness. It was not, in other words, new social commitments at home which undermined economic performance but rather a refusal to accept a changed economic role abroad.

12

THE LABOUR GOVERNMENT 1945–51

In 1945 the Labour party finally came of age. Before 1914 it had failed to establish itself as the main alternative opposition and after 1918 it had yet to prove itself capable of becoming a majority government. This chapter looks at the reason for Labour's sudden electoral success. It also deals with the economic and social changes introduced between 1945 and 1951, focusing on the key questions of how radical these really were and whether or not they can be regarded as an overall success.

THE 1945 GENERAL ELECTION

The British people were invited to cast their votes in the last year of both the First World War and the Second World War. There, however, the similarity ended. In 1918 the Prime Minister, Lloyd George, kept much of the wartime coalition together and rode to victory over the Labour party and others who were no longer willing to co-operate with his government. In 1945 the reverse happened. Churchill's wartime coalition broke up in May and British politics reverted to a strongly partisan course. In the election held in the autumn of 1945, Labour won 393 seats against the Conservatives' 213 and the Liberals' 12 (see Figure 9). This was the first time that Labour had ever achieved an overall majority in Parliament and came as a major surprise, not least to the Conservatives, who had been banking on a vote of confidence in Churchill's leadership.

Labour's victory has been attributed to a variety of factors. One is that the British electorate had been radicalised as a result of the experience of war, which had acted as a catalyst for increasing expectations about social reform (see Chapter 11). A popular view had been emerging since 1943 that Churchill was not fully committed to introducing the changes already agreed in outline by the coalition government. He had

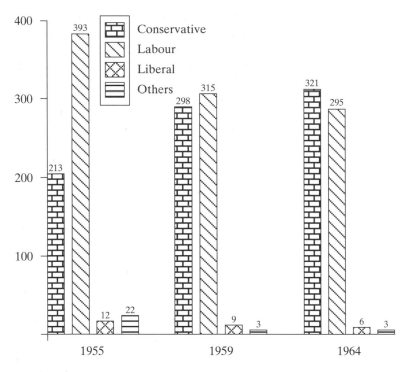

Figure 9 General elections 1945–51

said in a cabinet minute in 1943 that 'A dangerous optimism is growing up about the conditions it will be possible to establish after the war.' He added: 'The question steals across the mind whether we are not committing our forty-five million people to tasks beyond their capacity to bear.'[1] This attitude came into the open in the ABCA affair. The Army Bureau of Current Affairs, responsible for political education and discussion within the armed forces, issued a pamphlet at the end of 1942 on the Beveridge Report and its possible implications for the future. When this was suddenly withdrawn on the orders of the government, the ensuing outcry was so strong that copies had to be restored to discussion leaders. But the damage had been done and the suspicion that Churchill was decidedly lukewarm was confirmed when a number of Conservative MPs warned in the House of Commons in February 1943 not to expect too much from the government's response to the Report. Associated with a growing lack of confidence in the Conservatives as future reformers was a retrospective judgement on the record of the Conservative-dominated national governments during the 1930s; this applied especially to their handling of unemployment.

It is also agreed that Labour ran a more effective election campaign than the Conservatives. The Labour manifesto, for example, contained a much clearer undertaking to introduce the reforms the electorate were expecting. The Conservatives also lost the organisational battle. R.A. Butler maintained that the Conservative organisation was 'in a parlous condition, much harder hit than that of our opponents by the absence of agents and organizers on war service.'[2] Although this view has been challenged on the grounds that the two parties were likely to have been evenly affected by the war, there is no doubt that the overall trend was against the Conservatives. Between the wars they had had an enormous organisational advantage in reaching the working-class as well as the middle-class vote, a grass-roots approach which went back as far as the era of Disraeli and Salisbury in the late nineteenth century. The war removed this natural advantage and so for the first time the two parties contested the election on more or less equal terms. The Conservatives also owed little to the eccentric campaign conducted by their leader, who proved in the circumstances a liability rather than their main asset. Churchill made a disastrous miscalculation about the mood of the electorate when he tried to create a frightening image of Labour by associating their rather mild brand of socialism with totalitarian regimes on the Continent.

I declare to you, from the bottom of my heart, that no Socialist system can be established without a political police. . . . No Socialist Government conducting the entire life and industry of the country could afford to allow free, sharp, or violently worded expressions of public discontent. They would have to fall back on some form of Gestapo, no doubt very humanely directed in the first instance.

In the same speech he made a tactical blunder.

On with the forward march! Leave these Socialist dreamers to their Utopias or nightmares. Let us be content to do the heavy job that is right on top of us. And let us make sure that the cottage home to which the warrior will return is blessed with modest but solid prosperity, well fenced and guarded against misfortune, and that Britons may remain free to plan their lives for themselves and those they love.[3]

This speech, which was widely reported by the media, shows that Churchill was unable to adjust his talents as a war leader to the demands of political campaigning. His rhetoric, so reassuring in the wartime situation, seemed condescending and insulting in the context of an election.

These explanations suggest one of two overall conclusions. The first is the more common and traditional. Although the result came as a shock, it should not have done. It was as nearly inevitable as any general election result this century. Labour was riding the crest of radicalism created by the special circumstances of the Second World War and it is hardly surprising that they should have been entrusted with the task of consolidating the gains made in wartime. In rejecting Churchill, the voters were giving a retrospective judgement on old Conservative policies and the clearest possible indication that their expectations had moved on since the 1930s. Now that the war was won in Europe, the electorate swallowed their gratitude for his wartime leadership and revived their memories of his pre-war Conservative associations. Churchill therefore lost the election as the electorate adjusted its priorities during the transition from war to peace. Compared with this underlying momentum, election issues were peripheral. P. Adelman makes the point as succinctly as anyone: 'It is doubtful whether the detailed party programmes or the election campaign itself had much to do with the final result . . . most historians agree, the party's victory was due primarily to the voters' assessment of the past.'[4] A. Calder also maintains that Labour were all set to win the election quite irrespective of any speeches by Churchill.[5]

The alternative view is that there was not a great deal of difference between the policies of the parties – rather the timing was the key factor in implementing reforms in the future. D. Dutton has argued that there was, in fact, a strong basis of consensus during the war years within the context of the coalition government. The Beveridge Report (1942) and the White Paper on the National Health Service (1944) were both conceived as joint initiatives and there is no reason why the Conservatives should not eventually have put them into practice; according to Dutton: 'It is interesting that Beveridge himself had suggested that a Conservative government would be the best vehicle for carrying through his policies.'[6] Nor is it enough to assume that Labour had the irresistible momentum of history behind it. It may well be true that the radicalising influence of the war favoured the left. But the notion that the 1945 election result was a retrospective judgment on the Conservatives is less convincing. Why should the electorate have condemned only the record of the Conservatives in the 1930s? What about the failings of Labour, which included the deflationary budget of Snowden in 1931 and the refusal of most of the party to take part in salvaging the political and economic situation in the 1930s? For every voter reminded of Conservative measures there would have been another who recalled Labour's complete abdication of responsibility. All this suggests that there must have been more *immediate* reasons for the victory of Labour. The electorate were clearly convinced that Labour rather than the Conservatives would introduce the promised reforms. The reason for this was partly the longstanding caution of Churchill but, more likely, the impression given during the election campaign that the welfare state would be abandoned if the Conservatives came to power. A key factor in this was the impression given by Churchill himself. What he had to do in 1945, to stand a chance of defeating Labour, was to reverse the suspicion that he would not implement Beveridge. Because he lacked a positive programme and campaign he failed to do precisely that. If, therefore, he is to be given credit for winning the war, he must also carry the responsibility for losing the election. Perhaps there is in this no paradox after all.

LABOUR'S ECONOMIC POLICIES
1945–51

Labour emerged from its election victory with a mandate for reconstruction and reform. A traditional image of the new government is that it proceeded to take the first conscious step towards socialism in Britain, in the process breaking radically with government policies of the inter-war years. This explains why many Conservatives fought individual measures bitterly and regarded it as their duty to undo at least part of Attlee's legacy after coming to power in 1951. An alternative, and more balanced, view is that Labour was acting very much within the mainstream of British party and parliamentary traditions. Many of the policies introduced might well have come in – albeit more slowly – with the Conservatives. What Churchill and his successors later undid was minimal, indicating that there was between the parties a broad consensus which had originated during the Second World War. In any case, the composition of the Labour government was strongly dominated by the party's centre and right, including Clement Attlee, Herbert Morrison (Lord President of the Council), Ernest Bevin (Foreign Secretary) and Hugh Dalton (Chancellor of the Exchequer), all of whom had served under Churchill during the war. In addition,

Plate 7 Clement Attlee, 1950.
Reproduced by permission of 'PA' News.

Labour would not have had the chance to implement extreme policies even if it had wanted to. It was constrained by post-war economic difficulties and the need to bring about a revival of confidence in British industry and trade.

It might be thought that in the economy, at least, Labour would have attempted to introduce radical solutions to long-term problems. It was, after all, the party which advocated economic planning. In the early years there was an attempt, through the Steering Committee on Economic Policy, at macro-economic policies. But this is associated mainly with the chancellorship of Dalton (1945–7) and was soon replaced by a more immediate policy of economic survival when he was succeeded by Stafford Cripps (1947–50) and Hugh Gaitskell (1950–1). The last two were more influenced by neo-Keynesianism than by any visions of centralised economic planning, and the type of policy pursued usually differed little from what would have been carried out by a Conservative government.

This was because the possibilities for detailed planning were actually very limited. The war had caused the loss of a quarter of the national wealth, a threefold increase in the national debt and the decline of exports by two-thirds. The priority therefore had to be short-term reconstruction, accomplished by any means available; these included an American loan in 1946 and the inclusion of Britain in the Marshall Plan (1948). Accompanying this was a policy of austerity and rationing, normally associated with Cripps. Overall, therefore, 'The Government's first priority was economic survival, which meant survival of existing economic arrangements.'[7] The government raised many Labour eyebrows by deliberately encouraging the export of capital to replace the overseas investments which had been used up in financing the war effort. This was far from radical since it was to the benefit of the financial interests of the city and was very much in line with the policies of the 1920s and 1930s. There is even a case for saying that Labour's economic planning was much less pronounced than that in the European countries, where the leading economies stole a march on Britain in the ten years after the end of the war. A. Schonfield maintains that:

The striking thing in the British case is the extraordinary tenacity of older attitudes towards the role of public power. Anything which smacked of a restless or over-energetic state, with ideas of guiding the nation on the basis of a long view of its collective economic interest, was instinctively the object of suspicion.[8]

185

All three of the Labour chancellors continued to use the time-honoured medium of the budget to exert financial control, an emphasis which was to be retained by the Conservatives after 1951.

Did these policies work? Considering the enormity of the problem confronting it, the Labour government had a series of important successes. But these tended to be periodic highlights rather than an underlying momentum of sustained growth. There are several examples of this.

The first peak was reached fairly soon after the war, when an early boom favoured high employment and eased the task of demobilisation. This was in large measure due to the American loan of 1946. Unfortunately, this was reversed during the harsh winter of 1947, during which several crises emerged. One was the run on sterling, which forced the suspension of the earlier policy of putting the pound on convertibility with the dollar. There were also a fuel shortage (partly the result of deficiencies in Shinwell's organisation of supplies), a trade deficit of £500 million, and a fall in the reserves by £1,000 million. Recovery occurred quickly, with a second peak emerging in 1948. The balance of payments moved into a surplus of £30 million and exports were up by 25 per cent on the previous year. The upturn was due partly to more favourable international trade conditions, partly to a drop in imports through Cripps's policy of wage restraint. This was, however, followed by a second trough in 1949, largely as a result of depression in the United States and a run on sterling to which Cripps responded by a 30 per cent reduction in the value of the pound. A third, although lower peak resulted as the outflow of currency reserves was stopped. Exports increased rapidly, to the extent that by 1951 they were half as great again as they had been in 1938. Cripps tried to consolidate this by means of public spending cuts on areas such as housing and food subsidies. Then, during Gaitskell's term as Chancellor, Britain was once again confronted by a deficit in the balance of payments, caused by heavy imports from the continent and speculation over the pound.

Needless to say, such fluctuation had a generally negative effect on the underlying well-being of the British economy, which became increasingly susceptible to influences from abroad and to fluctuations in exports and imports. The main deficiency was industrial, particularly the absence of industrial investment. British industry had already appeared antiquated in many respects before and during the war, especially in terms of machinery and the training and education of the workforce. During the war the Cabinet Reconstruction Committee had argued that modernisation of the motor industry needed to be carried out urgently within a period of eight to ten years. After 1945, however, this type of recommendation was not accorded as high a priority in Britain as on the Continent, which partially explains the substantial advantages possessed by the latter during the 1950s.

We have seen, therefore, that Labour did not, despite expectations, follow a radical approach to economic regeneration. There is, however, a second area where rapid change was predicted by optimists and pessimists alike. There appeared a strong prospect of greatly increased state control through a rolling programme of nationalisation. This would be based on Clause IV of the Labour Party constitution of 1918, which advocated 'the common ownership of the means of production, distribution and exchange'.[9] Such socialist connotations had been extended in 1934, when the Labour party programme had called for 'public ownership and control of the primary industries and services as a foundation step'.[10] Labour's critics maintained that this clause crossed the frontier into Marxism and the Conservatives were highly apprehensive about its application. The nationalisation programme after 1945 was certainly bold and extensive; it included the Bank of England (1946), civil aviation (1946), coal, cable and wireless (1946), and electricity, gas and inland transport (1948). The nationalisation of iron and steel was based particularly heavily on political and ideological objectives. The industry was perhaps the most effectively run of all those taken over and could have been left in private hands without detriment to it. In fact, taking it over involved a major constitutional crisis that showed the full extent of Labour's determination to enforce a political principle. When the House of Lords resisted the nationalisation of steel, the government reduced its delaying power, through the Parliament Act of 1949, to two sessions (one year). This meant that the measure finally received royal assent and became operative in 1951.

And yet, the way in which nationalisation was implemented was anything but revolutionary, or even radical. The method used was highly traditional. Britain already had a long history of public ownership, ranging from local-government control over water and sewage services to the partial nationalisation which had been introduced between the wars; the latter had included the Central Electricity Board, the London Transport Board, and British Airways and Imperial Airways. There was very little structural upheaval in the enterprises now added to the list, since most were similar to the public corporations established earlier by the Conservatives and most were modelled on the BBC. They were run by Boards, such as the National Coal Board and the six boards of the British Transport Commission. Each of these was managed by experienced officials who were now given a salary. In fact, many of those on the boards had dominated the industries in the days of private ownership and there was only nominal representation for the interests of workers and trade unions. There was certainly no ideological attempt to redefine the relationship between capital and labour. This is why the left wing of the party expressed disappointment in the measures: according to Shinwell, they were 'little more than a technicality'.[11] With the obvious exception of the bill nationalising iron and steel, there was relatively little sustained opposition in Parliament from the Conservatives. The Liberal leader, Clement Davies, said of the Coal Bill, 'I am perfectly sure that, given a fair chance, this Bill will not only work, but will become one of the most epoch-making Acts of Parliament in our history'.[12] Churchill said in 1946 that he saw nothing immoral with the nationalisation of the railways, while Macmillan said to Morrison that on the nationalisation of railways and public utilities 'our views were not very far apart'.[13] Some right-wingers argued that Labour had a hidden agenda for a massive programme of nationalisation in the future. In 1949, however, a policy document entitled *Labour Believes in Britain* was issued. In this, according to K. Morgan, there was 'an evident downgrading of the standing of nationalisation in Labour's future priorities'.[14] Certainly there were no plans – or indeed later attempts – to take over the 80 per cent of industries and enterprises excluded from the 1945–51 programme.

In some respects the measures of nationalisation were necessary and effective. It made sense to drag the coal industry into the modern world and to try to avoid a repetition of the industrial disputes between militant miners and reactionary coal owners which had overshadowed the 1920s. There was also much to commend the way in which nationalisation was carried out: since the corporations retained considerable autonomy and were not directly integrated into the government departments concerned, there was no sudden overloading of the administration and civil service. There were, however, major drawbacks. Some of the industries, like iron and steel, were already functioning reasonably effectively. What Labour did here was to start a see-saw with the Conservatives between denationalisation and re-nationalisation, a clear indication that, in this case at least, pragmatism was subordinated to party dogma. Industries in a less healthy state required enormous amounts of investment to show a significant improvement. The problem here was the clash of priorities as, periodically, the government had to make cuts in the nationalised industries in order to meet the more immediate demands of financial crises. Nationalisation therefore had to be done on the cheap and had to compete with social priorities like the welfare state. This sometimes resulted in a credibility gap. The public who used the services became increasingly likely to blame any problems associated with them on the government which had nationalised them. Labour was storing up a problem of latent resentment against central control, particularly since the nationalisation programme did not build into the system an adequate means of complaint, accountability or representation. Indeed, it was actually more difficult to raise an issue in Parliament after an industry had been nationalised than it had been before. Above all, nationalisation redirected the target of trade union resentment away from the private owners towards the government – with ominous implications for the future.

LABOUR'S SOCIAL REFORMS 1945–51

The government introduced a variety of reforms between 1945 and 1951. The welfare state was based on five main measures. The first two were the Family Allowances Act (1945) and the National Health Service Act (1946). The latter provided for universal free medical treatment from general practitioners and dentists. Hospitals were nationalised and administered by local management committees and regional boards. The National Insurance Act (1946) provided sickness and unemployment benefit for all adults, together with pensions on retirement, at 65 for men and 60 for women. These were paid for by contributions from workers, employers and the state. The National Assistance Act (1948) provided a safety net for anyone not fully covered by National Insurance and also introduced services for the elderly or disabled. The National Insurance Industrial Injuries Act (1946) provided a system whereby, in return for regular contributions, the worker would be entitled to compensation for injury or to disability pensions.

There were also changes beyond the immediate scope of the welfare state. The 1944 Education Act was fully implemented, providing free secondary education to the age of 15. This was based on examination at 11 leading to a tripartite division between education in grammar, secondary modern and technical schools. LEAs were also to provide for meals, milk and medical services. Living conditions were improved by a major programme of Aneurin Bevan's Ministry of Health to replace the housing shortfall caused by the war. The environment was enhanced by two measures. By the New Towns Act (1946) the government took more general responsibility for planning for new areas of urbanisation, thereby avoiding the squalor associated with older conurbations. The results were fourteen new towns established between 1945 and 1951, including Stevenage, Hemel Hempstead and Harlow. A year later the Town and Country Planning Act required local authorities to produce development plans for rural areas and preserve the local heritage where appropriate.

E.J. Hobsbawm considers that this legislation was the most extensive change of the Labour government and that 'the welfare planning of the Labour era was . . . far more ambitious than anything which had preceded it.'[15] It is true that many of the proposals had been derived from the Beveridge Report and that Labour were building on foundations prepared by the wartime coalition. Even so, in the words of Childs: 'to many working people the post-war measures appeared revolutionary.'[16] Two further developments emphasised the scope of Labour's changes. One was the emphasis on arrangements being comprehensive and universal and, in the case of the NHS, free. All previous arrangements had been selective and exclusive. Second, the state played a more central role in administering all the schemes. Nationalisation was a means of achieving the medical side of the welfare state. It was intended by Bevan that GPs should also come under state supervision, although this eventually had to be abandoned because of the opposition of the British Medical Association (BMA). The application of the insurance schemes was directed by the administration and not by insurance companies, while the cost of the NHS was borne by general taxation, a new departure in financing the welfare state.

As with Labour's economic changes there is, however, a stronger case for stressing the underlying continuity of the social reforms. It could be argued that the real foundations for the welfare state had been laid by the Liberals before 1914, after which there had been a few subsequent additions in the inter-war period. The whole system had then been thoroughly examined by the Beveridge Report, which meant that Labour's changes actually constituted the fourth phase in a long and more or less continuous tradition. James Griffiths, a Labour minister, argued that the National Insurance Act was 'the culmination of half a century's development of our British social services.'[17] This could stand as a description of the development of the welfare state as a whole. It might also be said that the welfare state was based on a broad degree of consensus resulting from wartime discussion. An example of this was the National Insurance Act which, in the words of L.C.B. Seaman, 'must be regarded as a harvest towards which all three major parties had contributed'.[18] The details of the welfare-state legislation also contained direct links with past measures. The whole principle of national insurance was, for example, an extension of the 1911 National Insurance Act; the idea of a comprehensive health service had been put forward between the wars in the Dawson Report of 1920 and the Royal Commission on National Health Insurance (1926); and the time-honoured expedient of means-testing was maintained through the National Assistance Act. Finally, in the National Health Service, doctors were not made salaried state employees and a parallel private system continued, including the existence of private beds in NHS hospitals. The medical adviser to the TUC described the legislation as 'as fine a piece of compromise health work as is possible in this country at the present time'.[19]

How successful were Labour's social reforms? The main achievement was the sheer scope of their measures. The range of people covered by comparison with earlier schemes was far greater; the NHS was the only health care system in the west to include the entire population in its free medical care. The range of benefits was also far greater. The National Insurance Act, for example, released a series of grants in addition to unemployment and sickness benefit, including maternity and death grants. Quantitative criteria can also be applied in other sectors. After a relatively poor start, there was an impressive increase in the number of houses built: 55,400 in 1946, increasing to 139,690 in 1947 and 284,230 in 1948, followed by an annual average of 200,000. Another major achievement was in overcoming opposition and winning the support of the people. The revolt in 1948 by the BMA threatened the very foundations of the new welfare state. The NHS was opposed by 40,814 members and supported by only 4,734. The main fear, expressed as far back as 1943, was that

> doctors will no longer be an independent, learned and liberal profession, but will instead form a service of technicians con-trolled by bureaucrats and by local men and women entirely ignorant of medical matters.[20]

Bevan, however, held to his course. He conducted sensitive negotiations with the BMA, denying that he intended to turn doctors into 'civil servants'. The BMA eventually agreed to a compromise whereby doctors would receive a salary from the NHS but could also take private patients. The British public meanwhile remained firmly attached to the welfare state – more so than to nationalisation or, indeed, to any of the other measures.

Such popularity should not, however, be allowed to obscure the problems which emerged in the wake of Labour's social changes. One was the spiralling administrative costs, which in 1951 necessitated the imposition of prescription charges. This decision provoked the most bitter internal dispute of the whole administration as Aneurin Bevan, Harold Wilson and John Freeman resigned from the cabinet in protest. There were also missed opportunities – not least in education. It is true that Labour's hands were, to a certain extent, tied by the 1944 Education Act. But they lost the chance to influence the future of education or give careful consideration to the possibility of comprehensive schools, in which the majority of ministers really believed. Instead, they fully implemented the tripartite system – and then spent the next twenty years seeking to undo this. They also failed to come to terms with independent schools, leaving a legacy of growing hostility towards them. Finally, ministers showed little knowledge of educational theory: they accepted in its entirety the Norwood Report of 1943 upon which the 1944 Act was based. Indeed, it was probably disillusionment with secondary modern schools and concern about the 11 plus which alienated substantial numbers of the lower middle class who had been persuaded to vote Labour in 1945.

THE 1950 AND 1951 GENERAL ELECTIONS

It is unusual for a government which has introduced major policies to hold on to its original landslide majority five years later. After their sweeping victory in 1906 the Liberals only just clung to power in the first election of 1910. Attlee found himself in a similar position in February 1950 and, in an attempt to secure a workable majority, called a further election in October 1951.

The 1950 general election was a fairly low-key affair. Attlee decided to hold it in February rather than in the spring or summer (July was the latest possible date) possibly because he feared that he might be considered to have influenced the electorate after a favourable budget. Politicians now appear less constrained by such inhibitions and it might not be too uncharitable to argue that the budget has become a means of earning votes as well as balancing books. The election produced 315 seats for Labour, 298 for the Conservatives, 9 for the Liberals and 3 for the other parties (see Figure 9, p. 180). This result was a disappointment to Attlee, who had hoped for more than a majority of 10. The main reason for the slide in seats since 1945 was the reduction in the support of the middle class from 21 per cent to 16 per cent. The effects of the war in radicalising this part of the population had clearly worn off, even though the support of the working class was as firm as ever.

The electoral system also told against Labour. The redistribution of seats by the 1948 Representation of the People Act created constituencies of more equal size, which transferred a number of marginals from Labour to the Conservatives. This more than offset any advantage Labour received from the abolition of the business franchise and the plural vote in the university seats.

The 1951 general election produced a close but eccentric result. With 48.0 per cent of the popular vote, the Conservatives secured 321 seats and an overall majority of 17; Labour's 48.8 per cent of the vote won only 295 seats. In the process of losing the election, Labour secured nearly 700,000 more votes than in 1950 and 2 million more than in 1945. Its 13.9 million was the highest ever scored by any party until 1992.

Yet it lost – and for a variety of reasons. In the first place, it seemed to be a government growing weary of power, an impression intensified by problems in the cabinet between 1950 and 1951. Cripps was forced through illness and exhaustion to resign the chancellorship in October 1950, while Bevin went from the Foreign Office in March 1951, to be replaced by Morrison. Attlee, too, was in poor health at the time, which made the government vulnerable to any sustained attack. This, in fact, came initially from within the Labour party as Bevan attacked Gaitskell's proposal to introduce charges for spectacles and dentures. Bevan widened the debate into whether it was desirable to increase the defence budget from 7 to 10 per cent of national income. The strength of Bevan's personality and his obvious leftward leanings presented the Conservatives with an opportunity to revive the spectre of a Labour party being pulled down the path of socialism. Labour's election campaign was also not very effective. It took the defensive over the performance of the nationalised industries, using arguments based on dogma rather than making comparisons with their obvious deficiencies before nationalisation. To be fair, the Labour government was adversely affected by two factors beyond its immediate control. One was Britain's participation in the Korean War, which revived the prospect of austerity. The other was that Attlee had to time the general election to avoid a clash with the King's proposed visit to Australia; this greatly reduced any 'healing' time for the cabinet. Even so, it would be hard to argue against C.J. Bartlett's point that 'Labour contributed much both to their own fall and to the subsequent Conservative ascendancy'.[21]

A second reason for the defeat of Labour was clearly the revival of the Conservatives. This was due partly to a direct exchange of fortunes, as one party benefited directly from the other's problems. But it also depended on an increasingly positive image projected to the electorate. The Conservatives made it clear that they would not indulge in any wholesale reversal of Labour's achievements, apart from the denationalisation of steel. They were fully committed to maintaining the welfare state and the general principles of public control. The real strength of their case, however, was that they would be the party of consolidation after a period of innovation. The electorate were now opting for continuity and efficiency, by contrast with 1945 when they had chosen change and had been prepared to take a chance on the effectiveness of the method. The Conservatives also benefited from a revised perception of history. Their role in the austerity of the 1930s was now obscured by the more recent austerity under Labour. They were now the more confident party and managed to convince voters that they would overtake Labour's post-war record by, for example, building 300,000 houses a year.

Another major factor in the 1951 general election was the disintegration of the Liberal vote from 2.6 million in 1950 (slightly up on that in 1945) to a mere 731,000 in 1951. The main reason for this was a huge drop in the number of Liberal candidates. Most Liberal voters in the 80 per cent or so of the constituencies affected opted for the Conservatives as their first-choice alternative. This probably interacted with the eccentricities of the electoral system to give the Conservatives, with a quarter of a million fewer votes than Labour, an advantage of 26 seats. Labour tended to win their seats by larger majorities than the Conservatives, whose individual victories were remarkably economical. The Conservatives won Labour marginals, probably with ex-Liberal votes, in sufficient numbers to make a crucial difference. The whole process was further distorted by boundary changes of the 1948 Representation of the People Act, which resulted in Labour having to secure 2 per cent more of the popular vote than the Conservatives to win the same number of seats.[22]

Despite the closeness of the 1951 election, the balance had well and truly turned. The Labour party might have been expected to have made an early comeback. In fact, the reverse occurred and it remained out of power for the next thirteen years. In addition, it was confronted by an ever-growing conflict between the centre and the left that prevented an early recovery. To these themes we now turn.

13

THE CONSERVATIVE DECADE
Domestic Policies 1951–64

After 1951 there were thirteen years of uninterrupted Conservative rule under four successive Conservative Prime Ministers: Winston Churchill (1951–5), Anthony Eden (1955–7), Harold Macmillan (1957–63) and Alexander Douglas-Home (1963–4). The party won three successive general elections, a record exceeded in the twentieth century only after 1979. It is, therefore, not surprising that the period 1951–64 is often known as the 'Conservative decade'. Within this timescale there were two general trends. Between 1951 and 1960 Conservative domination was complete, while from 1961 to 1964 the governments of Macmillan and Douglas-Home came under increasing pressure, the latter eventually falling to a revived Labour party under the leadership of Wilson.

CONSERVATIVE ASCENDANCY 1951–60

During the 1950s the Conservatives won the highest proportion of the popular vote since the 1930s, when the collapse of the Liberals and the crisis of Labour had enabled them to reach artificial heights. After coming to power in 1951 they were remarkably consistent. In 1955 they won 49.7 per cent of the vote and 344 seats, in 1959 49.4 per cent of the vote and 365 seats (see Figure 10). On each occasion they scored comfortable majorities. The overall trend of support for the Conservatives had been sharply upwards; since their fiasco at the end of the war they grew in strength over four successive elections. In 1945 they had been 180 seats behind Labour; by 1950 the deficit had dropped to 17; in 1951 they converted this into an overall majority of 17, which was increased in 1955 to a majority of 58 and in 1959 to one of 100. This record was due to a combination of Conservative strengths and Labour weaknesses.

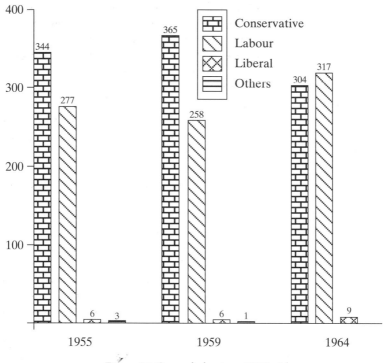

Figure 10 General elections 1955–64

A good starting point was a new image of moderation and efficiency. The Conservatives had learned a great deal from their electoral defeat in 1945, the extent of which had come as a profound shock. Almost immediately work had been launched on the party's rehabilitation by a combination of groups: the Research Department, the Advisory Committee on Policy and Political Education, and the Conservative Political Centre. These gave Conservatism a new appeal to see it through the 1951 election and sustain its support for the next thirteen years. The process was sustained by the Bow Group, which aimed, through consensus politics, at increasing Conservative support among the working classes. It is sometimes argued that the Conservatives learned from the defeat of 1945 to adapt to the welfare state and accept some of the principles, which they had originally strongly opposed when these had been introduced by Labour. If that had been the case, then the Conservatives would have undergone something of a revolution. Much more likely is that they had agreed in principle with many of Labour's measures, since these had come from the stable of wartime collectivism. They might have been unhappy about their timing, but now that the measures had been introduced, there was little cause for continuing opposition. The Conservatives had simply learned to adapt. According to R.A. Butler, 'As in the days of Peel, the Conservatives must be seen to have accommodated themselves to a social revolution.'[1] This 'accommodation' applied to a variety of areas. One was the welfare state, on which the Conservatives substantially increased government expenditure. There was also a commitment to full employment, to maintaining housebuilding targets and to keeping the public corporations.

Behind all this was a strong element of pragmatism. Butler said, referring to the electorate and the welfare state, 'if they want that sort of thing, they can have it, but under our auspices'.[2] Even Churchill had come to the same conclusion; in 1951 he said: 'I have come to know the nation and what must be done to retain power.'[3] After returning to power he said in Parliament in 1951: 'Controversy there must be on some issues before us, but this will be a small part of the work and interests we have in common.'[4] So strong was the consensus between Conservative and Labour policies that the composite name 'Mr Butskell' was invented in 1954 by *The Economist*. This combined the names of Butler and Gaitskell. There was no longer much to choose between the Conservatives and Labour over welfarism and broad economic policy. Thus the middle classes had no special reason, as they had had in 1945, to vote Labour, while an increasing proportion of the upper working class was enticed into supporting the Conservatives.

The Conservatives also had an advantage over Labour in terms of leadership. A new prime minister boosted the Conservative Party on two occasions. Sir Anthony Eden, who succeeded Churchill in 1955, was widely considered a very strong candidate and was unopposed within the party. He had resisted the official policy of appeasement during the 1930s and performed effectively as Foreign Secretary between 1951 and 1955. He brought to the Conservatives new life and a renewed vigour which proved a powerful electoral asset in 1955. Eden did, of course, fall into disrepute as a result of his handling of the Suez crisis in 1956. But his successor, Macmillan, was installed in sufficient time to bring about recovery from external problems and to give a benign and optimistic aura to the 1959 election. Macmillan was described by Shinwell as 'the most astute and able' of peacetime Conservative prime ministers, with a 'delicate blend of adroitness and unscrupulous in-fighting'.[5] Initially mocked as 'Macwonder' and 'Supermac', he eventually came to earn those names. He was projected

Plate 8 Harold Macmillan and Anthony Eden, 1954.
Reproduced by permission of 'PA' News.

during the 1959 campaign as a major world statesman and his tele-
vision performances were far more effective than those of Gaitskell.
Behind these leaders was a remarkably effective ministerial team. A new
generation of Conservatives had emerged who were as committed as
Butler to consensus, including Iain MacLeod, Reginald Maudling and
Edward Heath. The last of these was especially important. As chief
whip he had kept the Conservative party together during and after the
Suez crisis. Lord Hailsham also proved highly successful as Party
Chairman and was responsible for the success of the 1959 campaign
with its slogan 'Life is better under the Conservatives'.

Above all, the Conservative governments had the advantage of a period of economic growth during the 1960s. Whether or not they were fully responsible for this will be examined separately. What mattered was that a sufficient proportion of the electorate believed that they were and therefore returned them to power in 1955 and 1959. The 1950s were a period of affluence and increasing consumption, certainly by contrast with the austerity of the late 1940s. Macmillan captured the essence of this when he said in 1957 that the British people had 'never had it so good'. The chancellors were also able to cut income tax before both elections – by 6d. (2.5p) in 1955 and by 9d. (3.75p) in 1959. It is rare for a government to be thrown out during a period of prosperity. Elections are normally won at the edges by the transfer of marginal seats through the change by floating voters, and there was no economic reason for floating voters to do this in 1955 or in 1959.

Given these points, the government of the day had a hold on power which could be loosened only by the defection of whole blocs of supporters or by a major crisis. The Conservatives took care to prevent the former by appealing to the widest possible range of interests. In 1957 Macmillan stated that the Conservatives had never been 'and I trust that while I am your leader, we never will be, a party of any class or sectional interest.'[6] There was, of course, a foreign policy crisis in 1956, but it did not destroy the political equilibrium at home. The Lord Chancellor of the time, Lord Kilmuir, later maintained that: 'Suez did us no harm politically either in the short or in the long view.'[7] There was no internal split, no real chance for a Labour onslaught. Eden was removed not as a result of the crisis itself, which would have let in the Labour wedge, but rather as a result of ill health. His retirement prevented the more damaging alternative of resignation.

The electorate, meanwhile, was faced with an opposition party which had a strong recent record of government but which was now internally divided. The Labour party proved far less adept at recovery and internal reconstruction after 1951 than had the Conservatives after 1945. Instead, they indulged in serious – and public – argument about their future course. This made it look, for a while at least, much less like a party of potential government, a situation which has similarities to Labour's predicament in the 1980s (see Chapter 16). The greatest problem was a division between the Revisionists (or Gaitskellites) of the right, and the Fundamentalists (or Bevanites) of the left.

The key issue was the future of socialism. The Revisionists, especially Anthony Crosland, argued that there was no longer a need to over-throw capitalism, which had been 'reformed and modified almost out of existence'. The changes made by the 1945–51 Labour governments had ensured that capitalism was now under effective state control within the overall context of the mixed economy. Crosland believed that the emphasis should no longer be on economic change but rather on social equality. The left, on the other hand, were concerned about Labour's apparent swing to the right. Bevan published in 1952 *In Place of Fear*, which argued that capitalism, far from being transformed, was as strong as ever. Bevan argued:

> it is essential that we should keep clear before us that one of the central principles of Socialism is the substitution of public for private ownership. There is no way round this.[8]

Two more specific issues caused serious internal difficulties. The first was defence. Bevan opposed the party line, which was to support government proposals for the rearmament of Germany and her inclusion in NATO; he argued that this would permanently alienate the Soviet Union. Then, in 1955 Bevan was expelled for a while from the Parliamentary Labour Party for challenging official Labour policy on nuclear weapons. He represented a considerable level of support within the party for unilateral nuclear disarmament. This was not, however, shared by the majority of the electorate, despite the formation of The Campaign for Nuclear Disarmament (CND) in 1958. The second divisive issue was the future of Clause IV of the Labour party on nationalisation. Gaitskell tried to persuade the party to jettison it but this provoked bitter recriminations in 1959.

Finally, Labour's campaigns and leadership lacked the appeal of those of the Conservatives. Attlee appeared ageing, tired and ill at the time of the 1955 election and contrasted unfavourably with the new leader of the Conservatives with his impressive record in foreign affairs. During the 1959 campaign there was a strong public preference for Macmillan over Gaitskell; it seemed that the latter was unable to produce the charisma needed to counter the gravitas of the former and, in Bevan's uncharitable phrase, came across as a 'desiccated calculating machine'.[9] Above all, he was unable to persuade the electorate. Whereas the Conservatives made a point of reducing income tax in time for the 1959 election on the basis of a proven record of economic management, Gaitskell's promise that future social reforms by Labour would not involve an increase in income tax was simply not believed. The firm message delivered by the voters in 1959 was: why change from what seemed to work to what would at best be unpredictable?

CONSERVATIVE DECLINE 1961–4

The Conservatives appeared to have reached a new peak in 1959. The party had an unusually high feeling of confidence and Macmillan said that he was 'ready to set out on a new adventure'.[10] There followed a particularly active period of foreign policy (see Chapter 17) which enhanced his reputation as a statesman. Yet, within the following five years the Conservatives experienced an unusually wide range of problems and misfortunes that eventually led to defeat in the 1964 election. These were partly fortuitous, partly the government's own responsibility. Circumstances which were often external to the government reacted with it to create a deepening impression of decline.

Conservative dominance in the 1950s had been based more than anything else on economic growth and the party's reputation for sound financial management. By 1961 the economy took a sharp downturn and with it went the political fortunes of the Macmillan government. 1960–1 saw the pound under pressure and brought a balance of trade deficit. This was to be the first of many but was seen in 1961 as a matter requiring urgent remedies. Selwyn Lloyd therefore increased national insurance contributions and introduced a 'pay pause'. The government tried to provide longer-term remedies with the establishment of the National Economic Development Council (NEDC) and the National Incomes Commission (NIC). But these had no noticeable impact. Unemployment, which had not been a problem during the 1950s, reached 800,000 by the end of 1962, while there was also a significant increase in the number of strikes, especially in the docks. Especially damaging to the government's image were the comparisons made between crisis in Britain and continuing affluence on the Continent; both France and Germany had faster economic growth rates than Britain and a higher GDP per head.

Economic crisis nearly always generates political crisis. In July 1962 Macmillan sacked seven cabinet ministers and nine other ministers in an attempt to stop the economic spiral. As a direct result of this, he lost his earlier and more positive image, now becoming known as 'Mac the Knife'. He also damaged the unity of the party and endangered the future of the economic planning he had sought to implement through the NEDC. T.O. Lloyd argues:

> Planning required either a government which commanded enough prestige to force its will upon people or a system in which people could be confident that they would be treated fairly.

Macmillan did not possess either claim to authority after the ministerial changes.[11]

After 1962 the Conservative leadership never recovered its earlier popularity, as was indicated by a consistently poor performance in the public opinion polls.

This was partly due to the first significant intrusion onto the domestic scene of foreign affairs. There was a dual problem. The way in which the Cold War peaked in the early 1960s graphically demonstrated the relative weakness of Britain in the world at large; at the same time, the search for an alternative attachment failed. The Conservatives suffered from this concatenation of trends. One of Macmillan's strengths had been his reputation as a world-class statesman. After the 1959 election he worked on this further. But the initiative was snatched out of his hands by the Cold War crises in 1961 and 1962. The Berlin Wall and Cuban Missiles Crisis were dealt with by the United States in direct confrontation with the Soviet Union. Kennedy and Khrushchev had taken the centre stage and the weakness of Macmillan's position reminded the British electorate of what it did not wish to know – that, on such occasions, Britain did not count for very much. As Chapter 17 shows, this is perhaps an over-simplified view of Macmillan, but it is certainly one held by the electorate at the time. Popular disillusionment was aptly summarised by Dean Acheson, formerly US Secretary of State, who had said, 'Britain has lost an Empire and not yet found a role.'[12] This meant that more and more attention was paid to Europe. Unfortunately, Macmillan had, by 1962, failed in his attempts to seek entry for Britain into the European Economic Community (EEC). This had serious domestic consequences since he had given a great deal of publicity and effort to winning around public opinion. He had said in a broadcast to the nation on 20 September 1962:

> all through our history . . . we have still been very much involved
> in Europe's affairs. We can't escape it. Sometimes we've tried to
> – but we can't. It's no good pretending.[13]

The detailed negotiations, conducted on behalf of the government by Edward Heath, ended with a veto imposed on British entry by President De Gaulle of France.

Ailing governments often find themselves confronted by a rash of scandals. The Conservatives in the early 1960s had more than their fair share of these. One concerned the profiteering by a number of prominent men over property; some like Rackman used unscrupulous means to evict tenants for resale and all of them drove prices up. It was considered that the government was doing far too little to prevent what passed into the English vocabulary as Rackmanism. More serious were the Portland spy scandal (1961), the conviction of George Blake for espionage, and the defection of Kim Philby to the Soviet Union in 1963. But the most spectacular was the Profumo affair. This had all the elements which the press could use to whip up public indignation and, of course, to increase sales: an affair between the Minister of Defence and a model who was also sharing her favours with a Soviet intelligence official. To make matters worse, Macmillan was criticised by Lord Denning for not acting quickly enough:

> It is the responsibility of the Prime Minister and his colleagues, and of them only, to deal with this situation: and they did not succeed in doing so.[14]

It would, in the circumstances, be hard to disagree with Adelman that the Profumo affair 'delivered the coup de grace to the Conservative government'.[15]

The final factor in Conservative decline was a new – and far less effective – leader. Macmillan resigned his office in October 1963, partly because of the Profumo affair, partly through loss of public confidence in his leadership, and partly through ill-health. This need not have spelt disaster, as there were several candidates with considerable potential – especially Lord Hailsham and R.A. Butler. Macmillan, however, recommended Lord Home to the Queen. Hailsham had undermined his chances by indulging in an American presidential candidate-style campaign at the 1963 Conservative Party Conference. Ironically, Macmillan considered Butler too *low* key and there were concerns that he did not have the presence necessary to lead the party or win a general election. It is therefore generally argued that Home was his choice as the anti-Butler candidate after Hailsham's performance at Blackpool. Undoubtedly the weakest of the alternatives, Home had virtually no experience of domestic affairs, although he did have experience as Foreign Secretary. He was not popular with his cabinet, two of whom resigned, and was immediately overshadowed in the media by the new Labour leader, Harold Wilson. According to Bartlett, 'Home was never entirely at his ease as leader of the conservatives. He blossomed as an elder statesman once he had relinquished the leadership.'[16]

By 1963 all the electoral signs pointed to a major revival by the Labour party, which now began to surge ahead in the public opinion polls. It also began to win seats from the Conservatives in by-elections, for example Middlesbrough West in 1962.

Plate 9 Alec Douglas Home, 1969.
Reproduced by permission of 'PA' News.

The transformation in Labour's fortunes owed much, of course, to Conservative difficulties. At the same time, however, Labour were developing a new image under a new leader. Gaitskell's death in 1963 was in one sense a tragic loss and he came to be mourned in Labour ranks as the 'best Prime Minister Britain never had'. But it was also an opportunity to reunite the party under Harold Wilson. Originally a Fundamentalist in the early 1950s, Wilson had since become more flexible and pragmatic. This meant that he, more than anyone else, was able to bridge the gap between right and left. He reinforced this by adopting policies which avoided the language of the left–right faultline. Words like 'nationalisation' were dropped. The economy was to be 'modernised' and brought within the 'white heat of the technological revolution'.[17] Wilson was a more effective party manager than Gaitskell had ever been. He was also a gifted, if idiosyncratic speaker, with a flair for wit and repartee. He believed that the media should be more effectively exploited and made the tactically important decision to target the floating voter, convinced that this was the only way in which Labour would ever win power. A party team worked on an image to achieve this support, coming up with slogans like 'Let's go with Labour' and, above all, avoiding offputting ideological arguments and commitments. Suddenly, Labour appeared to be the party with ideas and vision. It also benefited from a cultural and psychological change in the early 1960s in which the government was constantly lampooned by *Private Eye*, or by programmes such as *That was the week, that was*. Widespread irreverence for the establishment made it easier to accept Labour's generalisation that the period of Conservative rule had amounted to 'thirteen wasted years'.

COMMENTS ON CONSERVATIVE POLICIES 1951–64

Such a view was diametrically opposed to Macmillan's belief that Britons had 'never had it so good'. Since both descriptions reflected partisan enthusiasm and bias, a fair assessment of Conservative domestic policies will obviously lie somewhere between the two.

The Conservative governments certainly presided over a major improvement in living standards. Wages rose by 72 per cent, prices by only 45 per cent. The differential meant a growth in purchasing power and hence in consumer products. Car ownership, for example, increased by 500 per cent between 1950 and 1964, and television ownership from 4 per cent of the population to 91 per cent during the same period.

There was also a much wider distribution of refrigerators, vacuum cleaners and washing machines. This prosperity was enhanced by tax policies. Income tax was raised after the Conservatives came to power, but thereafter it was steadily reduced; during the period as a whole it was reduced from 9s. 6d. to 7s. 8d. (47.5p to 39p). Conservative governments also delivered the improvements they had promised in living conditions. They generally met their building target of 300,000 new houses per annum, actually exceeding it in 1953 and 1954 with 327,000 and 354,000 respectively. The results were, on the whole, beneficial and a substantial drop in waiting lists for housing enabled the government in 1957 to return letting to the private sector by a measure of de-control. There was also a connection between prosperity and improved living standards as the proportion of people who owned their own homes increased from 25 per cent before the Second World War to 44 per cent by 1964.

Churchill said in 1954: 'We have improved all the social services and we are spending more this year on them than any Government at any time.'[18] It is certainly true that expenditure increased; as a share of the GDP it rose from 16.1 per cent in 1951 to 19.3 per cent in 1964.[19] Even in the period of economic crisis there were ambitious new hospital projects, with ninety to be built in the ten years from 1962. There were also extensions to health legislation. The Mental Health Act of 1959 was a much needed and humane measure that ended the former 'Lunacy Acts', which had required certification, and made most forms of treatment voluntary. Educational reform included pledges to raise the school-leaving age to 16 and to set up 6,000 new schools. Accepting the recommendations of the Robbins Committee Report, the government also expanded higher education by founding eleven new universities. Conservative ministers were prepared to be open-minded about the type of secondary education provided locally. On the one hand, they saw themselves as the natural inheritors of Butler's 1944 Education Act and strongly preferred the tripartite system. On the other hand, they were prepared to allow Local Educational Authorities to introduce a comprehensive system if they chose to do so. Labour accused the Conservatives of being inconsistent. But there were advantages to this. According to M. Hill, 'this was very much an era in which professional rather than political concerns were allowed to dominate the education agenda.'[20]

It is, of course, possible to give a very different perspective to Conservative economic and social policies. Seen retrospectively, and therefore in historical perspective, there is much that was disappointing about their record. Economic growth was taking place from a low level of post-war recovery and was set against the background of austerity and reconstruction. Barring sudden and catastrophic recession, economic growth was as near as possible inevitable. It was also due, at least in part, to objective factors like a world trade boom at the end of the Korean War. In comparative terms, Britain's growth-rate was unimpressive during the 1950s; France's was three times as rapid, Germany's four times and Japan's ten times. Britain's share of world trade shrank between 1950 and 1962 from 25 per cent to 15 per cent while, during the same period, Germany's grew from 7 per cent to 20 per cent. Even more telling was the difference during the 1950s between the growth of Britain's GDP (30 per cent) and the average growth in the GDP of the members of the EEC, which was as high as 80 per cent.

To what extent were Conservative governments responsible for this state of affairs? In July 1962 *The Times* argued:

> Britain's economy has been sick for years. The malady has outstripped too many Chancellors. They come; they apply their notions . . . they declare the patient will recover; they go. Before the public have had time to know much about their successor the trouble starts all over again.[21]

The six chancellors of the period – Butler, Macmillan, Thorneycroft, Heathcoat-Amory, Selwyn Lloyd and Maudling – all resorted to 'stop-go' policies. This was a term used to describe the pragmatic and short-term measures for dealing with underlying factors such as growth, inflation, balance of trade figures and unemployment. Policies varied primarily between controlling expenditure on the one hand and encouraging economic expansion on the other. The problem, seen largely in retrospect, is that clamping down during a period when there was a balance of payments deficit slowed down the possibility of recovery and a resumption of growth. Conversely, responding to growth by cutting income tax tended to increase expenditure and inflation, making a balance of payments deficit much more likely.

A cycle therefore developed, which successive chancellors tried to break. In 1951 Butler inherited a balance of payments deficit from Labour. He dealt with it by a credit squeeze and raising interest rates and controls on imports. The economy took a turn for the better between 1952 and 1954, giving Butler an opportunity to encourage expansion by reducing income tax by 6d. (2.5p) and reducing the bank rate. An increase in inflation followed between 1955 and 1956, in response to which Butler increased purchase tax. Macmillan then raised the bank rate to control consumer expenditure and reduce the demand for imports. After a balance of payments surplus in 1956, Thorneycroft cut taxes and removed credit restrictions. In 1959, Heathcoat-Amory followed an expansionist policy, lowering income tax by 9½d. (4p). The result, between 1959 and 1960, was a boom, leading to an increase in prices, overheating in the economy, wage demands and the worst balance of payments crisis since 1951. Selwyn Lloyd therefore introduced further credit restrictions, raised interest rates and purchase tax, and imposed a 'pay pause' on public employees. This pushed up unemployment to a new post-war peak of 800,000 by 1962. In an attempt to lower this, Maudling tried to hasten a return to expansion in 1963 by means of tax-cuts. But the gamble failed; instead of exports being stimulated there was a rapid increase in imports. The result was the failure of the latest 'go' policy and an increase in the balance of payments deficit to £750 million – which Labour inherited in 1964.

Below the surface of the 'stop-go' strategy lay other, more fundamental, deficiencies which affected long-term economic growth. There were numerous accusations that the government was doing too little to rebuild British industry. There was, for example, no co-ordinated attempt to modernise the staple or traditional industries such as shipbuilding or textiles, which had already experienced difficulties between the wars, or to reinvigorate new industries such as vehicle production. The Conservative government faced the chastening experience of the rapid recovery of Japan and Germany, whose industrial infrastructure had been largely destroyed, to the point that they were overtaking Britain, whose infrastructure had been left largely intact. Part of the problem was that it had the wrong priorities. Instead of modernising industry, the government aimed to revive former priorities like investments overseas and a strong sterling area. The former is emphasised by A. Shonfield, who refers to the 'folk myth that British greatness and wealth have depended on pouring out our treasure abroad'.[22] Maintaining the pound as a reserve currency has also been seen as a folly. According to S. Brittan:

> Britain now has to maintain the sterling area on a reserve less than half of Germany's and a good deal smaller than that of France. Yet neither country maintains an international currency . . . [23]

Official government explanations for the comparatively slow economic growth rate placed the blame elsewhere – usually on irresponsible consumerism or, more frequently, on industrial disruption. In actual fact, both were myths. Between 1951 and 1962, for example, in the number of hours lost per annum Britain was below the United States, Italy, Canada, Japan, Belgium, Australia and France. In any case, disruption was often a reflection on the lack of modernisation in British industry, which meant the persistence of antagonisms between management and labour. On the Continent, by contrast, the reconstruction of industries had brought a redefinition of these roles.

The governments of the 1950s have also been accused of allowing the social reforms introduced after 1945 to stagnate. The Labour opposition argued that whatever economic growth there was did not find its way proportionately into the welfare state. It is true that pensions were updated from time to time, but this was on an erratic basis. In the case of the NHS, government arguments about an underlying continuity between the 1950s and the 1940s were based on a misconception. The real factors were inaction and inertia. The Conservatives did little to deal with the complex and uneasy relationship between private and national services, allowing the temporary compromise introduced by Labour to end the doctors' dispute to stratify into a permanent dichotomy. Part of the problem was a lack of real interest by the leadership in social issues. Churchill had already shown his caution in 1945 and between 1951 and 1955 he was more interested in Conservative survival than in consolidating social change. Eden's priority was always with foreign policy and the Suez Crisis diverted him from all domestic issues. Macmillan was the most progressive of all the Conservative leaders of the period, but his ministry coincided with the worst economic crisis, which was bound to lead to a tightening up of expenditure on the welfare state. This state of affairs was inherited by Douglas-Home, who saw no reason to attempt anything more adventurous. It is hardly surprising that, by 1964, there was increasing scepticism about the previous maxim that the welfare state was safe in Conservative hands.

THE 1964 GENERAL ELECTION

There are times in British political history when an election campaign is charged with anticipation of change. This was the case in 1964. Labour expected to win the election and the Conservative government was not confident of preventing them from doing so. Wilson forced the pace, focusing on the need for modernisation and a second industrial revolution. He thus avoided the doctrinaire approach of which Labour had for so long been accused by the Conservatives. Douglas-Home, by contrast, fought a defensive campaign, warning – not very convincingly – of major setbacks in the future should Labour be elected to power.

The result was actually very close. Labour won 317 seats with 44.1 per cent of the total vote to the Conservatives' 304 from 43.4 per cent. Taking into account the 9 seats won by the Liberals, Labour achieved an overall majority of 4, an advantage which could be wiped out in two by-elections (see Figure 10, p. 196). This proved a disappointment to Wilson and showed that there was a swing towards the Conservatives at the last minute. This was possibly because some of Labour's potential supporters played safe and opted for the security of the status quo and recent experience of power. As Wilson entered Downing Street in October 1964, he must have been only too aware that he would soon be having to appeal to them again.

14

YEARS OF REFORM AND CRISIS 1964–79

The second half of the twentieth century saw two periods of Conservative ascendancy. The first was between 1951 and 1964, the second after 1979. Between 1964 and 1979 Britain returned to a more genuinely two-party system, with alternating governments. After narrowly winning the 1964 general election, Harold Wilson substantially increased his majority in 1966, only to lose to the Conservatives under Edward Heath in 1970. The election of February 1974 was indecisive. As leader of the party with the largest number of seats, however, Wilson returned to Downing Street and secured a working majority in a second general election in October. In 1976 Wilson retired in favour of Callaghan, who eventually lost the 1979 election to the new Conservative leader, Margaret Thatcher.

These fifteen years saw three developments which seemed at the time to override everything else, an impression which has not since been contradicted. First, it was a period of reform; various commissions recommended sweeping changes, and the political, social and economic sectors were all affected by a stream of legislation. Second, Britain was perpetually on a knife-edge, threatened by crisis after crisis. Governments were constantly challenged by balance of payments deficits, inflation, industrial disruption or political instability. And third, the post-war consensus that had been the basis of Labour and Conservative policies between 1945 and 1964 began to wear thin as both parties tried to find more distinctive solutions of their own. The failure of such attempts forced them back onto the middle ground but prepared the way for the real break, which came after the 1979 general election, one of the most decisive of the twentieth century.

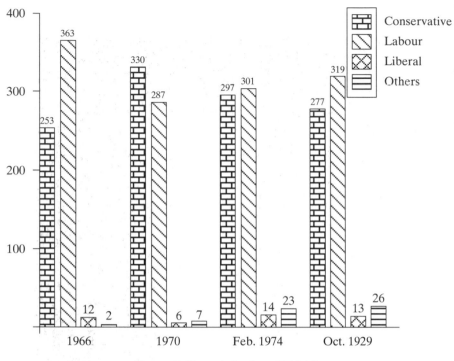

Figure 11 General elections 1966–74

YEARS OF REFORM?

As we have already seen in Chapter 13, the period 1951–64 was not a high point of reform. Depending on the political viewpoint of the analyst, its hallmark was either the careful and progressive consolidation of earlier changes or, alternatively, a serious loss of momentum and a growing inertia. The latter view is too negative; in many cases the 1950s and early 1960s contained the seeds for the reforms of the late 1960s and the 1970s. What had been missing was the urgency and the momentum, which undoubtedly accelerated after 1964. Particularly affected was the political sector. Writing in 1975, F. Stacey pointed to numerous 'planned changes which took place as part of an almost unprecedented quickening of activity in the re-shaping of our political institutions.'[1] To what extent is this view justified?

Central administration was certainly affected. The Civil Service experienced its first major changes since the late nineteenth century. The Fulton Report (1968) claimed that 'The service is still essentially

212

Plate 10 Harold Wilson, 1969.
Reproduced by permission of 'PA' News.

based on the philosophy of the amateur'[2] and, following its advice, Heath's government ended the rigid system of classes which had previously dominated its recruitment and promotion and substituted a more flexible structure of grades. There was, however, less success in coming to terms with professional training for civil servants or in increasing accountability to the public. The structure of the Civil Service was to be shaken up more radically by the Thatcher administration fifteen years later, while the Official Secrets Act, which had been rushed through in 1911, remained untouched. It is true that a new device was set up to channel public complaints against public administration. The Parliamentary Commissioner for Administration, or Ombudsman, was introduced in 1967, after being considered but shelved by Macmillan. This meant that grievances could now be handled by an impartial official and not by MPs, who were, after all, political figures. On the other hand, the British Ombudsman had far fewer powers than his European counterparts; he was not, for example, empowered to investigate complaints concerning the National Health Service, the nationalised industries or the police. There were, therefore, still many restrictions on the openness and accountability of central government.

Local government was more extensively restructured than at any time since the Middle Ages. The Local Government Act of 1972 introduced many of the recommendations of the massive Redcliffe-Maud Report. Local authorities were rationalised to cover either rural or urban areas. Six new metropolitan counties came into existence, subdivided into a second tier of metropolitan districts. The rest of England and Wales was given a modified county system which contained boroughs as a second tier. On the other hand, significant problems remained, including the rating system, which was unchanged until that nettle was grasped – unsuccessfully – by the Thatcher administration in the 1980s. Two other reforms were introduced by Heath's government, transferring major services to more specialised bodies. The Water Act (1973) established a National Water Board and ten regional authorities and the National Health Service Reorganisation Act (1973) set up a series of area health authorities based on the newly created counties. In 1973 there were also moves to provide a regional level of government. The Kilbrandon Commission recommended the devolution of power to Scottish and Welsh assemblies while, at the same time, retaining the essential features of the United Kingdom. The Labour governments of Wilson and Callaghan were, however, prevented from delivering these proposals by the results of referendums held in 1979 in Scotland and Wales.

Changes were introduced into the legislature as well as the administration. The House of Commons committees were extended to involve back-benchers to a greater degree. The Select Committee on Estimates, for example, was subdivided into six specialist sub-committees, including defence, overseas affairs, and technological and scientific affairs. Other select committees were added after 1966 for agriculture, education and science, race relations and immigration, and Scottish affairs. The electorate was substantially enlarged when the Representation of the People Act (1969) lowered the voting age to 18 to bring Britain in line with many other countries in Europe. It was also given an enlarged responsibility by being asked by Wilson's third government to participate in 1975 in a referendum on the EEC. Attempts had, in the meantime, been made to modernise the House of Lords. The white paper on Lords Reform (1968) proposed to end the right of the hereditary peerage to vote on legislation and to confine this to life peers and hereditary peers of first creation. The proposal was defeated when Enoch Powell, who opposed any changes, formed a tactical alliance with Michael Foot, who believed that the proposed reforms were entirely inadequate. Between them they mobilised the Conservative right in a rare alliance with the Labour left to stop this particular momentum.

Historians have also pointed to an impressive list of social reforms between 1964 and 1979. One of the key features of the 1960s was the use of private members' bills to secure changes in the law for specific groups within the population. This can, of course, be seen as an indication that normal government business was ignoring such priorities. Alternatively, it might be interpreted as an intelligent use by the government of time to relieve the pressure on an overcrowded programme. The private members' bills tended to cover those issues which were not party-political. The first was the Murder (Abolition of the Death Penalty) Bill of Silverman in 1964. This was followed in 1967 by the Sexual Offences Act; introduced by Leo Abse, this legalised homosexual acts in private between consenting adults over the age of 21. David Steel's Abortion Act (1967) legalised termination of pregnancies under certain clearly prescribed conditions, while George Strauss's Theatres Act (1968) removed the censor's pencil from plays performed in London. Government measures also remedied social anachronisms. The National Health Service (Family Planning Act) of 1967 made it possible for health authorities to provide free family planning and contraception. The reform of the divorce law meant that the irrevocable breakdown of marriage became the only grounds for divorce, removing the necessity of having to probe for evidence for grounds of adultery or cruelty. This was very much within the needs of the times, since there had been a rapid expansion of marital break-downs during the 1960s. Race relations legislation contained measures which were both restrictive and enabling. The former were in the Commonwealth Immigrants Act (1968) and the Immigration Act (1971), which defined more carefully – and unfavourably – the rights of immigrants to settle permanently in the United Kingdom. The emphasis on rights was more apparent in the Race Relations Act (1976) which made discrimination on the grounds of race unlawful. This was enforced by the Commission for Racial Equality, set up under the terms of the 1976 Act. This was directly in line with another important liberating measure. The Sex Discrimination Act (1975) disallowed occupational discrimination on grounds of gender and set up an Equal Opportunities Commission.

Finally, substantial changes were projected for the areas in which society and the economy overlapped. The first of these concerned the relationship between employers and employees. Heath's Industrial Relations Act (1971) required the registration of trade unions and major alterations in their rules to remove the use of strikes without preliminary ballots. Also banned were sympathetic strikes, strikes to secure a closed shop, or compulsory membership of one union within the workplace. The National Industrial Relations Court was established to enforce these measures. The legislation proved, however, to be the most unworkable of Heath's government. There was widespread resis-tance and refusal to register under the Act or observe its guidelines for conduct. It also made it very difficult to secure co-operation for the other important measure of the Heath era – the establishment of the Price Commission and Pay Board in 1973. Restrictions were placed on wage increases and on price rises, which had to be notified in advance to the Price Commission. But the attempt to institutionalise a pay and incomes policy came apart because of the lack of co-operation from trade unionists which culminated in the 1973 miners' strike.

Overall, the governments of Wilson and Heath should receive credit for an unusually hectic round of legislative activity. The political and constitutional proposals, whether successful or unsuccessful, had few precedents in the twentieth century. Against this it could be argued, however, that the Constitution was not fundamentally changed. There was no bill of rights, no redefining of the powers of the upper house, no examination of the electoral system, no progress on devolution, no commitment to open government. In the social and economic areas there was a considerable advance in achieving rights for minority

Plate 11 Edward Heath, 1983.
Reproduced by permission of 'PA' News.

groups and in creating a more open and tolerant society. But there was also disappointment, a typical example of which was Crosland's view in 1974. He concluded that Wilson's first two governments had failed:

> extreme class inequalities remain, poverty is far from eliminated, the economy is in a state of semi-permanent crisis and inflation is rampant.[3]

YEARS OF CRISIS

All the prime ministers of the period were painfully aware of the possibility of a crisis lurking around the next corner. The first area of major concern was the economy. During the 1950s this had caused periodic problems which had, however, alternated with the impression of prosperity and economic growth. By contrast, 'Labour's six years in office were characterised by continual economic crises.'[4] The process had already started during the period of the Macmillan government (see Chapter 13) and Labour had to deal immediately with an over-heated economy. Wilson, looking back from 1971, believed that 'It was this inheritance which was to dominate almost every action of the Government for five years of the five years, eight months we were in office.'[5] At first the Labour government tried, by establishing the Department of Economic Affairs, to avoid the hand-to-mouth measures and the stop-start policies of the Conservatives. The intention was to work out a longer-term plan for economic growth and for the revitalisation of industry. Then the pace of economic crisis increased. In 1966 there was a balance of payments crisis and a seamen's strike. These were so serious that the government had to reverse its macro-economic approach and return to crisis management. The options open to Wilson in 1966 were threefold: devaluation, public expenditure cuts or a prices and incomes freeze. At this stage a note of desperation entered into the government's economic policies. The Chancellor of the Exchequer, James Callaghan, refused to devalue the pound in July 1967, only to change his mind in November. The latter decision was considered necessary to bolster British exports. During the campaign to publicise the reasons for this, Wilson made on television his celebrated gaffe that 'this does not mean the pound in your pocket has been devalued.' The decline in the government's credibility over the issue was such that Callaghan was replaced as Chancellor by Roy Jenkins, who resorted to tougher measures in 1968, including cuts on government

Plate 12 James Callaghan, 1979.
Reproduced by permission of 'PA' News.

expenditure and increased duties on alcohol, petrol and tobacco. For the time being, these helped to improve the situation by producing a balance of payments surplus in 1969.

According to Budge and McKay, 'If the 1960s were years of periodic crises, the 1970s were years of unremitting economic crisis.'[6] Heath, the new Prime Minister, tried his own version of long-term planning to break the stop-start pattern. He believed that lower taxation and greater economic competition would provide the stimulus for recovery, especially if these were carried out within the environment of European integration. This is why Heath attached so much importance to British membership of the European Economic Community, which he finally accomplished in 1972. In preparation for the anticipated growth, Barber, the Conservative Chancellor of the Exchequer, had reduced taxes and credit restrictions. The result was disastrous and, like Wilson before him, Heath had to revert to crisis management. The balance of payments moved back into the red, reaching a deficit of £900 million by 1973. The other two manifestations of crisis also intensified: inflation and unemployment. The former increased from 6.4 per cent in 1970 to 9.4 per cent in 1971. In 1972 Heath had to alter his course to a freeze on prices and incomes and a reduction in public expenditure. He also hoped to control inflation through an incomes policy rather than by controlling the money supply, which was the device used in the later 1970s and the 1980s. His measures were, however, knocked off course by the sudden increase in oil prices announced in October 1973 by the Oil Petroleum Exporting Countries (OPEC) after the third Arab–Israeli War. Worse was to follow with the miners' strike and the three-day week. In the general election of February 1974 each side accused the other of crisis economics: Labour maintained that the Conservatives had generated the current crisis, while the Conservatives tried to convince the electorate that Labour would make a worse one in the future.

On returning to power in 1974, Wilson tried to reintroduce a planned economy. Almost immediately he hit problems: shortly after the end of the miners' strike there was a spate of pay demands. The government tried to deal with these in a reasonable manner by setting up the Conciliation and Arbitration Service (ACAS) and agreeing with the trade unions a Social Contract to promote voluntary restraint on wage increases. The hiatus in the economy saw Labour through the 1974 October election with a slightly increased majority. From 1975 onwards the economy went into the most serious crisis to date as inflation reached the unprecedented figure of 24.2 per cent. Sterling collapsed a year later and the pound fell to its lowest level ever. The Chancellor of the Exchequer, Denis Healey, now had to apply for urgent loans from the IMF to meet payments on debts. For its part, the IMF insisted on a reduction in public expenditure by £3 billion over the period of two years. This, and the incomes policy, resulted in the fall of inflation to 8 per cent. Ironically, at the very moment that the government appeared to have got the economic crisis under control, it headed for the worst yet confrontation with the trade unions.

This brings us to industrial relations, a second element of the years of crisis and one which was closely related to economic difficulties. In the words of D. Powell, 'the "Labour question" in all its facets re-emerged with a force it had not shown for a generation.'[7] After 1964 governments inclined more and more to a prices and incomes policy after the failure of earlier attempts at voluntary wage restraint. This provoked more militant responses from the trade unions which in turn deepened the economic crisis. The political parties resorted to different strategies to deal with the problem. The Conservatives went for legal controls based on the Industrial Relations Act, introduced by Robert Carr, the Employment Secretary, in 1971. This was enforced by an Industrial Relations Court which could insist on a 'cooling off period' before any strike took place as well as the holding of strike ballots. The TUC confronted the government by instructing all unions not to register. The Act proved unworkable and the whole attempt by the government to control industrial relations from above collapsed in the wage rounds of 1972 and 1973. The miners succeeded in gaining up to a 24 per cent increase in 1973 after a strike which had a serious effect on power services and forced the government to introduce a three-day week. But when the NUM prepared for a further strike in 1974, the government reimposed the three-day week, introduced restrictions to conserve fuel, and reduced television transmission times. Heath decided to go to the country with a 'crisis campaign', seeking the electorate's answer to the question 'who governs?' The manipulation of the crisis backfired in the narrow Conservative defeat of February 1974.

The approach of Labour governments to industrial relations was more cautious: they tried to temper wage restraint with trade union involvement and co-operation. This was epitomised by the White Paper *In Place of Strife*. Published in 1969, this guaranteed the rights of trade unions but allowed the government more powers of intervention in industrial relations, including the imposition of a 'conciliation pause'. But it aroused a storm of fury in the trade union movement, especially from the TGWU and the AUEW. Labour lost the 1970 general election before having to face the full consequences. On returning to power in February 1974, Wilson avoided a repetition of Heath's head-on collision with the trade unions and opted for a more equal partnership as a way of resolving the crisis. He now tried to involve the unions directly in the process of price and wage controls and, as a first step, repealed the Conservative legislation. But this policy immediately came under threat and the crisis re-emerged in a frantic free-for-all in the wage round of 1974-5. The impact on the economy has already been noted;

unemployment reached 1 million and inflation topped 25 per cent. Confronted with a crisis of a new dimension the government and the TUC sought a compromise in a voluntary wage restraint with a flat rate initially and then a graduated increase. The TUC, however, came under pressure from its members and, in 1977, demanded a return of free collective bargaining. In 1978 Callaghan took a unilateral approach by imposing a restriction of 5 per cent on any wage increase. The result was the worst series of strikes yet in the so-called 'Winter of Discontent'. The following spring Callaghan's government suffered the same fate as Heath's five years earlier.

Crisis therefore appeared in a third guise. Economic problems and industrial conflict provoked snap general elections in 1974 and 1979. These, in turn, revealed a growing difficulty within the electoral system itself. Normally this can be relied upon to produce a majority government out of a minority vote, a distortion which had consistently been defended by both major parties on the grounds that at least majority governments provided political stability. But, with the exception of that of 1966, the elections of the period were all very close. The election of 1964 therefore had to be followed by one in 1966, the election of February 1974 by one in October of the same year. The majority produced by the October election was soon dissipated in by-election losses, which meant that Labour had to do a deal with the Liberals and, for the first time since 1929, set up a Lib-Lab pact. Underlying the economic and industrial crises was therefore a feeling of political uncertainty, reflected by the inaccuracy of the public opinion polls, which got the outcome of the 1970 election completely wrong. The sense of crisis was deliberately understated by the Labour and Conservative parties but was very much pointed up by the Liberals, who argued for proportional representation as a means of 'breaking the mould' and liberating the British electorate from the tyranny – now increasingly uncertain – of an artificial two-party system. It seemed that the electorate had some sympathy for this viewpoint. In February 1974 the Liberals secured 6 million votes, the highest number in their history and over twice as many as their total in their landslide victory of 1906. For this they received 14 seats. From the Liberal perspective this discredited the whole notion of representative democracy.

There was also a political crisis in a regional sense. The period saw basic questions raised about the future of the United Kingdom as, in one part of the country, regional self-government was removed while, in another part, it was proposed but not delivered. Undoubtedly the most serious problem was Northern Ireland, which erupted into violence in 1969, forcing the British government to send troops to the streets of Belfast (see Chapter 21). Following the 'Bloody Sunday' incident in 1972, the Stormont assembly was suspended and direct rule introduced from Britain. The crisis in Northern Ireland dominated the regional policies for the rest of the period and cast a cloud over the more positive devolution proposals for Scotland and Wales. The failure of the Scottish proposals was especially disappointing in view of the disputed interpretation of the result of the referendum held in 1979: although the ballot secured a narrow majority in favour of devolution, the government had insisted that there had to be a majority of the entire Scottish electorate, not just of those who had voted. The disappointment felt by the Scottish National Party (SNP) was so extreme that they took a fearsome revenge. In February 1979 they tabled a vote of no confidence which resulted in the first defeat of a government by this method since 1924. Coming hard on the heels of the Winter of Discontent, this linked together all the different strands of crisis. The economic crisis of Callaghan's government had precipitated a crisis of industrial relations. The latter discredited the government, creating a political crisis as a result of the action of a minority party with a sense of crisis over failed devolution proposals. The problem – although not the solution – had been identified by Callaghan at the 1978 Labour Party Conference:

> Society today is so organised that every individual group has the power to distort it. How is their power to be channelled into constructive channels?[8]

BREAKING THE CONSENSUS?

One of the main characteristics of the period 1945–51 had been a broad measure of agreement, or consensus, between the parties on fundamental policies relating to the economy and to society. Between 1964 and 1979 – and especially between 1974 and 1979 – this was severely shaken. In summary, Labour and the Conservatives both attempted special remedies which involved moving away from the central ground they had previously occupied. Both were forced to give way to circumstances beyond their control and move back towards more familiar policies. Consensus therefore survived – at least for the moment. At the same time, however, each party was developing a radical wing which eventually predominated. The Conservative right won control from 1975 and the Labour left after 1979.

Dutton argues that 'It was the Conservative Party which made the first significant attacks on postwar consensus.'[9] This view has much to commend it. The 'attacks' came in three waves, each becoming more significant. The first was a fringe movement, consisting of the supporters of Enoch Powell, attracted by his radical ideas on reducing government control over the economy and repatriating Commonwealth immigrants. The second and more significant wave was Heath's attempt in 1970 to reverse the neo-Keynesian principles which had dominated almost all post-war economic policy. He believed that to tackle Britain's economic problems he had to challenge some of the previous tenets of consensus. The new Conservative policy, drawn up at the Selsdon Park Hotel in February 1970, emphasised increased competition and a return to free enterprise based on fewer restrictions. Heath was certainly conscious of the change he was proposing. He said in 1970, 'It is not just a lurch to the Right, it is an atavistic desire to reverse the course of 25 years of social revolution.'[10] Wilson saw it as the return to old Conservatism, 'not just pre-1964 but pre-Macmillan, pre-Butler.'[11] Heath was, however, forced to reverse many of his policies halfway through his government, having encountered unexpectedly strong resistance and other difficulties. His initiative therefore failed. Ironically, Heath's reputation in the future was as a moderate seeking to revive consensus after it had been eradicated by his successor.

This was Margaret Thatcher, who introduced the third wave, or the new radicalism. Ideologically she was indebted to Sir Keith Joseph, who went much further than Heath in redefining the policy of his party. 'It was only in April 1974 that I was converted to Conservatism. I had thought I was a Conservative, but I now see that I was not really one at all.'[12] He attacked the growth in the power of the state for removing the initiative from family and individual and for creating excessive dependence. The Centre for Policy Studies, established by Joseph and Mrs Thatcher in 1974, was intended to promote economic liberalism, influenced by economists such as F.A. Hayek and Milton Friedman. A decisive move had to be made away from consensus since, according to Joseph, 'the middle ground these days is a guarantee of a left-wing ratchet'.[13] Mrs Thatcher, meanwhile, was arguing that the Labour party had become increasingly socialist, even Marxist.

Her analysis was partly correct. Although she exaggerated the extent of the swing, she was correct about the swing itself. While in opposition between 1970 and 1974, Labour moved to the left under the chairmanship of Tony Benn. The party developed a series of policies which would have increased the involvement of the state – the very opposite of what was being attempted by the Heath administration. The main element was a proposed agreement between trade unions and government whereby the former undertook to control wage demands in return for the latter's control of prices. Several historians have commented on the significance of this. According to Dutton the party came up with the 'most radical agenda since the war',[14] while D. Coates goes back even further: 'the shift to the left in language and programme after 1970 was on a scale last seen . . . as long ago as 1931'.[15] The 1974 Labour manifesto pledged to 'bring about a fundamental and irreversible shift in the balance of power and wealth in favour of working people and their families.'[16] There was, however, a strong similarity to the experience of the Heath administration. The economy soon got completely out of hand and the Social Contract with the trade unions proved no more successful than had been Heath's policy of free enterprise. The Labour Chancellor, Healey, followed the sort of policies which were far from left-wing or socialist. Indeed, he moved sharply rightwards back to the centre, just as Heath had, against his inclination, been forced to move leftwards. So, according to W. Thompson, 'The Labour government of the 1970s adhered to the same essential priorities as its Labour and Conservative predecessors had done.'[17] This meant above all defending sterling and imposing controls over public expenditure.

The left-wing backlash against such policies was as fundamental as the right-wing movement against Heath among Conservatives, although it was delayed until after the 1979 general election. There is therefore a similarity in the overall development of party policies. From 1970 the leadership of each party moved away from the long-accepted point of consensus between the parties; Heath moved to the right and Wilson to the left. They took their parties with them so that, during the early 1970s, a gap opened between the Conservatives and Labour. Circumstances forced the leadership back into the position of consensus, as Heath retreated to the left and Callaghan to the right. But the new centres of gravity remained on the wings of the two parties, which were to be pulled further apart by the new radicalism of Thatcher and Joseph on the right and of Foot and Benn on the left.

THE 1979 GENERAL ELECTION

Hence the forces were drawn up against each other in 1979 for one of the most significant elections of the whole century. The Conservatives won 339 seats with 43.9 per cent of the total vote, against Labour's 269 from 36.9 per cent. This was Labour's worst electoral performance since 1931 when, in any case, the party had been split. Mrs Thatcher had a comfortable overall majority of 41, sufficient to prevent her from having to go to the country again within the first year of her new government.

A crucial reason for this outcome was the timing of the election itself. There were strong arguments for going to the polls in October 1978, which is what most people, members of the Labour party included, were expecting. The economy seemed relatively stable at that point, with wages going up by an average of 15 per cent and inflation by 8 per cent. All the indicators, however, suggested that the economy had peaked and was about to take a downward turn. Labour also led the Conservatives in the Gallup polls by 1.7 points and 54 per cent of respondents said they were satisfied with Callaghan's leadership, compared with only 37 per cent with Thatcher's.[18] But Callaghan thought that an October election might be too close to call and that Labour would do better to wait until 1979. That delay proved disastrous. The intervening Winter of Discontent completely discredited a government which had been riding the waves only a few months earlier. By February Labour had fallen 18 points behind in the public opinion polls as the public were shocked by the sheer intensity of the strikes by lorry drivers, engine drivers, local authority workers, water workers, refuse workers and many others. Worse was to follow when Callaghan lost even the option of waiting until October 1979 in the hope that Labour's credibility might recover over the summer. Losing the vote of no confidence tabled by the SNP in February meant that Labour had to fight the election at the worst possible time. It seems, therefore, that Callaghan had committed a major blunder. In his defence, it might be argued that he could not have predicted the full impact of the Winter of Discontent and, in any case, he was not alone in wanting to postpone the election: he was supported by Michael Foot, Merlyn Rees and David Owen against William Rodgers, Roy Hattersley and Shirley Williams, who all favoured October 1978.

Labour lost the election because of some marked changes of voting habits among different parts of the electorate. Most worrying was the working-class swing to the Conservatives, which was 6.5 per cent among unskilled and semi-skilled workers and as much as 11 per cent among the skilled. Even trade unionists could no longer be relied upon to give automatic support to Labour; nearly one third now voted Conservative.[19] New voters, traditionally more inclined to Labour or the Liberals, were more likely to cast an anti-government vote in the direction of the Conservatives. The greatest overall change, however, occurred among men. In the past the majority of men had voted Labour, probably because of their trade union membership, while the Conservatives had made up their numbers from women in the electorate. In 1979, however, men voted Conservative in significantly larger numbers, thus negating the worries of those Conservative organisers who feared that men might be put off by the prospect of a woman prime minister. There were also massive swings to the Conservatives in the Midlands and the South, especially in new towns like Basildon, which became a yardstick for new Toryism.

At the time, much of the credit for the Conservative victory – or blame for Labour's defeat – was given to Saatchi and Saatchi's carefully organised advertising campaign. It was also assumed that Mrs Thatcher had been more forceful and positive than Callaghan. In fact, these mattered less than was originally thought. According to I. Crewe, 'It was issues, not organization or personalities, that won the election for the Conservatives.'[20] In order of perceived importance, these issues were prices, unemployment, taxes, strikes, and law and order. The Conservatives were seen as the party more likely to succeed on taxes and law and order, in which they had massive leads in the opinion polls of 61 per cent and 72 per cent, and on strikes.[21] The Conservatives also emphasised more successfully a large number of specific proposals, such as the reduction of supplementary benefits for strikers and the lowering of income tax. The Conservative manifesto had far the greater impact, especially its proposals to ban secondary picketing, to sell council housing and to allow a free vote in the Commons on capital punishment. In 1979 personalities seemed to count less than issues. Throughout the campaign Callaghan remained more popular than Thatcher among voters; it seems that Labour lost and the Conservatives won *despite* their leaders, not because of them. Organisation and advertising were more effectively carried out by the Conservatives than by Labour, but probably did little more than change people's minds on the fringes. The real battleground proved to be ideas and policies.

Labour also had to face a longer-term problem, the true impact of which was only becoming apparent in the 1970s. For some time the Labour party's share of the vote had been moving downwards: from a peak of 48.8 per cent in 1951 to 46.4 per cent in 1955 and 43.8 per cent in 1959. After a brief recovery to 44.1 per cent in 1964 and 47.9 per cent in 1966, the decline resumed with 43 per cent in 1970. During the 1970s Labour never reached 40 per cent, managing only 37.1 per cent in February 1974, 39.2 per cent in October 1974 and 36.9 per cent in 1979. These figures were partly a reflection of dissatisfaction with

Labour policies, both in government and in opposition. But there were also significant changes in the structure of the working class, which opened it increasingly to Conservative influences, a process which had undermined the Liberals in the late nineteenth century. Upward mobility in social and economic terms often results in a new political affiliation to defend the change of status. The specific policies of the Conservatives in the 1979 election overlapped the aspirations and needs of this group more than ever before. The left wing of the Labour party argued the very reverse: that significant sections of the working class had defected because of the absence of socialist policies in Labour's manifesto. This was not shown in the election result; those parties which stood on an explicitly socialist policy fared extremely badly and, throughout the campaign, the personalities of Labour's left trailed in popularity to those of the centre and right.

Was 1979 the year in which the British electorate rejected the post-war consensus and opted for what came to be called 'conviction politics'? The Conservative leadership certainly thought so. The policies which appealed in 1979 were sharper, tougher and more specific than before. Mrs Thatcher openly attacked consensus, arguing that it had led to leftward looking and outmoded ideas. In so far as the Conservatives were returned to power, it seems that they won the arguments. But the majority of the population remained to be convinced and 50.7 per cent voted Labour or Liberal against the 43.9 per cent for the Conservatives. It would be fair to say that although the parties were further apart than they had been for some time, there was no mass rejection of the central ground. In a way the Conservatives knew this. Their manifesto in 1979 was the reverse of what was normal. Instead of containing a larger number of commitments than would actually be carried through, it resembled an iceberg, with much that was implied but not yet made explicit. Eleven years of Thatcherism would reveal just how much lay below the waterline.

15

THATCHERISM AND
AFTER, 1979–95

Mrs Thatcher entered Downing Street in May 1979 committed to a policy of economic and social transformation. For the next eleven years she dominated British politics more completely than any other prime minister of the twentieth century. There were periods in which she was vulnerable, but special circumstances gave her an apparently irresistible momentum which carried her through two further general election victories. In 1983 she won a majority of 144 seats, which she followed up in 1987 with a third successive win, this time by 102 seats. She interpreted these results as a mandate to maintain a course which was so radical as to make some observers refer to the 'Thatcher revolution', a phrase which has aroused considerable controversy.

Then, in 1990, came a strange twist as Mrs Thatcher was elbowed out of power by sections of the Conservative party which feared that she had become so stuck in her ways that she would lead them to electoral disaster. John Major, widely considered a compromise successor, saw the Conservatives through a fourth consecutive victory in 1992. But, almost immediately afterwards, the party fell into crisis which was all the more serious as it coincided with the recovery of Labour. The two parties also began to compete more openly for the central ground, leading some analysts to claim that the politics of consensus were being revived.

THE MEANING AND MOMENTUM OF
THATCHERISM

From the time she was elected leader of the Conservative Party in 1975, Mrs Thatcher made no secret of her dislike of political consensus between the parties, seeing it as 'the process of abandoning all beliefs, principles, values and policies'.[1] She expressed a commitment to 'conviction politics' which was so strong that she became the only

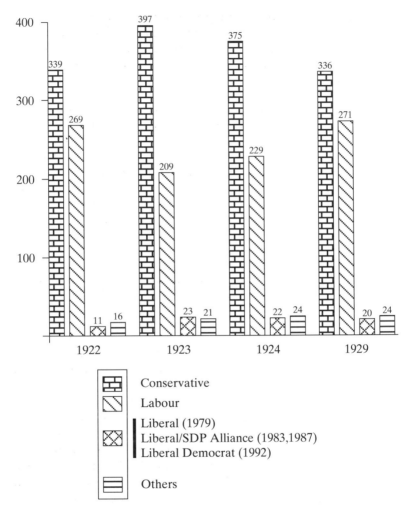

Figure 12 General elections 1979–92

British prime minister ever to lend her name to an ideology. In brief, 'Thatcherism' aimed to move Britain forward into the future by rediscovering what were perceived as the greatest strengths of her past. During the 1983 general election campaign she gave an insight into her own view of the past. She emphasised the Victorian achievement:

In fact, during Victorian times, as you know, conditions improved. That was the great improvement in industry, the great

230

expansion in industry, which gave us a chance to have a rising standard of living. . . . It was a time when you had great self-reliance – you lived within your income – great honesty, great duty, a great increase in Empire, and a great increase in self-confidence as a nation.[2]

She had six main priorities. She aimed to reduce the role of the state in the life of the individual; to develop a market economy in the hope that this would arrest Britain's economic decline relative to other countries; to promote popular capitalism through a process of privatisation; to destroy inflation; to end industrial conflict by cutting the power of the unions; and to enhance Britain's international position. All of these were rooted in past strengths, although some historians have interpreted the connection in a more negative way. W. Thompson, for example, argues:

> When the Prime Minister asserted with passion her commitment to Victorian values it may be surmised that the one she had chiefly in mind was the Victorian moral value of blaming the victims.[3]

This opens up the main ground for opposition to Thatcherism: that it was seeking to roll back the scope of the welfare state and therefore reverse some of the more compassionate achievements of the post-1945 consensus.

Mrs Thatcher's ideas were forcefully delivered and backed by a personal dominance rivalled in the twentieth century only by Macmillan. Like Macmillan, she spoke in simple terms. In 1979 she said: 'Unless we change our ways and our direction, our greatness as a nation will soon be a footnote in the history books.'[4] Her willingness to take personal responsibility for the country's image seemed at times to involve a confusion of identity between herself and Britannia. She imposed a more complete domination over policy than any other prime minister of the century. According to Lord Thorneycroft, 'the basic policy was Margaret Thatcher. She knew what she wanted to do before she got into office.'[5] She was renowned for leading and imposing her will on the cabinet: 'herself was the prime source of economic policy formation',[6] in which she had a particular interest. She exerted her control through careful and at times ruthless manipulation. She determined the cabinet agendas and the membership of cabinet committees and, when necessary, was willing to part with her colleagues through extensive cabinet reshuffles – the main casualties being Norman St John

Stevas, Francis Pym, Sir Ian Gilmour, James Prior and Nigel Lawson. She was influenced, in the American style, by personal advisers, such as Professor Alan Walters. These helped her formulate economic policies which were sometimes not submitted to full discussion in the cabinet. She invoked a deep hatred among some members of the opposition; according to a Labour backbencher, 'Mrs Thatcher refuses to admit she could be wrong, and brazens it out.'[7] In 1986 he added, over the Westland affair: 'I say that she is a bounder, a liar, a deceiver, a cheat and a crook.'[8]

The initial pace of Mrs Thatcher's policies was relatively slow. But the momentum soon increased as she concentrated on a strict control of the money supply and of public-sector expenditure. There was little immediate evidence of success. What did happen was that the new government helped bring on a recession by maintaining the high exchange rate in which the pound moved up to $2.40 and unemployment climbed steadily. By 1981 the Conservative government was deeply unpopular and had fallen over 20 per cent behind in the public opinion polls. To make matters worse, July 1981 saw a series of riots in Britain's inner cities, especially in Brixton, Toxteth, Wood Green and Handsworth. These came as a profound shock and it seemed that Mrs Thatcher's ministry was in crisis.

Then came the first reprieve – and opportunity. The Falklands War of 1982 (see Chapter 18) did more than anything else to bring about Mrs Thatcher's recovery and consolidate her power. With the front pages of every newspaper devoted for three months to the crisis and the campaign, attention was inevitably diverted from the economic problems that had made the Conservatives so vulnerable in 1991. Mrs Thatcher played an impressive role as war leader, on which she was congratulated in the House of Commons by the leader of the opposition – a rare tribute. The stakes had been high, since losing the war would have meant the end of Mrs Thatcher's administration just as surely as winning it meant the end of General Galtieri's. But the outcome of the war enormously boosted her own image and enabled her to ride a patriotic wave as a Churchillian figure. The impetus carried into 1983 and it was unquestionably the 'Falklands factor' that was directly responsible for the size of the Conservative victory in the general election that year.

By 1984 the euphoria had begun to wear off and Mrs Thatcher was encountering some of the criticism and unpopularity which had previously been apparent in 1981. This time she took advantage of another conflict, the miners' strike. Always at her most formidable when in confrontation, Mrs Thatcher now proceeded to dispatch

Arthur Scargill, although with rather more difficulty than she had seen off Galtieri. The miners' strike was not directly provoked by the government, but it does seem to have been a fight which the government relished. This was in obvious contrast with Callaghan's discomfiture over the Winter of Discontent (1978–9) or Heath's over the miners' strike of 1973. Certainly Mrs Thatcher's esteem increased and she had another confirmation of her power base. This she used to introduce her next wave of radical measures, especially privatisation and local government reform.

THE THATCHER ACHIEVEMENT: A REVOLUTION?

We have seen the considerable personal influence imposed by Thatcher, and the accelerating momentum of her changes. A more fundamental question now emerges: were her reforms part of a 'Thatcherite Revolution'? There is no doubt that she was conscious of bringing about a transformation in Britain, based upon an ideological change, and she said in 1983: 'we must win the battle of ideas'.[9] On the other hand, there were elements in her reforms which were strongly opportunist and which may well have developed in response to specific circumstances rather than as part of an overall plan. These two approaches need to be kept in mind in any analysis of specific changes.

The earliest reforms were those affecting the economy. These showed a particularly close combination of Victorian thinking and late twentieth-century theories: Thatcherism here was both backward- and forward-looking. Sir John Nott said in 1983 that both he and the Prime Minister were 'nineteenth-century liberals'.[10] And yet the main influence was modern – the post-Keynesian economic theories of the Monetarists. These believed that the increase in inflation was due primarily to the growth of money supply. Reductions in interest rates, intended to promote industrial production, would tend to increase the money supply and thereby fuel inflation. Keynesians had accepted this as the price for keeping down unemployment levels, but Monetarists like Friedman and Hayek saw unemployment as a longer-term result of inflation.[11] They also believed that public sector expenditure should be controlled more rigorously. This was the reverse of the Keynesian approach, which had been to stimulate industrial output and higher employment, financing the budget deficits through loans and higher taxation. Mrs Thatcher considered that monetarism was not an alien theory but rather a revival of nineteenth-century *laissez-faire*, a sort of updated version of the ideas of Adam Smith. It was, in her view, a thoroughly British approach to restore confidence to the open market.

Did this amount to an economic revolution? P. Jackson sees it more as a counter-revolution; he points to the paradox of monetarism being applied in Britain, 'the nation of the Keynesian revolution'.[12] But he also argues that it was partly a reaction against the 'stagflation' years of the 1970s, which bred disenchantment with Keynesianism. Callaghan and Healey had become receptive to some of the new ideas. To try to cut back on their previous deficit spending they secured a loan from the IMF. The condition for this was a reduction in public expenditure. 'The first UK monetarist government was, in fact, a Labour Government.'[13] Hence Mrs Thatcher did not suddenly plunge Britain into monetarism and reverse a thriving Keynesian system. Keynesianism had already come under pressure and elements of monetarism were already apparent. In one important respect, however, 1979 was a turning point. Before that date monetarism had been used as a short-term corrective; afterwards it became the basis of long-term macro-economics. According to Holmes, 'contemporary Conservatism has arguably been remoulded in such a fundamental way as to make a return to the Keynesian middle-way consensus impossible.'[14]

The policy had mixed results. On the surface, the most significant achievement of Mrs Thatcher's government was to lower the basic rate of income tax from 33 per cent to 25 per cent and the higher rate from 80 per cent to 40 per cent, the greatest tax cuts by any administration in the twentieth century. This seemed directly in line with the underlying policy of freeing capital for the open market. On the other hand, there was a corresponding increase in indirect taxation, especially in VAT and national insurance contributions. Indeed, it has been estimated that 'The tax burden as a percentage of gross domestic product (GDP) actually increased from 34 per cent to 37 per cent, 1979–1990.'[15] Perhaps more lasting was the reduction of inflation to levels lower than at any time since the 1950s. Mrs Thatcher also managed to do without the various economic trappings of the 1970s, including incomes policies, commissions on comparability, price and wage freezes, social contracts with trade union leaders, and growth targets. Even so, monetarism as a conscious policy was gradually laid to rest by Mrs Thatcher's government after 1985. The arguments had never won widespread appeal or even acceptance among the population and the Conservatives preferred to promote more attractive monetarist offshoots.

One of these was the policy of privatisation, an essential part of the

Conservative government's decision to roll back the frontiers of state control. This was applied to enterprises such as British Petroleum from 1979, British Aerospace from 1981, Cable & Wireless (1981), Amersham International (1982), National Freight Consortium (1982), Britoil (1983), Jaguar (1984), British Telecom (1984), British Gas (1986), British Airways (1987), Royal Ordnance (1987), Rolls Royce (1987), British Airports Authority (1987), Rover (1988), British Steel (1988), the ten Water Companies (1989), twelve Electricity Companies (1990), and National Powergen (1991).

The reasons appear to have been partly ideological, partly pragmatic. Ideological factors included the desire to reduce government intervention; in some respects this was a return to the principle of economic *laissez-faire*, whereby the government created the climate for economic competition but did not involve itself in a direct managerial role. This, it was held, would greatly increase efficiency by reducing impediments to economic growth and cutting public dependence on the state. Similarly, the public could be persuaded into accepting different expectations by being given a financial stake, as shareholders, in the private sector rather than a theoretical role, as voters, in the public sector. There were, however, pragmatic and party political reasons as well. One of the main obstacles to effective government authority during the 1970s had been the political strike. This had been made possible by the view of public-sector unions that the government, as employer, was the appropriate target for pressure. The Conservatives in the 1980s therefore accompanied their legislation to weaken the trade unions by measures which would deflect any strike action from the government to private employers. By privatisation the government cut itself off from direct pressure from public sector unions; Sir Keith Joseph saw this as a means of breaking their hold on the national 'jugular vein'.[16] Equally strong was the fiscal motive. Privatisation had a double spin-off. It reduced the extent to which the government needed to provide in the future for public corporations, thereby cutting its borrowing requirements. To the cynical – or realistic – observer, privatisation also created a series of cash windfalls which enabled the Conservatives to plan cuts in income tax to coincide with general elections.

Did privatisation amount to a revolution? According to J. Foreman-Peck, it was 'the most radical restructuring of British industry at least since 1951'.[17] M. Pirie goes further: the privatisation programme involved 'the largest transfer of property since the dissolution of the monasteries under Henry VIII'.[18] This can be borne out by the sheer scale of the enterprise, which involved over sixty companies and corporations, as well as increasing the number of shareholders from 7 per cent to 21 per cent of the adult population.[19] This was a complete reversal of the nationalisation programme which had been introduced by the Attlee Government after 1945 and retained by Churchill, Eden, Macmillan, Douglas-Home, Wilson, Heath and Callaghan. And yet it could not be said that the policy of privatisation was not a systematic one at the outset. It received only four paragraphs in the 1979 manifesto. The first of Mrs Thatcher's governments concentrated more on monetarism and the reduction of the public sector borrowing requirement (PSBR), privatisation playing a subordinate but useful role. It was only during Mrs Thatcher's second and third governments that privatisation acquired a strong ideology and became the flagship of Conservatism. According to Foreman-Peck, 'Only in 1986, with the White Paper on water privatization, were all the Government's objectives for privatization fully stated.'[20]

The response to privatisation was mixed. The public joined enthusiastically in the purchase of shares. But some of the more important changes caused extensive opposition. The new water companies, for example, became extremely unpopular with the public, who complained about poorer services, higher costs and excessive salary increases for top officials. The government did seem more interested in raising revenue in the short term rather than in improving overall efficiency in the long term. In some cases there were serious threats of reduced services, as with the break-up of British Rail. It is true that the government established agencies to monitor the standards of the new companies, such as the Office of Gas Supply (OFGAS) and the Office of Water (OFWAT), but these were widely considered to be ineffectual in preventing rising costs and poorer delivery. John Major tried to follow the Thatcher momentum but encountered a backlash among the public, and within his own party, against his attempts to privatise the Post Office in 1994. By the beginning of 1995 the whole policy was beginning to seem a liability and there was a strong possibility that, like monetarism, it might begin to fade into the background.

Mrs Thatcher's government found the welfare state a particularly delicate area. Her own views were quite clear. She placed emphasis on the Victorian values, especially those of self-help and care within the family, and tried as far as possible to personalise welfare. She therefore promoted private provision, whether in health or education or housing, even pensions. The welfare state was seen increasingly as a safety net for those who could not provide for themselves rather than as the normal means through which basic provision was to be made for all. In practice this meant freezing child benefit as a universal concession and directing specific help towards the needy. This was done by family income support, which took the place of supplementary benefit. She also removed the 16–17 age group from automatic unemployment benefit, developing instead the Youth Training Scheme (YTS). In the NHS and education she aimed for greater efficiency by making competitive tendering compulsory for certain services. As a result, under Mrs Thatcher, Britain experienced heavier cuts to social welfare and reductions in manpower than elsewhere in the European Community.

On the other hand, Mrs Thatcher was never given the opportunity to dismantle the welfare state. Popular and party resistance to any such suggestion was just too strong. It seems that the British public were much more attached to the welfare state than to the nationalised industries, regarding it as an inalienable inheritance from the Second World War. Public opinion polls from 1990 showed that most of the electorate supported increased funding to the NHS and to education even if this should mean tax increases. Besides, the impact of monetarist economic policies meant that the welfare state was needed more than ever to deal with the growth of unemployment and poverty. Between 1979 and 1985, for example, the number of people below the poverty line and in receipt of supplementary benefit increased by 55 per cent and to 17 per cent of the entire population. It could be argued that the Thatcher government drove more and more people into dependence on the welfare state instead of weaning them off it. Despite her intentions, therefore, expenditure on welfare services steadily increased in health, while in education between 1979 and 1989 the spending on each pupil increased in real terms by 42 per cent.[21]

The measures to change the economy, to reverse nationalisation, and to pull back the scope of the welfare state could not have been introduced without a concerted campaign against the trade unions. All three of Mrs Thatcher's ministries produced legislation which achieved far more than Wilson and Heath had even attempted. She started with the Employment Acts of 1980 and 1982. Between them these banned secondary picketing, limited the closed shop and imposed penalties for unofficial strikes. The Trade Union Act (1984) imposed secret ballots before strike action could be taken, while the Employment Acts of 1988 and 1990 enforced the use of ballots in the election of trade union officials and gave members rights of redress against their union. The government's objectives were clear, although too ruthless to be articulated publicly. Unless it could tame the trade union movement the government would not succeed in the rest of its policies. The impo-sition of the free market through monetarism required a compliant labour force, not one which would resort to industrial action in defence of established procedures. Wages had to reflect more accurately their market value, which again meant that the shadow of strike action had to be removed from wage negotiations. Privatisation could not be considered as long as the public-sector trade unions retained the power to take on the government; otherwise it was possible that almost every attempt to reverse the earlier policy of nationalisation would incur the wrath of some trade union or other. A national, or general, strike was not inconceivable. Finally, the government's campaign for efficiency in the public sector meant slimming down the National Health Service and the Civil Service, objectives which would certainly have provoked major action in the 1960s and 1970s.

Considering the wave upon wave of trade union action in the 1970s, it may seem surprising that Mrs Thatcher was able to introduce and then enforce her policies in the 1980s. There are three main reasons for her success. One was that the state of the economy drove unemploy-ment up very sharply so that it reached a peak of over 3 million in 1985. Since changes had been made in the collection and collation of statistics, the actual figure could well have been over 4 million. This compared with an average of 1.4 million when Callaghan was prime minister and half a million under Heath. The Conservatives undoubtedly used the shadow of unemployment to make the workforce place a higher value on their jobs and to reduce their willingness to risk losing them as a result of militant trade union action. The second reason was the sheer determination of the government not to give way. In this respect, Mrs Thatcher possessed a ruthlessness lacked by any of her predecessors. She took tactical advantage of the 1984 miners' strike. An overall scheme had already been drawn up to take on and defeat the miners, widely seen as the most militant of the trade unions, as the first step in taming the rest. In this respect, Arthur Scargill played right into Mrs Thatcher's hands. The futility of his efforts and the violence of some of the incidents embarrassed the other parties sufficiently to distance themselves from the strike. A third factor was that the trade unions had to become more cautious and defensive. Many of their members were already voting Conservative; some had become white collar workers with the shrinking proportion of working-class members; and above all the overall membership of the trade unions declined steadily throughout the 1980s.

How permanent the subjection of the trade unions would be was an open question in the early 1990s. Their influence had certainly not been eradicated and by 1987, membership, although down on 1979, was still up on 1966. There was also a sign of improved recruitment after Tony Blair became leader of the Labour party in 1994. To some union leaders the correct strategy was now to aim at recovery and wait for a future Labour government to repeal at least some of Mrs Thatcher's measures. There is a school of thought that a revival of trade union power is a strong possibility anyway. Pimlott maintains that unions are always weakened 'in times of high unemployment and of depression'; he adds 'when inflation is slackening, the unions become much weaker. Their ability to mount industrial action becomes less and their ability to win it less still.'[22] The corollary to this is that future economic revival and higher levels of employment could be expected to strengthen the trade unions. Perhaps this would coincide with a period of Labour government, in which case, one of the most radical achievements of Thatcherism would be under heavy pressure.

Many authorities speak in terms of an 'administrative revolution' under Mrs Thatcher. There are two themes here. One is the paradox that, in aiming to pull back the role of central government, Mrs Thatcher actually strengthened it. The other is logically connected with this. In strengthening central government, she brought about major changes in Whitehall and in its relationship with the local authorities. Her main target at the centre was undoubtedly the Civil Service. According to P. Jackson, this had been one of the main influences behind consensus between 1945 and 1979. Mrs Thatcher preferred to think that continuity in policy had been due to bureaucratic inertia, which was, therefore, one of the factors which needed to be swept away before any fundamental economic changes could be made. How could this be accomplished? One way was by introducing advisers from outside the scope of Parliament and the Civil Service. Another was to introduce radical changes within the Civil Service. For example, Mrs Thatcher reduced the number of civil servants from 732,000 to 565,000, transferring some of their functions to private bodies. The Civil Service came under close financial scrutiny in the Financial Management Initiative (1982), which was intended to make Departments define their objectives, set targets, measure their performance against these, and make effective use of resources by giving VFM ('value for money'). In 1988 the Next Steps programme emphasised the distinction between the two main roles of the Civil Service – advice on policy and delivering services. The latter function was hived off into a series of agencies like the Central Statistical Office and the Teachers' Pensions Agency. Altogether, these amounted to an even more extensive package of changes than those introduced by the Heath Government following the Redcliffe-Maud Report. They were also more radical in the sense that they aimed to redefine the functions of the Civil Service, whereas earlier changes had concentrated on its structure. On the other hand, Mrs Thatcher never got as far with the reforms as she had intended and it could be argued that the full extent of the transformation was not seen until after 1991, when Major's government introduced the 'competing for quality' programme which went to the logical – and drastic – conclusion of privatising civil service functions through competitive tendering.

Local government was also extensively overhauled by the Conservatives. The process started with the offensive against Labour strongholds. The government took the offensive by forcing local authorities to sell off assets and council houses, and to put services out to competitive tender. It also reduced central government funding and then rate-capped those authorities who refused to comply with the financial guidelines set up. Some authorities tried to defy this by refusing to set a rate at all, which simply played into Mrs Thatcher's hands, enabling her to point out that they were being totally irresponsible. The Conservative changes embodied both radicalism and opportunism. The radical element was the forceful application of Conservative policies on finance and public expenditure by the removal of much of the financial autonomy which the local authorities had previously enjoyed. The opportunist element can be seen in two ways. The first was the advantage taken of the behaviour of the far left group, Militant Tendency, in Liverpool. This appeared to justify the policies of the Conservative government which might otherwise have carried the taint of party self-interest. The second was the elimination of the Greater London Council (GLC), an authority set up as recently as 1964. This was done for manifestly political reasons and left London alone among the major European capitals without a unified system of municipal government.

So was there a 'Thatcher revolution'? If we define revolution as a sharp break with existing theory and practice we get one perspective; if we focus on the word *re*-volution and see it as a return to the principles of a past age we get another. It seems that the answer should include both, and that it should also establish the extent to which the changes were based on ideology. A case can be made that Mrs Thatcher *did* introduce a revolution; she broke the consensus which had dominated British politics since 1945 and returned to some of the basic principles of the Victorian era – in both respects a fundamental change. The

240

process was deliberate and ideological, a combination of modern economic theory in the form of monetarism and of nineteenth-century *laissez-faire*. It involved a political transformation as well: Thatcherism meant an increase in the power of central government in order to enforce the right ideological environment to withdraw government involvement in the economy. This has strong parallels with government policy over *laissez-faire* in the nineteenth century.

An alternative argument is that Mrs Thatcher was above all an opportunist. It is true that many of her changes were radical but her overall approach was dogmatic rather than doctrinal. Pimlott maintains that her most remarkable achievement was the length of her time in office, 'which can be largely ascribed to the combined generosity of General Galtieri and the British opposition. For the rest, most of the positive claims of Thatcherism and some of the negative ones are a coincidence of timing'.[23] There is also the view that increasing the power of government was accompanied by a deliberate reduction in its responsibility; the more it could offload the less it could be held directly accountable for what went wrong. This goes against the trend of a revolution, in which power is generally sought to *take* responsibility. There is also the case that Thatcherism was part of an overall trend within Britain. In some respects her economic policy had been anticipated before 1979; what she did was to formalise and accelerate the measures already used by Callaghan. Pimlott argues that these and developments like the sale of council houses 'would have happened anyway, albeit with a different rhetoric, under Labour, and probably with much the same kind of rhetoric under Heath.'[24] Also, similar trends were taking place in Europe and North America. The main reason is that the more traditional industries were everywhere in decline and a period of economic adjustment was necessary in Germany, France, Italy and the United States as well as in Britain. The working classes had shrunk in size and pressures had been placed on welfare states. Mrs Thatcher was part of a western as well as a British trend, although her supporters prefer to think that she dictated it and set the example which others followed.

CONSERVATISM AFTER MRS THATCHER

For much of the electorate, Conservatism had become synonymous with Thatcherism. No one since Lord Liverpool had won three consecutive general elections and no one since Attlee had brought about such a transformation internally. No one since Churchill had had such an impact on the international scene. But her apparent invulnerability had always been something of a myth. She could have fallen in 1982 but had survived to win a landslide election the following year. Yet in 1990 the unthinkable actually happened and Mrs Thatcher became the first prime minister this century to be removed by his or her own party in peacetime.

The trouble started when she committed herself totally to replacing rates with the poll-tax as the main form of local government finance. This was part of a policy to undo the welfare state and end the redistribution of wealth. The rating system had been a compromise between flat-rate payments for services and local income tax. The Thatcher government, however, intended to 'assimilate public services as far as possible to the form of a cash transaction'.[25] This was certainly consistent with the theories behind privatisation. But it was also the most unpopular policy of her entire administration and it aroused the most forceful and wide-spread opposition. Mrs Thatcher was determined to press ahead despite warnings from colleagues in the cabinet and on the back benches, who were increasingly worried about the revelations of the public opinion polls in 1989 and 1990. These showed two disconcerting developments. One was a consistent lead for Labour, which now appeared to be well on the way to recovery. The other was the growing unpopularity of Mrs Thatcher herself. It became increasingly obvious that the Prime Minister was the main obstacle to the Conservatives winning the next general election. But it was Mrs Thatcher's clash with Sir Geoffrey Howe in the House of Commons over her policy towards the European Union which precipitated the dramatic events that resulted in her replacement. After Howe's resignation from the cabinet, Sir Anthony Meyer gave notice that he intended to challenge Mrs Thatcher for the leadership. When Michael Heseltine entered the race Mrs Thatcher narrowly failed to secure the overall majority which she needed to avoid a second ballot. Submitting to strong pressure from other members of the cabinet, she stood down. Her preferred candidate, John Major, went on to defeat Heseltine and Douglas Hurd for the leadership.

This could be interpreted as the overthrow of an *ancien régime* or, alternatively, as the ending of a revolution which had become personified. Either way, the short-term result was gratifying for the Conservative party. In the run-up to the 1992 general election, John Major had a honeymoon period in which he projected himself as a moderate. The Gulf War of 1991 also gave him the opportunity to pose as a national leader and statesman. His strong instinct for survival persuaded him to withdraw the poll-tax and replace it by a new council

Plate 13 Margaret Thatcher and John Major, 1992. Reproduced by
permission of 'PA' News.

tax. He did just enough to reverse the gravitational pull of Thatcherism
and to see the Conservatives through the election. In its late swing
to Major the electorate showed a preference for security and the known
rather than for experimentation and change. Labour had been gam-
bling that Mrs Thatcher would lose power through her unpopularity.
The change in the leadership had been made just in time for the
Conservatives to survive.

The problem was that Major proved more adept at winning a new
term of power than at using it. There was no period of calm and
stability. Instead, the Conservative party seemed to plunge headlong
into crisis. It was dogged by an unusual sequence of scandals, involving
adultery and sexual deviations by a number of Conservative MPs.
These were widely reported in the media and contrasted strangely

243

with the ill-fated 'back to basics' campaign launched at the 1993 Conservative Party Conference. One after another, ministers made their contributions to the debate on morality. Michael Howard, the Home Secretary, stressed the disadvantages of one-parent families and the stigma of illegitimacy. Peter Lilley, the Secretary of State for Social Security, said in 1994 that children should ideally have two parents.[26] George Young, the Housing Minister, said that unmarried mothers should not be given priority in housing lists. Similar statements were made by other ministers, including John Redwood. The problem was that the government came to appear both insensitive and, in the circumstances, hypocritical. In some respects the campaign was a return to Thatcherite ideology in a period when many Conservatives were becoming nostalgic for the strength of her leadership.

There were also difficulties over financial issues. Faced with increasing pressures for public expenditure, the government had to make unpopular decisions about taxation. Since any increase in income tax was considered out of the question, Value Added Tax (VAT) was imposed for the first time on fuel. This created another public outcry, which was embarrassing for the government as it involved highly publicised campaigns on behalf of vulnerable social groups like pensioners. Even more serious was the crisis over Europe. Mrs Thatcher had aimed to create 'zero inflation' through Britain's membership of the Exchange Rate Mechanism (ERM). But this proved too much for the pound, which sank rapidly in value. In September 1992 Britain had to withdraw from the ERM and the media made the government appear directionless. The sacrificial lamb was Norman Lamont, who was sacked as Chancellor of the Exchequer shortly afterwards. As a result of his treatment he became an inveterate opponent to Major. Bad enough in itself, this was followed by a series of divisions and back-bench rebellions within the Conservative party. There was some opposition to the back-to-basics programme, but the worst fury erupted over a rebellion by several MPs, including Teddy Taylor and Teresa Gorman, who at the end of 1994 voted against the government's measures to increase Britain's financial contribution to Europe and to raise the level of VAT on domestic fuel.

To make matters worse, the Conservative party experienced a decline in membership and funding. The latter normally came from affiliation fees, constituency quotas and donations. By 1993 the party had accumulated a deficit of some £19 million, over £10 million of which had been used to win the 1992 election.[27] The main reason for this was the financial recession, which greatly reduced donations from those corporations that considered that the Conservatives might actually have brought it about. There were also allegations of improprieties, particularly a connection between donations and honours. For example, the Labour party maintained that the top ten corporate donors between 1979 and 1993 received 7 peerages and 8 knighthoods.[28] These difficulties came at the worst possible time, as the Conservatives really needed to throw everything into the task of holding off a revived and newly confident Labour party.

By 1995, therefore, the position of John Major had become precarious. There were four depressing indicators. The first was the European elections of June 1994, in which the Conservatives slumped to 27 per cent of the national vote and won only 18 seats. This compared very unfavourably with Labour's 44 per cent and 62 seats. It was suggested at the time that this was not so much a vote on European issues as a protest vote against the domestic performance of the Conservative government. Second, the local government elections of April 1995 proved an unprecedented disaster. Of the 1,161 seats contested, the Conservatives won only 82. They now controlled far fewer councils overall than the 127 they had held in 1987 and the 29 in 1991. Even more serious was that they controlled not a single county in 1995, a complete reversal of their almost continuous domination of the county councils since their formation in 1888. In England, once their stronghold, the Conservatives became the *third* party within local government – behind Labour and the Liberal Democrats.[29] A third indicator was a series of by-election defeats, including the loss of one of the party's few remaining Scottish seats, Perth and Kinross (May 1995). Finally, the public opinion polls revealed a consistent and very substantial lead for Labour. No other government to that time had ever remained so long on a deficit of more than 29 per cent to the main opposition party.

What could be done about all this? The last time that the Conservatives had been in such trouble was in 1990, when the solution had been to change the leadership. They had then surged to victory in the 1992 election. Many within the party wanted to repeat the experience and there was increasing pressure from the right wing of the party for Major to stand aside. The latter opted for a bold pre-emptive strike. On 22 June 1995 he resigned as party leader and invited a leadership election, in which he would himself stand. This was an unprecedented act, clearly designed to flush out the opponents within his party so that he could subsequently defeat them and re-establish his authority. This was, of course, a gamble. The first round might have seen a stalking horse attracting sufficient dissident votes to deprive Major of a convincing majority; his position might then have been seen as untenable, resulting in a straight contest between Michael Heseltine of the left of the party and Michael Portillo of the right. As it was, the outright challenge emerged in the first round, but from the right alone. John Redwood put up a good but hardly overwhelming performance and Major was re-elected leader by 218 votes to 89. This proved a vindication for Major's decision and certainly lessened the degree of internal disunity in the immediate aftermath of the election.

The leadership issue therefore seemed to have been resolved – at least for the moment. But what about Conservative policy? There still appeared to be some indecision as to whether to continue with Thatcherism – or to bury it. A compromise was attempted with the development of a new right-wing initiative in 1995, which would open up 'clear blue water' between the Conservatives and Labour. This would have the advantage of reconciling the right within the Conservative party. Perhaps it might also drag Labour still further to the right and encourage the left to break away – much as Labour's slide to the left had lost it its right in 1980. There was an early indication that this might succeed when Arthur Scargill announced the formation of a rival party on the left – the Socialist Labour Party (SLP). On the other hand, there were dangers that the Conservative left might be destabilised, as was shown by the defections of Alan Howarth and Emma Nicholson. It remains to be seen, therefore, whether the policy represented a temporary rightward wobble by the Conservatives in an otherwise post-Thatcherite return to consensus politics, or whether it indicated a post-consensus return to Thatcherism.

16

THE SECOND CRISIS OF
LABOUR 1979–92

After losing the 1979 general election the Labour party entered its worst crisis since the split of 1931. The electoral record was particularly depressing: Labour lost four successive general elections – in 1979, 1983, 1987 and 1992. In the 1983 election the party won a lower proportion of the popular vote than at any time since 1918. It also experienced a struggle for identity, threatened alternately by internal conflict and by external encroachment from the parties of the centre. Even the long-term sociological signs seemed unfavourable, with a declining working class and population movements that favoured the Conservatives.

Labour's first crisis, dealt with in Chapter 14, concerned a party struggling to achieve maturity. The second crisis was seen by many as an attempt to stave off death. Is this a fair assessment, or, to adapt Mark Twain's famous phrase, was the diagnosis of death an exaggeration?

THE SHORT-CUT TO DECLINE

Labour's underlying problem was that it covered a very broad ideological spectrum, which ranged from centrists and former Liberals on one wing to radicals and Marxists on the other. This was an uneasy coalition, the various parts of which were out of balance with each other. Part of the reason for this is historic. In most continental countries the First World War brought a split between moderate socialists and revolutionary socialists, most of the latter becoming Communists. The process was accelerated between the wars by the widespread use of proportional representation. This had meant that there was no incentive for socialists of different shades to stick together: they could survive effectively as smaller parties without becoming part of a broader coalition. The British Labour movement, on the other hand, remained heterogeneous and the wide range of ideological positions could at times prove severely disruptive. The greatest threat to its cohesion came with the lurch to the left after 1979.

Why did this happen? In part the impetus preceded 1979. Much of the party had lost confidence in consensus during the 1970s. Under the third Wilson administration and Callaghan the Labour party lost its way and its complex eclecticism became a liability. The threat of break-up was accelerated by the 1979 general election. Callaghan's policies on the trade unions and wage restraint had already alienated the left and he was now blamed for the inept timing of the election (see page 15). In a way, the crisis of 1931 was being played out again after 1979. In both cases, the left considered that Labour's leadership had sold out to a policy of gradualism that had become indistinguishable from some of the measures of the preceding Conservative government; there were even dark comparisons between Wilson and Callaghan on the one hand and MacDonald on the other. The Labour Conference of October 1979 saw the first determined push by the left, with demands that included the regular reselection of MPs. The National Executive Committee was given control over the selection of the party's manifesto and there was to be a committee enquiring into new methods of electing the Labour leader. This was taken further at the 1980 Labour Party Conference in Blackpool, at which the mandatory reselection of candidates was confirmed. Shortly afterwards Michael Foot was elected leader upon Callaghan's retirement. He was committed to the policies of the left, including unilateral nuclear disarmament, more extensive nationalisation and withdrawal from the European Community. It was also decided that future leadership elections would be conducted by three parts of the party – the trade unions, the Parliamentary party, and the constituency parties.

A direct result of this leftward momentum was the secession of the right wing of the Labour party. On 25 January 1981 three Labour MPs – Shirley Williams, William Rodgers and David Owen – joined with Roy Jenkins in announcing the Limehouse Declaration. This accused the Labour party of having moved 'steadily away from its roots in the people of this country and its commitment to parliamentary government'. What was now needed was 'a realignment of British politics'.[1] Hence they established the new Social Democratic Party (SDP), which aligned itself with David Steel's Liberal party in an electoral pact known as the Alliance. This produced several spectacular by-election victories: in 1981 William Pitt won Croydon and Shirley Williams Crosby, while Roy Jenkins won Glasgow Hillhead the following year. By October

1981 the Alliance were topping the public opinion polls with well over 50 per cent of popular support, well ahead of both the Conservative government and the Labour opposition. Already the parties of the centre were talking in terms of breaking the traditional pattern of British politics and of combining to replace the Labour party as the main opposition to the Conservatives. There were many in 1981 and the beginning of 1982 who believed that the Alliance was a potential government; most believed that the next election would produce at the least a three-way split in Parliamentary seats, with the Alliance holding the balance of power. Either way, Labour seemed set for rapid decline.

The secession of the right was followed by an assault from the far left, which comprised various Marxist groups. The most striking of these were the Trotskyists, who had a strange history. Between 1917 and 1927 Trotskyism had been associated mainly with the spread of revolution from Russia to other countries – in other words its emphasis had been openly ideological. After his removal and exile from 1927 onwards, Trotsky had become more pragmatic, recommending that the best way of taking over was not by overt revolution but by covert penetration. This meant that Marxists should become involved in democratic politics, but with the ultimate purpose of effecting a communist take-over. Trotsky had recommended that British activists should enter the Independent Labour Party (ILP) as a distinct group and thereby gain publicity. But as the ILP disappeared the Trotskyists transferred to the mainstream Labour party. Thus Trotskyism was equivalent to entryism, a deliberately parasitic strategy by a minority seeking to take eventual control over the whole party and subjecting it to an alien ideology. The most important Trotskyist group was Militant Tendency. Formed in 1950, this expanded during the 1970s, especially under Ted Grant and Peter Taaffe and stood 'on the foundations of the ideas of Marx, Engels, Lenin and Trotsky'.[2] In the late 1970s it was already claiming a unique position and influence:

> What guarantees the superiority of our tendency – the tendency of Marxism – from all others inside and outside the labour movement is our understanding of all the myriad factors which determine the attitudes and moods of the workers at each stage.[3]

But it also monopolised the 'correct' interpretation of Marxism. It attacked Labour and the leadership of the trade unions for

> shoring up decrepit and decaying capitalism. They do not see that by doing so, they are merely prolonging the death-agony of the system and lending it a more violent and convulsive character.[4]

The connection between Militant Tendency and the Labour party was strengthened by Tony Benn who, although not himself a Trotskyist, openly welcomed the Militants in the process of 'participatory democracy'. This explains why Militants had a higher regard for Benn than for any other prominent Labour politician. The connection exposed Labour to the accusation that it was riddled with Marxism. Members of Militant made it clear that the crisis of capitalism was at hand, and they even equated Thatcherism, in the context of the recession of the early 1980s, with Fascism in the early 1930s. Clearly such arguments severely damaged Labour's image with the electorate and handed the other parties a weapon they could use as propaganda. And yet for several years the party tolerated such influences. The reason for this is paradoxical. On the one hand, Labour had a long tradition of tolerance, based on the sort of heterogeneous support which the Liberals had once boasted, and was more open to internal debate than were the Conservatives. On the other hand, groups like Militant Tendency were alien to Labour's tradition and, for a while, threatened to undermine that tradition. It claimed to represent the true feelings of the working class, but within the context of an ideology which had never taken root within Britain. Benn's policy of tolerating Trotskyism was therefore an actual danger to Labour's own roots, as the leadership realised after 1985.

The influence of the mainstream left, which was also under pressure from the Trotskyist left, resulted in a swing towards socialism. Was this a liability to Labour? Not according to Tony Benn. In his view, what was needed was a new impetus, a new commitment to changing the capitalist system. He said at the 1979 Labour Party Conference:

> We have seen twenty years of surrender. Since 1959 the Parliamentary leadership of the Labour Party has been going along with the idea that the post-war consensus built upon full employment and the welfare state was a permanent feature of life in Britain. . . . That response has failed to command the support of our people because they have seen first that it did not contain within it any element whatsoever of transformation. . . . That policy could not bring about growth and could not extend freedom.[5]

Two recent observers disagree fundamentally with Benn's analysis. Kavanagh maintains that

> Labour voters are not attracted by many 'socialist' policies, that is greater public ownership, comprehensive education, extending

trade union rights, and redistribution. Such policies appear to unite supporters of other parties in rejection while serving to *divide* Labour voters.[6]

A similar point is made by W. Thompson:

The essence of the left's error was in the presumption that a left wing programme would be self-validating with the electorate, that it only needed to be put before the voters to generate spontaneous acceptance, thus that its validity could be taken for granted.[7]

There was an assumption within the left of the party that socialism was the natural philosophy of the working class – and both the Marxist and non-Marxist socialists believed this. Others within the party consistently warned against such an assumption.

Socialism was the driving force behind the policies in the Labour manifestos of 1983 and 1987; these changed rapidly after the party's internal reorganisation and the leadership elections of 1980–1 and went far beyond any commitment to undo contentious Conservative measures. In addition to reversing Thatcher's policy of privatisation, Foot undertook to nationalise areas which had previously been left alone by Attlee and his successors. He also reversed the previous consensus with the Conservatives on Britain's nuclear deterrent; Labour entered the elections of 1983 and 1987 committed to unilateral nuclear disarmament. The absence of a convincing explanation alienated many Labour voters, who felt that there was too close a connection between the Labour party and a specific pressure group, the Campaign for Nuclear Disarmament (CND). The Conservatives, meanwhile, had a field-day probing Labour's alternative defence programme, concluding that the consequent increase in conventional weapons would exceed the nuclear budget. Unilateralism also caused difficulties within the Labour party: Callaghan opposed it and Healey was deeply unhappy, declining – uncharacteristically – to talk about it. A third policy which caused consternation was Labour's commitment to withdraw Britain from the European Community, despite Wilson's acceptance of permanent membership after the 1975 referendum. Other areas of contention were proposed increases in public spending, which would have meant reverses in Conservative tax cuts; the abolition of the House of Lords, which raised concerns about an imbalance in the constitution; and import controls, which had already proved a graveyard for many party aspirations in the past.

The Labour party was also beset by leadership problems. On Callaghan's retirement in October 1980, Michael Foot was elected by 139 votes to Healey's 129. He was seen as a candidate of reconciliation, the first clearly left-wing leader since Lansbury in 1933. In some ways he was admirable. He had deep convictions; he was a brilliant, although eccentric, orator; and he was cultured and widely read. He shared one of these three qualities with Mrs Thatcher. The Prime Minister, however, had a single-mindedness and ruthlessness which is the true hallmark of the successful leader. The tragedy of the Labour party at this stage was that the man who combined the qualities of Foot and the aggression of Thatcher was confined to the position of deputy leader. Denis Healey, former Chancellor of the Exchequer, was admired by many but hated by the rest; he therefore reopened the conflict within the party which the election of Foot had been intended to stop. Neil Kinnock, Labour leader after the 1983 election, proved much more robust than Foot. But even he was unable to project himself as a real alternative to Mrs Thatcher or, after 1990, to John Major. He had no ministerial experience and his techniques were faulty in the House of Commons; he was not, as the Prime Minister tartly pointed out in her response to a question in 1988, always fully in command of his financial material.

So far we have considered the ways in which the Labour party can be said to have contributed to its own decline. There were, however, more fundamental factors. One was the decline of its traditional identification with the working class. Even by 1979 'Labour had undergone the most spectacular electoral decline of any socialist party in Western Europe. It lost votes at every general election bar one between 1951 and 1979 and its vote tumbled from 47 per cent in 1966 to 37 per cent in 1979.'[8] During the 1970s and the 1980s there had been a substantial change in the composition and affiliations of the working class. The so-called 'new working class' was more likely to own property, less likely to be unionised, and generally lived in the South. In these categories working-class support for Labour substantially declined, making it increasingly difficult for Labour to win any seats in the South outside a handful of constituencies in the Greater London area. The process of embourgeoisement meant that the Conservative party had gained considerable support by 1983. Mrs Thatcher's policies also began to shape the electorate in the Conservative image. The proportion of workers in the private sector rose, while in the public sector it declined; the former were also more likely to be home-owners, perhaps even to have benefited from the Conservative policy of selling council houses.

Above all, Labour was affected by the changing pattern of trade unionism. As Mrs Thatcher's legislation on trade union reform began to take effect, there was a decline in union activism, with occasional exceptions such as the miners' strike. This accelerated a long-term decline in union membership – from over 1 million in 1952 to 300,000 in 1979. This was closely paralleled by a contraction in the membership of the Labour party itself – from 1 million in the 1950s to 700,000 in the early 1970s and 261,000 by 1992.

All these problems occurred alongside a period of remarkable success for the Conservatives. Labour's failure and Conservative strength were relative to each other and each was affected by the other's state of health at a particular stage in the 1980s. It was, therefore, logical to expect Labour's recovery to be associated with Conservative decline. The key question for both parties in the 1980s was: would either ever happen?

THE LONG, HARD ROAD TO RECOVERY

For much of the 1980s Labour's recovery seemed unlikely and the death of Labour was being widely predicted. The election result of 1987 was only slightly less crushing than had been that of 1983 and Labour was still supported by less than a third of the electorate. On the other hand, the Liberal party had been similarly written off during the 1890s, only a few years before it won a landslide in the 1906 general election. Recovery was unlikely to be sudden or continuous, but early signs were detectable even in the midst of the general political gloom. This recovery involved two processes. One was the creation of a more homogeneous party. The other was the adoption of more pragmatic and less ideological policies. But the whole process was more arduous than most had anticipated. At each stage in the recovery there was gathering confidence, which then was dashed by electoral defeat. It would have been surprising if Labour had seriously expected to win in 1983. But 1987 was a disappointment and 1992 even more so. Each effort had to be followed by another and there was a constant need for 'one more heave'.

In retrospect, the earliest sign of recovery can be seen in the contest for the deputy leadership in 1981. Benn only just lost to Healey, but the result was highly significant for the future. Thompson argues that had Benn won, Foot's position as leader would have been impossible. Benn might have succeeded Foot and this would have led to a massive influx of Labour MPs to the SDP. In fact, the number of defections was limited and it could be argued that Healey's victory helped staunch the flow in 1981 and prevent a second flow later. There were also signs that Foot was becoming increasingly concerned about the activities of Militant Tendency: certainly Trotskyism was recognised as a problem well before he retired from the Labour leadership in 1983. A more direct approach was, however, taken by Kinnock. He took full advantage of the disastrous reputation of Derek Hatton in Liverpool City Council to launch an attack on Militant Tendency at the party conference of 1985. He also changed the image of the Labour party, substituting the red rose for the red flag and changing the colour of its campaign material from red to grey. It focused on more identifiable campaigns, such as 'Putting People First'. There were some rumblings about presentation at the expense of policy, but Kinnock argued that the essential priority was to modernise Labour's image and eliminate the widespread fear the electorate seemed to have of the far left. Kinnock's service was therefore to remove the party within the party and soften the image of what remained.

These changes did not, however, have the desired results. The 1987 election still produced a majority of over a hundred for the Conservatives and Labour had to rethink its strategy for the future. The key lesson was that presentation had only been part of the problem; very little had changed in terms of policy. This was now addressed with some urgency.

At the 1987 Party Conference Kinnock introduced a fundamental policy review which went on in 1989 to produce some major changes to Labour's commitments. Labour no longer undertook to pull Britain out of the European Community. It also came to terms with some of the policies introduced by the Conservatives, including the sale of council houses. It withdrew its earlier undertaking to renationalise those enterprises that had been privatised, stating that this was no longer a high priority. Instead, it would use the government's own share to enforce a stricter form of supervision. This could be seen as a growing awareness of the commitment of the electorate to privatisation, through their shares, but also a willingness to take advantage of the public's disillusionment with some of the inefficiency shown by the privatised companies. There was even a commitment to the market system and to controls over public spending. Labour promised not to reverse the basic-rate tax cuts made by the Conservatives and to confine any increase in the higher rate from 40 per cent to 50 per cent. Above all, Kinnock took note of the views of the electorate and abandoned Labour's promise of unilateral nuclear disarmament. Overall, Labour's policy became more flexible. According to Brian Gould: 'The key to the issue is flexibility and pragmatism. The objective is what matters, not the means by which it is achieved.' That 'objective' was to 'secure certain social benefits'; this could be done in other ways than through '100 per cent public ownership'.[9]

Labour's recovery was assisted by the problems of the other political parties. The first boost came from the fracturing of the centre. The Liberal-SDP Alliance had never succeeded in breaking through the electoral barrier. This was partly because the Conservatives recovered from the Alliance threat as a direct result of the emergency of the Falklands War of 1982 (see Chapter 18). Strangely, this did Labour a favour since the Alliance had regarded Labour as its main target. It might be argued that Labour's crushing defeat by the Conservatives in 1983 was preferable to what might have happened without the Falklands diversion: an Alliance government and a Conservative opposition. From the mid 1980s the Alliance began to break up because of a disagreement between David Owen and the Liberals, whom he found too left-wing. The result was a unified centre party in the form of the Liberal Democrats. This, however, could be more easily squeezed by Labour and was seen as the old Liberal Party writ large.

The Conservatives, unintentionally of course, assisted Labour in several ways. Paradoxically, Mrs Thatcher did more than anyone else to force the Labour party to develop a new image. Her success at the polls convinced Kinnock of the need for new methods and policies. At the same time, her own toughness was bound to leave Labour with the image of the 'caring' party. There was another benefit. The retraction of government involvement under the Conservatives meant that Labour had fewer commitments to make to the electorate, while Mrs Thatcher's taming of the trade unions removed the voters' fear about the tyranny of the 'greedy' and 'self-interested' union barons once projected in right-wing newspapers. There is a neat irony here. Labour, in time, came to benefit from the backlash of Conservative measures. By the 1990s perceptions had changed. The controllers of the newly privatised companies were being seen as self-seeking oligarchs, awarding themselves huge pay increases while, as in the case of the gas companies in 1994, planning to cut the wages of their workforce to more 'competitive' levels. The political concept of a 'greedy baronage' was now associated with the Conservatives rather than Labour. Mrs Thatcher once expressed her intention to destroy socialism in Britain and her preference for an opposition which was non-socialist. In fact, she assisted greatly in reviving the Labour party through the very measures that weakened its appendages.

Labour were, therefore, much more confident by 1990. Yet, in 1992, they lost the fourth general election in succession. This was a stunning blow, since Labour had clearly expected to win it. The public opinion polls all predicted a slight majority for Labour; the BBC poll of polls gave Labour a lead of 2 per cent during the election period. In practice the result was a difference of 7.5 per cent of the vote and 21 seats. Labour achieved only 34.4 per cent of the total vote, the lowest achieved by either main opposition party since 1945, apart from Labour's performances in 1983 and 1987. The main reason is probably that the Conservative party, with the insight which occasionally strikes it, had come to identify Mrs Thatcher as a potential electoral liability. Its reaction was ruthless but effective. Mrs Thatcher was replaced by a more moderate prime minister who had the benefit of a 'honeymoon period'. This was enhanced by John Major's leadership during the Gulf War in 1991. Labour would much rather have fought Mrs Thatcher than Major and failed to adjust its election campaign properly to their new adversary. They could not believe that the electorate were willing to give the Conservatives – but not Mrs Thatcher – another chance.

In the short term this was clearly a disappointment for Labour. In the longer term, however, it worked to Labour's benefit. It allowed the Conservatives time to decay as a government. Almost immediately after the 1992 election there was an inexorable feeling of decline, which was accelerated by a series of mishaps faced by the Cabinet (see Chapter 15). Major was unable to provide the same sort of leadership in the face of adversity which had been given by Mrs Thatcher in such circumstances. Labour's recovery was, by contrast, remarkably rapid. The leadership changed again as John Smith succeeded Neil Kinnock, who stepped down after Labour's defeat. Smith appeared to possess the gravitas that Kinnock lacked and he was widely tipped to be Britain's next Prime Minister. This was, however, prevented by his sudden death in 1994. Labour now took the opportunity of 'skipping a generation' and electing Tony Blair. Like Kinnock, Blair was a former left-winger who had come to the conclusion that pragmatism had to prevail if Labour was ever to have another chance of power.

His focus was on the removal of Article IV from Labour's constitution, which pressed for the 'common ownership of the means of production, distribution and exchange, and the best obtainable system of popular administration and control.' It was a campaign which Blair had to win. This he did. According to one authority,

> The campaign was a brilliantly successful gamble, marking out Tony Blair as a politician of depth, courage and unusual elan.

... In retrospect we can see the reform of Clause Four as one of the most brilliantly successful political campaigns since the war; perfectly planned and perfectly executed.[10]

It also enabled Blair to show his toughness as a politician and reassured the electorate that Labour had really pulled itself well away from the left. This undoubtedly helped to increase middle-class support, most of which had previously leaked away to the Conservatives. An amended version of Article IV was accepted by a Special Conference on 29 April 1995. It stated:

The Labour Party is a democratic socialist party. It believes that by the strength of our common endeavour, we achieve more than we achieve alone so as to create for each of us the means to realise our true potential and for all of us a community in which power, wealth and opportunity are in the hands of the many not the few, where the rights we enjoy reflect the duties we owe, and where we live together freely, in a spirit of solidarity, tolerance and respect.[11]

When this went to a vote by the whole party in April the constituencies were 90 per cent in favour and the unions 57 per cent.

This was a final vindication of what Gaitskell had tried to do in 1961. Gaitskell's failure meant that the whole process had to be undertaken again. As B. Bivati points out:

Without challenging the destination of the Labour movement he had little hope of revitalising its image. . . . The possibility would always exist for the antediluvian opponents of change to claim that they represented the real soul of the Party. The sorry history of the Alternative Economic Strategy and the Bennite surge of the 1970s, culminating in the 1983 manifesto, illustrates the degree to which Gaitskell was right.[12]

By 1995 comparisons were springing to mind, not so much with Gaitskell as with the youthful and modernising image of Harold Wilson, who had steered Labour through the 1964 election.

THE CRISIS RESOLVED?

The long-term prospects of Labour depend very much on the overall shape of British party politics between 1995 and 2005. There has been much controversy over this, with three main scenarios emerging. The first is a Labour victory in the first general election after that of 1992, followed by an era of revived Labourism. The second is a Labour victory, but giving way to a Conservative recovery in the subsequent election and a further period of Conservative domination. The third is a series of continuing and uninterrupted Conservative victories and Labour setbacks. The key question is: has Labour's long haul to recovery been sufficient to ensure the first of these possibilities rather than the second or third?

Some observers maintain that the British political system had become by the 1990s a one-party state. There seems to be strong support for arguing that there has been, from 1886, a long-term advantage for the Conservatives against which any other party can do no more than exert a temporary challenge. And even that was becoming more and more difficult. For one thing, the Conservatives benefited increasingly from the predominance of the vote in the south; 55 per cent of the seats of the United Kingdom are in the south, and the Conservatives won 74 per cent of these in 1992. Labour's natural constituency remained in pockets in the North and in Scotland. It was also in the 18–21 age-group, which was steadily declining as a proportion of the population, and the working class, which had contracted from 52 per cent in 1974 to 39 per cent in 1994 and a projected 33 per cent by 1996.[13] A more fundamental argument for Labour's disadvantage is put by W. Thompson. The failure of Labour in the 1992 general election was an indication of the longer-term decline of Labourism associated with the contraction of industry and of trade unionism. Further damage was inflicted by the policies of Mrs Thatcher's government. Labour's own contribution was an inability to move away from an authoritarian structure or from its close relationship with 'state structures': this has meant that Labour has been unable to accommodate effectively the various components of the left. Thompson also maintained that Labour was returning to the Liberalism of the centre:

> The Labour Party was increasingly taking on the features of what the Liberal Party might have become had it survived as a contender for office beyond 1918; the labour movement's roots in liberal politics were increasingly asserting themselves, more than a century after its beginnings.[14]

This view might, however, be too restricted. Labour was not so much retracing its own historical roots as falling into line with developments in the rest of Europe and coming to terms with the impact of Thatcherism at home. But the question remained whether Labour had done enough to offset the natural advantages of the right.

There is, however, another side. The 'decline' of Labour can be seen as a misnomer. The term 'crisis' is a better one: strictly speaking, this is analogous with a severe illness, which is followed either by death or by recovery. The more pessimistic analysts have not allowed for the extent of Labour's recovery; other observers argue that Labour could win an election with 'one last heave' to add to the changes in the vote already made in 1987 and 1992, when they had increased their share of the vote by 3.3 per cent each time, and by 20 and 42 seats respectively. There is also an increasing number of people who have not benefited materially from the long period of Conservative rule (especially social groups C2 and DE) and evidence of the return of significant support to Labour from the traditional Conservative AB and C1 sectors. There are also more promising signs for the Labour party, as the election of Blair to the leadership added some 50,000 new members in 1994. In addition, Labour had, by the end of 1994, amassed a campaign fund of £9 million, considerably more than that available to the Conservative party (see Chapter 5).

Labour has also been assisted by a slide towards crisis by the Conservatives themselves. Major's government after the 1992 general election showed all the signs of one which had lost its way. Its reputation for sound economic management was affected by the deepest recession since the 1930s. It ran into trouble over proposals by British Coal to close thirty-one pits. There have been numerous embarrassments to the government over Conservative MPs' involvement in the 'sleaze factor'. Back-bench rebellions occurred in 1994 over increasing Britain's contribution to the European Union and over the proposal to increase the rate of VAT on fuel. In any case, the Conservative hold on the electorate is, according to M. Moran, a tenuous one:

> What is most remarkable about the years of Conservative domination is the slender base on which the impressive structure rests. Control of the House of Commons has depended less on success in capturing electors than on the workings of the electoral system and the divisions in the left of British politics. The ideological inheritance of Thatcherism is not wanted by the population at large. We seem, in other words, to be looking at something more limited and transient than the hegemony enjoyed by movements like social democracy in Scandinavia.[15]

Does the study of other periods of British politics help to anticipate future trends? Can we detect any precedents or underlying dynamics? We cannot, of course, expect past trends to repeat themselves precisely.

But we can use them as broad indicators of what might happen. There are two examples.

The first is the broad pattern of party politics over the past two centuries. There are several precedents in British political history for runs of party success. The existence of a two-party system does not necessarily mean governments alternating between the parties. Alternation tends to happen as an exception, not as a rule. It occurs mainly during times of consensus, as, for example, between Gladstone and Disraeli or between MacDonald and Baldwin. There have been numerous examples of the opposition despairing of ever getting back into power again: the Conservatives after 1830 and again after 1846, the Liberals in the 1890s, and Labour in the 1930s – in each case the party's demise was predicted. Each crisis was, however, followed by recovery and electoral victory: the Conservatives in 1841 and 1874, the Liberals in 1906, and Labour in 1945. These successes followed a change in the party's image after a period of confusion, internal wrangling and strong performances by the governing party.

A more specific historical precedent can be drawn upon. In 1830 the Whigs, rejuvenated by the leadership of Earl Grey, defeated a Tory party which had recently experienced a major crisis over Ireland. Two years later, in 1832, they crushed the Tories in a Whig landslide. So far, there are similarities with the Conservative victories over Labour in 1979 and 1983. In 1835 the Whigs won again, this time by the narrower margin of 112 seats. A comparison can be drawn with the Conservative victory by 102 seats in 1987. In the meantime, the Tory leader, Robert Peel, had endeavoured to offset the paralysing influence of the Tory right and to give his party a more modern image – a possible parallel with the endeavours of Neil Kinnock against Labour's left? The next election, in 1837, was a close contest in which the Whig majority was down to 32 seats; the 1992 election resulted in a Conservative majority of 21. The trend was completed when, in 1841, Peel's reformed party at last defeated the Whigs by 78 seats. History does not, of course, repeat itself precisely, and a convincing win by Labour in 1996 or 1997 is by no means inevitable. But, given that the British electoral system has never yet allowed an opposition party to remain at an ebb indefinitely, it does seem likely.

17

FOREIGN POLICY AND DEFENCE 1945–70

In the decades following the Second World War, Britain was forced to adapt to a new role in the world. F.S. Northedge maintains that 'the most striking fact is, of course, the decline of British power continuously over that period.'[1] This included a contraction of Britain's military and naval strength, a retreat from her imperial commitments and, in the longer term, a move towards integration within Europe.

The term 'continuously' is perhaps misleading. It took some time for British governments to come to terms with a changing role and the administrations of Attlee and Churchill had an optimistic – even over-ambitious – view of British power. They viewed Britain and the United States as equal partners in leading the defence of the free world against the threat of Soviet aggression. During the 1940s, at least, Britain actually took the initiative on several occasions to spur the United States into action. As the first part of this chapter shows, Britain still had aspirations to be one of the superpowers. By the beginning of the 1950s consciousness of British decline was beginning to dawn and plans were being considered for changes in Britain's defence and over-seas commitments. The Suez Crisis, dealt with in the second part, greatly accelerated this trend. The adjustment became more conscious and deliberate between 1957 and 1970, and, as the third part shows, decline had become self-acknowledged. It was certainly apparent to analysts at the time; according to J. Frankel: 'Britain, a member of the victorious Big Three at the end of the second world war, has in little more than twenty-five years accepted the status of a major second-rank power and has decided . . . to seek entry into a regional grouping.'[2]

1945–56: BRITAIN AS A WORLD POWER?

In the period immediately after the Second World War, politicians of both major parties were confident about Britain's continuing role as a great power. Churchill, then leader of the opposition, said at Fulton, Missouri, in 1946:

> Let no man underrate the abiding power of the British Empire and Commonwealth . . . do not suppose that we shall not come through these dark years of privation as we have come through the glorious years of agony or that half a century from now you will not see 70,000,000 or 80,000,000 Britons spread around the world and united in defence of our tradition, our way of life and of the world cause we and you espouse.[3]

On the surface there seemed to be good reasons for holding this view. Britain was one of the victors of 1945 and, as late as 1951, still had conscription and a standing army of 827,000. It was still a major economic power, the centre of a revived sterling area and equal in its manufacturing output to France and Germany combined. What was not yet recognised was the long-term damage inflicted by the war. Britain had suffered devastating financial losses, even if the physical damage had been less severe than in Germany and Japan. These would soon become apparent, as would the lack of real cohesion in the British Empire. Churchill's illusions were more appropriate to the period before the First World War than that after the Second: the Fulton speech was reminiscent of the days of Joseph Chamberlain.

Given that there was a gap between the perception and reality of British power, what were the actual intentions of the governments of the period? Two contrasting interpretations have been put forward. The traditional view is that Britain followed a moderate course immediately after the Second World War, seeking to co-operate with wartime allies in effecting reconstruction. A. Bullock, for example, maintains that for over a year after 1945 the British government tried to create an agreement with both the United States and the Soviet Union. V. Rothwell has also argued this: that between 1945 and 1947 'Britain still had hopes of salvaging something from the wartime Anglo-Soviet alliance.'[4] Unfortunately, the Soviet Union proved so opposed to this that Britain had no option but to seek a special relationship with the United States and a new multilateral format within NATO. There is, however, a revisionist interpretation. From the start, Britain sought an equal partnership with the United States. As part of a process of realigning her policy, Britain contributed directly to the growth of the

Cold War in Europe. According to J. Kent and others, Britain aimed to be a third force, one of the three power blocs, but allied with the United States against the Soviet Union. Within this third force would also be Europe and the Empire, but under British leadership.[5]

The latter approach can be used to reverse the original argument that Britain followed the lead of the United States in developing a policy to contain the Soviet Union. Instead, it can be shown that Britain actually forced the pace and that the United States was sometimes an unwilling partner. After two decades in isolation in the 1920s and 1930s, the United States was involved in a delicate diplomatic area with little recent experience. Between 1945 and 1947 Britain forced the confrontation against the Soviet Union much more firmly than did the United States, just as Churchill had already taken a tougher line than Roosevelt at Yalta. Britain also had a strong historic distrust of Russia which went far back into the nineteenth century. Her antipathy to the Soviet Union was not just ideological – it was the residue of a great-power antagonism. In 1945, Bevin attached some importance to the view of his private secretary that 'the main objective of the Russians is access to and a base in the Mediterranean.'[6] The fact that Britain was still considered a Mediterranean power is significant. This was an area in which the United States had not yet developed a vital interest and British officials were the first to warn of Soviet expansionism in the region.

There were plenty of other examples of Britain seizing the initiative and pulling the United States along with it. Churchill's Fulton speech provided, in the 'Iron Curtain', the catch-phrase of the Cold War. More specifically, Britain reacted more firmly than the United States to the failure of the Soviet Union to pull out of Iran on time in 1946. Britain also forced the United States to recognise the threat posed by the Communists to the future of Greece. In 1947, the Chancellor of the Exchequer, Hugh Dalton, warned that it would have to end its aid to the Royalists in the Greek Civil War. This provided the strongest of hints that the United States had to pick up a responsibility previously held by Britain. The result was the announcement of the Truman Doctrine and of Marshall Aid, referred to by Bevin as 'the birth of the Western bloc.'[7] It was previously assumed that these initiatives grew out of American perceptions of British economic problems by 1947. These may well have accelerated the decision, but more important was the persistent influence of the British government and of the leader of the opposition in keeping an American focus on European issues and preventing the possibility of another American retreat into splendid isolation. According to D. Reynolds, therefore, Britain made 'important contributions in firming up the Marshall Plan and in creating the Atlantic Alliance'.[8]

Meanwhile, Britain had taken the lead over the future of the German zones. The Soviet Union had removed much of the infrastructure from the eastern zone and refused to co-operate with the west on future trade or production levels within Germany as a whole. The British zone was particularly hard-pressed, since it had to provide most of the food for the western part of Germany, including the American and French zones. Bevin accepted advice from Foreign Office officials that all three western zones should be consolidated and provided with a single currency. There was a slight delay in implementing this while US policy came into line. Although the creation of a joint economic zone was a mutual decision, it is now evident that Britain had forced the pace of the decision.[9] The same happened over the Berlin blockade of 1948. It was Bevin who first developed the airlift as the main option and who articulated the western powers' determination not to be forced out of Berlin by Stalin's manoeuvres. Finally, the British government took the initiative in developing the Brussels Pact between Britain, France, Belgium, the Netherlands and Luxembourg. This was extended to the North Atlantic Treaty Organisation (NATO) in 1949 – in effect, an American superstructure upon a British foundation. Sir Nicholas Henderson maintained that 'if one person was responsible at the time for canalizing the mood of Western Europe into the idea of the Treaty, this was Ernest Bevin'.[10]

By the beginning of the 1950s, however, there were obvious signs that Britain was severely overstretching herself. The major problem was, of course, economic: here there were three interconnected influences. One was the impact of the Second World War, which had destroyed Britain's overseas investments and commercial links – all of which were having to be rebuilt. At the same time, the British government was deliberately undertaking, with the foundation of the welfare state, the most expensive internal changes ever attempted. Then, in 1951, just as it appeared that there might be an upturn in economic performance, Britain became involved in the Korean War. Although the brunt of this was borne by the United States, Britain was badly affected by the additional increase in military expenditure and by the sudden rise in world prices of essential raw materials. By the time the war ended in 1953 the Conservatives had been back in office for almost two years and, although Churchill was still endeavouring to maintain Britain's world role, there was a noticeable dilution of his rhetoric on the subject.

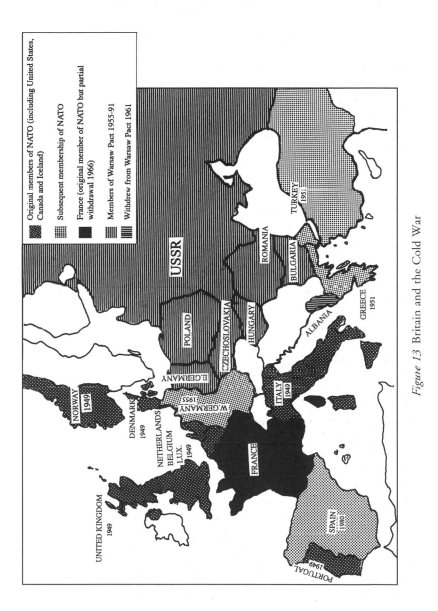

Figure 13 Britain and the Cold War

Another obstacle to Britain's continuing role as a superpower was that this was not accepted by the United States on Britain's terms. Put simply, Britain wanted equal partnership with the United States in terms of making policies affecting the world at large but, at the same time, a special relationship in which the United States would take special note of British interests and also share with Britain the latest developments in nuclear technology. Neither Truman nor Eisenhower showed much enthusiasm for this rather one-sided vision. The latter wrote in his diary in 1953 that Churchill

> has fixed in his mind a certain international relationship he is trying to establish. . . . This is that Britain and the British Commonwealth are not to be treated as other nations would be treated by the United States in complicated foreign problems. On the contrary, he most earnestly hopes and intends that those countries shall enjoy a relationship which will recognize the special place of partnership they occupied with us during World War II.[11]

He went on to say that 'In the present international complexities, any hope of establishing such a relationship is completely fatuous.'[12] As long as Britain made the case for equal partnership there was bound to be the possibility of clashing interests. In particular, the United States was suspicious of Britain's aspirations to retain an imperial role and about her involvement in the Middle East. As far as Eisenhower was concerned, Britain had to recognise that any special relationship could carry only inequality. This new scenario is precisely what emerged from the chaos of 1956.

THE SUEZ CRISIS (1956) AND ITS IMPACT

By far the most spectacular and important single incident involving British foreign policy in the 1950s was the Suez Crisis. There has always been considerable controversy about its handling and effects.

Britain had a longstanding interest in the Middle East which both Churchill and Eden were determined to maintain, even if this was not entirely consistent with her decline as a major power. Early involvement in the region was not unsuccessful. With American help, the British government engineered the fall of the radical regime of Mussadiq in Iran in 1953, the result of which was a series of concessions to the Anglo-Iranian Oil Company (British Petroleum). In a sense, however, this was an unfortunate precedent. Two lessons were drawn from it:

that Britain could bring about the collapse of governments hostile to her interests, and that the United States would back her to the hilt. Both assumptions were to prove disastrously wrong.

By 1956 a new threat had emerged, this time in Egypt. Colonel Gamal Nasser, who seized power in 1954, dreamed of setting up a pan-Arabist state. For this reason, he was regarded at the outset with suspicion by Britain and the United States and as a possible threat to the Baghdad Pact, formed in 1955 between Britain, Turkey, Iraq, Iran and Pakistan. At first Britain and the United States had jointly proposed to finance the construction of the Aswan Dam in Upper Egypt. Eden, however, was convinced that Nasser's regime was inherently expansionist and that he would seek to establish Egyptian control over the whole of the Middle East; in fact, Eden went so far as to equate Nasser with Mussolini. Eden also assumed that Nasser was moving inexorably towards Communism, especially when, in July 1956, Nasser recognised Communist China. Consequently the Anglo-American loan was withdrawn on 19 July. Nasser's immediate response was to nationalise the Suez Canal Company. This comprised shares held mainly by the British government and by financiers in both Britain and France.

Eden immediately applied an anti-appeasement policy, seeking to avoid any repetition of the sort of concessions made by the British government in the 1930s. He therefore formed the Egypt Committee from key members of his cabinet and from the chiefs of staff of the armed forces. Operating in almost total secrecy, this aimed at re-establishing British control over the Suez Canal and at bringing about the fall of Nasser himself. Britain and France drew up plans for co-ordinated landings of troops at Port Said and, in the meantime, signed with Israel the Protocol of Sèvres. The terms were that the Israelis would advance on the Canal through Sinai. Britain and France would then issue an ultimatum for a ceasefire, which Israel would obey. This would be followed by Anglo-French landings to enforce the armistice and, at the same time, secure the Canal.

This enterprise, which smacked of the ruthlessness of the secret diplomacy of the late nineteenth century, initially went according to plan. The Israelis attacked Egypt at the end of October 1956. When, as expected, Nasser rejected the Anglo-French ultimatum, British aircraft suddenly destroyed much of the Egyptian airforce on the airfields. This was followed by the landing of 45,000 men. At this stage, however, things went badly wrong. Strong opposition was expressed by the United States and very little support came from the Empire and Commonwealth. Eden eventually gave way to a United Nations resolution calling for complete withdrawal from the Canal zone. This was done early in December and the British part in the intervention was widely recognised as a fiasco.

There were several practical reasons for the failure of Eden's policy. The first was the delay caused by Britain's need to be certain of being able to overcome the Egyptian defences. These included an airforce of 270 aircraft (a substantial proportion of which were Soviet Mig-15s), 100,000 ground troops, and modern equipment and arms supplied by Czechoslovakia. Britain's resources in the area did not match up to these.[13] This meant that there had to be a surprise attack, which involved Eden in duplicitous diplomacy with France and Israel. Eden faced a major problem over preparing a landing force and a staging-post from which it could embark, a process which involved several changes of plan extending over a period of at least six weeks. In the earlier crises affecting her overseas and imperial interests, Britain had been able to react quickly. But since 1949 Britain had had extra commitments in Europe in NATO which greatly weakened her capacity for swift improvisation. Hence Britain's response was slow, even though the situation was urgent.

This gave the opposition to Eden's action a chance to mobilise. It was particularly strong in the United States. President Eisenhower was in the middle of an election campaign and had no wish to see an American involvement in a Middle East disaster. He therefore exerted financial pressure on Britain, refusing to provide any backing for sterling unless British troops were withdrawn. Such threats precipitated opposition within Eden's cabinet. Harold Macmillan, then Chancellor of the Exchequer, realised what damage the United States could do to the British economy. He therefore polarised a growing sentiment within the government which wanted to bring the enterprise to an end. This came sooner rather than later because of the deteriorating relations with France. The latter had, throughout the crisis, pushed for speedier action while, at the same time, expecting Britain to carry the brunt of the campaign. The break came in November, when Britain ignored France's opposition to the United Nations' resolution and announced that British troops would be pulled out.

Was there any justification for Eden's policy over Suez in 1956? Given his desire for swift action to secure British interests, there is a strong underlying logic to what he did. The initial problem was the view of the chiefs of staff that such an attack would take some six weeks to prepare. If he still wished to go ahead, what option did he have but secret diplomacy with Israel and France? It was not as if Nasser had made any reasonable proposals to prevent the need for intervention. Throughout the crisis he flatly refused to consider an international body to run the canal, as suggested by the United States in September, even though this would not reverse Egyptian sovereignty. It would seem, therefore, that the only alternative to immediate force, or secret diplomacy, was capitulation to Nasser's demands.

There were also broader issues. Eden later argued in his own defence that he had prevented the expansion of Nasser's influence in a way which had not even been attempted against Mussolini in the 1930s. It is certainly possible that Nasser might otherwise have become an Arab hegemonist. He subsequently merged Egypt and Syria in a United Arab Republic, but was denied the opportunity of creating a much wider state including Libya, Iraq, Lebanon and Jordan. British action also forced the United States into accepting a greater degree of responsibility in the area and recognising the existence of the Soviet threat there. According to Eden: 'The extent of Soviet penetration of the Middle East has been exposed, with the result that the United Sates at last seems to be taking the action for which we pleaded in vain throughout 1956.'[14] The result was the Eisenhower Doctrine, which emphasised the need of forces and resources in the Middle East 'to secure and protect the territorial integrity and political independence of such nations, requesting such aid, against armed aggression from any nation controlled by International Communism.'[15]

It is, however, easier to criticise Eden than to defend him. He was the classic case of the politician helping to make history but failing to draw appropriate lessons from it. During the 1930s Eden had strongly opposed the policy of appeasement pursued by Chamberlain in his diplomacy with Hitler. But that particular memory was entirely inappropriate in dealing with Nasser's nationalisation of the Suez Canal. Indeed, most subsequent references to historical precedent have come to polarise around Chamberlain and Eden. The former has become synonymous with under-reaction and caution, the latter with over-reaction and recklessness. If the analogy with the 1930s were pressed further, Eden might actually be seen to have repeated mistakes rather than to have avoided them. Mussolini had been antagonised by the ineffectual application of sanctions so that he moved away from the western camp towards Hitler. Nasser was similarly infuriated by Eden's policy so that he realigned Egypt and much of the Arab world with the Soviet Union.

Eden was also thoroughly secretive about his handling of the crisis, implying that he was ashamed of his own role. It is now known that he ordered the destruction of any documentation relating to the Sèvres Protocol, even though there were copies available in French. He also denied to Parliament that there was any secret deal with Israel and France and said that he knew nothing in his memoirs. Suez has therefore become synonymous with a blunder underscored by deceit: the last thing that could ever be claimed of Eden was that he remained proud in error. He could not even claim that time would prove him right; in at least one respect, future developments made his intervention pointless. Eden was acting partly to prevent large increases in the cost of oil which would result from the use of the Cape route rather than the Suez Canal. These, in fact, did not occur. Rising oil costs were in the future due more to political than to geographical factors – not least the powerful resentment against the West within the Arab world. Transport costs, meanwhile, had been greatly reduced by the use of a new generation of supertankers, which were too large to use the Suez Canal: in the long term, therefore, it made little difference whether oil was carried through the Suez Canal or via the Cape of Good Hope.

What was the significance of the Suez Crisis for the future? There has been a particular conflict of opinion on this issue. The traditional interpretation is that the Suez Crisis was of vital importance in its own right. It lost the West the moral high ground in the Cold War by diverting attention from the bankruptcy of Soviet policy in Hungary. Instead, the Soviet Union was able to cancel out its oppression in Hungary by seeming to champion the Egyptians by leading an offensive in the United Nations against Eden's policy and by threatening a missile attack on the West in defence of Egypt. The Suez Crisis also accelerated the end of British colonialism in Africa (see Chapter 20) and helped prepare British public opinion for this. According to D.R. Devereux, 'Suez shattered the exaggerated public perceptions of Britain's role as a great imperial power.'[16] More seriously, the British failure over Suez completely discredited the West with the Arab world and allowed a long period of Soviet connection with the Middle East. In 1958 the pro-western regime in Iraq was overthrown and by the end of the 1960s Iraq, Syria and Libya were all looking to Moscow for their weapons. The damage to the West was not undone until the diplomacy of the US Secretary of State, Henry Kissinger, in the late 1970s.

Finally, as a direct result of Suez, Britain was forced to choose a special relationship with the United States at the expense of the earlier rapprochement with France. The result was that France and Britain moved ahead on different paths. France became profoundly suspicious of both Britain and the United States, to the extent of vetoing Britain's applications to join the European Economic Community and partially withdrawing from NATO. Overall, Britain was tipped into irreversible decline as a major power, dependent on the United States and trying, against French resistance, to seek revival in Europe.

A more recent view is that Suez was not a cause of British decline. Rather, it was a symptom of what was already happening and it accelerated changes already being considered in Britain's role in the world.[17] It is true that it confirmed the inadequacy of Britain's military preparedness in terms of equipment and assault ships. But such short-comings had already been shown during the Korean War. Suez therefore showed the need not for a sudden change but rather for a thorough review of military priorities; this would eventually have happened without Suez – although there would have been less urgency behind it. Similarly, the Suez Crisis did not inevitably lead to Britain developing a special relationship with the United States. Again, this was very much on the cards before 1956. The crisis did, however, speed up the process. In the first place, it meant the early replacement of the traditionalist Eden by the more progressive and pro-American Macmillan who had a real need to rebuild relations with the United States. He also had to make some early decisions about the nuclear component of Britain's defences to remedy the deficiencies exposed by Suez; these, however, required American co-operation. As for the decline of Britain's imperial role, this had already been accepted by 1956. The Indian sub-continent had been given its independence nine years earlier and plans were already being drawn up for similar concessions to the Gold Coast and other African states. Suez did not initiate this trend. Yet the speed with which Britain subsequently decolonised Africa – during a period of Conservative rule – must have been affected by the growth of anti-colonialism as a world-wide force; this, in turn, was accentuated by the events of 1956.

Serious as it was, the impact of the Suez Crisis on western interests in the Middle East should not be exaggerated. British influence in the region did not suddenly collapse. According to Selwyn Lloyd, 'in 1964 we were certainly as powerful in the Persian Gulf as we had been in 1956.'[18] The eventual withdrawal of British troops and presence east of Suez was due less to the Suez Crisis itself than to the desire of the Labour governments after 1964 to make domestic savings at the expense of defence expenditure. The loss of Britain's control over the Suez Canal provided the justification rather than the cause for this decision. Nor can Eden's policy in 1956 be blamed entirely for subsequent American difficulties with the Arab world. Although Suez did lead to a period of disenchantment with the West, a more specific irritant for the Arab states was the continuing support of the United States for their enemy, Israel. This was a policy which was influenced by internal pressures within the United States and not by any residual effects of 1956.

Thus the Suez Crisis did not impose a sudden change in the course of British foreign policy; it cannot, therefore, be seen as a revolution. It did, however, accelerate a trend which was being tentatively adopted; in this sense it can be called a watershed.

BRITAIN'S CHANGING WORLD ROLE 1956–70

The immediate impetus behind these changes was a new prime minister, appointed in 1957. He was confronted by a number of urgent problems which forced him to make some major decisions about Britain's long-term role in the world. One was the economic crisis which had been exacerbated by the expenditure on the invasion and the US refusal to hold up sterling. Another was relations with the United States and with the Commonwealth. A third was the need to modernise Britain's defences. Given the other two problems, modernisation would have to mean reduction and this would be justified in the name of rationalisation. Macmillan therefore wasted no time in instructing Duncan Sandys, at the Ministry of Defence, to prepare a new defence policy for Britain. The White Paper that followed had major implications for the future of Britain's defences in two areas: conventional and nuclear.

The starting point of the review was the constraints of what Britain could afford financially: 'in the true interests of defence . . . the claims of military expenditure should be considered in conjunction with the need to maintain the country's financial and economic strength'.[19] This meant an inevitable reorganisation with the emphasis on streamlining to enhance efficiency along with cutting to reduce costs. Over the next few years, therefore, substantial changes occurred in Britain's conventional defences. National service was ended and Britain's armed forces were reduced by nearly half to 375,000. Troops were withdrawn from a number of overseas posts, but three aircraft carriers were stationed in the Indian Ocean. To some extent this was the culmination of earlier thinking, but the Suez Crisis forced Britain to develop a more remote naval role using carriers, as several Arab states now refused to allow her permission to overfly their territory. Such a policy meant that drastic cuts had to be made elsewhere.

The most effective way of making such savings without seriously compromising Britain's defence was to develop the nuclear option. This was an important part of the Sandys White Paper, which recommended that Britain should have a 'nuclear deterrent power of her own'.[20] Sandys also argued that the element of deterrence was most likely to act as an indefinite guarantee against war. The conventional forces of Britain should be reduced, modernised and more fully integrated within NATO.

This course, more than anything else, confirmed Britain's decline from the status of the world's third major power. The nuclear option was intended to provide Britain with a defensive cover which was relatively inexpensive. It was not, however, an effective basis for the revival of an assertive foreign policy: nuclear weapons are so awesome that what they gain as a deterrent they lose as an aid to diplomacy. Options for worldwide intervention required a large conventional force and Britain's reduction of this indicated that her worldwide role was contracting rapidly. This was in complete contrast to the period between 1945 and 1951, when Britain was seeking to become a nuclear power to confirm the importance of her world role.

The focus on nuclear weapons had another important effect: it confirmed that Britain had to have a 'special relationship' with the United States. This was because Britain was incapable of bearing the expense of conducting the research necessary to enable her to become an entirely independent nuclear power. The assistance of the United States was therefore essential. This was agreed in 1957, leading to full nuclear collaboration for the first time since the connection had been broken in 1947. Macmillan undertook to allow the stationing of sixty US intermediate ballistic missiles in Britain, in exchange for which Britain was provided with access to the latest nuclear technology by the Atomic Energy Act and the Anglo-American Agreement for Co-operation on the Uses of Atomic Energy for Mutual Defence Purposes, both in 1958. From 1960, Britain was able to procure the latest weapons from the United States, including Polaris: since these were missiles which could be launched from submarines, they were the ultimate deterrent.

We have seen that the nuclear option was a formal acknowledgement that Britain's foreign policy had contracted to a primarily defensive role. This had certain advantages to the United States. There would be less scope for Britain to exercise a foreign policy which might, as in 1956, conflict with American interests. Britain as a nuclear power but as a smaller conventional power therefore fitted neatly with the American perception of its dominant role while, at the same time, ensuring that

Britain undertook ultimate responsibility for its own defence. For this reason, both Eisenhower and Kennedy worked to maintain the 'special relationship' to which Macmillan and the Sandys White Paper had attached so much importance. At the peak of the Cold War Britain was consulted more than any other power and Kennedy took care to seek Macmillan's views on the 1962 Cuba Missiles Crisis. On the other hand, Macmillan was never able to claim equality with Kennedy in any decision-making, as Churchill, Attlee and Bevin had with Truman after 1945.

How did Labour's victory in the general election in 1964 affect the new course of British foreign policy? The Conservative party manifesto argued that the strongly unilateralist trend within the Labour party would eventually prevail upon a Labour government to abandon Britain's nuclear deterrent and that no provision would be made to increase expenditure on conventional weapons proportionately. In fact, the Labour leadership was not influenced by the anti-nuclear camp. Both Gaitskell and his successor, Wilson, maintained a consensus with the Conservatives about the need to keep the nuclear deterrent. Wilson's government also wanted to maintain the Conservative policy of maintaining at least some British presence overseas for as long as possible. The White Paper of 1965 actually considered the possibility of extending Britain's presence east of Suez, especially in Hong Kong, the Persian Gulf and Malaysia. Indeed, Denis Healey, Labour's Defence Secretary from 1964 to 1970, was initially more in favour of this than of boosting Britain's commitment to Europe.

But it soon became evident that Britain could not afford to meet these continuing commitments and that further reductions would be necessary. Wilson and Healey saw these as the completion of the process started by the 1957 White Paper. Three factors now led to an acceleration of Britain's retreat from a world role.

One was the end of the British Empire in Africa, which reduced the need for a naval role in the Indian Ocean. The newly independent Commonwealth nations were not particularly closely connected to Britain and did not need defending. The one possibility for British military intervention was against Ian Smith's regime, which illegally declared Rhodesia independent in 1965. But the British government expressly renounced the use of force as an option and therefore negated any need for its Indian Ocean facilities.

The second reason for the contraction of Britain's world role was her search for a regional alternative – in Europe. Wilson re-applied for British entry into the European Economic Community in 1967.

Although this was vetoed by De Gaulle, who feared that British membership would bring with it the growing influence of the United States in European affairs, Wilson was following the course of Macmillan in a fundamental re-orientation of British priorities that did not require large forces overseas.

The third, and most pressing, reason was the recurrence of economic crisis during the late 1960s (see Chapter 16). This meant that foreign policy had to be subordinated to urgent domestic needs. Since there was no question of abandoning the nuclear commitment, the only course which now made sense was to withdraw Britain's forces from where they were not immediately needed. The 1967 White Paper therefore argued for further reductions in Britain's conventional forces, while in 1968 Wilson announced that all British forces east of Suez would be pulled back except for small units in Hong Kong, Belize, the Falklands and Gibraltar.

Although this was greeted with horror by the Conservative opposition, it was entirely within the logic of the long-term trend since 1945. The argument of this chapter has been that, after an initial attempt to perpetuate it, Britain gradually reduced her role as a world power. The watershed was the Suez Crisis of 1956, which accelerated changes already under consideration. The rationalisation of Britain's defence was carried out by the Sandys White Paper (1957) which set the pattern for reducing Britain's conventional role while developing a nuclear deterrent. This switched the emphasis from an active foreign policy to a convincing defensive one. The whole process meant the contraction from a world to a regional power. How would Britain now adjust to this transition?

18

FOREIGN POLICY AND DEFENCE 1970–95

British foreign policy between 1970 and 1995 experienced a large number of twists and turns, most of them unexpected or unintentional. During the 1970s the Conservatives aimed to expand Britain's conventional defences, only to be forced into further contracting them. Labour, normally committed to defence cuts, went in the opposite direction until 1979. The first part of this chapter seeks to explain this anomaly.

The second part deals with the 1980s. These opened with a Conservative decision to upgrade Britain's nuclear defences, which was strongly contested by Labour. Rationalising defence expenditure meant, however, another reduction in the conventional sector, with the navy taking the brunt. This probably precipitated the Falklands War of 1982. Although the conflict was unwelcome and unexpected, victory revived the fortunes of a flagging government and enabled Mrs Thatcher to project a much stronger image on the world scene. She was assisted in this by a close relationship with the United States and a shared antipathy towards Communism.

By the time of her resignation in 1990, however, the revival of British prestige had worn off. Her successor, John Major, was confronted with the need to make further defence cuts and with the difficulty of coming to terms with the end of the Cold War. By 1995 the way ahead was thoroughly obscured by uncertainties over the former Soviet bloc, the European Union and the United States. This is the theme of the third part.

THE 1970S

There is a paradox about British foreign and defence policies in the 1970s. The Conservatives came to power in 1970 committed to expanding Britain's role; instead, they further contracted it. Labour undertook in 1974 to cut defence expenditure; they increased it. In each case, natural preferences had to be subordinated to extraneous factors, both domestic and foreign.

During the late 1960s the Conservatives had strongly criticised Labour's policy of withdrawing from east of Suez. It therefore seemed likely that the next Conservative government would reverse some of Labour's measures or, at least, slow down the contraction of Britain's role overseas. After winning the 1970 general election, Heath certainly appeared to move in this direction. There was a sudden increase in commitments as, along with Australia and New Zealand, Britain undertook to contribute to the defence of Malaysia and Singapore. At the same time, the British government agreed jointly with the United States to build a naval base in the Indian Ocean at Diego Garcia and also revived Britain's lease of the Simonstown naval base, which had been cancelled by Labour.

Initial policies were, however, misleading. There was no real long-term change. Heath only increased defence expenditure fractionally – from 5 per cent to 5.75 per cent of the GNP.[1] There was no systematic attempt to revive Britain's world role. Indeed, there could not be, for several reasons. One was the growing economic problem, exacerbated by a spate of industrial unrest which culminated in the 1984 miners' strike; all this meant that Heath's priorities were overwhelmingly domestic (see Chapter 14). Second, the Conservatives were faced with the need to maintain a permanent military presence in Belfast from 1972 as a result of the crisis in Northern Ireland (see Chapter 21). Third, Heath's successful application to take Britain into the EEC inevitably committed Britain more completely to a European than to a world role.

There was also less reason now to support US policy abroad. Indeed, the 'special relationship' had recently been severely tested by the Vietnam War and by American support for Pakistan in the war with India. This antagonised Britain, which had tried to remain neutral in the conflict between two Commonwealth members – and it also increased the threat from the Soviet Union, which immediately strengthened its ties with India. Britain was also dragged by the United States into a crisis in the Middle East. American support for Israel in the 1973 Yom Kippur War provoked from OPEC a retaliatory increase in oil prices by up to 70 per cent. This particularly affected western Europe and served to accentuate the economic crisis in Britain. Heath's attempts to deal with this resulted in the Conservatives being elbowed out of power in February 1974.

But not before he had warned of dire consequences for Britain's defence if Labour were elected. At first, his worst fears appeared to be justified. Wilson's government of 1974–6 gave absolute priority to buttressing the welfare state, which was severely under siege. To that effect, the 1974 Defence Review announced a reduction of defence expenditure as a proportion of GNP from 5.5 per cent to 4.4 per cent within ten years. The areas to be maintained would be the nuclear deterrent, the defence of the British approaches and the contribution to the NATO defence of Europe – specifically the British army on the Rhine. Another White Paper, which followed in 1975, recommended further cuts. By 1977 Britain had to reverse Heath's commitment and pulled out of her undertaking to contribute to the defence of Malaysia and Singapore.

Then a strange development occurred as a Labour government actually committed Britain to an increase in defence expenditure. This was part of a wider European concern that levels of defence were too low. What could have happened to precipitate this new commitment at the very time that Britain was having to apply for loans from the IMF to deal with a domestic economic crisis?

The answer was a sudden reversal of US foreign policy which had a profound impact on the world at large. In the wake of the Watergate Crisis, President Nixon was forced to resign his office in 1974. His successor, Gerald Ford, was the first non-elected president in America's history, the Vice President, Spiro Agnew, having already followed the corruption route into political oblivion. In reaction to these events, the American electorate in 1976 elected Jimmy Carter on the purity ticket. This was followed by four years in which the United States retracted its overseas commitments. The result was a rapid expansion of Soviet foreign policy under Brezhnev. The European members of NATO reacted with alarm and undertook to increase their contributions by 3 per cent per annum. Britain was included in this.

Unfortunately, Britain's underlying economic problems reasserted themselves to prevent Callaghan from taking a vital decision on updating Britain's *nuclear* defence. The problem was that Polaris was reaching the end of its effective life and production of the missile system had been discontinued in the United States in 1975. Callaghan was also reluctant, in the general atmosphere of restraint, to make a substantial pay award to the armed services as recommended by an independent body. The prospects for an active role by Britain in world affairs seemed even more remote by 1979 than in 1970. According to the Central Policy Review Staff:

In the past 20 years our share of the total Gross Domestic Product of the OECD countries has fallen by a quarter and our share of the world trade has fallen by more than a half. In today's world a country's power and influence are basically determined by its economic performance. Inevitably therefore the UK's ability to influence events in the world has declined and there is very little that diplomatic activity and international public relations can do to disguise the fact.[2]

MRS THATCHER'S PREMIERSHIP 1979–90

This was not to be Mrs Thatcher's understanding of Britain's position in the world. At the outset she made it clear that she would be making defence a top priority and agreed to provide a pay award of 33 per cent to the armed forces. Within a year, however, the familiar economic problems began to exert their constraints. The result was that Conservative policy moved back into line with the broad trend since 1957 – maintaining a strong nuclear deterrent while, at the same time, rationalising conventional defence expenditure.

Far more conscious than any of her predecessors of the Soviet threat, Mrs Thatcher gave absolute priority to nuclear deterrence. She therefore made the decision which Callaghan had deferred and, in 1980, announced that Britain would replace Polaris with the more advanced Trident system. She also implemented Callaghan's decision to allow US cruise missiles to be installed in Britain, something which was also happening in Italy and Germany. These decisions were greeted with outrage by the Labour opposition, which was in the process of abandoning the consensus on nuclear weapons and moving towards a unilateralist stance.

Along with the nuclear option were heavy conventional defence commitments to Europe. The problem was that Britain was hit by a severe recession in 1980 and Mrs Thatcher's government had to make severe cuts in government expenditure. Despite being a 'favoured' sector, defence had to take its share; indeed, it had already exceeded its financial guidelines in 1980. The brunt was taken by the navy. The Defence Review of 1981 therefore announced that the navy's role would be related more directly to Britain's nuclear defence and that its conventional role would have to be further downgraded. This would involve the decommissioning of two out of Britain's three aircraft carriers.

It was particularly unfortunate that Argentina's dictator, General

Galtieri, chose this moment to invade the Falkland Islands and involve Britain in overseas conflict for the first time since the Suez Crisis.

The Falkland Islands had been part of the British Empire since the late eighteenth century. Claimed by Argentina, which had always called them the Malvinas, they had long been a source of diplomatic friction between London and Buenos Aires. For the British government the key issue was that the inhabitants did not wish to come under Argentinian rule. There had been various attempts at a settlement, including a British proposal that sovereignty might be transferred to Argentina on a lease-back agreement. But this was not acceptable to the islanders themselves. Then two factors converged in 1982 to hasten Argentinian intervention. One was the crisis experienced by the military government of General Galtieri. Confronted with an escalating economic crisis and discredited by an atrocious record of human rights abuse, Galtieri sought to divert attention and unite the nation behind him by emphasising Argentina's historic irredentism. In this situation Britain's proposed naval cuts came at the worst possible time and telegraphed the misleading message to Galtieri that Britain was about to abandon her interests in the South Atlantic.

The Argentinians invaded at the beginning of April. Within days Mrs Thatcher's government had assembled a task force, which reached the Falklands early in May. Goose Green was recaptured on 29 May and the final surrender of Argentinian forces took place on 14 June. There are clearly two sides to the government's record on these events. The conflict showed up the worst and the best of reactions to the crisis and preparations for military victory.

On the negative side, the war was totally unexpected. There was no accurate prediction or warning from British intelligence and the government had taken no anticipatory measures. It had not even delivered an ultimatum to Galtieri during the build-up of Argentinian forces immediately before the invasion. Nor had it taken account of Galtieri's quest for an external diversion from Argentina's domestic crisis. All the government had done was to announce defence cuts which would particularly affect the South Atlantic: it had even removed HMS *Endurance* from the area. For these reasons it was strongly criticised from all sides of the House in a Commons debate on 3 April. The other side of the picture was an apparently stunning success in regaining the Falklands from Argentina. The war was not of the government's making, yet the response to it was remarkably swift and decisive for a country which had faced no comparable emergency for twenty-six years. Within days of Galtieri's invasion, Mrs Thatcher despatched a task force of naval and merchant ships, grouped around two aircraft carriers. The professionalism of the British troops ensured a rapid victory against a numerically superior enemy. Throughout the crisis Mrs Thatcher showed the resolution and courage generally associated only with the great wartime prime ministers of the past, and, on the successful outcome of the campaign, she was warmly congratulated in the House of Commons by the Leader of the Opposition, Neil Kinnock.

Even so, there are several remaining reservations about the war and its effects. First, certain deficiencies became apparent in British equipment, particularly the inadequacy of the armament of destroyers like the *Sheffield*, sunk by an Argentinian exocet missile to which British forces had no effective counter. Second, the subsequent cost of garrisoning the Falklands (£5 billion) proved much greater than the cost of the war itself (£700 million). Finally, the Falklands War was in a sense an irrelevance and an anachronism – the last example of a colonial war fought between a defunct imperial power and a Third-World dictatorship. There were complex cross-currents as Britain's various associates within NATO, the United Nations and the European Community were individually and collectively embarrassed. The war created serious problems for the United States, which was forced to choose between its special relationship with Britain and its attempts to maintain close relations with Latin America. The European Community was cool in its response to what it saw as a throwback to Britain's earlier and pre-European role, while Spain openly sided with Argentina. Much of the Third World was strongly critical of Britain, especially through the United Nations, and the Soviet Union was able to score several propaganda successes by depicting it as a North–South confrontation which overlapped with the more traditional East–West one. Russia, in other words, was able to restore to Communism its earlier anti-imperialist emphasis.

Despite these shortcomings, the Falklands War did revive British prestige abroad and for the rest of her time in power Mrs Thatcher was able to project a more assertive face for British foreign policy. The arena she chose was the Cold War and in this she made common cause with the United States. Relations between the two countries had been strained by the Falklands crisis, but there was an underlying empathy between Mrs Thatcher and President Reagan which was far stronger and more ideological than that between Macmillan and Kennedy or between Callaghan and Carter. Mrs Thatcher and President Reagan had in common their faith in the policy of monetarism, their dislike of any form of socialism, and their anti-Soviet rhetoric. In practical terms the revived connection enabled Mrs Thatcher to exert more influence than was now usual for British premiers. Her stance has been given at least some of the credit for the eventual collapse of the Soviet Union, just as Thatcherism in the economic sector showed the way for a number of eastern European governments in their rejection of Communism. Mrs Thatcher was also able to play a conciliatory role, especially when Gorbachev became Soviet President in 1985, and act as a mediator between more powerful protagonists, as in the 1987 agreement between the USA and the USSR on the reduction of intermediate range nuclear weapons.

On the other hand, the post-Falklands revival of British influence in world affairs was as illusory as any military recovery. There was no real substance to British power and the closer relationship with the United States was unequal, leaving no room for Britain to disagree with her senior partner. On two occasions Mrs Thatcher's government came close to being humiliated. In 1983 Britain suffered the indignity of having to sit back and watch Grenada, a member of the Commonwealth, being invaded by US marines. Then, in 1986 the government was obliged to allow the use of airbases in Britain by US aircraft attacking Tripoli in an attempt to kill President Gaddafi. It could also be argued that the part played by the 'Iron Lady' in the fall of the Soviet Union was minimal; the real factors were the crisis of the Soviet economy and the constant pressure exerted by the Reagan administration. Britain simply did not have the resources to make any difference and these could not be replaced by rhetoric, no matter how forceful.

How radical was Mrs Thatcher's foreign policy? Was there a counterpart to the 'Thatcher revolution' at home? On the whole, it would seem not. Although she took the bold decision to update Britain's nuclear weapons system, this was not a new departure; if anyone abandoned the consensus on foreign policy it was Michael Foot and Labour's unilateralists. Mrs Thatcher was also continuing the tradition of the 1957 White Paper by rationalising Britain's conventional forces. Mrs Thatcher's government did not introduce the enormous increase in defence expenditure that characterised Reagan's first administration; indeed, the Conservatives claimed that they were merely fulfilling the pledge made by Callaghan to Britain's European partners. Even Labour had no cause to criticise this, except that Foot argued for the end of the nuclear role and the further strengthening of the conventional one. The Conservative counter-argument was that this course would actually prove more expensive and would severely affect the funding of domestic priorities. There was certainly nothing radical here. Any actual increases in Britain's world role were temporary – the result of exceptional circumstances like the Falklands War and the special relationship, not so much between Britain and the United States as between Mrs Thatcher and President Reagan. In retrospect, therefore, it seems that Mrs Thatcher was a little over-optimistic when she said in 1988: 'I believe that Britain's role and standing in the world have increased immeasurably. . . . We are now able once again to exercise the leadership and influence which we have historically shown.'[3]

THE 1990S

John Major was a strong contrast to Margaret Thatcher. He possessed little experience of foreign affairs, except for three months as Foreign Secretary, and showed a very different style. In the words of W. Wallace,

> There was . . . no distinctive Major 'tune'; no new vision of Britain's place in the world to substitute for his predecessor's British Gaullism or Michael Heseltine's proposed shift towards Europe. John Major was a political manager rather than a visionary in style, whose interests were more domestic than international.[4]

He also came to office at a time when two significant decisions had already been made about the future. He inherited a defence review which, according to L. Freedman, was to lead to 'the defence budget being reduced more sharply than at any time since the post Second World War demobilization'.[5] Mrs Thatcher had also made commitments to the United States to assist Kuwait against Saddam Hussein. To some extent, therefore, Major was presented with a set agenda and had little room for manoeuvre.

Almost immediately, he was confronted by a crisis as, early in 1991, Britain found herself at war for the second time in nine years. This time, 45,000 British troops were committed to the Gulf to assist the United States and its Middle-Eastern allies to recover Kuwait from the grip of Iraq. Because of the overwhelming superiority of the allied military technology, the result of the war was never in doubt. Unlike the Falklands conflict, the Gulf War carried virtually no risk to Britain. Even so, Major's quiet style of leadership and the comparatively low cost of British involvement went down well with the British public and quite possibly helped win the 1992 general election for the Conservatives. There is little doubt that Major's reputation reached its high point at this stage.

From 1992 onwards, however, British foreign policy began to appear less decisive. The main problem was the adjustment of Britain's defence role to a rapidly changing world. Between 1989 and 1991 had occurred some of the most amazing events of the twentieth century – the collapse of Communism in Poland, Hungary, Czechoslovakia, East Germany, Bulgaria and Romania; the end of the Warsaw Pact; and the collapse of the Soviet Union itself at the end of 1991. The Cold War had therefore completely disappeared. To some, this offered a real prospect for defence cutbacks. Labour leftwingers, including Tony Benn, argued that the Soviet Union had never been the threat claimed and that the removal of even its shadow now provided an opportunity to cancel the Trident programme. The Major government disputed this interpretation but nevertheless used the opportunity to continue the cutbacks in Britain's conventional defences, a further milestone in the long road since 1957. By 1996, British defence expenditure was to be only 75 per cent of the level of 1986, with a corresponding reduction from 5 per cent to 3 per cent of the GDP. Further cuts were planned for the end of the century. The main casualty was the army, which was to be cut back in Germany.

This certainly seemed to make sense. But there was another perspective. The end of the Cold War was likely to be followed by dangers and problems in the future which were less predictable than at any time since 1945. Mrs Thatcher clearly believed this when she argued in February 1990 that 'Great plans for peace can precede great wars. Cool headedness, commonsense and vigilance are never more important than when Europe is convulsed by change.'[6] There were several possibilities for the future. One was the emergence of some authoritarian system in Russia which would make it as great a threat as the Soviet Union had once been: this was a strong argument for not abandoning the nuclear option. At the same time, Britain also needed to be alert to the rise of a second-rank power which, in the absence of the constraining influence of the Cold War, might well pose a serious threat in *conventional* military terms.

Getting the balance right between the two types of defence was therefore more crucial than ever. Unfortunately, the state of the economy left no room to manoeuvre between them. One solution might have been closer integration within the European component of NATO, but Major's confrontation with the European Union over issues which were also splitting the Conservative party (see Chapters 15 and 19) effectively prevented this. A more obvious approach would have been to return to the 'special relationship' with the United States.

But there was a problem here too. British governments had generally got more out of a relationship with Republican administrations, especially those of Eisenhower in the 1950s and Reagan in the 1980s. The Democrats were inclined to be more distant, like Carter in the 1970s and Clinton in the 1990s. The latter accused the Conservative government of blatant bias during the 1992 presidential elections: the Home Office, he alleged, searched its files for information about his views on US involvement in Vietnam whilst a student at Oxford in the 1960s. On becoming president, Clinton fell out with Major in 1993 over the extent of US and British involvement in Bosnia. The British government was furious when, in 1995, the United States issued a visa to Sinn Fein leader Gerry Adams. Even the longstanding consensus between the two governments on nuclear weapons was affected. In March 1995, Clinton suggested that Major should give up at least part of Trident, a policy which the United States could if it wished enforce, since it handled all the refurbishment and replacement contracts. Clinton's reasoning was that the end of the Cold War meant that Britain should reduce her nuclear weapons to bring them, in comparative terms, into line with the reductions made by the United States and Russia.

There is, therefore, some justice in W. Wallace's assertion that Major's government was caught between continental and American pressures: that it 'had no foreign policy: no sense of Britain's place in the world or how best to use diplomacy to achieve national objectives.'[7]

19

BRITAIN AND EUROPE
SINCE 1945

The idea of European unity had roots as far back as the eighteenth century, while the term 'United States of Europe' was coined in the nineteenth. During the inter-war period serious proposals for unity were advanced by the Austrian statesman Coudenhove-Kalergi and the French politician Aristide Briand. It was not, however, until after 1945 that integration exerted an appeal which was sufficiently widespread for it to become a feasible proposition. This was due largely to the cataclysmic experience of the Second World War and to the growing belief among politicians on the Continent that nationalism needed more constraints than had been the case in the past. Various forms of collaboration therefore developed.

One was based on the more traditional style of intergovernmental co-operation. This applied to the Organisation of European Economic Co-operation (OEEC), set up in 1947 to co-ordinate the distribution of American aid through the Marshall Plan. This was followed in 1948 by the Brussels Treaty between Britain, France, Belgium, the Netherlands and Luxembourg, which in turn expanded into the North Atlantic Treaty Organisation in 1949, a traditional style of military alliance. In the same year the Council of Europe was established; comprising most of the non-Communist states of Europe, this was intended to co-ordinate intergovernmental negotiations on a variety of issues. Overall, however, this was not the route to integration or supranationalism or what many had originally considered the European ideal.

Instead, this began to emerge with the formation in 1951 of the European Coal and Steel Community (ECSC) between France, West Germany, Italy, and the Benelux countries. The same 'Six' expanded this into the European Economic Community and Euratom by the Treaties of Rome (1957). These allowed for a transitional period of twelve years for the establishment of a customs and economic union between the

286

member states. Ultimately, it was envisaged, progress would be made towards the transfer of political sovereignty to a supranational authority. The ECSC, EEC and Euratom were merged in 1965 into the single European Community (EC). The economic objective was highly successful, but the political dynamic slowed down during the 1960s and 1970s. Instead of political integration, therefore, the European Community aimed at enlargement, bringing in Britain, Ireland and Denmark in 1973, Greece in 1981 and Spain and Portugal in 1985.[1] Then, during the second half of the 1980s, the momentum for integration was revived as France and Germany, especially, rediscovered a zeal that their individual governments had shed during the 1960s and 1970s. Under their impetus the Treaty of Maastricht (1992) set a new agenda for complete economic union and left the door open to a supranational political sovereignty as well.

This chapter considers Britain's reaction to the various stages in the evolution of European integration. In outline, the argument is as follows. Britain had consistently opposed the integrationist route, always opting for internationalism rather than supranationalism. At first she was instrumental in confining the OEEC, the Brussels Treaty and NATO to intergovernmental co-operation: there was nothing new in any of these. Labour and Conservative governments alike considered that anything more was inappropriate for Britain. They were therefore not tempted by the prospect of membership of the ECSC in 1951.

Gradually, however, the ECSC evolved into a broader economic co-operation between the Six. As this began to threaten Britain's future economic standing in Europe, Eden's government attempted in the mid-1950s to secure a special connection between Britain and the Six in the form of a Free Trade Area (FTA). This did not, however, materialise and when the Six drew closer together in the EEC and Euratom in 1957, Britain countered by drawing up the European Free Trade Association (EFTA). But this was not the answer to Britain's economic needs and between 1961 and 1973 successive governments recognised that British interests would be best served by membership of the EEC, especially since this was the period when the integrationist trend was in apparent decline. French opposition, however, prevented the success of the British application until 1973. Even then, there were no immediate solutions to Britain's economic problems. There was strong disappointment in terms of what Britain was actually getting out of the EEC. Heath (1970–4) tried to secure more generous regional grants; Wilson (1974–6) renegotiated the terms of British entry; and Mrs

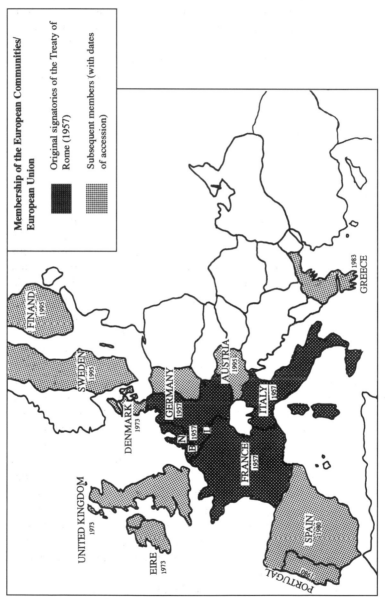

Figure 14 Britain and the European Community

Thatcher (1979–90) became involved in a series of budgetary wrangles. Underlying the whole relationship with Europe was an unchanged British suspicion of integration. Europeans, and some pro-European Britons, accused British governments of seeking to subvert the European ideal and to force the EEC into the non-integrationist channel which Britain had always favoured. In other words, Britain had entered Europe only to try to unpick previous trends, even reverse the inevitable.

REMAINING ALOOF 1945–60

From the end of the war in 1945, Britain considered it essential to have a form of European co-operation that would operate on two levels: between individual states on the continent and between Britain and these states. The Foreign Secretary, Bevin, believed that a 'third force' or 'western union' was necessary to counterbalance the superpowers. But the scheme was limited to co-operation over defence and the economy which, according to S. Greenwood, 'makes it an antecedent of NATO rather than the European Economic Community'.[2] Bevin's initial priority was to safeguard Britain's interests as a world power. He envisaged 'the closest possible collaboration with the Commonwealth and the overseas territories, not only with British but French, Dutch, Belgians and Portuguese'.[3] This concept he referred to as the Western Union. But any ideas going beyond this were impeded by other cabinet ministers, as well as by officials in the Foreign Office and the Treasury. From the start, therefore, there was virtually no possibility of a British-led initiative to achieve a more extensive form of European integration.

In the meantime, however, a French pattern of collaboration was beginning to emerge, which sought precisely what Britain was anxious to avoid – a closer political integration in Europe to prevent the possibility of another world war in the future. Integration would, in other words, be a means of controlling Germany. This was not a course approved by the British government which, in any case, regarded the Soviet Union at this stage as a greater threat than Germany. For a while Britain influenced the pace of multilateral negotiations, moving them away from the integrationist pattern and ensuring that the new agreements and institutions which emerged were based on internationalism rather than supranationalism.

The first of these was the Dunkirk Treaty with France (1947), which was broadened the following year into the Brussels Treaty with France, Belgium, the Netherlands and Luxembourg. Meanwhile, the Committee for European Economic Co-operation (CEEC) had been set up in 1947 to co-ordinate the flow of Marshall Aid to western Europe. This was succeeded by the Organisation for European Economic Co-operation (OEEC). The formation of NATO in 1949 was for Britain the logical conclusion of her dialogue with Europe. It comprised the members of the Treaty of Brussels, together with Norway, Denmark, Iceland, Italy, Portugal, Canada and the United States. The inclusion of these last two powers showed how Bevin had moved from his original idea of a European counterpoise to the two superpowers and was now seeking a 'special relationship' with the United States (see Chapter 17). In a sense, all these early measures represent the failure of the first attempt to realise a European ideal. NATO was as much Atlantic as it was European, while the OEEC failed completely to move down the road to integration. 'That the OEEC . . . was devoid of any supranational implications was principally Britain's doing.'[4]

The alternative approach, the search for integration, was revived at the beginning of the 1950s. This was, however, entirely a continental initiative and Britain refused to be part of it.

The main influence behind the new impetus was Jean Monnet, a French civil servant, who believed in the establishment of 'a vast continental market on a European scale'.[5] He argued that the European economies should be integrated stage by stage and sector by sector. The first stage was to unite the coal and steel sectors of the Ruhr in Germany and Lorraine in France. His reasoning was that binding these closely together would prevent the emergence of another German war machine and would weld together the future interests of France and Germany. The result was the formation of the European Coal and Steel Community in 1951. This did not, however, fit the strategy of the newly formed Conservative government. Although he had once extolled the idea of European unity, Churchill's view had changed by the 1950s. In opposition he had often criticised Labour's caution on Europe but was forced to adopt the same stance when he returned as Prime Minister in 1951, when he said: 'I never thought that Britain or the British Commonwealth should, either individually or collectively, become an integral part of a European federation'. He added

> Our first object is the unity and consolidation of the British Commonwealth and what is left of the former British Empire. Our second, the 'fraternal association' of the English-speaking world; and third, United Europe, to which we are a separate, closely and specially related ally and friend.[6]

This was strongly suspected by Monnet, who considered that Britain had rejected the Schuman Plan because she 'had no confidence that France and the other countries of Europe have the ability or even the will effectively to resist a possible Russian invasion.'[7]

The Europeans had one or two false diversions before making further progress towards integration. One of these was the attempt at a European Defence Community (EDC), proposed by the French Prime Minister, Pleven, whereby European countries would pool their military resources along similar lines to coal and steel in the ECSC. This did not, however, come into existence and, predictably, Britain refused to have anything to do with it, still trying to find alternatives to being drawn into the integration channel. Anthony Eden, Foreign Secretary to 1955 and Prime Minister 1955–7, proposed the Western European Union (WEU) as an alternative to the EDC. This was really an extended form of the Brussels Treaty of 1948, the intention being to prepare the way for the admission of West Germany to NATO without risking any loss of sovereign control over each individual country's armed forces as adherence to the EDC might incur. The WEU seemed therefore a significant British success for the traditional line of NATO against the newer form of integration.

The next stage was, however, far more successful for the Europeans. The principle of integration, relaunched at the 1955 Messina Conference, was firmly embedded in the 1957 Treaty of Rome, which set up the European Economic Community (EEC) and the European Atomic Energy Community (Euratom). At this point Britain lost the opportunity of joining and contributing to the process. Although Eden's government sent a representative to the Messina conference, it subsequently withdrew from future negotiations. The view of most historians is expressed by S. George, that 'this was possibly the biggest tactical mistake that Britain made in its attempt to create the sort of Europe that it preferred.'[8]

What, precisely, was Britain seeking as an alternative? It seems that the government's strategy was a confused compromise based on the misapprehension that Britain was still a world power but that she was also in need of a closer connection with Europe. Hence it followed the contradictory policy of resisting any tightening of the Community while, at the same time, seeking closer association with it. Britain clearly preferred the idea of a free trade agreement to the EEC policy of a customs union since the former would allow governments to pursue their own policies rather than have a supranational solution imposed upon their economies. It would allow for the relaxation of tariffs by individual governments rather than their external removal. Britain therefore tried to persuade the Six to develop a Free Trade Area with which she would be closely associated. This was a deliberate attempt to divert the Six from a closer union. Macmillan put the same point slightly differently:

> We must not be bullied. . . . We could if we were driven to it, fight their movement. . . . We must take positive action in this field, to ensure that the wider Free Trade Area is more attractive than the narrower Common Market of the Six.[9]

When this failed to prevent the formation of the tighter EEC, Britain still tried to press the FTA link. In 1957 negotiations were started. But in 1958 de Gaulle imposed a number of obstacles in Britain's way – largely for political reasons. Britain therefore responded with the formation of the European Free Trade Association (EFTA), in the Stockholm Convention of 1959. This included a number of European states outside the EEC, such as Sweden, Norway, Denmark, Austria, Portugal and Switzerland: it came to be known, in contrast to the 'Inner Six', as the 'Outer Seven'.

Why was Britain so reluctant to go along with other major European states like Germany, Italy and France in accepting integration? The psychological impact of her experience between 1939 and 1945 must have had some bearing. Britain was one of the few states to have gained inward unity and outward prestige from the experience of war. The British had never been more nationalistic and it was not surprising that they found it difficult to accept in the late 1940s or the early 1950s that Britain's world role was in decline and that she needed to adjust to a European dimension. Second, it took some time to recognise what was happening to the British economy. During the early 1950s Britain's performance still appeared very strong. Her GNP in 1951 was twice that of West Germany and three times that of France, while her industrial production was greater than both combined, accounting for one-third of the output of all of the OEEC countries. Why, therefore, should it be necessary to enter a European arrangement with strong political undertones when there was still room to manoeuvre with the idea of more liberal trade arrangements in other ways? And third, the Empire was still a powerful concept in the late 1940s and early 1950s. Official advice given in 1956 was that 'less than one-third of our trade is with Europe; entry into the Common Market would be bound to damage much of the other two-thirds, particularly that with the Commonwealth'.[10] To do otherwise would mean disrupting a system which already existed for the purpose of opting for an organisation with an unknown future.

In any case, Britain had not taken an irrevocable decision. She was retaining her freedom of action, which would have been lost had she committed herself to integration during the early 1950s. There was a strong inclination therefore to 'wait and see'. According to A.S. Milward, 'what became all too visible by 1960 was only just perceptible in 1950 and certainly anything but irreversible.'[11]

SEEKING INVOLVEMENT

In a radio broadcast on 20 September 1962 the Prime Minister, Harold Macmillan, announced to the nation that Britain would apply for membership of the EEC. In characteristically simple phrases, he explained the need to do this: 'all through our history . . . we have still been very much involved in Europe's affairs. We can't escape it. Sometimes we've tried to – but we can't. It's no good pretending.'[12] The Labour party was critical of this change of policy as its leader, Gaitskell, was strongly opposed to the Common Market. But his successor, Harold Wilson, also took up the cause from 1964. Between the two political parties there was therefore an eventual identity of purpose. This change in Britain's policy can be explained in both economic and political terms. The former set the pace, while a reappraisal of the latter removed the main obstacle.

Realisation dawned very soon after the formation of the EEC that Britain could not compete with it economically. Britain's economic performance since the early 1950s had been far less impressive than that of the Six. Her exports, for example, had increased between 1953 and 1963 by under 40 per cent, while the average growth of the Six over the same period had been 140 per cent. Of course, it might be argued that Germany, France and Italy were recovering from a very low economic base following the catastrophic effects of the war on their economies. Even so, the scale of Britain's comparative decline was unprecedented and the reasons for this are analysed in Chapter 13. Part of the problem was that Britain had paid for her wartime involvement through the sale of many of her overseas assets and investments. These had previously been used to convert an increasingly regular balance of trade deficit into an overall balance of payments surplus. At first the true extent of Britain's losses had been concealed by American loans. But during the 1950s Germany rapidly reconstructed her shattered industries and, in the process, replaced the type of obsolete plant used in Britain. Gradually, the grim truth emerged that Germany's bomb damage was less difficult to repair than the contraction of Britain's overseas investments.

Nor was Britain at the centre of a viable trading bloc which would provide a permanent alternative to EEC membership. The case for relying on Imperial preference was weakening all the time, as members of the Commonwealth like Canada and Australia were developing stronger trading connections with the United States and Japan. Overall, during the 1950s Britain's trade increased with the Empire and Commonwealth by only 29 per cent from £1.24 billion to £1.6 billion. This was at a time when her trade with the Six grew by 230 per cent from £463 million to £1.53 billion. The trend seemed inexorable. But the problem was that Britain lacked the free access to the necessary European markets because of her Commonwealth attachments. S. Greenwood argues that the Commonwealth was therefore a disadvantage for the post-war British economy.

> Tied to markets which were more diverse and less vigorous than those developing in post-war Europe, Britain was deprived of the necessary competitive thrust to maintain early post-war growth. The very opposite happened on the Continent where intra-European competition between a group of expanding economies allowed growth to be sustained.[13]

Britain's attempt to secure access to European trading privileges – without losing the special relationship with the Commonwealth – was unsuccessful. The idea of the Free Trade Area, linking Britain with the Six, might have worked for a while, but the latter rightly considered it a threat to their own interests. The alternative, EFTA, was from the outset a poor substitute for association with the EEC. There was an inherent imbalance between the size of the British economy and those of the other members: Austria, Switzerland, Portugal, Sweden and Norway. Macmillan was fully aware of the disadvantages of EFTA by comparison to the EEC when it came to exporting British manufactured goods. 'How', he said, 'are we going to sell them if the base, the home market, is only a quarter of theirs?' In any case, British trade was growing more rapidly with the Six, even without concessions, than with the Seven. By the 1960s, therefore, Britain was clear that EFTA was not in her interests and that the EEC would be much more appropriate after all. Access to a greatly enlarged free market could accelerate British economic growth, while continued isolation from it could only accentuate its sluggishness.

Up to that point Britain had always been deterred from seeking closer accommodation with the Six through fear that this would lead to political union. But during the 1960s and early 1970s the cause of political integration received a major setback at the hands of the two largest members of the EEC, France and Germany, both of whom made it clear that they wished to pursue their own interests. This was highly significant, since it had been the growing accord between France and Germany which had started the early trend towards integration in the form of the ECSC. Now their paths seemed to be diverging and weakening the whole process. The priority of President de Gaulle was to revive France's influence in Europe and he expressed quite openly his preference for nationalist-based policies. These involved the development of an independent defensive capacity and partial withdrawal from NATO; a cooling of French relations with the United States and a search for *détente* with the Soviet Union; and, above all, the open pursuit of French interest within the EEC. In 1965, for example, he precipitated a crisis within the Community by imposing a veto on certain agricultural policies that were acceptable to the other five members of the EEC. This gave Britain the strongest signal that it was possible to pursue individual policies within the EEC. This was confirmed by the Luxembourg Agreement of 1966, which acknowledged the right of any member state to insist on unanimous agreement. A less assertive, but not dissimilar line was taken by the West German Chancellor, Willy Brandt, who was determined to follow a national foreign policy that would mend German relations with the Soviet Union and eastern Europe. Britain's earlier apprehensions about political integration had therefore been allayed. Edward Heath maintained, 'That situation is fully safeguarded and we should not frighten ourselves by false apprehensions about these matters.'[14] This was echoed nine years later by Sir Geoffrey Rippon, who was involved in the second round of negotiations. 'There is no question of the imposition of theoretical solutions from above; no threat of instant federation.'[15]

Other political factors, quite unconnected with fears of integration, also influenced Britain's change of mind on Community membership. By the 1960s it had become all too evident that Britain was a power far set into decline and that its former world role was contracting into a regional one. The Suez Crisis of 1956, while not precipitating that decline, eventually brought an acceptance of it (see Chapter 17). Similarly, the Commonwealth seemed to be slipping away from Britain's leadership. The emergence of independent states lessened the likelihood of automatic support of Britain on key issues and, as their reactions to Suez indicated, the Dominions were fully capable of open criticism. Nor could Britain hope any longer to exert an automatic influence in Europe – unless this could be done on the inside. A committee of senior civil servants advised in 1960 that 'on political grounds – that is, to ensure a politically cohesive Western Europe – there was a strong argument for joining the Common Market.'[16] Nor was Britain's 'special relationship' with the United States an impediment. Quite the contrary: after a visit to Washington in 1961 Macmillan was convinced that 'the shortest, and perhaps the only, way to a real Atlantic partnership lay through Britain's joining'.[17] For their part, successive American presidents considered the EEC a vital bloc for the future and British prime ministers feared that an isolated Britain might be excluded from future links between the United States and Europe.

Of the political parties, the Liberals had always been in favour, while the Conservatives were converted during Macmillan's premiership. The first application for British membership, made in 1962, was vetoed by de Gaulle in 1963. Labour opposed the first application, but under Wilson, who assumed the leadership after the death of Gaitskell, the official policy of the Labour party changed. Wilson therefore reapplied in 1967, only to be frustrated by a second use of the French veto. The third application was made by Heath's Conservative government in 1970. Heath was more enthusiastic about entry than any of his predecessors but the Labour party now officially opposed entry, arguing that Heath's terms were unacceptable and that he was selling Britain short. At the same time, Wilson tried to persuade Labour to accept the principle of membership. Heath's renewed negotiations succeeded and Britain formally joined by signing the Treaty of Accession, along with Eire and Denmark, in 1972. She became a full member of the EC on 1 January 1973.

Why the dramatic change in fortunes? Why did the first two applications fail and the third succeed? There were initial difficulties in the way of British membership, including arrangements between the Six and Britain's current trading partners in EFTA and the Commonwealth. But these could well have been resolved. The major block was undoubtedly the opposition of President de Gaulle. The relationship between Britain and France was complex and paradoxical. Above all, there was a strong mutual distrust. Britain's distrust of France acted as an impetus for her to join the EEC to reduce French influence in Europe, while France's of Britain meant a deliberate stalling tactic to keep Britain on the periphery. De Gaulle disliked Britain's preference for Atlanticism and was convinced that she was not genuine about her application. He argued in 1963 that

> the nature and structure and economic context of England differ profoundly from those of the other states of the Continent. In the end there would appear a colossal Atlantic community under American dependence and leadership which would soon swallow up the European Community.[18]

Britain would also interfere with France's more nationalistic ambitions embodied in the *force de frappe*, or independent nuclear deterrent, and would in two ways dilute the French influence on the EC. First it would bring into association with the Community a series of Commonwealth states and would therefore expand its base beyond Europe. And second, it would lead to the increased influence of the United States via Britain. He was especially concerned about the US decision to supply Britain with Polaris nuclear weapons: this would place Britain far ahead of France and would mean continued British dependence on the United States well into the future. In a variety of ways, therefore, Britain was seen as a Trojan Horse for American influence in the European Community.

The late 1960s did not see a sudden reversal of the economic difficulties confronting British entry. Not the least of the obstacles was the Common Agricultural Policy (CAP), which would result in an increase in food prices in Britain. Another issue was the protection of West Indian sugar producers and New Zealand dairy produce. The third was the question of Britain's budget contribution. Nevertheless, the way was suddenly cleared between 1970 and 1972. In part, this was because Heath preferred not to hold out too strongly on economic details but to sort out differences once Britain had joined the EC. But even more important than Heath's obvious eagerness was de Gaulle's resignation in 1969, following the student disturbances in Paris in 1968 and the defeat of the president's proposals for constitutional change in a referendum. De Gaulle's successor, Georges Pompidou, was much more sympathetic to the idea of British entry and was a personal friend of Heath. Bilateral negotiations therefore replaced the previous cloud of Anglo-French suspicion and greatly eased the multilateral settlement of remaining economic issues. It seems, therefore, that Britain's eventual accession to the Community, like the delay leading up to it, had as much to do with the influence of personalities as with the resolution of issues.

FIGHTING A CORNER OR FINDING
AN IDENTITY?

It soon became apparent that British membership of the European Community would be far from problem-free. Indeed, each of the next five prime ministers focused on the difficulties as much as on the opportunities, although they had different methods of addressing these. Heath (1970–4) gave priority to securing membership of the EC before dealing with difficulties, his intention being to solve the latter from the inside. He secured a transitional period of six years until British contributions to the EC budget would reach their full amount but, even so, the cost of membership was still considered too high, especially since Britain was in the midst of an economic crisis. Hence Heath followed a second strategy of trying to secure aid from the Community for the more depressed areas via a proposed European Regional Development Fund (ERDF). This was not set up until later. These attempts were interrupted by industrial disputes at home and by his defeat in the February 1974 general election.

The method followed by Wilson (1974–6) in dealing with the cost of membership was very different. He committed his government to renegotiating the whole basis of British entry to the Community. His main targets were the amount of the British contribution to the central budget, greater flexibility on monetary union, more emphasis on regional development and better trade terms for Third World countries in the Commonwealth. Wilson was able to claim by 1975 that these had all been achieved, although to an extent the reasons were not directly of his making. For example, the Development Fund was established anyway; the Community produced a trade agreement with the Third World as a whole in the form of the Lomé Convention (1975); and the recession of the 1970s put paid for the time being to monetary union. Wilson put the whole issue of continued membership to a referendum in June 1975. The result was a 2 to 1 vote in favour of continued membership, on a turnout of 64 per cent.[19] This should have eased the path for Callaghan (1976–9), but he faced opposition from much of the Labour party and had to adopt a broadly pragmatic course with the emphasis on the pursuit of British interests. He had three main objectives. The first was to maintain existing levels of national sovereignty and to prevent any increase in the powers of institutions in Brussels or of the European Parliament. The second was to insist that governments should be free to pursue their own economic policies. The third was a further reform of the Community budget.

The most difficult of the British Prime Ministers with whom the Community had to deal was Mrs Thatcher (1979–90), who sought satisfaction over two areas: a budget rebate and the preservation of national sovereignty. Her style was much more abrasive than that of any of her predecessors. According to Roy Jenkins, former Labour minister and President of the Commission, Mrs Thatcher had a considerable impact on the Strasbourg Summit (1979); she 'performed the considerable task of unnecessarily irritating two big countries (France and Germany), three small ones (Netherlands, Denmark and Eire) and the Commission within her opening hour of performance at a European Council.'[20] Her methods, nevertheless, partially succeeded, as she managed at the Fontainebleau Summit (1984) to secure a substantial rebate. There was one area of accord: the pursuit of the single market which was seen by Britain and the other states as of common interest. This also seemed to accord with Mrs Thatcher's emphasis within Britain on free enterprise. Unfortunately, this was accompanied by the revival of a previous pattern which had never been acceptable to Britain. The President of the Commission from 1985, Jacques Delors, saw the single market as a means of reactivating the integration process. France and Germany especially considered that it should involve greater institutional involvement. Mrs Thatcher, however, considered that extra layers of bureaucracy would be an unwarranted interference in the operation of market mechanisms and a threat to British sovereignty. She took her stand especially on the Commission's White Paper which pressed for the removal of customs and immigration controls ('physical barriers'), 'fiscal harmonisation' and the removal of 'technical barriers'. These were the result of the Single European Act (SEA) of 1986. Mrs Thatcher was also highly suspicious of economic and monetary union (EMU). By 1990 she had become more abrasive than ever and was criticised in the House of Commons by Sir Geoffrey Howe for her attitude. This precipitated a challenge on her leadership and subsequent resignation as Prime Minister.

Major's policy towards Europe from 1990 was less confrontational than Mrs Thatcher's had been. He even referred to placing Britain 'at the heart of Europe'. He also signed the Maastricht Treaty in 1992, for which he was strongly criticised by Mrs Thatcher. In the process, he held out against pressure from the right within the Conservative party which voted against ratification of the Maastricht Treaty in 1993. Major took a tough line by withdrawing the party whip from the 'Euro-rebels'. When criticism continued he voluntarily put himself up for re-election as party leader in June 1995. Overall, therefore, Major seemed to have taken a step towards co-operation rather than confrontation. On the other hand, Major maintained continuity with previous governments over the extent of integration. For example, he was obliged to take Britain out of the Exchange Rate Mechanism and he made a number of important conditions to Britain's acceptance of Maastricht. One was Britain's right to opt out of the Social Chapter. Another was his insistence that the British Parliament should take the final decision on whether Britain joined the EMU. Above all, he insisted on the principles of subsidiarity and intergovernmental co-operation.

The complexities of renegotiation and the bitterness of talks on budget rebates led many within the Community to accuse the British of being bad Europeans. Britain had, in fact, acquired a consistent reputation for awkwardness. First, she had refused to co-operate at the time of the establishment of the three communities. Then she had sought association on exclusive terms in the form of the FTA. Having secured membership in 1973 she began to haggle about the terms and to resist the long-term process of integration which had always been part of the rationale of the Community. To make matters worse, it seemed that there was a constant intrusion of domestic issues in the form of economic crisis and forcefully expressed views between and within the political parties.

The obverse side, of course, was whether Britain was actually benefiting from membership of the Community. British political parties and public opinion generally returned a split verdict; this reflects the difficulty of coming to a firm conclusion as most statistical evidence is capable of at least two interpretations.

The economic effects of membership are particularly difficult to assess. There is no doubt that the impact of the Community on Britain's trade pattern was considerable. In 1958 Britain's imports from the Six accounted for 21.8 per cent of her total, and her exports to the Six 21.7 per cent. By 1990 these had increased to 51.0 per cent and 52.6 per cent respectively. The patterns remained fairly constant with the United States and showed a measurable increase with Japan. Imports from other areas dropped from 45.6 per cent in 1958 to 16.2 per cent in 1990 and exports from 46.8 per cent to 19.8 per cent.[21] Whether this would have occurred without membership of the EC is debatable. It does on balance seem that Britain joined in recognition of a trend which had already started and that, even without membership, the trend would have continued. But would it have been so rapid and, without freer access to the 'common market', would Britain's exports have increased in proportion to her imports?

300

There is a similar problem in attempting to interpret figures for Britain's Gross Domestic Product (GDP). During the period of her membership Britain showed a large overall increase, but was overtaken by both France and Italy. Britain's GDP in 1955 stood at £19 billion and in 1965 at £36 billion, climbing in 1975 to £106 billion and in 1987 to £396 billion. Italy's figures were £9 billion in 1955, £22 billion in 1965, £86 billion in 1975 and £408 billion in 1987.[22] Britain was also overhauled by Italy during the 1980s in terms of her percentage of the world's total exports of manufactured goods. These figures could indicate damage caused by the EC or, alternatively, it could be said that Britain's performance would have been even worse outside the EC. The rate of GDP growth in Britain is also not very helpful in coming to a conclusion on this. Between 1961 and 1973 the average annual growth rate was 3.2 per cent. Between 1974 and 1981 it was 0.7 per cent. On the other hand, it steadily recovered to 3.8 per cent in 1987 and to 4.2 per cent in 1988, before dropping back again in the early 1990s. We cannot with any degree of certainty attribute these figures to specific influences either within or outside the EC; they must be a combination of the two.

There seems to be a clearer picture about the inequitable extent of Britain's financial contributions to the Community. Even the most ardent pro-European politicians did not attempt to defend these. In terms of budget transactions with the Community Britain was in debit every year, with the single exception of 1975. By the end of the 1970s her annual budget payments had risen to £1 billion and Britain looked set to replace Germany as the largest contributor. This was despite having the fourth largest Gross Domestic Product (GNP), after West Germany, France and Italy. Another particular difficulty faced by the British government was the movement towards monetary union, revived in the 1980s by France and Germany and given a specific timetable by the Maastricht Treaty. This defined three stages to complete union. The first and second involved the exchange rate mechanism (ERM) being tightened up, with other currencies pegged to the Deutsche Mark (DM). Britain, however, experienced a serious crisis as a result of this. A combination of factors was responsible. One was the pressures exerted on the German economy by reunification in 1990. The rise in German inflation necessitated an increase in interest rates. Britain's domestic policy was geared to sustaining economic recovery by keeping interest rates low. But the pressure from Germany made this difficult to sustain. Investors suddenly switched from sterling to marks and Britain, confronted by financial crisis, withdrew from the ERM in

September 1992. Her future here remained more unsettled than that of the other EU members, some of whom remained in the narrow band of the ERM, others settling, for the moment, for the broader band.

Social legislation within the Community also proved difficult for Britain, although in this case there was a difference of opinion as to whether Britain would benefit or not. The two main changes were the Commission's Social Charter (1989) and the Social Chapter of the Maastricht Treaty (1992). Successive Conservative governments argued that policies on employment, pay, working conditions, benefits, and health and safety would unnecessarily hamper the competitiveness of British industry and that such areas were already adequately covered by British law. There would also be strong economic consequences: higher social provision would be bought at the cost of lower economic performance and rising unemployment. An altogether different perspective was taken by the trade union movement in Britain, who saw the Social Charter and Social Chapter as a guarantee of employees' rights at a time when trade union powers had been cut back by Mrs Thatcher's legislation in the 1980s.

The political implications of Britain's membership also attracted considerable criticism. In some instances there was a conflict between Community law and British Parliamentary law. One of the strongest arguments of the anti-EU lobby was that Britain's Parliamentary sovereignty had gradually been eroded. This called into doubt Heath's contention in 1972 that 'There is no question of any erosion of essential national sovereignty.'[23] There were, of course, parliamentary checks operating through question time and select committees, together with a number of standing committees on EU issues, set up in 1989. But Conservative back-bench critics were convinced that these did not constitute all that much of a check on the increasing intervention of the European Commission in British domestic issues.

Another area of potential difficulty was local government. The general trend within Europe was towards stronger regional governments within the nation state. Even France, traditionally the most centralised and unitary state in Europe, went down this road during the 1980s. Britain, on the other hand, did not adopt the policy of devolution which had looked a likely prospect in the late 1970s. During the long period of Conservative rule from 1979 local government was further reduced in terms of powers and initiative (see Chapter 15). On the other hand, there were some compensations: as Chapter 21 shows, the regional dimension of the Community could prove extremely useful for the implementation of any future 'all-Ireland' solution.

This brings us to the question of Britain's future prospects in Europe. There are three broad possibilities. One would be a soft-pedalling on integration and a further pursuit of the widening process, which happened in the 1970s. This would mean extending the catchment area to eastern Europe. This is Britain's preference, as was indicated by Mrs Thatcher, but it does carry certain risks. For example, the centre of gravity could move increasingly towards Germany, which was greatly enlarged through reunification in 1990 and which already dominates the economies of eastern Europe.

A second possibility would be the intensification of the process of unity based on Maastricht and focusing especially on the tightening links between France and Germany. For Britain, this is the least favoured option since it would be against everything successive British governments have avoided.

The third alternative is a 'two-track' Europe, with an inner group seeking accelerated integration and an outer band which would be associated more loosely with them. A possible scenario is that Britain will opt for the outer layer, only to find herself impelled to seek further involvement in the future; the dynamics of the late 1950s and 1960s could therefore repeat themselves. In these circumstances it is difficult to see how Britain could succeed in holding out against the revived forces of integration or continue being in Europe but not of it.

20

THE BRITISH EMPIRE
AND COMMONWEALTH
IN THE
TWENTIETH CENTURY

The British Empire had developed as a result of very different cycles of growth. During the eighteenth century, the colonisation of India and North America had been based on commercial exploitation and military conquest, usually in wars against France. Then, for much of the nineteenth century there was a reluctance at Whitehall to increase the number of dependencies, largely on the grounds of expense. From about 1870 onwards, however, the Empire expanded rapidly in the hitherto largely untapped areas of Africa and the Pacific.

By 1914 the Empire covered nearly one quarter of the earth's land surface, including self-governing Dominions such as Canada, Australia, New Zealand and South Africa; in Asia, the British Raj, Malaya, Singapore and Hong Kong; in the East Indies and Pacific, New Guinea, North Borneo, and Fiji; in central America, Guiana and Honduras and a series of West Indian islands including Jamaica, Trinidad and Barbados; in Africa, Basutoland, Swaziland, Bechuanaland, the Rhodesias, Nyasaland, Kenya, Uganda, the Sudan, Egypt, Nigeria, the Gold Coast, Sierra Leone and Gambia; and, in the Mediterranean, Gibraltar, Malta and Cyprus. The twentieth century, however, saw the gradual reduction of this array of colonies until, by 1995, the only formal dependencies left were Hong Kong (due to revert to China in 1997), Gibraltar and a handful of remote island colonies, the largest of which were the Falklands.

This chapter considers the two main stages in the process of the weakening of the Empire: between the two world wars and the period since 1945. There are really two sides to the same coin: the decline of formal imperial rule and the emergence of the British Commonwealth. As one faded and expired, the other grew and matured. The first cannot, in retrospect, be considered surprising. As J.R. Ferris argues

The British Empire could not have lasted forever; no polity has yet managed that feat, let alone this unlikely candidate, in which so many owed so much to so few. The wonder is not that the British Empire fell but that it took so long in the falling.[1]

Conversely, it might be added, there is no precedent for a successful association of ex-colonies, which makes the rise of the Commonwealth more remarkable than the decline of the Empire.

DEVELOPMENTS BETWEEN THE WARS

The British Empire reached its greatest extent immediately after the First World War. To the already considerable core of 1914 were now added a series of mandates from the defeated powers. These were of two types. German colonies, like Tanganyika, part of Kamerun and the Solomon Islands, were undeveloped and therefore added to the British Empire for the indefinite future. The Arab areas of the Ottoman Empire were another matter; they were more advanced economically and British rule was intended to prepare them for independence within the foreseeable future. These included Iraq, Transjordan and Palestine.

During the 1920s there was tremendous confidence about the future of the British Empire. Germany had been the main rival before 1914 in terms of naval supremacy and empire-building. But the Treaty of Versailles had systematically dismantled the German Empire and imposed drastic restrictions on German armaments. Other powers also appeared less threatening. The French Empire remained intact, but France had been weakened more than Britain by the war. Japan emerged strengthened, but at this stage was still an ally of Britain. The Russian Empire had collapsed and the new Soviet state was concerned primarily with survival. The British Empire was still seen as a positive and beneficent force, while the First World War had demonstrated the importance of the imperial contribution in the defeat of both Germany and Turkey. There were also possible advantages for the future, especially in economic terms. This became more and more important during the inter-war period. Between 1910 and 1914 25 per cent of Britain's imports and 36 per cent of her exports were with the Empire. Between 1925 and 1929 the corresponding figures were 28 per cent and 42 per cent; between 1935 and 1939 39.5 per cent and 49 per cent.[2]

There were, however, also incipient problems. More than at any other time in her history Britain found her resources stretched almost to breaking point in dealing with the Empire. Demobilisation was an economic necessity after the First World War and altogether Britain had to rely upon total armed forces of 200,000 plus another 100,000 Indian troops for her defence needs and for the protection of the Empire. The extent of this vulnerability was less apparent in the 1920s, when the strength of possible rivals was artificially low as a result of the outcome of the First World War (see Chapter 17). During the 1930s, however, a major threat emerged in the Far East, the climax of which was the fall of Hong Kong and Singapore to the Japanese in 1942.

A second problem was Britain's changing economic relationship with the Empire. Before 1914 Britain had still had a considerable balance in her favour in terms of overseas investments and could regard the colonies as markets for her industrial goods. By the end of the First World War Britain had been obliged to sell many of her investments in order to pay for the war effort, a process which was to be completed between 1939 and 1945. In addition the balance of trade had altered perceptibly; Chapter 8 shows how India had become a significant competitor to Britain in textile production and how her own imports were as much from Japan as from Britain. This was a key factor in the decline of textiles as one of Britain's staple industries during the period.

Third, Britain faced the problem of future relations with the various parts of the Empire. These differed according to the stage of development reached. The greatest advances had been achieved by the Dominions, which now underwent a series of constitutional refinements. The least developed parts of the Empire were the African, West Indian and Pacific territories, for which future arrangements hardly arose at this stage. Between the two poles was the Indian subcontinent, which was beginning to exert pressure for a redefined status – and which posed the most difficult problem of all. Outside all of these categories were the Arab states, most of which were mandates, and which were left out of the refinements of discussions about dominion status.

The concession of dominion status and full sovereignty to Australia, New Zealand, Canada and South Africa had been accomplished before 1914. Each of these possessed its own legislature before 1914 and they had all contributed to Lloyd George's Imperial War Cabinet. But during the 1920s and 1930s several refinements were made to dominion status. These cleared up a great deal of the previous uncertainty about the extent of the Dominions' constitutional powers. The need arose as a result of several constitutional difficulties during the early 1920s. In 1924 the Nationalist Party came to power in South Africa under Hertzog, who was determined to secure the fullest possible recognition of South Africa's internal sovereignty. The following year the Canadian Prime Minister, William Mackenzie King, complained at unwarranted interference by the British Crown when he was refused a dissolution of the Canadian Parliament by the Governor-General. Both Hertzog and Mackenzie King supported an earlier resolution by General Smuts that what was now needed was a declaration of constitutional rights guaranteeing that Westminster had no remaining control over the Dominions in either domestic or foreign policy.

The first specific statement was the Balfour Declaration, agreed at the 1926 Commonwealth Conference. This defined Dominions as 'autonomous communities within the British Empire, equal in status, in no way subordinate one to another in any aspect of their domestic or external affairs, though united by a common allegiance to the Crown, and freely associated as members of the British Commonwealth of Nations'.[3] The second was the Statute of Westminster (1931). This repealed some of the earlier constraints imposed by the Colonial Laws Validity Act (1865). It removed the condition that dominion laws could not be 'repugnant' to British law or 'to the provisions of any existing or future Act of Parliament of the United Kingdom, or to any order, rule or regulation made under any such Act'.[4] It also stated that British law could apply to the Dominions only if this was accepted by the dominion parliaments. Finally, it enabled the Dominions to enter their own diplomatic relations with other countries, although they first sent diplomats abroad at different dates: Canada in 1927, Australia in 1940 and New Zealand in 1941.

Clarification of constitutional status was often accompanied by a more open pursuit of individual interests, sometimes in opposition to Britain; Canada, for example, opposed the renewal of the Anglo-Japanese Treaty in 1920. Foreign policy issues between the wars attracted lukewarm responses on occasion. For example, Lloyd George's request for support for Britain's action at Chanak in 1922 received no support at all from Canada, Australia and South Africa. Dominions were also beginning to make their own diplomatic and commercial agreements – as, for example, with the halibut fishing agreements between Canada and the United States in 1923. Above all, one of the influences on the policy of appeasement pursued by Britain during the 1930s was the feeling that the Dominions would be reluctant to go to war over an issue like the Sudetenland.

Clearly, therefore, a great deal had changed since 1914. Britain and the Dominions had moved somewhat apart between the wars as self-government became actual independence. There were indications, too, that the whole structure of the Commonwealth was loosening. The Afrikaner population was anxious to distance South Africa from

Britain; the Irish Free State was in a trade war with Britain during the 1930s, and relations between Britain and Australia came close to rupture in the 1932–3 'bodyline' cricket tour. The Ottawa Conference of 1932 also failed to provide a fully integrated system of imperial preference on tariffs, instead setting up a series of individually negotiated agreements between Britain and the Dominions.

On the positive side, there remained a great deal of mutual affection and loyalty. This was sustained partly through family connections, brought about by extensive emigration and settlement, and partly by shared historical traditions, the focus of which was the British monarchy, always held in higher esteem than the British government or Parliament. The ultimate test came with the support of all the Dominions for Britain's declaration of war on Germany – with the exception of the Irish Free State and a strongly expressed opposition within South Africa to official government policy there. Overall, it seemed that the relationship between Britain and the Dominions had changed. Although they had weakened in terms of centralised sovereignty, they had strengthened in terms of voluntary association and support over crucial issues.

At the other extreme from the Dominions were the less developed areas in the Pacific, Africa and the West Indies. These were under the control of an array of governors, who were ultimately responsible to the British Crown. The inter-war period saw the actual growth of the Colonial Office, that part of the British government which was responsible for dependencies. The future of these was never firmly established at this stage. On the one hand the ultimate logic was that they too would be prepared for eventual self-rule and dominion status. On the other hand, there was no agreed timetable. This was partly because none of the other colonial territories belonging to France, Belgium, the Netherlands, Italy and Portugal were the subject of any schemes for self-rule: why should British territories be different? There was also a consciousness that they were somewhat less developed than the Dominions, with lower educational attainments, lower Gross Domestic Products and less contact with the Westminster system of government. There was still a widespread belief that unless government was in white hands it would lack the necessary experience of effective democracy. The only real compromise was therefore in the case of Southern Rhodesia where, in 1923, the ruling white minority were given internal self-government, although admittedly with sufficient constraints to prevent this from being construed as dominion status. Elsewhere in Africa it was considered enough that there was already a system which functioned on delegated authority, fitting into a traditional tribal hierarchy under the benevolent guidance of Crown representatives who took the real decisions. This seemed to be the natural form of government for two reasons: it was relatively inexpensive and it could be justified as an alternative to dominion status in that it seemed to allow for indigenous participation. What it did not, of course, do was to allow for the expression of any form of nationalism, which ended up by being totally opposed to the continuation of tribal structures. But all this lay very much in the future.

Britain's most consistent imperial problem between the wars was India. This was far in advance of Africa in its development of internal opposition to British rule; the main challenge came from middle-class movements like the Congress party, led by activists like Gandhi and Nehru, and from the Muslim League. Here Britain faced a different test to the two types of problem already examined. The traditional form of delegation through the Indian princes was no longer adequate, which meant that the problem could not be ignored as in Africa. Nor could it simply be adjusted by conferring full dominion status, as with Australia and New Zealand.

The problem was compounded by the growing confrontation between the authorities and the elements demanding home rule for India. There were occasions when the British government was clearly embarrassed by atrocities on the spot, like the Amritsar massacre of 1919 which resulted in the death of 379 people at the hands of troops under General Dyer. More persistent was the campaign of civil disobedience organised by Gandhi which, more than anything else, forced the British government to consider some form of compromise for the future. The proposals in the 1919 Government of India Act for responsible self-rule in the distant future were too gradualistic, based as they were on local legislative responsibility on low-level issues. They were therefore replaced in 1935 by the 1935 Government of India Act, which proposed a sort of apprenticeship to dominion status. There would be a federation with an elected parliament, a broader franchise and partial responsibility of the executive to the legislature. On the other hand, the traditional powers of the princes would be retained and the overall control would still be with the British viceroy. Comparatively little progress had been made in implementing this scheme before the outbreak of war in 1939. In any case, there were major differences of opinion about it. Conservative politicians such as Churchill believed that it went much too far, while Indian activists like Gandhi saw it as totally inadequate. Clearly this was a major area of unfinished imperial business.

Another area for which decisions had to be made was the Middle East. But here the policy was not to hold on to colonies or to redefine the constitutional status. Instead, Britain hoped to cut her losses and grant independence, on the understanding that British interests were in no way endangered. This was applied with reasonable success to three Arab states. Egypt, occupied by Britain in 1882, was made independent in 1922 with special arrangements for British control over foreign policy and, from 1936, for a British force to protect the Suez Canal. Iraq and Transjordan, former provinces of the Ottoman Empire assigned to Britain as mandates, were also given independence under specially installed kings favourable to Britain: Feisal in Iraq and Abdullah in Transjordan. The Palestinian mandate proved more complex. With the best of intentions, the 1917 Balfour Declaration had undertaken to provide British support for the 'establishment in Palestine of a national home for the Jewish people'. This created a considerable problem with the majority Arab population, who fiercely resisted the immigration of Jews from Europe, especially during the 1930s when numbers went up as a result of persecution in Nazi Germany. Britain tried desperately to find a solution – not by keeping Palestine within the Empire, but by handing it a workable form of independence. It considered first of all a partitioned state in 1937, then a federated state in 1939. But the war intervened before anything could be settled here. Palestine, too, had to look to the future for a resolution of its constitutional status.

During the inter-war period, therefore, the British government encountered different problems with various parts of the Empire in different stages of development. By and large, however, any changes which actually occurred were unspectacular and there seemed no logical reason why the British Empire should not last a considerable length of time in its existing form, allowing, of course, for the settlement of the problems of India and Palestine. After 1945, however, there was an inexorable movement towards ending the Empire altogether. What made the difference?

DEVELOPMENTS SINCE THE SECOND WORLD WAR

It is possible to argue that, up to 1939, the British Empire was actually in decline while it was still expanding. During the nineteenth century, for example, dominion status was being conferred on Canada and Australia even before the completion of British expansion into Africa. This was refined and extended during the 1920s and 1930s at the same time that Britain was adding mandated territories to her imperial responsibilities.

After 1945, however, the process of decolonisation was extraordinarily rapid. India and Pakistan were given their independence in 1947, Burma and Ceylon in 1948. These were followed by the Sudan (1956), Malaya and Ghana (1957), Cyprus and Nigeria (1960), Sierra Leone and Tanganyika (1961), Jamaica, Trinidad and Uganda (1962), Kenya (1963), the union of Sabah and Sarawak with Malaysia (1963), Zambia, Malawi and Malta (1964), Gambia (1965), Guyana, Lesotho, Botswana and Barbados (1966), Aden (1967), Mauritius and Swaziland (1968), Fiji (1970), Bahamas (1973) and Zimbabwe (1980). By the 1980s the only areas still under British rule were Gibraltar, the Falkland Islands and Hong Kong (which, in any case, was due to revert to China in 1997 as a result of the 1984 Anglo-Chinese Hong Kong agreement).

The end of the British Empire was in all cases a voluntary surrender of power. According to J. Darwin, it

> did not come about in a sudden and violent conflagration, or as a result of irresistible colonial insurrections. Almost everywhere, on the face of it, British rule came to an end as the result of decisions taken, or ratified, in London about the terms and timing of a transfer of power.[5]

This contrasts with the experiences of other colonial powers after 1945. France and the Netherlands attempted to cling on to their possessions, only to release them with unprecedented alacrity after experiencing military defeat. Britain's decolonisation was more gradual and led to the redefining rather than abolition of relationships, in the form of the Commonwealth.

The French assumed that the defeat of the Japanese would be followed by the recovery of French Indo-China. In 1954, however, they were humiliated by the Viet Minh at the Battle of Dien Bien Phu. A significant change of heart followed as the Prime Minister, Pierre Mendes-France, told a shocked nation that France would have to give up parts of North Africa. When De Gaulle came to power he adopted a policy of the voluntary dissolution of France's remaining colonies. The Dutch, too, were forced to give up their remaining colonies as a result of defeat by nationalist guerrillas, this time in Indonesia. Having learned the hard way that imperialism was no longer viable, both countries were able to justify ending it on economic grounds. Earlier fears that the loss of the East Indies would ruin the Dutch economy proved completely groundless, since firms that had previously operated in Indonesia now redirected their capital and management skills to the home market, contributing to the boom experienced by the Netherlands in the mid-1950s. For both France and the Netherlands, preserving colonial empires seemed suddenly less important than seeking closer integration in Europe in the form of the ECSC and the EEC (see Chapter 19).

Because the end of the British Empire was less spectacular and more prolonged than this, explanations are somewhat more complex. They cover four main areas: domestic influences, economic realities, international pressures and nationalist reactions within the colonies themselves.

There is no doubt that public opinion had become far less attached to the concept of Empire. Indeed some historians, such as C. Barnett, maintain that Britain experienced after 1945 a moral revulsion against imperialism.[6] Others consider that this is somewhat overstating the swing of opinion, which was influenced more by a choice of priorities. After 1945 the main alternative was the welfare state, which Britain would not be able to afford if she also retained her imperial responsibilities. The electorate showed in 1945 that it was overwhelmingly in support of social change. For the working class, this was especially important, and even the working-class Conservative voters, of whom there were many, had lost the taste for glory abroad that had been so carefully nurtured in the late nineteenth century by Disraeli and Salisbury.[7] The middle classes benefited also from the welfare state and were also unlikely to be drawn into imperialist diversions. The Second World War had given most people enough external campaigns to last them a lifetime and their emphasis was now on internal reconstruction. Another important social ingredient has been added to this by A.P. Thornton,[8] who argues that the declining role and influence of the aristocracy accompanied the reduced interest in the empire from the public.

This lack of enthusiasm among the electorate was underscored by the consensus between the political parties that the colonial role should be reduced. The same consensus eventually allowed the colonial role to be wound up altogether. This, of course, took time to emerge, partly because of the debate within the two major parties. Labour, for example, had always possessed a strongly anti-imperialist wing but, in the immediate post-war period, this had been muted by official government policy – to see through the independence of India and Palestine but not to rush into decolonisation elsewhere. During the 1950s, however, Labour could afford from the opposition benches to be more critical of the whole concept of Empire. This was partly due to the arguments of Fenner Brockway who, with Anthony Wedgwood Benn, founded the Movement for Colonial Freedom in 1954. Labour also believed that the Empire could be converted into the Commonwealth, which would act as a channel for more positive relations between Britain and free Third World countries. It might even be the focus of North–South harmony which could reduce the impact of East–West tension caused by the Cold War. The Conservatives moved in much the same direction. Although a minority, led by Lord Salisbury, favoured retaining the Empire in its existing form, the mainstream of the party was pragmatic. It was Macmillan who signalled the acceleration of decolonisation in his 'wind of change' speech given in South Africa in 1961, while Iain MacLeod was given the post of Colonial Secretary to prepare the way for the transfer of power.

Several arguments have been put forward concerning the influence of economic factors on winding up colonial empires. One is really a modern version of the theory of colonial exploitation. According to G. Wasserman, the search for new outlets for investment no longer focused on underdeveloped parts of the world since these could no longer fulfil the demands of the metropolitan economies in an age of growing international finance and multinational companies.[9] More specifically related to Britain is the view of B. Lapping and others that Britain could not have sustained imperial commitments while, at the same time, undergoing a contraction in her economic base.[10] There is much to support this: Chapter 11 deals with the reduction of Britain's overseas assets and the conversion of the favourable balance with the colonies before the war to an unfavourable one after it. Finally, R. Holland argues that Britain's economic condition meant that she had to adjust to new economic networks – based more on Europe.[11] This can certainly be supported by the decline in British trade with the Empire and Commonwealth. Exports, which had been 47.7 per cent in 1950, fell back to 40.2 per cent in 1960 and 24.4 per cent in 1970, while the respective figures for imports were 41.9 per cent, 34.6 per cent and 25.9 per cent.[12] Membership of the European Community and winding up the British Empire were therefore logically connected.

There were also several international factors influencing the pace of decolonisation – all beyond Britain's control. One was the declining status of the imperial powers in a new bipolar world. Imperialism had depended on Europe being the centre of the word's political gravity. After 1945 this was no longer the case: the periphery had taken over, with the emergence of the United States and the Soviet Union as the two superpowers. Both were strongly anti-imperialistic, one through its historic traditions and the other through its ideology. In this new order, priorities began to change. The Cold War brought new commitments. It is true that there was a touch of the historic anti-Russian sentiment involved. But this was because of the perceived threat on Europe rather than the traditional concern about Russian threats to the Empire. Britain therefore had to make choices, and the urgency of defence in Europe outweighed the needs of imperial defence. The most dramatic sign of this change was that the navy, which had always been the most important of Britain's forces, took the brunt of any rationalisation or cuts (see Chapter 17).

How important were the international pressures surrounding the 1956 Suez Crisis in forcing the pace of British decolonisation? One view is it was a turning point in British attitudes to empire. Before Suez Britain had been consciously pursuing a world role based partly on the Empire, whereas after Suez Britain's role contracted increasingly into a European one. The other interpretation is that Suez was less a turning point than an accelerator. This seems to make more sense. Britain had made arrangements before Suez for the independence of the second batch of colonies: Ghana and Malaya, with proposals also for a third batch, including Nigeria. According to J. Darwin, 'Suez did not trigger an imperial implosion nor instigate a sudden revulsion against colonial rule among the policy makers.'[13] It did, however, show the danger of antagonising the United States, as well as members of the Commonwealth, and it demonstrated the military difficulty of undertaking the sort of imperial action that Britain had once taken for granted. In this respect, Suez confirmed in the clearest possible way that the commitments of empire were a costly irrelevance.

Finally, it would be a mistake to see the impetus of decolonisation entirely as a one-way process. It also owed much to the growth of indigenous nationalism. This was already apparent in parts of Asia before the Second World War but became a major factor in large parts of Africa only after 1945. Nationalism was not in itself sufficient to destroy colonial structures, as the inter-war period had proved. Instead, a major shock was needed to the whole system of European rule in Asia. This was administered by the Japanese occupation of the Dutch East Indies, French Indo-China and British Malaya, Singapore and Hong Kong. For the French and Dutch colonies this had two main effects. It disrupted their pre-war administrations and it evoked powerful resistance movements, directed initially against the Japanese and then against the attempted return of the Europeans. India was not directly part of this experience since it had not been invaded. Nevertheless, the wave of nationalism sweeping through Vietnam and Indonesia against the French and Dutch respectively gave further strength to the drive for Indian independence – and a greater sense of urgency for Britain to concede it in 1947.

The development of nationalism in Africa had pre-war roots but was undoubtedly given a huge impetus by the success of anti-colonial movements in Asia and the inclusion of new Asian members of the United Nations. There was therefore a powerful 'domino effect' which provided a major boost to leaders in British African colonies during the late 1950s and early 1960s: Nkrumah in Ghana, Kenyatta in Kenya, Obote in Uganda, Banda in Malawi and Kaunda in Zambia. There were also 'functional' reasons for the spread of African nationalism. One was the spread of the English language, which cut across tribal linguistic differences. Another was the use by nationalist leaders of a variety of specific discontents with colonial rule to unite a heterogeneous population in opposition to it. Unintentionally the British contributed to this by trying to raise educational and medical standards, which meant an inevitable increase in the levels of taxation.

One of the reasons that the British Empire had remained intact for so long was that Britain had always governed with the co-operation of indigenous agents or collaborators. The growth of nationalism gradually reduced the supply and the same groups moved into opposition to colonial rule. Faced with this the British government's policy was now to prepare the way for colonial withdrawal. By and large, Britain's response to nationalism was positive; most politicians and officials considered it to be an inevitable consequence of exposure to western democratic ideas on representation. Successive British governments therefore argued that self-government had always been the long-term intention and that the Empire was evolving naturally into the Commonwealth.

THE MODERN COMMONWEALTH

Two major organisations helped ease the transition to the post-colonial world: the British Commonwealth and the French Union. Both were intended to provide a permanent bond between the former metropolitan power and its ex-colonies. The French Union, however, gradually faded, while the Commonwealth survived and prospered to become, after the United Nations Organisation, the largest international structure in the world. It has been defined as 'a voluntary association of extremely diverse, fully sovereign states, which are internationally equal but which have in common a historical background with a period of British rule and a political evolution which led up to responsible government.'[14]

We should not seek explanations for its survival and growth in the achievement of any historical objectives. The original Commonwealth was intended as a means of updating the Empire and was therefore part of the movement towards integration which many, like the historian Lionel Curtis, favoured; his book, *The Commonwealth of Nations*, published in 1916, sought to promote a federal union with constitutional links covering all dominions. He was very much in the line of imperialist 'centralisers', like Joseph Chamberlain, who wanted to update imperial links, but at the same time to unify. But this is not the direction the Commonwealth took at all. Rather, it was the means of decentralising and reducing any overlapping powers. According to A.J.R. Groom it is 'clearly inter-governmental, rather than supranational in character'.[15] Instead of being a more advanced form of imperial union, therefore, the modern Commonwealth was one of the loosest organisations ever constructed.

Nor has the modern Commonwealth produced any specifically defined purpose. It has never, for example, developed into an economic trading bloc. None of the earlier attempts at imperial tariffs, made by Chamberlain and MacDonald, were repeated. Nor is it a channel for redistributing wealth. Aid to its third-world members comes either bilaterally from donor states such as Britain or Canada, or multilaterally through the agencies of the United Nations. It has no defensive or political obligations; it has not, for example, managed to prevent wars between member states – especially between India and Pakistan. Nor can it be relied upon to provide Britain with moral support in times of conflict. Many members of the Commonwealth sympathised with Argentina over the 1982 Falklands conflict, identifying it as a North–South conflict and Britain's action as a revival of neo-colonialism.

On the other hand, the very ambiguity of its structure and purpose is the Commonwealth's strength. This is in complete contrast with the French Union. In some respects the latter was the more attractive proposition in the 1960s. Close association with the metropolitan country could offer security and economic viability. The disadvantages were, however, manifest. One was the divided allegiance of the metropolitan power between the European Community and the former members of the empire. Another was the indigenous nationalism which would not be given a proper chance to develop. It was once said that the French Revolution devoured its children; the French Union

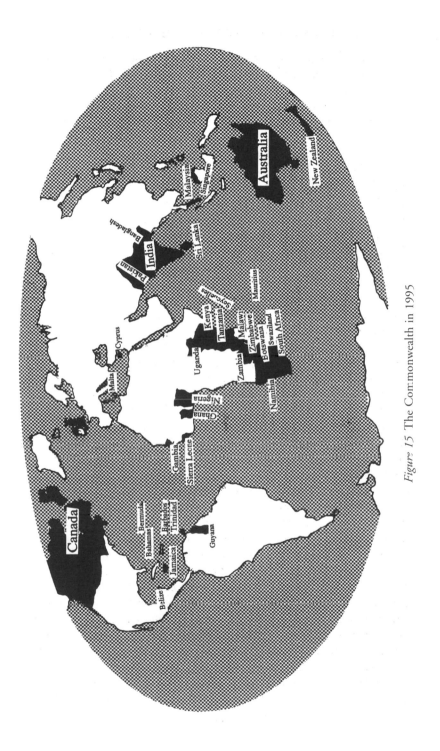

Figure 15 The Commonwealth in 1995

similarly threatened to smother its offspring. By contrast, the British Commonwealth seemed initially unpromising: it offered no close ties with the metropolitan power and no material reason for continued membership. But in a sense it is inappropriate to judge it by the tightness of its structure and the cohesiveness of its objectives since any emphasis on these would most probably have sent it the same way as the French Union – into the past. As it is, only five states out of over eighty have withdrawn, and three of these – Pakistan, South Africa and Zimbabwe – have subsequently considered it worthwhile rejoining.

The Commonwealth has proved highly adaptable. Although Britain has deliberately stood back from being the focal point, the Queen is its formal head. At one time this would have required all members to acknowledge the monarch as their nominal head of state as well. Now, however, several Commonwealth countries, including India and Pakistan, have converted themselves into republics of the Common-wealth. There is a compromise here, which smacks of British politics generally: the Queen carries a constitutional role for some states but not for all. The functional head of the Commonwealth is the Secretary General, but there is no dominant centre. There is certainly no equivalent to the Security Council in the United Nations, with special powers conferred on its five permanent members. This makes the Commonwealth one of the most democratic of international organisations. What the member states have most in common is their primary use of English, the main language in the world outside China. French, by contrast, is the seventh, behind Chinese, English, Hindi, Russian, Spanish and Portuguese.

The Commonwealth also has scope for further development in the future. Although it has so far avoided any form of closer association, it provides plenty of potential for collaboration on specific issues. In October 1991, for example, the Harare declaration, drawn up in the capital of the host, Zimbabwe, pledged the support of the member states to democracy, independent judiciaries, free trade and market economies. Four years later the Commonwealth Conference, held in New Zealand, carried out this resolution by suspending the member-ship of Nigeria. This was in protest against the repressive regime of General Sani Abacha, his actions against the Ogoni people of the Niger delta, and the execution of the writer Ken Saro-Wiwa and other dissidents. As a contrast to punitive action, the Commonwealth might also contribute to the solution of specific problems. One of the most complex issues in recent history has been the Irish question. A possible outcome in the future might be an 'all-Ireland' policy, which is analysed in Chapter 21. This might, as part of the package, involve Ireland rejoining the Commonwealth. And why not? The label 'British' has long since been dropped; republics are now common within the organisation; and the search for a solution to the Northern Irish issue has increased the general residue of goodwill between London and Dublin.

CONCLUSION

The British Empire reached its greatest territorial extent after the First World War. But this was also the time when Britain was having to address the varied problems of imperial states in differing stages of development. Some, the Dominions, were given confirmation of their independence. Others, the less developed colonies, were not dealt with at all. Specific solutions were attempted for the problems of India and Palestine, but had to be deferred after 1939. At this stage, however, there was nothing to indicate that the Empire might disappear in the future.

The Second World War accelerated the decline of British power in the Empire in a variety of ways, especially by changing the population's perceptions of the need for empire, by reducing Britain's economic strength to sustain it, by throwing up alternative international and military obligations, and by promoting indigenous nationalism into an anti-imperial campaign. Britain responded with considerable pragmatism to the changed circumstances and used the model of the Commonwealth as a means of ending the Empire. But this was not the British Commonwealth that had originally been intended. Instead, it was a looser association of nation states in which each had other commitments and involvements. But the essential point is that the Commonwealth survived because it was no longer British.

21

THE IRISH ISSUE 1914–96

Ireland was linked to Britain in 1800 by the Act of Union. Following extensive violence during the First World War, this arrangement ended in 1921 as the three southern provinces became the Irish Free State and two-thirds of the northern province, Ulster, remained within the United Kingdom. For a period of nearly fifty years the two parts adapted to a separate political existence. The Irish Free State severed its last remaining link with Britain when, in 1949, it left the Commonwealth and became the Republic of Eire. Ulster, meanwhile, developed within the United Kingdom as a province with devolved power, which meant that it was represented in two parliaments and had its own government at Stormont. This was not a formula for lasting peace as, from 1968, a series of disturbances occurred which led eventually to the replacement of devolution by direct rule from London. For the next thirty years Ulster remained on the brink of civil war – until more promising signs of a political settlement began to emerge in 1994.

REVOLUTION AND INDEPENDENCE
1914–22

Throughout the nineteenth century there had been opposition to the nature of the relationship between Britain and Ireland. The first half had seen a series of campaigns by Daniel O'Connell, first for the admission of Catholic MPs at Westminster, then for the repeal of the Act of Union. He succeeded in his first objective but at the time of his death in 1851 the second was nowhere in sight. The mid-century crisis, brought by the terrible potato famine, for a while distorted all the issues. But gradually two separate solutions began to emerge for the future of Ireland; one might be categorised as 'republican', the other as 'nationalist'.

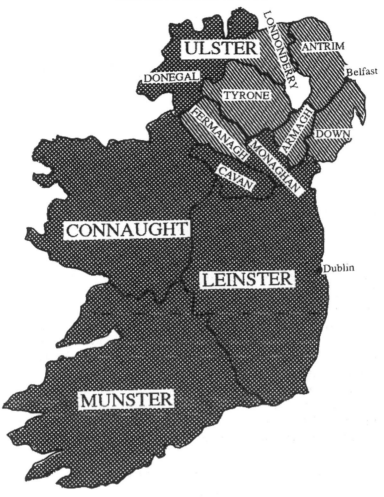

 NORTHERN IRELAND (comprising 6 counties of the province of ULSTER)

 IRISH FREE STATE/EIRE (comprising the provinces of MUNSTER, LEINSTER and CONNAUGHT, and 3 counties of the province of ULSTER)

(Counties shown only for the province of ULSTER)

Figure 16 Ireland in the twentieth century

Republicanism was advanced by the Fenians, set up in 1858 by James Stephens. The members were expected to 'swear allegiance to the Irish Republic',[1] and to prepare for armed revolution. They opposed any constitutional negotiation and had no interest in social or land reform: their quarrel with Britain was entirely political and ideological. Known from 1865 as the Irish Republican Brotherhood (IRB), they provided the roots for the future organisation of Sinn Fein and the Irish Republican Army (IRA). They resorted to a series of bombings and an unsuccessful rebellion in 1867. But for a while the initiative passed from them as more moderate proposals were advanced by the Irish Nationalists, led by Isaac Butt and Charles Stewart Parnell. These policies comprised a separate parliament in Dublin that would provide autonomy for Ireland in all but foreign affairs, security and trade. 'Home Rule' was formally adopted by Prime Minister William Gladstone in 1885, but his attempts to introduce it were defeated in Parliament in 1886 and 1893; this caused a split within the British Liberal party, a minority of which sided with the Conservatives in opposing any concessions to Ireland.

Yet, by 1914, Home Rule was on the verge of being achieved. Asquith's Liberal government got the third Home Rule Bill through the Commons in 1912 and had only to wait until 1914 before it reached the statute book, because the House of Lords' power of veto had been reduced by the 1911 Parliament Act to one of delay only. The Irish Nationalists had co-operated fully and their leader, John Redmond, said in 1912:

> We on these benches stand precisely where Parnell stood. We want peace with this country. We deny that we are separatists, and we say we are willing, as Parnell was willing, to accept a subordinate Parliament created by statute of this Imperial Legislature as a final settlement of Ireland's claims.[2]

Even more significant was the total hold of the Irish Nationalists on all the Irish seats at Westminster in the two elections of 1910: they controlled all 84, while their opponents, the Irish Unionists and Sinn Fein, had none. In these circumstances, Home Rule would appear to have been the logical, even inevitable, outcome of nineteenth-century Anglo-Irish relations.

History, however, is littered with examples of an unexpected twist which nullifies an apparently inexorable trend. Ireland is one of these. By the time of the 1918 general election the strength of the Irish Nationalists had been totally destroyed. They managed to win only 7 seats, while the Irish Unionists claimed 25 and Sinn Fein 73. What had happened between 1914 and 1918 was a considerable increase in support for two more extreme parties at the expense of the moderate Irish Nationalists. The Irish Unionists, concentrated especially in the province of Ulster, had already emerged as an obstacle to a negotiated settlement before 1914, while Sinn Fein developed partly as a backlash against the Ulster Unionists and partly as a protest against the additional burdens placed on Ireland by the British government during the First World War. In this way the war acted as a catalyst for revolution and the eventual settlement was very different to that envisaged in 1914.

The resistance within Ireland to Home Rule came from people of Anglo-Irish and Scots-Irish descent. The desire to retain the union with Britain was in part a fear of the Catholic majority: increasingly, 'Home Rule' was projected as 'Rome Rule'. In part it was economic, since Ulster was more heavily industrialised and had much closer economic connections with the mainland, relying heavily upon it for raw materials and markets. The problem was that an independent Ireland might seek to protect itself with tariff walls. It might also fall prey to the agricultural interest of the peasantry, which would undermine the industrial growth that had taken place in the late nineteenth century. Ulster had also been less badly affected by the famine and the land wars of the nineteenth century, and its population had actually increased while the rest of Ireland's had declined.

The campaign in Ulster against Home Rule began in 1886 with the formation of the Ulster Loyalist Anti-Repeal Union, which was replaced in 1904 by the Ulster Unionist Council. These established close links with the Conservative party at Westminster in a desperate bid to outmanoeuvre the Liberals and Irish Nationalists. For a while they succeeded, the Conservative opposition managing to defeat Gladstone's first Home Rule Bill in the Commons and his second in the Lords. During this period the activities of the Ulster Unionists were relatively restrained. There was, after all, a guarantee that the permanent Conservative majority in the House of Lords would be able to veto Home Rule; the Ulster Unionists were content, therefore, to act as the Irish conscience of the British Conservatives.

By 1914, however, the situation was very different. The Lords had lost their permanent veto – as a result of the 1911 Parliament Act – and the Conservatives were helpless to prevent Asquith's third Home Rule Bill from reaching the statute book by the end of 1914. The Ulster Unionists therefore took matters increasingly into their own hands.

They put pressure on the House of Lords to delay the Home Rule Bill as long as possible while they mobilised for direct action. The delay between 1912, when the Bill passed the Commons, and 1914, when the suspensory veto finally lapsed, was crucial. The Ulster Unionists had time to organise a Volunteer force of 100,000 men, smuggle in rifles and to make it absolutely clear that Home Rule would be resisted by force. Edward Carson, a barrister and former Irish Solicitor-General, set up a provisional government in Ulster, acting on a warning he had already given in 1911 that

> We must be prepared, in the event of a Home Rule Bill passing, with such measures as will carry on for ourselves the government of those districts of which we have control. We must be prepared – and time is precious in these things – the morning Home Rule passes, ourselves to become responsible for the government of the Protestant Union of Ulster.[3]

To make matters worse, the outbreak of the First World War prevented the British government pushing ahead with the policy it had come increasing to favour: Home Rule with special guarantees for the North. The whole question was frozen until Britain had dealt with the German threat.

By the time this option was picked up again by Lloyd George in 1916 there had been further changes. The rapid increase in the influence of Ulster Unionism in the North had a serious backlash: the dramatic rise of Irish republicanism in the South. To the Irish Republican Brotherhood (IRB) was added Sinn Fein, formed in 1905 by Arthur Griffith. Its name 'Ourselves Alone' indicated an early rejection of the Home Rule solution and a demand for a constitution based entirely on separate governments. The economy would be protected and English influences would be eradicated. In response to the mobilisation in Ulster, Sinn Fein and the IRB established a force of 200,000 Volunteers in the South. At first the Irish Nationalists tried to maintain a degree of control over this, but were gradually superseded by the republicans, who planned and launched the Easter Uprising against British rule in 1916. This resulted in the deaths of 450 rebels and 103 soldiers and the executions of 14 leaders, including the organiser, Padraic Pearse. The executions, although understandable within the context of the war, damaged Britain's reputation in Ireland and created martyrs for the republican cause. There was a sudden increase in popular support for Sinn Fein and for the paramilitary organisation it formed, called the Irish Republican Army (IRA). Lloyd George, who at this point led a coalition government in Britain, tried to win back the initiative by introducing Home Rule immediately rather than waiting for the end of the war; this, however, foundered on the question of Ulster and on the determination of Sinn Fein and the IRA to win complete independence. Sinn Fein's performance in the 1918 general election confirmed the increased support for the republicans. To publicise their proposal to break altogether with Britain, Sinn Fein refused to take up their seventy-three seats at Westminster, instead setting up the *Dail Eireann* in Dublin and electing Eamon de Valera the new Irish leader. To all intents and purposes, Home Rule was now dead.

The First World War had been a decisive factor in these developments, as is shown in Chapter 2. The events in Ireland between 1916 and 1922 were unquestionably part of a revolution within the United Kingdom in the sense that they produced within a short period an outcome which was at variance with all longer-term trends. It is true that the first blows to Home Rule were delivered *before* the war by the Ulster Unionists. But the backlash, which saw the defeat of the moderate nationalists by the more extreme republicans, occurred *during* the war, and is explicable only within the context of the war. Perhaps the most important factor was the attempt made by the British government in April 1918 to extend to Ireland the 1916 conscription law. This was widely opposed, to the great benefit of the republicans. It has been argued that even by 1918 Sinn Fein had not established themselves fully in Ireland, and that the Easter Rising had somewhat undermined its credibility. What the conscription law did was to provide Sinn Fein with a new focus that could be used to good effect in the 1918 election. E. Norman goes further: 'The anti-conscription movement had revived the fortunes of Sinn Fein at a time when they would otherwise have wilted into extinction.'[4] This is, of course, impossible to prove. It does indicate, nevertheless, that the rise of Sinn Fein was by no means inevitable; even within the destabilising context of war it took the crisis caused by the conscription issue to bring it to the verge of power.

There is an unexpected twist here. The impact of a wartime measure interacted with the peculiarities of the British electoral system to convert a less than total shift in popular support into an electoral landslide. In the 1918 election Sinn Fein won 70 per cent of the Irish seats at Westminster with 47 per cent of the Irish vote. As a proportion of the total United Kingdom vote, Sinn Fein achieved 4.5 per cent, compared with 2.7 per cent for the Ulster Unionists and 2.2 per cent for the Irish Nationalists, or a combined opposition to Sinn Fein of 4.9 per cent.

Ironically, the destabilising impact of the war was converted into a political revolution by the continuity of the British electoral system.

On the 1918 election results, the South had an overwhelming case for independence as a republic and the North for partition and continued union with Britain. Events between 1919 and 1921 confirmed this trend. The IRA carried out a series of attacks on the British authorities to lend credibility to Sinn Fein's claims to control the South. The British government responded by using ex-service volunteers, who were nicknamed the 'Black and Tans', and the auxiliary division of the Irish Constabulary, or the Auxis. In the ensuing chaos Lloyd George decided that the only feasible solution was independence and partition. The 1920 Government of Ireland Act divided Ulster into two parts. Six counties of Ulster were to remain within the United Kingdom, while the remaining three were to join a separate Irish state, along with the provinces of Connaught, Leinster and Munster. In both cases, Britain would retain overall control: the proposed constitution was therefore not dissimilar to that intended in 1914. The Ulster Unionists accepted the Act and established a government under Sir James Craig. In the South, however, Sinn Fein rejected the scheme and, in 1921, the British government was forced to acknowledge the new Irish Free State.

DIVERGENT DEVELOPMENTS: SOUTH AND NORTH 1922–68

The experiences of the South and the North could not have been more different after 1922. The South went through violence and civil war before eventually achieving stability through moderation. The North, by contrast, saw half a century of political stability before lapsing into violence and sectarian strife.

The key force for moderation in the development of the Irish Free State was the rejection of Sinn Fein and the emergence of a new party system. This took time to achieve and was accompanied by considerable upheaval. The initial problem was the Anglo-Irish Treaty of 1921, ratified by Westminster in 1922. This was rejected by the IRA and its political wing, Sinn Fein, because it included two terms which were widely opposed – an oath of allegiance to the British Crown and the secession of the six counties. A general election showed that most of the population favoured accepting the Treaty and there was a majority in the assembly for non-Republican members. At this point the IRA attempted a violent takeover and assassinated the Irish president, Arthur Griffith. But his successor, W.T. Cosgrave, made it clear that the terms of the Treaty would be implemented and proceeded to frame a new constitution. He also took the strongest possible measures against the IRA. Between 1922 and 1923 some 12,000 IRA activists were imprisoned and 77 were shot, more than six times as many as had been executed by the British after the Easter Uprising of 1916. The IRA and Sinn Fein were so badly discredited that the latter secured only a handful of seats in the new assembly. These were not taken up because Sinn Fein refused to accept the verdict of the Irish electorate. From 1923 onwards the party which had, only a few years earlier, experienced such a meteoric rise, was cut back to a resentful and marginalised minority with no chance of political power. Deprived of a role in the South, it turned its attention increasingly to the North with results which will be analysed in the next section.

A more moderate political alignment now emerged as Ireland gradually reorganised its parties. One grouping was *Cumann na Gaedheal* (Society of Irishmen), eventually to become *Fine Gael* (Soldiers of Ireland); the other was *Fianna Fail* (Warriors of Ireland). At first the pendulum of power took broad sweeps from one side to the other, before eventually settling down into a more rhythmic alternation. *Cumann na Gaedheal* dominated the scene from 1923 until 1932 and Cosgrave did much to improve the efficiency of farming, to develop hydro-electric schemes, and to reform local government, the judiciary and civil service. Between 1932 and 1948 *Fianna Fail* took over, under the leadership of De Valera. This party soaked up much of the earlier republican wing of Irish politics, including the more moderate members of Sinn Fein. De Valera redefined the relationship with Britain, abolishing the oath of allegiance to the Crown and being careful to keep Ireland neutral in the Second World War. A swing back to the other bloc followed, as John Costello headed a *Fine Gael* government between 1948 and 1957. This stole some of *Fianna Fail*'s support – and policies – by taking Ireland out of the Commonwealth in 1949. The period 1957–73 saw the return of *Fianna Fail* but, thereafter, governments changed more quickly: *Fine Gael* formed a coalition with the smaller Labour party between 1973 and 1977, after which Ireland was ruled by *Fianna Fail* (1977–81), with further alternation between *Fine Gael* and *Fianna Fail* in the 1980s and 1990s. Ireland had therefore become one of the best examples in Europe of a successful two-party system.

The reverse was the case in the North. While the South evolved, the North ossified, fixed in the image of its creation in 1922. The South threw off Sinn Fein and the IRA to discover moderation. The North, on the other hand, based its whole rationale on unchanging Unionism, which meant that there could be no moderate course or genuine two-party system.

The main problem in Ulster was the huge divide between the Catholic and Protestant communities. The latter's slight overall majority was enshrined in a permanent Unionist domination over the Stormont parliament and government. From 1929 onwards proportional representation was abolished, which meant that the Catholic parties never had more than 20 per cent of the seats. In any case, the opposition was treated with contempt. According to the *Irish News*, whenever opposition MPs rose to address the House, 'the Prime Minister and other ministers and many of their followers retired ostentatiously and deliberately to the smoke room.'[5] The Stormont regime also institutionalised discrimination at the level of local government, achieved by 'gerrymandering', or the careful redrawing of electoral boundaries to ensure a Protestant majority. The Cameron Commission (1968) revealed that in Londonderry the boundaries of three wards were fixed so that 14,429 Catholics elected 8 opposition councillors, while the Protestant electorate of 8,781 produced 12 Unionists.[6] This was reinforced by weighting local votes according to rates paid, which meant that some Protestant businessmen had as many as seven votes each.

Discrimination also took social and economic forms. Unemployment among Catholics was consistently higher than among Protestants. Catholics also held the majority of the lower-paid and menial posts and a small minority of jobs in the higher levels of the Civil Service, the police force and the universities. The situation was exacerbated during the 1930s by the onset of depression, which affected the textile and ship-building industries hit heavily especially. Particularly badly affected were the skilled industrial workers, most of whom were Protestant. As unemployment figures reached 28 per cent, the future Prime Minister of Northern Ireland, Sir Basil Brooke, argued in 1933 that preference should always be given in the allocation of jobs to Protestants rather than to Catholics. It is difficult to know whether discrimination was always systematic and government-directed but certainly individual companies operated a policy of employing Protestants rather than Catholics, irrespective of suitability and qualifications. Similarly, while it might have been difficult to prove a deliberate policy of discrimination in the allocation of housing across the province as a whole, there were certainly areas where this was very much the practice – Belfast, Londonderry, Armagh and Dungannon, for example.

These examples would appear to indicate that society in the North was becoming more and more divided. Yet there was some hope. The introduction of the welfare state in the United Kingdom after 1945 led to a gradual improvement in the standard of living, so that the Catholics in the North were, by the 1950s, materially better off than those in the South, where welfare services had not yet been developed. According to E. McCann:

> Compulsory national insurance, increased family allowances and the Health Service all helped to shield Catholics from the worst effects of unemployment and poverty . . . and since such benefits were not available south of the border the tendency to regard the achievement of a united Ireland as the only way to make things better began to weaken.[7]

But the key question by the 1960s was whether the Unionist government could see its way to consolidate this advance by well-timed political concessions.

NORTHERN IRELAND IN CRISIS 1968–94

The situation looked promising when Terence O'Neill, more progressive than the normal run of Unionists, became Prime Minister in 1963. Yet by 1969 the province was sliding rapidly into chaos. What happened?

The 'troubles' started innocuously enough with a reawakening of reformist demands. The Northern Ireland Civil Rights Association (NICRA), which comprised Catholics and liberal Protestants, sought an end to entrenched abuses such as plural voting, gerrymandering, distorted housing allocations, and other forms of institutionalised discrimination. There was also strong opposition to the use of special powers and the Ulster B-Specials. Civil rights marchers were attacked by Unionist supporters and by members of the Royal Ulster Constabulary at Burntollet Bridge near Londonderry and there was extensive rioting in the Bogside area of Ulster's second city. The Ulster government tried to contain the situation by the promise of moderate reform, but O'Neill was immediately criticised by the right wing of his party, which accused him of traitorous behaviour. Although he narrowly won the 1969 general election, he was unable to cope with the escalation of violence and gave way to James Chichester-Clark, who followed a more obviously defensive policy of containment. Even so, he was forced to agree to the stationing of the first British troops in Belfast in 1969. He was succeeded by Brian Faulkner, a typical Unionist hardliner, who put the reforming programme into reverse and sought to rediscover firm government. By now, the IRA, for so long marginalised in the South, had discovered a new mission in the North and proceeded to attack army personnel. The situation had deteriorated so badly by March 1972 that Ulster was brought under direct rule from Westminster.

Why did this crisis occur? The nineteenth-century French writer De Tocqueville once observed that a bad system is most in peril when it begins to liberalise. A modern equivalent is the view of D. Quinn that 'Stormont was a reactionary system of government which attempted to reform itself. The result was disaster.'[8] It could be argued that reactionary systems can only hope to reform effectively through self-transformation, as occurred later in De Klerk's South Africa. Anything less cannot meet the expectations which have been built up. This applied to the changes made by Terence O'Neill: although more progressive than any of his predecessors, he was nevertheless considered too conservative by the Catholic minority while, at the same time, he appeared dangerously radical to the traditionalist elements within his own party. In a sense, the civil rights movements fully expected O'Neill to fail. The People's Democracy Movement, which soon outbid NICRA for militant support, constantly raised the demands, while campaigners like Bernadette Devlin and Eamonn McCann made it clear that this was no time for restrained protest. According to the Cameron Commission:

> We are driven to think that the leaders must have intended . . . to increase tension, so that in the process a more radical programme could be realised. They saw the march as a calculated martyrdom.[9]

Even the year was significant: 1968 was the crest of a world-wide radical movement, ranging from the student riots against De Gaulle, to the anti-American riots in Grosvenor Square and the protests against the Soviet invasion of Czechoslovakia. Paris, London, Prague: why should Belfast remain immune to the wave of anti-establishment disturbances?

As the crisis deepened, cross-splits developed on each side of the dividing chasm. The fundamental division was between the Nationalists and the Unionists. Originally all Nationalists had been united in their demand for independence from Britain and for a united Ireland. But the form this would take had caused major differences, as far back as the beginning of the century, between moderate Nationalists

330

and radical Republicans. The modern equivalent of that division is the alienation between the moderate Social Democratic and Labour Party (SDLP) and the radicals. The SDLP was established in 1970. Led from 1979 by John Hume, it was strongly opposed to Unionist domination, arguing for 'an autonomous Northern Ireland state within a federal Ireland and an Anglo-Irish Council providing the institutional link with Britain, which would provide for British citizenship.'[10]

The radicals, meanwhile, distanced themselves from the moderate SDLP and experienced some splintering within their own ranks. As we have seen, Sinn Fein and the IRA had been marginalised in the South. After an unsuccessful campaign of terrorism in Britain in the late 1930s and against Northern Ireland in the 1950s, they withdrew into a non-violent pursuit of Marxist policies. But not before two new organisations had broken away from them in 1970: the IRA Provisionals (or the 'Provos') and their political arm, Provisional Sinn Fein. A second offshoot emerged in 1974 in the form of the Irish National Liberation Army (INLA). The Provisional IRA and INLA pursued a campaign of deliberate terror against British rule and the Protestant community. They attempted to mobilise the Catholic community into demonstrations and, if possible, acts of violence; to undermine military and police security in Northern Ireland; and to terrorise the British government by, for example, bombing a Conservative Party Conference at the Grand Hotel in Brighton in 1984 and mortaring a cabinet meeting in Downing Street in 1991. Meanwhile, Provisional Sinn Fein, latterly under the leadership of Gerry Adams, focused more directly on gaining Catholic support in local government elections; it did, however, remain tarnished by its obvious association with the IRA and was certainly kept at arm's length by the majority of the Catholic population which, if anything, supported the SDLP.

The Unionists also split into wings – with great acrimony. The larger group was the Official Unionist Party (OUP), from 1979 to 1995 under James Molyneux. This was further subdivided into 'devolutionists' and 'integrationists'. The former wanted the return of Stormont and partial independence, while the latter felt that the true logic of Unionism was full integration with Britain, a course which was strongly argued by Enoch Powell. The latter, who had left the Conservative party, was elected for the OUP in 1974 and became the party's main theorist. More extreme was the Democratic Unionist Party (DUP), under the Reverend Ian Paisley, which was implacably opposed to any possibility of union with Ireland.

Our fathers rejected the attempts of the British Parliament, swayed by the Irish Nationalists, to force home rule on Ireland. If the Crown in Parliament decreed to put Ulster into a United Ireland, we should be disloyal to her Majesty if we did not resist such a surrender to our enemies.[11]

The DUP was essentially backward-looking. By the early 1990s Paisley was advocating the return of Stormont, no doubt with its built-in Unionist majority, with a few concessions to the minority population: this was more or less the position reached by O'Neill in 1969. Going well beyond both the OUP and the DUP were the Protestant para-military organisations, especially the Ulster Defence Association (UDA) and the Ulster Defence Force (UDF). Often referred to as 'loyalists', these were the counterparts to the IRA and the INLA and, during the late 1980s, became increasingly involved in retaliatory sectarian killings.

The fundamental conflict between the two main groupings was usually seen as a religious one: it was obviously sectarian and it was between Catholic and Protestant. The Reverend Dewar believed in 1959 that an Orangeman 'should love, uphold and defend the Protestant religion. . . . He should strenuously oppose the fatal errors and doctrines of the Church of Rome.'[12] The views of Ian Paisley seemed to be straight out of the sixteenth century Reformation; he referred to 'popery' and 'papism', associating these with 'the devil' and 'anti-Christ'. On the other hand, the religious commitment of the Unionists had been strongly *politicised*; allegiance was as much historical as it was ideological and it was perpetuated by parades commemorating events of the 1690s such as the Battle of the Boyne and the lifting of the siege of Londonderry. Hence 'the link between religion and politics within the Unionist Party continued to be maintained by the Orange Order'.[13] Since religious labels were often synonymous with political stances, there is a certain logic to pre-1968 job advertisements such as: '*Wanted – Reliable cook-general: Protestant (Christian preferred)*'. The sectarian explanation seemed less obvious to the Nationalists, who saw the conflict as one between the 'haves' of a privileged establishment seeking to repress the 'have-nots' of an historic sub-class. The SDLP aimed not so much to represent Catholics as Catholics, or Catholics against Protestants, as to advance a left-of-centre view within the tradition of the British Labour party and the continental Social Democrats. Sinn Fein and the IRA were more radical, aiming at a united Ireland in which the politics of the far left would eradicate religious differences altogether. They therefore perceived sectarian rivalry as a facade for class conflict – very similar to a Marxist analysis. They also emphasised another ingredient. Britain was the main enemy, cast in the role of an imperial power which had to be forced to surrender the last vestiges of its occupation of Ireland. To the class war, Sinn Fein and the IRA therefore added a struggle for liberation against colonialism, an image which brought it much support, largely misguided, from groups within the United States.

ATTEMPTS AT RESOLUTION SINCE 1968

Successive British governments had to get used to being hated – to being seen, on the one hand, as turncoats seeking to force an alien union with Ireland upon its kith and kin and, on the other, as imperialists seeking to prevent that union. In the early days of the crisis, frustration led to ministerial slips. On a visit to Northern Ireland, Reginald Maudling (Home Secretary between 1970 and 1972) said, with feeling: 'What a bloody awful place!'[14] Nevertheless, British policy over the period between 1968 and 1995 showed a careful and sequential development, starting with containment, moving via direct rule to 'power-sharing', before ending up with an 'all-Ireland' solution.

The initial policy of containment was intended to control the violence by means of a military presence in Belfast, while giving the Stormont government a chance to regain its legitimacy through a package of reforms. When this failed to materialise under James Chichester-Clark and Brian Faulkner, the British government abandoned containment and took the initiative for the reforms which Stormont had been unwilling to deliver. The initial step was to declare direct rule in 1972 and to consider measures to achieve a consensus among Catholics and Protestants. The first attempt was made by William Whitelaw, appointed Secretary of State for Northern Ireland by Edward Heath. He developed the concept of 'power-sharing', which meant that any future executive in the province should contain representatives of the two political traditions and should not be the exclusive preserve of the Unionists. In 1973 a new assembly was elected and a power-sharing executive followed in January 1974, comprising the Official Unionists, the Alliance Party and the SDLP. But so strong was the opposition to power-sharing that it fell apart in May 1974. The British government, however, considered this fundamental to its policy and tried several times to revive the power-sharing experiment. For example, Merlyn Rees attempted in 1975 to reconvene discussions in the form of the Constitutional Convention.

These collapsed. Roy Mason tried to reopen talks between the various groups in 1977. He failed. The Conservative government of Mrs Thatcher initially followed the same course from 1979 to 1982 under Humphrey Atkins and James Prior. But another conference, in London in 1980, solved nothing. Prior introduced a more sophisticated form of power-sharing in his 'rolling devolution' scheme in 1982; this would elect an assembly which would scrutinise the work of the Northern Ireland departments even if it could not agree on constitutional proposals.[15] The problem was that the Nationalists failed to co-operate, especially the SDLP, which considered that the solutions were too narrow.

By the mid-1980s it had become apparent that power-sharing was no longer a feasible solution. History had moved on and the British government accepted that the only logical course now was one which involved the Irish Republic as well. The 'all-Ireland' approach was a clear departure from the earlier emphasis that Northern Ireland was essentially a British problem. A huge step forward was taken in 1985 when Mrs Thatcher and the Irish Prime Minister, Garret Fitzgerald, signed the Anglo-Irish Agreement. Its main terms were that the constitutional status of the North would be changed only with the consent of the majority of the people there, but that lines of co-operation would be opened up with the South; in particular, an Anglo-Irish Conference of Ministers would be set up to consider issues affecting Northern Ireland and its relations with the Irish Republic. The hope was that a solution would eventually emerge that would guarantee the rights of both 'traditions' in the North and satisfy the aspirations of those who wanted closer links with Britain or with the South. There can rarely have been a more ambitious project. It was, of course, roundly condemned by both Unionist parties, which did not wish to water down the connection with Britain, and by Sinn Fein and the IRA, which maintained calls for a fully integrated Ireland.

Yet the British government persevered, with the ever-increasing co-operation of successive Irish Prime Ministers. Ten years after its introduction, the 'all-Ireland' policy was given renewed impetus in the document *Frameworks for the Future*, published in 1995 with the purpose, in John Major's words, of bringing to an end 'the dialogue of death'.[16] The main proposals were for a new assembly to be elected by proportional representation and to have legislative and executive responsibilities; an all-Ireland body of elected representatives from the Northern Ireland assembly and the Irish parliament with 'harmonising powers'; the end of any Irish claim to Northern Ireland; guidelines for increased collaboration between the British and Irish governments; the acknowledgement of the right of the people of Northern Ireland to choose their own future; a charter of rights to cover everyone living in Northern Ireland; and, finally, separate referendums in Ireland and Northern Ireland before any of the proposals could come into force. The overall emphasis was on bringing the two sides ever closer together: 'In this spirit, both governments offer this document for consideration and accordingly strongly recommend it to the parties, the people in the island of Ireland and more widely.'[17] The Irish Minister for Foreign Affairs, Dick Spring, sought to reassure the people of Northern Ireland that the interests of all were guaranteed by what he called a 'quadruple lock' against the predominance of any individual group. This comprised 'the rule of consensus, democratic accountability, mutual interest and reciprocity'.[18]

The reaction of the Unionists was mixed. The DUP was predictably hostile; Paisley called the document 'a declaration of war' and saw it as evidence that 'successive British governments have been implicated in a dastardly scheme to remove Northern Ireland from the union into an all-Ireland republic.'[19] There were, however, promising indications that the OUP, under their new leader, David Trimble, might eventually be drawn into negotiations and even the UDA gave the initiative a cautious welcome. But the most promising development was the 'outbreak of peace' which had occurred a few months earlier when, on 31 August 1994, Sinn Fein and the IRA announced an end to the campaign of violence. For the first time in Northern Ireland's history, therefore, an important constitutional initiative coincided with a period of peace.

The IRA's decision to announce a ceasefire was certainly unexpected. Although there has not yet been time for a proper perspective to emerge, the following is offered as a provisional explanation for their decision. By the early 1990s the IRA had lost their war. This was not through military defeat, but rather because any logic behind this war had disappeared. In the first place, the radical left was in decline everywhere in Europe and once-active terrorist organisations like the Red Brigades, the Red Army Faction and *Action Directe* were virtually defunct; the IRA had therefore become increasingly isolated. Second, the fully integrated Ireland at which it aimed was rendered obsolete by the 'all-Ireland' approach. By the early 1990s no one wanted unconditional reunification. The mainly agricultural economy of the South had benefited from membership of the European Community and there was apprehension that full reunification with the North might bring severe economic dislocation. Catholics in the North, meanwhile, had become conscious that their standard of living was generally higher than that in the South. There was also an acute awareness of the practical problems brought about by the reunification of the two Germanies in 1991. Third, what was now on offer from the British and Irish Governments seemed increasingly feasible. Within the European Union were many political structures and arrangements, so that even the complex combination of different levels of authority envisaged for Northern Ireland could be accommodated. It seems, therefore, that the IRA and Sinn Fein had been marginalised in the North, repeating its experience sixty years earlier in the South. Finally, the tide of history had swept away three of the world's apparently irreconcilable problems: the Arab–Israeli conflict, the Cold War between the Soviet Union and the West, and the apartheid system in South Africa. What was so unique about the crisis in Northern Ireland that it should not eventually join the falling bastions?

The IRA ceasefire of 1994 and the Anglo-Irish *Framework Document* of 1995 were no guarantee that the problem of Ulster had finally been solved. During the course of 1995 the peace process became bogged down, despite the intervention of President Clinton, while the detonation of a bomb in London in February 1996 raised fundamental doubts about the validity of the IRA ceasefire.

CONCLUSION

Developments in Ireland have been so complex that it is worth summarising the main trends identified in this chapter. In the first place, the natural solution to Ireland's historic problem in the nineteenth century was Home Rule – arrived at after considerable upheaval, not least in the realm of British party politics. But this Irish Nationalist solution, sponsored by the British Liberals, was impeded before 1914 by the resistance of the Ulster Unionists, whipped up by the British Conservatives. In the exceptional circumstances of the First World War there was a powerful Republican backlash (under Sinn Fein and the IRA) against the Ulster Unionists, while the moderate Nationalists were squeezed between the two extremes. By 1922 Home Rule had been replaced by partition; two Irelands therefore came into existence, each polarised around an extreme position. The South gradually overcame its radicals. During the civil war of 1922–3 it destroyed the influence of the IRA and gradually evolved into a bipartisan democracy. The North, by contrast, set into half a century of one-party rule until

Unionist power was challenged by the disturbances of 1968. The situation was complicated by the switch of Sinn Fein and the IRA from the South, where they had clearly been marginalised, to the North, where they transformed a crisis into a terrorist campaign. Faced with the intransigent position of the Unionists on the one hand, and Sinn Fein and the IRA on the other, the British government moved through a series of policies towards a solution which, it recognised, would have to involve the whole of Ireland. It remains to be seen whether the IRA ceasefire will hold and whether an all-Ireland solution can finally be achieved.

22

EQUAL OPPORTUNITIES AND WOMEN'S RIGHTS IN TWENTIETH-CENTURY BRITAIN

Before 1914 women, who constituted slightly over half the total adult population of Britain, had been conceded only a handful of rights. By the Married Women's Property Act of 1882 they had been given ownership of their own possessions within the context of marriage; they had also been allowed since 1876 to register as doctors, and since the 1890s to vote in local government elections. Women did not, however, have the vote in parliamentary elections, they could not enter the Universities of Oxford or Cambridge or practise law, and they had virtually no protection or rights in employment.

This chapter will analyse the further progress made by women in attaining equal opportunities with men between 1914 and 1995. Within this period, it will be seen that the pace of change varied and that progress was far from steady or consistent.

THE GROWTH OF EQUAL OPPORTUNITIES 1914–45

The First World War brought a considerable step forward; the major change in the status of women was the achievement of the vote. This was conceded in 1918 by Lloyd George's Coalition Government: the Representation of the People Act had enfranchised women over 30 provided that they were graduates, householders, or the wives of house-holders. Securing the vote for women had been the object of extensive campaigns before 1914, especially from the National Union of Women's Suffrage Societies (NUWSS) and the Women's Social and Political Union (WSPU). The latter had been the more radical, resorting to militant measures such as smashing windows, burning letter boxes, attacking MPs and chaining themselves to railings. Both organisations had suspended their activities on the outbreak of war, although some members of the WSPU, including Sylvia Pankhurst, opposed the war on principle.

The usual interpretation for the enfranchisement of women is that they had earned the vote through invaluable service during the war rather than by specious pressure before it. Asquith, who had opposed their pressure, succumbed to their service. In 1917 he said:

> How could we have carried on the war without them? Short of bearing arms in the field, there is hardly a service which has contributed, or is contributing, to the maintenance of our cause in which women have not been at least as active and efficient as men.

Hence

> I . . . find it impossible to withhold from women the power and the right of making their voices directly heard.[1]

On the other hand, it is very unlikely that suffrage would have been granted to women *without* the pre-war activities of the Suffragists and the Suffragettes. The former had presented with indisputable logic the case for the vote, while the latter had shown equally clearly the passions which could be aroused by the rejection of those arguments. Before 1915 Asquith's government felt that it could not surrender to the suffragettes without losing its image of being in control. There is, however, little doubt that the majority of Liberals would have granted the suffrage in order to end the disturbances if only the opportunity had presented itself. This, of course, did occur with the war. But war is a temporary, even if devastating, phenomenon. Socially, the special conditions it creates can soon slip backwards unless there is also a *pre-war* impetus. Thus the activism before 1914 was necessary to remind the government of what lay in store if it did *not* change, while the war broke the psychological barrier to making that change.

How did the First World War affect women's employment? It certainly limited the numbers of women in domestic service and enormously increased those working in munitions and factories, along with those in nursing and auxiliary services. Even so, there is some controversy as to whether the First World War had a positive effect on women workers. On the one hand, some historians argue that it did. Horizons were expanded, responsibilities increased and opportunities enhanced. War, in other words, was a catalyst for social change. On the other hand, S. Lewenhak maintains that the effect of the war was minimal. The change was in scale, not in type. 'Few of the kinds of work they did were totally new to women.'[2] Women had, after all, worked in munitions as early as 1862. What really brought the impression of radical change was the publicity given to middle-class women 'for doing what working-class women had been doing before'.[3] It has even been argued that the effect of the First World War was damaging to women's interests. Women were prepared to accept much longer hours than those which had been developed before the war. Besides,

> Most of the women who rushed into war industries in the various belligerent states, had no trade union experience. They accepted whatever conditions they were offered out of a sense of patriotism. They did not see that they were undermining the standards of pay and conditions built up over many years and through many weary struggles and privations. Employers played on women war workers' eagerness, but experienced men and women trade unionists and workers reacted with suspicion and hostility. The effect of the First World War was not to cement the growing unity . . . of working people, but to disrupt it.[4]

In particular, the war aggravated tensions between men and women in the labour force. Employers underpaid women and had lower expectations of their ability and potential. Men feared for their jobs and also felt that women were undermining their hard-won trade union rights. This hostility was sustained immediately after the war and there were extensive demands from men to be given priority in the job market on demobilisation.

As important as the issue so far considered – whether the First World War affected women's rights and opportunities in the short term – was the war's continuing impact during the 1920s and 1930s. Did conceding the vote to women have knock-on effects for the future? Or were these dissipated in the readjustment to peace?

On the positive side was the continuation of political and legal emancipation. The 1928 Representation of the People Act completed the extension of the franchise by giving the vote to all women over 21. Baldwin was, however, obliged to do this because of an impromptu remark in a speech by his Home Secretary, Joynson-Hicks. Meanwhile, women had entered the House of Commons for the first time, Lady Astor being returned in 1919 at a by-election in Plymouth Sutton. After the 1922 general election there were two women MPs and in 1923 eight. An inter-war peak of fifteen was reached in 1931, but this fell to nine in the 1935 election. Changes in legal status were initiated by the Sex Disqualification (Removal) Act of 1919, which stated that gender or marriage should not disqualify any person from exercising a public function. A long-overdue educational step was taken in 1920 when the University of Oxford decided to award degrees to women. Professional concessions followed when, in 1921, women were eligible to become barristers and, for the first time, to sit on juries.

There were also social and economic developments. The new fashions and social conventions of the 1920s were seen by many as a liberating force, while the amount of drudgery was reduced in the home by the introduction of labour-saving devices such as the washing machine and the vacuum cleaner. The immediate post-war boom for a while extended the demand for women workers and this was eventually revived by the growth of the new industries. This applied especially to the motor-manufacturing industry, with its needs for carpets and upholstery. Employers were particularly anxious to use what they considered to be the traditional skills of women within the context of a new market.

There is, however, an alternative perspective. This takes more account of the underlying conditions of the economy as a fundamentally regressive force which slowed down the pace of change. Especially important here was the growth of unemployment which was, in turn, related to the contraction of the staple industries (see Chapter 8). Men demobilised from the forces were given priority in the job market and there was no legislation to prevent employers from practising what they no doubt interpreted as positive discrimination. The shortage of jobs also undermined any prospects of legislation to protect conditions of service for women in employment. During the First World War the Atkins Committee had recommended the principle of equal pay, based on productivity, but this was not implemented. If anything, the situation actually deteriorated. In the 1920s and early 1930s the argument was that men should have the jobs for economic and social reasons. By 1935 the government was denying equal opportunities as a point of principle. Duff Cooper expressed the view of the majority of the Conservative party who, of course, had a huge majority in Parliament, when he said that the government would not be influenced by 'a slogan which [it] did not believe to represent the facts'.[5] For the majority of women the inter-war period saw a return to a domestic role. This was justified by the growing use of labour-saving devices in the home – the hoover and washing machine especially. For a while these made domestic chores more exciting by revolutionising the mechanics of housework, just as the computer was later to change the procedures of office work. Or at least this is how the men who still had work viewed the purchases made with their hard-earned money.

Faced with these problems, it is hardly surprising that some of the original suffrage societies should have transformed themselves into groups pursuing women's social and economic interests. Again, however, they were overtaken by events before they had achieved their objectives.

THE SECOND WORLD WAR AND AFTER

In its impact on women's rights the Second World War has been the subject of as much debate as the First. A. Marwick, for example, argues that the war was an important departure for women, leading to 'new social and economic freedom'.[6] Furthermore, these changes continued to apply after the end of the war in 1945. He maintains that the disruption of war liberated women from their traditional roles and, in the absence of men, gave them experience of managing households. The key factor was the mass mobilisation of women for the war effort, an experience which undermined segregation and gave more confidence.

A rather different view is put by H. Smith.[7] He argues that women's work was still primarily domestic, and included suddenly imposed burdens like the hosting of evacuees. More women were still housewives than workers (8.8 million as opposed to 7.3 million), and many of those in work during the war years reverted to their traditional roles after hostilities had ended. In any case, most of the work done by women was either not men's jobs at all or men's jobs which were heavily downgraded. There were also special pay schedules for women and the marriage bar, temporarily lifted, was generally reimposed after the war. It is true that the Civil Service and teaching kept jobs open to married women, as did Boot's Pure Drug Co.; but the majority of employers, including Rowntree and Cadbury, did not. A. Carter's summary, therefore, is that 'As a result of the war women did make some gains, but these were fairly negligible.'[8]

It might be thought that a change of government immediately after World War II would have benefited women. In fact, it probably made little difference. Labour's emphasis on social change did not include the further emancipation of women. This was partly because Labour was strongly tied to trade unionism which, on gender issues, acted as a conservative force. Thus the government failed to introduce even the most basic measures and any gains made by women were by-products of the welfare state, such as the introduction of free school meals in 1944 and the Family Allowances Act of 1945.

The underlying trend of the late 1940s and the 1950s was the slow pace of change. A variety of factors were responsible for this. The widespread acceptance of stereotypes was one: it was the man's function to be the breadwinner, the logical consequence of which was that many men considered that financial provision should be accompanied by personal control. Many women accepted this and their acceptance of a subordinate role in employment meant that there was no real impetus for change. Women's attitudes could thus be a significant barrier to progress. To an extent they were influenced by weekly publications like *Woman*, which advised 'It is safe to say that most women, once they have a family, are more contented and doing better work in the home than they could find outside it.'[9] Views like this perpetuated the notion that women's roles were essentially limited to cleaning, cooking, support and childcare – all in the name of domestic skills. This is quite possibly what many individual women actually wanted, but the stereotype reduced the element of choice for the many who did not, and who would have preferred to pursue a career. Those women who did pursue careers were often regarded from two extremes: either they were paragons, able to rise above the limitations of their sex, or they were considered unnatural within the prevailing social atmosphere.

The main problem confronting those women in employment was continuing discrimination. This showed itself in two ways. First, women were not paid on equal terms as men for the same job and, second, they filled most of the menial posts and only a tiny proportion of the top jobs. Generally they were employed as waitresses, secretaries, cleaners, telephonists or factory workers. The main professions in which they were involved were nursing and teaching. Some professions had made no progress at all: in 1951 only 8 per cent of lawyers and doctors were women, compared with 6 per cent in 1911. Overall, it has been estimated, women earned only 53 per cent as much as the average wages paid to men[10] while, at the same time, receiving less overtime and fewer fringe benefits. Women were also disadvantaged by the lack of provision for maternity leave or childcare facilities. There were few opportunities for redress, since trade union membership was held by only 25 per cent of the female workforce, as opposed to 50 per cent of men. This was due to the type of work women were most likely to do, to their part-time work, and to the traditional connection of trade unionism with men.[11]

There were also instances of discrimination in the educational and financial worlds. The 11-plus examination was 'equalised' by many Local Education Authorities, which meant that girls had to secure a higher mark than boys to pass. Many schools failed to encourage girls to take science or technology subjects. Even the main educational committees of the time suggested special courses for them. The Newsom Report said that women must be educated for 'their main social function' because women are 'biologically and psychologically different from men.'[12] Women were also financially vulnerable. Wives were regarded for the purpose of tax collection as part of their husbands' affairs; it was difficult legally to enforce maintenance payments after divorce; and the different ages of retirement created hardship since women had to live on pensions longer than men. Women also found it more difficult than men to secure loans or take out hire-purchase agreements – usually requiring a husband's or father's signature. Even in politics the progress of women was slow: in 1970 there were only 26 female MPs in the House of Commons, out of a total membership of 630; this compared with 24 in 1945. The political parties put forward very few women candidates and virtually none of these had safe seats. Part of the problem was the political realism of selection committees and their fear that women were less likely to attract votes. Another factor is that women felt more constrained than men – for economic and social reasons – from coming forward as candidates.

During the 1960s and 1970s major changes occurred, culminating in legislation which affected women more fundamentally than at any time since the First World War. To some extent these were due to long-term economic trends such as the ever-increasing number of women in the workforce, to the social revolution of the 'swinging sixties', and to the educational opportunities provided by the enormous increase in the number of places available in higher education. Women were also liberated sexually, the contraceptive pill giving them more control in their relationships with men. Finally, there was a rapid expansion in the press directed towards women, providing a channel for new ideas and arguments.

There was certainly no shortage of these. Some came from the Labour party; other sources were extra-parliamentary groups like the Fawcett Society. More diffuse was a general trend called women's liberation. This was based partly on the literature of the period, including Germaine Greer's *The Female Eunuch*, which maintained that:

> The essential factor in the liberation of married woman is understanding of her condition. She must fight the guilt of failure in an impossible set-up. She must ignore interested descriptions of her health, her morality and her sexuality, and assess them all for

herself. She must know her enemies, the doctors, psychiatrists, social workers, marriage counsellors, priests, health visitors and popular moralists. She must analyse her buying habits, her day-to-day evasions and dishonesties, her sufferings and her real feelings towards her children, her past and her future. Her best aides in such an assessment are her sisters.[13]

The emphasis was on recruiting younger women, especially those at university. By and large women's liberation leaned to the political left and was more active in the Labour and Liberal parties than among the Conservatives. The main aims were equal pay with men, equal opportunities, nursery provision, and contraception and abortion on demand.

How influential was the women's liberation movement? To some women it was as unpopular as the suffragettes had been at the beginning of the century. For others it articulated the arguments and views of those who felt discriminated against by social attitudes and the employment market. It was, however, by no means the only form of pressure being applied. Other organisations included the British Federation of Business and Professional Women, the Equal Pay and Opportunity Campaign, the National Joint Council for Working Women's Organisations, and the Status of Women Committee. There were also movements within the Labour party and Baroness Seear exerted an important influence among Liberals. By the 1970s it had become the rule rather than the exception to accept the case for equal opportunities, even though there were strong voices of dissent within both sexes which held that feminism was incompatible with femininity.

WOMEN'S RIGHTS SINCE THE 1960S

There can be little doubt that, at the legislative level, women's rights have substantially improved since the 1960s. The governments between 1964 and 1979 introduced a wide variety of changes which are examined in Chapter 14 as part of an impressive reforming programme. The Abortion Act of 1967 allowed an abortion if the health of the mother or foetus were endangered, as defined by two doctors. Since easier abortion was linked to greater sexual freedom, women's movements have seen it as an issue in which women claim absolute rights over their own bodies and not the imposition of some external moral constraint. The Divorce Reform Act (1969) made divorce possible after two years' separation and removed the necessity to prove cruelty or adultery. From 1973 the length of separation needed to obtain a divorce was reduced to twelve months. Easier divorce was soon reflected by an increase in the number of proceedings initiated by women against men – about 70 per cent of all cases. The Matrimonial Proceedings and Property Act (1970) provided that a woman could claim a share in the house after a divorce even if she had not been a joint mortgagee with her husband. The Guardianship Act provided that custody for and responsibility for bringing up children should be divided equally between husbands and wives. The Sexual Offences Amendment Act (1976) provided that women involved in a rape case could remain anonymous, whereas the man accused could be named.

More central to the cause of equal opportunities were two pieces of legislation affecting the occupational status of women. The Equal Pay Act of 1970 enforced the payment of the same wages for equivalent jobs carried out by men and women, thus ending the anomaly which had been apparent – even in the Civil Service – of two salary scales. The same principle applied also to overtime rates and holiday provision. Even more important was the Sex Discrimination Act of 1975. This had been preceded by two private members' bills and a bill introduced by Heath's government in 1973. The measure of Wilson's government was, however, strongly influenced by the women's movement within the Labour Party and went much further. It made illegal any form of discrimination in employment, whether in recruitment or dismissal. Both the 1970 and 1975 Acts were enforced by the Equal Opportunities Commission, set up in 1975. Meanwhile, other measures had also plugged possible loopholes in the enforcement of equal opportunities. The Social Security Pensions Act (1975) brought all women into pension schemes, and the Employment Protection Act of the same year made compulsory provision for maternity leave.

Despite these measures, a number of problems remained, indicating that legislation was not entirely effective. The Equal Pay Act was based on the principle of equal pay for like jobs, but there was a major difficulty in applying the proof of similarity. The Sex Discrimination Act was even more difficult to interpret and fewer cases of discrimination were brought to the tribunals than cases on unequal pay. Part-time employees, the largest proportion of women workers, were not fully covered by the legislation and they were never really likely to achieve parity with men: even though there might not have been actual discrimination, earnings per hour tended to be lower in part-time than in full-time jobs. Those women who did establish themselves on an equal footing with men, especially in the professions, found that the prospects for promotion to the top posts had not greatly increased. The number of women making it to the position of permanent secretary in the Civil Service was minute. Even in professions with a large proportion of women, fewer women occupied the top managerial roles. For example, women constituted 45 per cent of the teaching force but occupied only 16 per cent of the headships. The chances of promotion in higher education were even less, only 2 per cent of university professors being women.[14]

How did the Conservative government led by the first woman prime minister affect women's opportunities? On the one hand, the rise of Mrs Thatcher was an immense boost to the image of women in politics, taking place as it did within a party in which women had generally made comparatively little progress. On the other hand, Mrs Thatcher's spell in power has been considered a retarding influence politically, economically and socially. Although a woman had risen to the top in political terms, there was no appreciable increase in the number of women MPs. In 1983 there were only twenty-three, less than the average for the years between 1945 and 1979. With such a low statistical base, it was impossible to see where the next woman prime minister could come from. Also, Mrs Thatcher did very little for the advancement of women in her government. In all her time in power (1979–90) she appointed only one woman to her cabinet.

Government policies during the 1980s also had generally negative effects on women's place within the economy and society.[15] There was no attempt after 1979 to extend earlier equal opportunities legislation and some measures actually reduced the impact of earlier successes. The 1980 Employment Act, for example, increased the complexity for claiming maternity leave and other benefits. This intensified the problems of women returning to work after childbirth. The situation was much worse than in the United States: 'In Britain there is much less upward mobility and the result is a decline in the average occupational status of women after children are born. The employment position of women is therefore considerably worse than that of their American counterparts.'[16] Women's opportunities were also affected by the cutbacks made by the Conservative governments in the 1980s, especially in the Civil Service and the armed forces. Such problems were exacerbated by the economic recessions of the early and late 1980s which may, or may not, have been the side-effect of government monetarist policies (see Chapter 15). They caused a contraction in the job market and increased the rate of unemployment, which hit part-timers particularly hard: these were generally women and generally the first to be laid off.

The recessions also increased the use of marginalised labour, including homeworkers, to cut production costs. This invited heavy exploitation, which was often beyond the detectable scope of the law.

There was also a social backlash during and after Mrs Thatcher's premiership because the Conservative emphasis on family life revived earlier stereotypes. Sir Keith Joseph, for example, argued that more women should consider giving up their jobs in favour of childcare. The 'back to basics' policy of the early 1990s emphasised the importance of the patriarchal family and resulted in those single mothers who cohabited losing their social security payments.

The real test of a government's popularity is the verdict of the electorate. The Conservatives won four general elections in a row – in 1979, 1983, 1987 and 1992. Yet there was a substantial change in voting behaviour. In most elections before 1983 over half of the Conservative vote came from women and over half the Labour vote came from men. Between 1983 and 1992 this pattern was reversed, indicating perhaps that the Conservatives had missed an opportunity over equal opportunities and that an increasing proportion of women feared that possible inroads into welfare state provisions would affect them more fundamentally than men.

UNFINISHED BUSINESS?

From the arguments used in this chapter can be drawn an overall dynamic of change. During the earlier part of the twentieth century women's legal rights grew more rapidly than their occupational opportunities. Women achieved equality in the franchise and equality before the law but there remained an inconsistency between these rights and what could actually be done with them. This inconsistency was the main reason for the periodic growth of feminism. Women's movements seemed to come in waves, at points where a particular log-jam seemed to have developed: during the 1920s, and the period 1965–75. Further revivals seemed possible in the 1990s, in response to the relative stagnation of women's opportunities over the previous decade due largely to economic circumstances and to government policies. The emphasis since 1979 was very much on the value, within employment and the economy generally, of the unsupported or self-supporting individual. This approach, heavily influenced as it was by neo-liberalism (see Chapter 15), was unlikely to make special exceptions for the advancement of specific groups. By 1995 there was some ambivalence over the future direction of equal opportunities.

One solution was seen as increased support for women. This would offset the disadvantages women experienced within the job-market, through family responsibilities, and enable them to compete on equal terms with men. One author emphasised the particular need for a revised look at responsibility for raising families. She therefore argued for 'equal sharing of the costs of family labor between men and women' and an automatic right to childcare facilities.[17] Other observers suggested an altogether different route into the future, even abandoning the consensus that legislation on equal opportunities was on the whole desirable. They challenged the notion that 'differences in the positions of men and women at work are the result of the absence of equal opportunities'. Legislation on equal opportunities came in for special criticism.

> Such interventions into the free market do not enhance justice; they undermine it. They weaken the institutions of private property, freedom of contract, and equality before the law which form the foundations of a free society on which the prosperity of women and society at large depends.[18]

Somewhere between these alternatives the political parties were, by 1995, positioning themselves for the next general election. They all inclined more to the first view and were considering the expansion of nursery education; only Labour, however, was promising a universal entitlement to this. Ultimately, further developments in equal opportunities were likely to have to compete, within the constraints on public expenditure, with other priorities, although they might be pushed along from time to time by special intervention from the institutions of the European Union (see Chapter 19).

23

IMMIGRATION, RACE RELATIONS AND THE PLURAL SOCIETY

Until the 1950s Britain was regarded as a cosmopolitan power and the core of a worldwide empire. It is hardly surprising, therefore, that Britain should eventually have developed as a multi-cultural society based on a variety of ethnic groups from those areas which she had once colonised and a few she had not. This chapter focuses on the two main developments associated with this plural society. The first was the gradual build-up of substantial ethnic minorities through the process of immigration. And the second was the extent to which they harmonised with the existing population through the process of integration.

IMMIGRATION AND GOVERNMENT POLICY

There were five main waves of immigration into Britain. The first was from Ireland – an almost continuous stream throughout the nineteenth century and well into the twentieth. The second occurred between 1880 and 1905, when an estimated 120,000 Jews fled to Britain from Russia, Romania and other parts of eastern Europe to escape persecution and the pogroms. The period of the Second World War saw the settlement of a similar number of Poles, who had been integrated into the British forces, including the RAF, to fight against Nazi Germany. During the 1950s by far the largest wave of immigrants arrived in Britain. This came from the Commonwealth, especially from the West Indies and the Indian sub-continent. Some immigrants from these areas were invited into the country by the British government, which was trying to offset a decline in the British workforce caused by the reduction in the average number of children per family from 3.37 in 1914 to 2.2 by 1939.[1] The labour shortage was felt especially in transport and the newly established National Health Service. Most public-sector jobs were less well paid than those in the private sector and the competition for labour in the days of comparatively low unemployment meant that immigration was a means of solving market difficulties. The numbers involved were substantial, averaging 46,000 per annum by 1956, and accelerating to 57,700 in 1960 and 136,400 in 1961. The fifth wave occurred during the late 1960s and early 1970s as Asian minorities fled from the regimes of Jomo Kenyatta in Kenya and Idi Amin in Uganda.

How did successive British governments respond to these immigration patterns? The first controls were introduced before the First World War, largely as a result of the pressure of Conservative MPs trying to revive the flagging fortunes of the party by mobilising an extra dimension of the patriotic and imperialist vote. This was the first blatant use of the racist card with the electorate. By the Aliens Act (1905) the Home Secretary assumed powers to prevent immigrants who were unable to support themselves and their families. Asquith's Liberal government followed suit. The Aliens Restriction Act of 1914 gave the Home Secretary unlimited discretion over immigration. This was extended by the 1919 Aliens Restriction Act which, at the same time, repealed the 1905 Act. In 1920 an Aliens Order was passed which empowered the Home Secretary to remove any alien from Britain, an example of a temporary power which became permanent – at least until 1971. It has been argued that much of this legislation actually stirred up hatred for minority ethnic groups. Legislation was usually the result of campaigns; campaigns stirred up antipathies which were often expressed in extreme forms. For example, the publicity given to the arguments before and after the First World War helped prepare the way for public consciousness about the immigration of Jews. This, in turn, played into the hands of Oswald Mosley's British Union of Fascists during the 1930s. According to Z. Layton-Henry, 'The anti-immigrant campaign contributed to a negative official attitude to Jewish refugees fleeing from Nazi Germany after Hitler's rise to power in 1933.'[2]

These early measures were, however, discretionary and there was no systematic attempt to impose any quota or limit on numbers. The first move in this direction came during the 1950s, culminating in the more restrictive legislation of the 1960s. The Conservative party, in particular, took the initiative. It tuned into the growing concern within the working class about the perceived threat to their jobs. This was given a racist edge, made respectable by the official endorsement of Winston Churchill, who said in 1954 that Britain faced the prospect of becoming a 'magpie society' which 'would never do'.[3] The pressure was sustained by a number of Conservative MPs, including Cyril Osborne and Norman Pannell, and by grass-roots organisations like the Birmingham

Immigration Control Association, set up in 1960. The two levels – MPs and local pressure groups – interlinked and placed such pressure on the Conservative party that the issue of immigration control was aired at successive party conferences in the late 1950s. Gradually there developed a self-sustaining momentum, and a self-fulfilling prophecy. The more immigration was taken up as a political issue the more it was assumed in the 'sender' countries that controls would soon be imposed, and the more likely it was that relatives would seek to join workers in Britain. Hence numbers did increase steeply at the turn of the decade, thus reinforcing the argument of those who had pressed for immigration controls in the first place. The logical outcome was therefore the Commonwealth Immigrants Act (1962), which confined permission to immigrants in receipt of vouchers issued by the Ministry of Labour. Category A vouchers covered the offer of a specific job in Britain, Category B the possession of skills needed by the British economy, and Category C other applicants with some lesser claim.

What, in the meantime, was the position of the Labour party? During the 1950s the leadership had been firmly against the introduction of immigration controls and the Labour party had fought the 1962 Act in the House of Commons. Yet, by 1968, Labour had apparently accepted the need for further legislation. Why was this? One reason was that the party was catching up with the basic feeling at the grass roots. There is no doubt that it had lost votes over the issue in 1964 and again in 1966: Patrick Gordon-Walker, shadow Foreign Secretary, was defeated in Smethwick in 1964 because he was known to be opposed to immigration controls. It therefore made sense for Labour to try to establish some sort of consensus with the Conservatives and remove immigration from the arena of party politics. This was accelerated by the change of leadership from Gaitskell to Wilson. The latter switched the focus away from supporting free immigration to adopting moderate forms of control, thereby minimising the difference between the two main parties. At the same time, Wilson stressed the need to balance immigration policies with legislation to achieve more effective integration of immigrants already in Britain. The passing of the Race Relations Act in 1965 (see page 355) meant that he could reasonably claim that Labour's measures were also positive.

And yet Labour introduced constraints on immigration. Why were these considered necessary? Why did Labour not simply sit on the Conservative measure of 1962? The main reason is that another emergency occurred in the late 1960s. The recently independent government of Kenya pursued a policy of internal controls over the Kenyan economy, which involved a threat to expel large numbers of Kenyan Asians, most of whom held British passports. The main year of flight from these discriminatory policies was 1967–8. In order to prevent a mass influx into Britain, Wilson tightened immigration controls in 1968 by the Commonwealth Immigrants Act. This stated that any citizen of the Commonwealth who held a British passport would be subject to immigration control unless a parent or grandparent had been born or naturalised in the United Kingdom. This meant the end of any large-scale immigration – except at the discretion of the government in special circumstances. It also ensured a significant degree of consensus between Labour and the Conservatives. This was maintained into the 1970s, even when it was challenged by the right wing of the Conservative party, especially by Enoch Powell. Heath's government sought in 1971 to round off the immigration issue with its own legislation to supplement Labour's in 1968. The Immigration Act of 1971 replaced employment vouchers with work permits, which allowed only temporary residence in Britain and no automatic right of entry for dependants. But the pressure from the Ugandan Asians to enter Britain, after their expulsion by the atrocious regime of Idi Amin, created a new scare and placed Heath's government in considerable difficulties. To his credit, Heath honoured the government's commitment to the Asians and Conservative policies were actually more generous than those of Labour over the Kenyan Asians.

For a while it seemed that consensus over immigration might be under threat. Labour moved to the left on immigration issues and opposed the tightening of immigration regulations in the 1971 Act. This move was not, however, taken to its logical conclusion during the next period of Labour government between 1974 and 1979: neither Wilson nor Callaghan attempted to repeal the Conservative measure. The change of leadership in the Conservative party was a somewhat greater threat to the consensus. Mrs Thatcher aimed to revive the connection between Conservatism and populism and to extend the scope of immigration control to the secondary sphere of dependants. Her intention was therefore to introduce legislation to influence the extent of future non-white population growth rather than non-white settlement. The commitment was to allow the essential reunification of families – but no more. To some extent, Mrs Thatcher articulated some of the earlier fears, especially when she referred in 1978 on television to the possibility of the British people 'being swamped' by 'alien cultures'.[4] The 1981 Nationality Act therefore closed the immigration door on any remaining peoples within the Commonwealth in possession of British passports. Needless to say, this was strongly opposed by Labour.

The 1981 Act did not, however, represent the permanent triumph of the right wing of the Conservative party. Nor was it followed by any proposals for planned repatriation as Enoch Powell had once suggested. In any case, Mrs Thatcher's government was faced with two exceptional circumstances – of the type which had confronted Wilson in the late 1960s and Heath in the early 1970s. One was resettlement in Britain of 20,000 Vietnamese refugees, the other the impending crisis in Hong Kong. In 1987 the British government agreed to allow in up to 225,000 Hong Kong Chinese, if they chose to leave the colony once it was handed over to China in 1997. Labour found little to contest here, and so the consensus gradually re-emerged. For one thing, the reviving Labour party needed to fight for every vote and if it was prepared to abandon unilateralism in nuclear weapons (see Chapter 16) it could hardly be expected to risk losing votes by unpicking Conservative immigration policy. It is not surprising, therefore, that many authorities considered that the immigration issue was dead by the late 1980s.

INTEGRATION INTO BRITISH SOCIETY

But the implications of past waves of immigration for life in Britain were still very much alive. Many feared that immigration could not lead to integration – that the peoples from the Commonwealth could not be absorbed into British society. The strongest and most notorious exponent of this view was Enoch Powell. In response to a question put by Bishop Trevor Huddleston on 9 June 1969, as to whether he saw the presence of minority groups as a danger, Enoch Powell said: 'Certainly, and I would have thought that a glance at the world would show how easily tensions leading to violence arise when there is a majority and a minority . . . with sharp differences, recognizable differences, and mutual fears.'[5] In a speech delivered in Birmingham in 1968 Powell was more radical in his wording. 'We must be mad, literally mad, as a nation, to be permitting the annual inflow of some 50,000 dependants who are for the most part the material of the future growth of the immigrant-descended population.' He also said: 'Like the Roman, I seem to see "the River Tiber foaming with much blood!"'[6] Inaccurately labelled the 'rivers of blood' speech, this followed up a pessimistic analysis of the prospects of integration by a call for voluntary repatriation of immigrant communities. The solution was rejected by all sections of the moderate political spectrum – but was the prognosis correct?

Up to the 1960s two main problems were apparent in Britain's race relations. One was the incidence of race riots, the result of endemic hostility to immigrant communities. These occurred as far back as 1911, when the Chinese community in Cardiff was attacked for failing, it was alleged, to take part in a strike involving seamen and firemen. In 1919 there was a wave of riots which started in London's East End before spreading to Newport, Cardiff, Liverpool, Tyneside and Glasgow. Again, the targets were minority ethnic groups: these were accused of taking the available jobs and consorting with white women. During the 1930s the situation deteriorated further with the activities of Mosley's British Union of Fascists, which targeted British Jews as the cause of unemployment problems. The Second World War drove racism underground for a while but it re-emerged after 1945 in another series of racially inspired riots in Britain's cities. The first occurred in Liverpool in 1948, where white crowds broke into and ransacked black clubs. Worse followed in Nottingham city centre in 1958, where there were clashes between whites and non-whites, and in London, where Teddy Boys went on the rampage. Finally, in 1962, there were riots which lasted over a period of four nights as white gangs sought to defy police attempts to prevent them from invading immigrant areas in Dudley.

Less violent and spectacular, but more insidious and ultimately more damaging, was the incessant discrimination experienced by non-white communities. This was widespread in accommodation, employment, even in trade unions. The most notorious phrase used was 'No Coloureds', shown in the windows of flats or rooms to let. Mortgages were more difficult to find, along with houses as estate agents found themselves under pressure from residents to prevent changes in the ethnic composition of residential areas.

The period after 1960 saw a determined effort by successive governments to tackle the problems of racism and racial discrimination. On the positive side, there were three major Acts of Parliament, each making the law tighter than the last. The Race Relations Act of 1965, introduced by Wilson's Labour government, made racial discrimination illegal and set up a Race Relations Board. There were, however, limitations. Breaking the Act was not considered a criminal offence and the Board had few powers to investigate grievances brought before it. Labour proceeded, for two reasons, to remedy these deficiencies. The first was the energy of the Home Secretary, Roy Jenkins, who expressed a particular interest in race relations and set in motion much of the preliminary work. Second, Labour's decision to restrict the entry of Asians from Kenya was taken badly by the pro-immigration lobby and was seen as a surrender to the arguments of the right. The 1968 Race Relations Act was introduced partly to counter allegations that Labour had gone soft on racism. The new measure made it a criminal offence to discriminate according to race in the allocation of housing, or in employment, or in the provision and use of other services. The Race Relations Board was given enhanced powers, including resort to legal procedures should the preferred option of conciliation fail.

The Race Relations Act of 1976 was part of a general offensive by Labour on behalf of disadvantaged groups, with the focus on women and ethnic minorities. The government's intention, according to the 1975 White Paper, was 'to see genuine equality of opportunity'; hence 'the government is convinced, as a result of its review of race relations generally, that a fuller strategy to deal with racial disadvantage will have to be deployed than has been attempted so far'. The Act extended illegal discrimination from *direct* to *indirect* measures – to those measures which were non-discriminatory on the surface but which had the practical effect of excluding ethnic minorities. This was a significant advance, especially once the Commission for Racial Equality replaced the Race Relations Board and, again, was given enhanced powers. This measure followed official action taken by the Conservatives in 1972, when the Ugandan Resettlement Board had been established. A political consensus had therefore emerged between the parties on racial equality just as it had on immigration.

Official policy was accompanied by informal measures to remove discrimination within education, the professions, the armed services and other areas. Despite these efforts, however, racism remained endemic within the attitudes of a significant minority of influential people. This applied, for example, to several police forces, where, despite attempts to eradicate racism, officers were found wanting on a number of occasions, especially in their handling of inner-city disturbances.

The main threats to full integration came from the violence shown by the far right in Britain. This was expressed in two main forms, which often overlapped. One was political, the other a sub-culture. The main political grouping was the National Front; originating in 1967 with a merger between the British National Party and the League of Empire Loyalists, this expanded its appeal in the 1970s. It was violently anti-black, arguing that immigration was responsible for general British decline. Its solution was the forcible repatriation of all 'new' Commonwealth immigrants. This should be effected immediately to prevent an inevitable increase in the non-white population. The

National Front attracted an opposition group formed by the Trotskyist Socialist Workers' Party (SWP) in 1977, which also comprised collaborators within the Liberal and Labour parties. This was the Anti-Nazi League. The rival organisations became involved in a series of clashes reminiscent of the events of the 1930s. Support for the National Front peaked between 1976 and 1978 and both groups declined from 1979. But the residual influence of the far right was still apparent in the 1990s, mainly as a social and para-military force, operating through sub-groups like the skinheads. These had a major impact on Europe as well as on Britain and there were extensive links with skinhead groups in Germany in particular. In 1990 the European Parliament's Committee of Enquiry into Racism and Xenophobia referred to Britain's 'racist and violent sub-culture of the skinheads'.[7]

Confronted by violently expressed racism by a small but determined minority, it is not surprising that immigrant communities remained defensive and, in many cases, suspicious of the rest of the white population in Britain. But there were other reasons for their retaining a separate identity. One was negative and involuntary; the many immigrant communities lived in inner-city areas and experienced a cycle of deprivation which, through inadequate educational and employment opportunities, trapped them in those areas. In other ways the separate identity of ethnic minorities was more positive, an attempt to preserve the heritage of language, culture and religion. At times, however, this has been called into question by the more assertive majority 'British' culture. At the trivial end of the scale, West Indians, Indians and Pakistanis have been criticised for supporting visiting cricket teams in test matches at Headingly, Edgbaston or the Oval. More fundamental, however, was the occasional confrontation between ethnic traditions and British law, over, for example, the Sikh objection to wearing crash helmets while riding motor cycles and the questioning by orthodox Muslims of some of the areas of legislation on equal opportunities for women.

Finally, much has been made of the return of inner-city rioting from the late 1970s, after a comparative lull from the mid 1960s. Violence occurred first at the Notting Hill carnivals in 1976 and 1977, spreading to other parts of the country during the 1980s. Bristol erupted in 1980 and a series of major disturbances followed in 1981 in Brixton (south London), Toxteth (Liverpool), Moss Side (Manchester), and Handsworth (Birmingham). Another low point came in 1985, with serious riots in Handsworth and at Broadwater Farm in Tottenham (North London). Further violence broke out in Wolverhampton and Notting Hill in 1989.

Where these motivated by racial tension? There was certainly a racial component and all the disturbances took place in areas of high immigrant population. Lord Scarman's view, expressed in 1981, was that 'racial disadvantage is a fact of current British life. It was, I am equally sure, a significant factor in the causation of the Brixton disorders.' It would, however, be a mistake to equate them directly with the race riots which had taken place before 1962. In one major respect the pattern of violence had changed by the 1980s. The previous trend had been attacks by whites on immigrants, with the police attempting to restore order. During the 1980s the police themselves became the main target and there were numerous cases of white youths and immigrants joining in a common offensive against the forces of authority. Some sources tried to provide more traditional explanations for the violence. The *Daily Mail* observed in 1985:

> Either they [the non-white communities] obey the laws of this land where they have taken up residence and accepted the full rights and responsibilities of citizenship, or they must expect the Fascist street agitators to call ever more boldly and with ever louder approval for them to 'go back from whence they came'.

This was clearly confusing a more complex recent phenomenon with the cruder conflicts of the earlier period. In many respects violence inspired by race hatred had withered with the decline of the National Front, to be replaced by a resurgence of attacks on authority.

PLURALISM AND EQUAL OPPORTUNITIES

The problems of pluralism covered in this chapter overlap with those of equal opportunities, dealt with in Chapter 22. Women are, for example, doubly disadvantaged if they are immigrants and black. In the first place, legislation on immigration was geared to working structures and societies controlled by men. For example, the 1968 Commonwealth Immigrants Act allowed in a quota based on United Kingdom passport holders who were heads of households. In almost all cases this applied to men. For similar reasons, the Equal Opportunities Commission considered that the 1983 immigration rules, based on the 1981 Act, were 'fundamentally sex-discriminatory'.[8]

Even when they were admitted into the United Kingdom, black women in society were heavily disadvantaged. According to A. Carter, 'they automatically have to contest both racial prejudice and prejudice against women, and in addition the majority of them are the poorest sector of society.'[9] They are likely to be socially isolated and deprived of educational opportunity. They are also at the margins of the economy. Most homeworkers are black women, who are targeted because they cannot enter the job market. This might be for two reasons: the lack of qualifications and the refusal of their husbands to allow them to leave the home.[10] There is, therefore, a major problem left unresolved by the 1990s. British society, under the influence of three decades of legislation, has come to accept the rights of women workers and of black workers. But it has not dealt with the complex social, educational and religious cross-currents which still disadvantage *black women* workers.

24

PRIMARY SOURCES FOR BRITISH POLITICAL HISTORY 1914–95

This book concludes with a survey of the different types of primary sources available for the student of twentieth-century history. A similar approach was provided in the final chapter of the volume preceding this one – *Aspects of British Political History 1815–1914*. In some instances, general points will be common to both, although examples and chronological references obviously differ. The reader of both volumes will therefore detect some overlapping, but also a number of contrasts between observations on the sources of the two periods: 1815–1914 and 1914–1995.

Primary sources are produced during the period being studied, which means that in this case some will be nearly a hundred years old (and classifiable by collectors as 'antiques'), while others will be contemporary. Primary sources have been described as the raw material from which history is made and they play a vital role in interpretations to be found in secondary sources. Interest in primary sources was initiated by the nineteenth-century German historical school but, during the second half of the twentieth century, has been given a new focus within the British educational system. The scope of primary sources has also expanded enormously over the past hundred years, the proliferation of written documents being the result of two technological revolutions: the typewriter and the word processor.

Every student of history is now familiar with the shades and variety of primary sources and with the questions which need to be asked of them: are they reliable and are they useful? The overall response generally given to this question is that reliability and usefulness depend entirely upon what the historian envisages as their function. This will be considered in greater depth in relation to diaries, memoirs and autobiographies; official documents; speeches; cartoons; newspapers; statistics; and novels.

DIARIES, MEMOIRS AND AUTOBIOGRAPHIES

The most personal of all primary sources is the diary. One motive for keeping a regular account is to prepare a reliable *aide-memoire*. This would be useful as a systematic record either for the eventual preparation of personal memoirs or for subsequent reference for speeches, diplomatic negotiations, or even cabinet meetings. Another motive might be to provide an outlet for personal views, impressions and frustrations. Either reason would involve the interaction between the author and the events of the day, the author helping shape the events and, at the same time, commenting on them.

As such, diaries provide the historian with the first-hand and vivid descriptions, which can be used retrospectively to supplement more formal records such as cabinet minutes. The personal views they contain illustrate and enliven the more formal approach of official documents. When kept over a long period of time, they provide perhaps the greatest form of continuity, illuminating changing attitudes as well as constant principles. A detailed and frank diary might confirm – or modify – the conventional evaluation of a particular individual personality, revealing especially personal charisma and eccentricities. At times, a diary might convey information or details not otherwise available and it is especially informative to compare two or more diaries covering the same period.

On the other hand, all diaries are open to question as to the motivation by their entries; this must inevitably affect their reliability as a source. The historian needs to consider the position of the diarist, since here there is an unusual opportunity to exaggerate (or, alternatively, to minimise) the author's role in particular events. There is also a considerable scope for bias. This may be expressed directly, in the form of commitment or antipathy, or indirectly through the selection of material. The latter raises the additional questions of the motives for inclusion and exclusion and the historian has to undertake the difficult task of assessing the extent of the diarist's concern for personal posterity and reputation. Finally, the habits of the diarist will undoubtedly affect the overall character of the work. A daily record is likely to provide a more precise recall of detail but will also contain a great deal that is redundant. A weekly diary, on the other hand, is more likely to have a sense of underlying perspective but, since this is based on selection, may be more prone to distorting the events covered.

Typical examples of twentieth-century diaries are those of Beatrice Webb, written between 1912 and 1924,[1] and of George V. Lord Riddell's diary contains some exceptionally candid observations, including a record of the view of the Labour leader, Ramsay MacDonald, about the outbreak of the First World War. Although a known pacifist, MacDonald could hardly have done other than express in public a commitment to the national interest. In private, however, he let slip a clear reference to his interest in forming a Labour government: 'R. MacD. smiled and said, "They are all wrong. In three months there will be bread riots and we [the Labour Party] shall come in".'[2]

Memoirs and autobiographies have certain similarities with diaries. They, too, are personal recollections based on the interaction between an individual and the society in which he or she lived and worked. On the other hand, memoirs and autobiographies are based on a more ordered and systematic selection of material; they have a more obvious development of themes and argument; and they put more emphasis on the 'times' as well as the 'life' of the subject. They may also contain more obvious self-justification, a greater emphasis on motivation over a longer period of time, and the use of non-personal, often privileged, material. Autobiographies and memoirs may well use diaries as their raw material, which in itself poses problems of distortion. What would be the motive for omitting certain diary entries? Could this amount to a new form of bias? Alternatively, if memoirs are not based on diaries, how accurate is the memory of the writer? How much of the material is third-hand and not personal at all?

Harold Nicolson's *Peacemaking, 1919* (1933)[3] contains anecdotes about key events which might, at first glance, categorise this work as a diary. But Nicolson's work transcends the format and intention of the diary in its detailed and reasoned assessment of the negotiations leading to the 1919 Versailles Settlement. It is true that he expressed his reservations about the process, but his own role was never seen as more than peripheral; his views on the settlement were far more central than any comment on his own contributions to it.

Perhaps the most famous example in the twentieth century is Lloyd George's *War Memoirs* (1934). In addition to detailed references to his personal role, this contains some more general assessments: external as well as internal observations. For example, he said of the key stage of the war, 1917:

> Had it not been for the inexplicable stupidity of the Germans in provoking a quarrel with America and bringing that mighty people into the War against them just as they had succeeded in eliminating another powerful foe – Russia – the Somme would not have saved us from an inextricable stalemate.[4]

Another key example was the *Memories and Reflections* (1928) of the Earl of Oxford and Asquith,[5] which contained reflections on the decline of the Liberal party, including the conflict between himself and Lloyd George. L.S. Amery is a much quoted writer on the inter-war period: perhaps his most celebrated observation is on the General Strike: 'Thus began the mildest-mannered revolution that ever tried to coerce a constitutional government.'[6] Harold Macmillan, meanwhile, had a reputation as one of the progressive Conservatives of the late 1920s and 1930s. The extent to which this represented a genuine commitment to reform is, however, debatable. Was Macmillan seeking to unsettle the Baldwin establishment? Similarly, did he later accept the welfare state merely because, like Churchill and Eden before him, he had no alternative? Perhaps there is a personal clue to his real motives in the memoirs he published in 1966. Referring to the height of the depression in the 1930s, he wrote:

> I shall never forget those despairing faces, as the men tramped up and down the High Street in Stockton or gathered round the Five Lamps in Thornaby. Nor can any tribute be too great to the loyal, unflinching courage of the wives and mothers, who somehow continued, often on a bare pittance, to provide for husband and children and keep a decent home in being.[7]

An equally candid view, although in a political rather than social context, was put by Baroness Thatcher in 1993. Commenting on the succession to her leadership two years earlier, she wrote:

> But there was one more duty I had to perform, and that was to ensure that John Major was my successor. I wanted – perhaps I needed – to believe that he was the man to secure and safeguard my legacy and to take our policies forward. So it was with disquiet that I learnt a number of my friends were thinking of voting for Michael Heseltine. . . . I did all I could to argue them out of this.[8]

The examples given so far have been political. There are, however, vivid personal accounts from humbler levels which represent the experiences of those who lived and died by political decisions. Siegfried Sassoon's *Memoirs of an Infantry Officer* (1932) provide a vivid interpretation of the reactions of the common infantryman in the trenches during the First World War. Referring, for example, to the destruction of his trench, he wrote:

Now it was wrecked as though by earthquake and eruption. Concrete strong-posts were smashed and tilted sideways; everywhere the chalky soil was pocked and pitted with huge shell-holes; and wherever we looked the mangled effigies of the dead were our *memento mori.*[9]

Such an account shows the perceptions of the poet rather than of the politician. Nevertheless, they transcend the diary's emphasis on the writer's own part in events just as surely; the difference is that they explore the inner spirit rather than the external situation.

OFFICIAL DOCUMENTS

'Official documents' is a generic term for a variety of materials produced for and by the British government. This section concentrates on papers produced internally by the Civil Service and externally through agreements with other governments.

Internal documents follow a common format. The general principles of government policy are provided by government ministers; these are then fleshed out and refined by civil servants. In the process, civil servants add extra layers of interpretation: it is part of their function to examine government policy for possible flaws before putting out a version which is as watertight as possible. This means that almost all official documents will have emerged from the classic civil-service format of arguments for, arguments against, and recommended approach. Legal advice is also sought in more controversial cases. Hence, behind each official policy, publicly promoted, lies a considerable volume of formative material which provides a wealth of evidence for the historian.

Much of this, however, remains under the wraps of secrecy for periods of up to thirty years, under legislation rushed through the House of Commons in 1911 and generally known as the Official Secrets Act. When it is eventually permitted, detailed study of this material will show the extent to which politicians reacted to the advice of officials by amending original proposals which may have been more substantial; or the impact of pressure groups on the development of proposals at their various stages. When it is released, Civil Service material may, on the one hand, confirm established views on how policy originated or, on the other, provide a new insight into a process which was uncertain, perhaps even tortuous. This applies, for example, to the Civil Service papers behind Macmillan's announcement that Britain should join the EEC. On the surface, the government's conversion was logical and straightforward. Behind the scenes, however, the Civil Service papers, released after thirty years, show a complex analysis of the options and a feeling that the issue would have to be presented in very simple terms to a public which might not otherwise understand them. This goes some way towards explaining why Macmillan's statements on the subject were so generalised.

There has been a considerable increase in the sheer quantity of documentation produced by civil servants during the course of the twentieth century. In the early decades this was the result of the introduction of the typewriter and its eventual association with carbon paper. The volume was further extended by the use of the photocopier and again by the widespread adoption of word processing and internal communications networks. Photocopying and word processing have led to a proliferation of draft copies. Most documents now go through several preliminary stages, each draft sent out for comments from interested officials and experts, comments from whom are incorporated into subsequent drafts. The finished document is therefore more than ever a collective piece of work – an anonymous product of an anonymous system. The historian will therefore find it more and more time-consuming to try to unravel the different influences entering policy at the different stages of its formation.

Occasionally the historian is left bemused by a civil-service memorandum which seems to depart from these basic principles. An example is the paper of a senior official in the Treasury, Sir Otto Niemeyer, prepared on 2 February 1925 to justify to Winston Churchill, then Chancellor of the Exchequer, the return to the gold standard. He stated that

> on a long view . . . the gold standard is in direct succession to the main steps towards economic reconstruction and is likely to do more for British trade than all the efforts of the Unemployment Grants Committee[10]

Here the historian would, however, need to know several things to interpret this advice fully. What were the terms of reference provided by the minister to his officials? Was he asking for justification of a political decision already taken? Or was he requesting views on whether it was the right decision? What form did the previous comments take before the concluding recommendation? Were other points of view put, as has always been the normal civil-service procedure? Or was this a case of a senior civil servant being asked to short-circuit the whole process? And if so, why?

The type of external document most commonly quoted is the treaty. This normally has two elements. One is the 'reflective' purpose, which is to provide a comprehensive settlement and so neutralise the causes of past tension and conflict. The other element is 'projective', the focus of which is on future territorial settlement or arrangements for military security or for economic and social co-operation. Examples include the Locarno Treaties of 1925, in which Britain played a prominent part, the Charter of the North Atlantic Treaty Organisation (1949), the accession to the European Communities (1973) and the Maastricht Treaty (1992).

Treaties of the twentieth century, like those of the nineteenth, tend to have a common format. This comprises a summary of the official ideology behind the treaty; a series of clauses or articles which contain the details of the agreement; and additional protocols which might be secret. There are several benefits in such documents for the student of British history. For one thing, they are the easiest to authenticate and are therefore the least likely to be forged. For another, their preambles contain an excellent summary of the multiplicity of viewpoints, which might even be seen as an agreed balance of biases. On the other hand, there must be reservations about the use of diplomatic documents. Treaties are by their nature legalistic and, as such, offer a very restricted understanding of the background of a particular situation. This is because a 'balance of biases' is achievable only through a 'balance of omissions'. Treaties rarely exist in isolation and have to be seen within the context of voluminous correspondence, official and secret, and the records and minutes of related meetings and conferences. These reveal the details of the process leading up to the formation of a treaty and the difficulties which have to be overcome. The main problem here is that the Official Secrets Act places severe limitations on what is available to the historian, a counterpart to the constraints placed on information on the development of internal policy.

SPEECHES

The main advantage of the speech as an historical source is that it provides an insight into the speaker's character through the use of vocabulary and tone. The greatest speeches of the nineteenth century were made in Parliament, usually in the House of Commons, and the skills of Canning, Palmerston, Gladstone, Bright and Disraeli were carefully honed to make the fullest possible use of that forum. This was partly because speeches were made for posterity, to be recorded in print by Hansard and read by an educated minority within the population. This inevitably conditioned the style employed: many speeches were delivered with all the precision and grammatical complexity which a classical education could bestow.

During the twentieth century the most obvious development has been the diminution of the grand oratorial style of the parliamentary debate. This is very obvious from any regular or, for that matter random, perusal of Hansard. The change can be followed up by the historian as a direct comment on the changes in the scope of Parliament and in the conditions under which it operates; indeed, there is here considerable scope for research by the historian of British politics.

In the first place, one can see a far greater restriction on parliamentary time as a result of the vast increase in legislation brought by the foundations and development of the welfare state. Hence the House of Commons gradually has become less concerned with formal debating than with presenting – or opposing – contentious legislation. A second factor is the widening of the franchise, which has meant that the speeches in the Commons have had to exert a broader appeal. Quantitative assessment of policy matters more than qualitative appreciation of delivery. It therefore pays to keep speeches shorter, simpler and to the point; among the first to perfect this technique was Stanley Baldwin. And third, the recording and televising of Parliament has added more emphasis to the style of debating characterised by 'point scoring': the lucid argument and systematic presentation of a case is all too often replaced by the sharp 'one-liner' intended as a 'put-down'. Public perceptions of the abilities of party leaders can actually be shaped by performances in Prime Minister's Question Time – which has become the focal point for most people's interest in Parliament.

The real skills of debating have been seen more frequently in the House of Lords especially since, from the 1950s, the creation of life peerages has meant that former party politicians could put behind them the hectic pace of party politics and seek a more measured and considered form of expression. They, not their counterparts in the Commons, have become the real heirs to the skilled debaters of the nineteenth century. This has undoubtedly enhanced the prestige of the House of Lords, making it much more difficult to consider abolition. The relative lack of detailed publicity in the press has also proved an advantage, since the quality of speeches need not be compromised by the need to achieve instant impact.

The twentieth century differs from the nineteenth also in the variety of alternatives to the Parliamentary speech. For example, each of the major political parties holds annual conferences. These provide the historian with a range of views from within a party which is rarely seen in the party's Parliamentary context because of the latter's operation of a whip system. This range is twofold. Within the conference there is an official diversity of approach to policy that leads through debate to reconciliation and synthesis. The purpose of the orator here is to rally opinion to a particular cause, with the overriding emphasis placed on the sinking of differences to the common good. Outside the conference, however, much can be gauged about the real state of party unity from what is said in 'fringe' meetings.

The style in radio and television broadcasts differs from both Parliamentary debate and the party conference. Regular broadcasts focus on annual events such as the explanation of the budget by the Chancellor of the Exchequer (and the reply from the shadow Chancellor). The almost uniform approach here is for the former to express a restrained optimism tempered by firmness and a sense of responsibility, while the latter shows restrained anger with the policy announced and disappointment at opportunities missed. More than any other type of speech, such an event has developed into a refined stereotype. More variety is shown in the ad hoc addresses to the nation, usually by the Prime Minister. Occasions have included the announcement of a general election, the declaration of war or some state of emergency, or the explanation of a change of policy such as Macmillan's announcement of Britain's decision to apply for membership of the EEC.

The politicians of the twentieth century may have lacked the opportunity – or inclination – to emulate W.E. Gladstone or Edmund Burke, both of whom were quite capable of speaking for over four hours with minimal notes. There has been, nevertheless, an array of talent. Lloyd George made his mark as a speaker in the Commons and on the hustings, the last of the great orators before the arrival of the airwaves. Less mercurial but adept at using the new medium of the wireless was Stanley Baldwin, whose style of address spoke volumes about his general political approach and pursuit of moderation (see Chapter 5). He was also conscious that parliamentary speeches would be edited and reported in the press to a public who wanted to read a few reassuring catchphrases. He therefore provided them (see Chapter 11). Winston Churchill was renowned for his stirring rhetoric on the wireless during the Second World War. There was, nevertheless, a strange inconsistency in the 1930s in his treatment of militarism and fascism. Earlier oratory shows quite another Churchill: even in the late 1930s he could say of Japanese expansion in China:

I do not think the League of Nations should be well advised to have a quarrel with Japan. . . . I hope we shall try in England to understand a little the position of Japan, an ancient state, with the highest sense of national honour and patriotism and with a teeming population and a remarkable energy. On the one side they see the dark menace of Soviet Russia. On the other, the chaos of China, four or five provinces of which are now being tortured under Communist rule.

Of the post-war politicians the first to make his mark as a public speaker was Harold Macmillan who, like Baldwin, chose to address the public in simple and reassuring terms, whether on the economy (see Chapter 13) or on the decision to apply for membership of the EEC (see Chapter 19). In complete contrast was Harold Wilson, with his sharpness and his ability to handle hecklers in public meetings and opposition back-benchers in Parliament. He was especially impressive during the mid-1960s when he emphasised the need for Britain to become more aware of its scientific, technological and educational potential: indeed, it would be a fair question for a historian to ask whether the ideas and techniques of Harold Wilson have had a conscious – if undeclared – influence on the presentation of 'New Labour' by Tony Blair.

The historian can also empathise more effectively with some of the more eccentric speakers of the second half of the century, especially Enoch Powell and Michael Foot. Both were speakers in the classic style, crafting arguments which aimed to persuade and which were based on the highest standards of expression. In the case of Powell, however, skills which might have served the highest levels of mainstream politics were diverted to the cause of fringe groups. The historian is entitled to ask whether his political views shaped his oratory – or were shaped by them. In this instance, therefore, recordings of Powell's speeches are far more useful than the transcripts. The same can be said of mainstream politicians who emphasised inflection, modulation, delivery and pauses. Mrs Thatcher was one of the most self-conscious speakers of the century, changing her delivery but not her ideas. Perhaps her oratory reflected her policy: a flexible presentation of fixed beliefs, or a pragmatic pursuit of ideology.

CARTOONS

One particular type of source may, at first sight, be seen as inappropriate for use by the historian. The cartoon is, by its very nature, one-sided.

All humour depends on the display of bias: after all, whoever heard of the balanced joke? To some extent, therefore, the historian needs to suspend the usual striving for impartiality to appreciate the point being made. On the other hand, the joke can reveal a great deal about the society in which it was produced and the people at which it was aimed.

During the nineteenth century the style employed underwent a considerable change. The cartoons of the early decades were far more complex than those which eventually replaced them. The cartoons of Cruikshank, for example, involved a considerable amount of detail and extensive dialogue, even though the issue itself may have been straight-forward. Gradually the focus sharpened and the cartoonist's intention was to convey the point immediately and succinctly. Until well into the twentieth century, however, the majority of cartoonists provided a literal portrayal of politicians: the drawings of Bernard Partridge, for example, were very much within the tradition of the nineteenth century, even to the inclusion of dialogue in some of his captions. A contrast gradually emerged between this traditional approach and the more distinctive style of Low, arguably the greatest political cartoonist of all time. He combined a simplified drawing style, which aimed to capture the essence of the subject through the accentuation of selected features, with a rare perception of the historical importance of events as they occurred. His approach influenced a whole succession of artists who now aimed to distil a situation to its essence while developing a personal style which was instantly recognisable. Examples since the Second World War include Vicky, Cummings, Gibbard, Garland and Frankland.

As in the nineteenth century, outlets for cartoons also underwent something of a change. Then the process was a gradual change from broadsheets and papers to satirical periodicals like *Punch*. In the twentieth century *Punch* continued to be an important channel for political cartoons but was increasingly pushed aside by the national newspapers, each of which produced its own cartoonists: Low in the *Evening Standard*, Cummings in the *Daily Express* and Gibbard in the *Guardian*. By the 1990s *Punch* had gone out of circulation and the daily newspaper had triumphed. The reason for this is paradoxical. On the one hand, the non-political sense of humour of the majority of the population had changed so much that a weekly magazine like *Punch* became uneconomic. Instead, the population sought humour in smaller, more concentrated extracts in other publications. Expectations from the political 'joke', however, remained fairly constant. One of the characteristics of *Punch* in its later years was that political cartoons became less and less evident: these migrated almost entirely to the daily and Sunday press. This was because the political cartoonist was expected to provide an instant reaction to events rather than a more considered perspective which had always been the hallmark of *Punch*.

The examples of the cartoons provided on pages 372–83 fall into two categories. The first is a unanimous interpretation in response to a particular crisis. This was the case with Ramsay MacDonald's formation of the 1931 National Government. *The Master Chemist* (Figure 17) points clearly to the political difficulties lying ahead, while *The Splendid Sword* (Figure 18) is a reflection on the need to make effective use of the largest majority ever given to any British prime minister in a general election. Both convey an awareness of the historic uniqueness of the situation – and of the need to succeed. The Second World War provided an even stronger reason for unanimity: in this instance the cartoon was harnessed to survival and victory. The government itself entered the medium in the form of the propaganda such as *Careless Talk Costs Lives* (Figure 19). At the same time, individual cartoonists suspended their normal satirical sense and lent themselves to the campaign. Low, for example, produced two cartoons which embodied the spirit of Britain at war. *Very well, alone* (Figure 20) was published in the *Evening Standard* on the day that France surrendered to Germany. It represents British determination to see through the conflict, although with some apprehension about impending invasion. The other, *All behind you, Winston* (Figure 21) was an exhortation to support the new coalition government. Perhaps Low had a certain satisfaction in the removal of Chamberlain, who had always been a special target for his wit.

Three issues, by their very nature, attracted rival interpretations. The two cartoons shown on the General Strike reveal the establishment and opposition view. Figure 22 from *Punch* shows the red flag of the TUC challenging the legitimate authority of the British government, represented by John Bull and the Union Flag; this was a widespread view held at the time and officially sponsored in the media by the Prime Minister, Baldwin. The imagery of this cartoon is directly challenged in the response of *Labour Weekly* (Figure 23), in which the Union Flag flies over the capitalist, who is protected in his exploitation of the working man by the forces of law and order.

There were also polarised interpretations of Chamberlain and appeasement, which find a parallel in the views of modern historians (see Chapter 10). A positive approach can be seen in Figure 24, which conveys Chamberlain's mission to Munich as a necessary search for peace, while Partridge's version (Figure 25) shows John Bull, standing

THE MASTER CHEMIST.

PROFESSOR MACDONALD. "NOW IF ONLY THESE RATHER ANTAGONISTIC ELEMENTS
WILL BLEND AS I HOPE, WE'LL HAVE A REAL NATIONAL ELIXIR."

Figure 17 The master chemist, Punch 1931 (?)
Reproduced by permission of *Punch*.

THE SPLENDID SWORD.

"THE BEST BIT OF WORK I'VE EVER DONE; AND I FEEL SURE YOU CAN BE TRUSTED TO USE IT WELL."

Figure 18 The splendid sword, *Punch* 4 November 1931. Reproduced by permission of *Punch*.

Figure 19 Careless talk costs lives

"VERY WELL , ALONE "

Figure 20 Very well, alone

anxiously beside his hastily prepared bomb-shelter being re-assured by
Chamberlain about the likely outcome of the crisis. In each case the
demeanour of the subject indicates a certain sympathy with the peace
process which the historian is entitled to take as representing a substantial range of opinion at the time.

A similar dichotomy can be seen in the views on the development of
the welfare sate after 1945. Figures 26 and 27 embody the fears that
the welfare state would crush individual initiative through excessive
'nannying' and heavier taxation. In each case, the cartoonist captured
and illustrated a political metaphor. In another cartoon of the period,
Low shows a more considered view reflecting the concern about the
welfare state in conjunction with the requirements of defence. The
point being made concerns the balancing of priorities rather than the
rejection of change altogether. A similar observation is made by Vicky
(Figure 28) about the 1951 split within the Labour party following the
imposition of prescription charges. Attlee, Bevan and Gaitskell are
confronted by the leftists: Bevan, Foot, Mikardo and Wilson. In the

Figure 21 All behind you, Winston

process, Vicky contrives to balance the caricature by representing the two sides as 'toffs' and 'louts'.

In the last three decades of the twentieth century, the cartoon became increasingly rivalled on television by the mimicry of Mike Yarwood and Rory Bremner and the puppetry of *Spitting Image*. The latter proved ultimately to be the more genuine extension of the cartoonist's art since it allowed the distillation of the essence of an issue or controversy through the calculated, often grotesque, exaggeration of a politician's vulnerability. It also attracted more intense interest. Political figures portrayed on *Spitting Image* felt that they had 'arrived', although at times there were allegations that the programme was crossing the boundary between legitimate satire and blatant character assassination. Perhaps this can be seen as a partial return to the cruder and more preposterous observations of the cartoonists of the late eighteenth and early nineteenth centuries.

UNDER WHICH FLAG?

JOHN BULL. "ONE OF THESE TWO FLAGS HAS GOT TO COME DOWN—AND IT WON'T
BE MINE."

Figure 22 Under which flag?, *Punch* 12 May 1926.
Reproduced by permission of *Punch*.

UNDER WHICH FLAG?

Figure 23 Under which flag?

STILL HOPE

Figure 24 Still hope, *Punch* 1938.
Reproduced by permission of *Punch*.

A GREAT MEDIATOR

John Bull. "I've known many Prime Ministers in my time, Sir, but never one who worked so hard for security in the face of such terrible odds."

Figure 25 A great mediator, *Punch* 1938.
Reproduced by permission of *Punch*.

THE WELFARE STATE

Figure 26 The Welfare State, *Punch* (? any date).
Reproduced by permission of *Punch*.

Figure 27 Wife, child and welfare state to support, by Gais, *Punch.*
Reproduced by permission of *Punc*

" SOCIALISTS! "

Figure 28 Socialists!, *News Chronicle* July 1951.
Reproduced by permission of Solo Syndication Ltd.

NEWSPAPERS

The most transitory of all written sources are newspapers. They lack the degree of self-consciousness of some other forms of material because, in the words of G. Wilkinson, they are 'time-specific and do not have an eye for posterity'.[11] This has a distinct advantage. No other source provides such a detailed account of and reflection on events at daily intervals. Their deliberate obsolescence means that their comments will lack the sort of manipulation which goes to make a long-term reputation. On the other hand, they will be more prone to short-term sensationalism, partly through the need to develop an immediate comment on an event in a way that will attract a transient readership. The historian also has to establish the precise nature of the relationship between the newspaper and the society it serves. To what extent does it

383

reflect contemporary views and to what extent does it manufacture them? All newspapers claim to articulate the view of the common man and woman, when the role they are generally fulfilling is to present the interest of the paper's owner. This may seem to reduce the usefulness of the newspaper as a source. The historian can, however, find in such manipulation a commentary on the formation of public opinion and on the channels used. In any case, the extent of bias can generally be cross-checked by comparing the views of different newspapers on the same issue. Substantial parts of any paper will be relatively free of editorial bias, providing a considerable amount of detail in the form of minor articles and advertisements which reflect the social life at the time, especially taste, leisure and fashions.

The development of the press in the twentieth century is in itself a reflection on the growth of a mass society. Until 1896 newspapers had been aimed exclusively at the middle and upper classes. By far the most important was *The Times*, which sold three times as many copies as all its rivals combined. A major change, however, occurred with the launching by Alfred Harmsworth of the *Daily Mail*, intended as a mass-circulation rival to *The Times*. Other rivals soon followed, in the form of the *Manchester Guardian* and the *Daily Telegraph*, while in mass circulation terms the *Mail* was challenged by the *Daily Express*, the *Daily Mirror* and the *Daily Herald*. Several notable trends occurred after 1945. In the first place, the differences between the various newspapers became more pronounced as they searched for the sort of individuality which would increase sales. They all polarised during the 1950s and 1960s into one of two formats: the tabloid and the broadsheet. The former was easier to handle and was ideally suited to a more sensational coverage of the news with a single front-page story; its political and international coverage was reduced, to be replaced largely by 'human interest stories'. The broadsheet maintained a more traditional approach, actually increasing the extent of news-reporting and carrying sections of commentary and background analysis. Both tabloids and broadsheets eventually made use of colour from the 1980s onwards, a particular benefit in sports reporting and in the presentation of graphics.

Most of the newspapers were, at one stage or other, bought up by a small number of wealthy proprietors. The *Sun*, *The Times* and *Today* were acquired by Rupert Murdoch (who also owned the *News of the World*), and the *Mirror* group by Robert Maxwell. Meanwhile, their political slant had been accentuated. The *Sun*, the *Daily Express*, the *Daily Telegraph*, the *Mail*, *Today* and the *News of the World* were consistently pro-Conservative, while the *Mirror*, the *People* and the *Guardian* were more inclined to Labour. The establishment of the *Independent* in 1987 was partly an attempt to recapture the non-partisan ground which had once been seen as the special role of *The Times*. All competed aggressively with other forms of the media, such as television. The latter seemed to have the advantage of being able to guarantee a more immediate and visual presentation of the news. But newspapers showed a remarkable capacity for adapting to changed conditions, with the exception of *Today*, which had to be wound up in November 1995. They also rediscovered an interest in 'social values', especially during the 1980s and 1990s. The historian needs, however, to be aware that the motivation for this varies widely. Some papers attempt a genuine assessment of social issues, while others use personal stories within the context of more direct moralising. A question to consider is whether this reflects a reversion to earlier values or whether it is used as justification for the increase in sensational revelations which are clearly designed to sell copy. Will the future historian see in the 1990s an underlying puritanism or a superficial prurience? The press will, no doubt, provide evidence for both.

STATISTICS

Statistics are the product of the modern technological society. They cover population growth and distribution, the breakdown of layers of the workforce, the distribution of industries and agriculture, the volume of production, imports and exports, the variation of wages, the cost of living, the development of inflation, the patterns of government expenditure, and the incidence of crime, disease and poverty. Such material is often considered one of the most inherently reliable forms of primary source on the grounds that it is likely to be the most neutral. It has, for example, a specific index, normally numerical, which is not directly attached to a political or ideological framework.

On the other hand, it may well have been manipulated. This could have been done by contemporaries seeking to support a particular thesis. The historian therefore needs to be aware of the possibilities of selection, omission, even distortion – all amounting to the expression of party bias. There is also the possibility of figures being falsified through accidental error at some stage in their compilation. The historian therefore carries a major responsibility. In the first place it is necessary to interpret a mass of data which has an underlying logic but no inherent meaning. There is also a need to make appropriate use of data and to avoid distortion through inaccurate comparisons between different types of figures. Finally, the historian has to beware of simplistic generalisations based on superficial reading of the figures; for example, statistics showing a rapid increase in industrialisation need to be related to the original industrial baseline since the rate of growth from a low baseline is likely to be significantly higher than from a more developed one.

One of the major problems with statistics is the suspicion that they can be politicised. This works in two ways. First, political parties are able to select material on unemployment or crime to present entirely different cases. Indeed, without the use of statistics the British two-party system would lose much of its edge. Where would Parliamentary Questions be without statistics? Many PQs request information from Government Departments in an attempt to embarrass the governing party; the questions are dealt with by civil servants who, in their follow-up notes, provide ministers with a defensive brief by advising on the positive interpretation of the statistical information given in the answers. Second, the rules may be changed for the collection of statistics. During the 1980s the Conservative government's reinterpretation of the basis of unemployment was particularly controversial. It was challenged on a number of occasions by the Labour opposition, which produced a second figure, calculated each time on the 'old' criteria.

The formats used for statistics are well known. The purest type is the table, which comprises a selection of figures, perhaps under a number of comparative headings. Recent compilations might well be the refinement of more detailed computer print-outs: these have an almost infinite capacity for cross-comparison. On the other hand, the analysis provided within tables, whether or not the latter are generated by computer, is only as good as the information which was previously fed in. The historian therefore needs to question the collection of data as well as the way in which those data are processed for tables.

Statistics presented in non-tabular form have undergone an additional stage of refinement. This makes their interpretation easier but, at the same time, more directed. Graphs are generally used to indicate the change, during a defined period, in population or unemployment figures. They provide an instant visual impact which invites immediate deductions about causation. Their main limitation is that they are too generalised to show smaller-scale fluctuations and the historian may well have to examine in greater detail material on the period between the points on the graph. If graphs are useful to show a general trend, bar charts are more appropriate for comparisons between several items. The best examples are the comparative productivity of the economies of different countries, or the results of a series of general elections. Pie charts go a stage further, apportioning the distribution on a percentage basis. Both are essentially limited to comparative analysis and invite particular attention to the motivation for using this approach to present statistics.

NOVELS

There is a certain common ground between history and the novel, in that both cover connecting links between events and therefore deal with causation. The underlying approach is different in that the historian aims to explain what has actually occurred and the motivation of individuals who really lived. The novelist, on the other hand, explores the human psyche through imaginative constructions. Where history and literature overlap is in the attitudes of a particular period. The literary analyst will wish to explore the novel's potential for, in Shakespeare's phrase, holding 'the mirror up to nature', while the historian will adjust the mirror so that it reflects contemporary society and social attitudes. There is, however, an obvious deficiency here. The reflection of society will be one-sided and hence incomplete; the novelist can hardly be expected to aim at the level of impartiality to which the historian aspires, since this might devalue the effectiveness of the plot or characterisation. Where possible, the historian will need to cross-check social descriptions in novels with details from other sources and, ideally, to compare two fundamentally contrasting approaches to the same issue within two different novels. The range of novels available for the twentieth century is massive; in this section it is only possible to point to the light thrown by a few selected British novelists on a handful of themes.

The first of these is the changes in society brought by the First World War. The leisurely life of the well-to-do in Edwardian England is vividly captured by L.P. Hartley (1895–1972) in *The Go-Between*. On the other hand, since this book was published in 1953, it should really be seen as a secondary source on an earlier period. Historical authenticity is therefore more likely to have been assembled through retrospective research than through contemporary experience. The reverse is the case with *The Forsyte Saga* of John Galsworthy (1867–1933). A description of a family through several generations, this was published between 1906 and 1928, as *The Man of Property, In Chancery, To Let, The White Monkey, The Silver Spoon*, and *Swansong*. More than any other works this century these provide an evocative account of a changing society and of the social impact of the First World War. Since they were contemporaneous with the period they portray they can be regarded as a genuine primary source.

Galsworthy was also interested in the impact of poverty at the turn of the century, especially in the *Island Pharisees* (1904). But more popularly associated with the description of social conditions is D.H. Lawrence (1885–1930), whose *Sons and Lovers* (1913) is of dual interest to the historian. First, it provides a vivid description of life in a Nottinghamshire mining community in the first decade of the century. Second, it is in effect an autobiography, in which the historian could gauge the extent of exaggeration, literary licence and personal indulgence, through a comparison with a biography. Lawrence was also notable for his regional emphasis as, more recently, has been Stan Barstow (1928–) whose *A Kind of Loving* (1960) provides a graphic account of working-class life in Yorkshire. This was followed by *Ask Me Tomorrow* (1962) and *Joby* (1964).

A major concern of twentieth-century Britain has been the steady and progressive emancipation of the individual, whether politically, socially, or psychologically. The novel contributed to this process through the 'stream of consciousness' and 'interior monologue': two terms especially associated with James Joyce (1882–1941). The historian can learn much about the growth of individual awareness in literature from *Ulysses*, published in 1920. Also of interest is the shock expressed by some critics at the explicit nature of this book, an indication of the more conservative and traditionalist influences in Britain between the wars. Much the same applied in the emancipation of sexuality: Lawrence's *Lady Chatterley's Lover* should have been a milestone but, because of the outrage it caused on its private publication, it had to be expurgated before it was released in London in 1932. Perhaps the most interesting aspect of this book was the trial of 1959 in which Penguin Books were prosecuted under the Obscene Publications Act. Their acquittal may be seen as the symbolic beginning of the era known as the 'swinging sixties'. Extracts from the transcript of that trial also illustrate the conflict between different values: at one point, for example, the jury were asked by the prosecuting counsel whether they would let their 'families and servants' read this book.

A major theme of the twentieth century was the emancipation of women. This is also strongly reflected in novels written by women largely about women. The second novel of Virginia Woolf (1882– 1941), *Night and Day* (1919), includes extensive references to the suffragette movement. Her works were considered increasingly important during the 1960s and 1970s by the feminist movement, which saw her *A Room of One's Own* (1929) as a feminist classic, along with its sequel, *Three Guineas* (1938). Perhaps her main social contribution was to provide a feminist input into the stream of consciousness movement. The feminist theme was also taken up by A.S. Byatt (1936–), and, more recently, by Margaret Atwood (1939–). The whole process became more self-conscious when, in 1973, Virago Press was launched by women for women writers. It described itself as 'a feminist publishing house'.

A counterpoint to feminism was the emergence of the 'angry young man', a term usually associated with the play *Look Back in Anger* (1956) by John Osborne (1929–96). From the mid-1950s onwards there was a sense of alienation both from accepted social norms and from some of the conventions which were beginning to replace them. The target was therefore very broad. The most celebrated novel of Kingsley Amis (1922–95) was his first, *Lucky Jim* (1954), a description of a radical lecturer in one of Britain's 'new' universities and an attack on what Amis perceived to be the pretensions of the academic establishment. Other novels of this genre were Alan Sillitoe's *Saturday Night and Sunday Morning* (1958) and *The Loneliness of the Long Distance Runner* (1959). The former explores the disillusionment of a factory worker in Nottingham, the latter the refusal of a borstal boy to meet the establishment half-way.

Power is another major preoccupation of the twentieth century. There was a vast outpouring of popular novels on the workings of government and Parliament, with details of political intrigue: Jeffrey Archer and Edwina Currie are two examples of politicians-turned-novelist. At a higher level, C.P. Snow (1905–80) wrote a series of novels which included *The Masters, The New Men, Homecoming,* and *The Affair,* all published between 1951 and 1960. In these he provided detailed perspectives on both the academic and administrative worlds; indeed, 'The Corridors of Power' became a catchphrase in the English language. The surrender of power was also captured. Paul Scott (1920–78) was closely involved in the complex events in the Indian sub-continent. He served in the Indian army during the Second World War, after which he focused on Anglo-Indian relations. His best known work here was the *Raj Quartet,* which comprised *The Jewel in the Crown* (1966), *The Day of the Scorpion* (1968), *The Towers of Silence* (1971) and *A Division of the Spoils* (1975). These aimed to provide a variety of perspectives and points of view on the complex events leading up to partition. The detailed way in which the whole picture is gradually revealed involves some of the skills more generally associated with the historian. Scott's work contrasted clearly with E.M. Forster (1879–1970), whose *A Passage to India* (1924) reflects the situation in India while it was still under British rule. On the other hand, it, too, deals with clashes and crises between different cultures and in many ways presages the problems of the transition to independence.

Finally, several major novels of the twentieth century can be read and interpreted at different layers of complexity and meaning. *Lord of the Flies* (1954) by William Golding (1911–93), for example, initially appears to be a commentary on the different types of behaviour of a group of schoolboys marooned on a deserted island – an inversion of Ballantyne's more idyllic nineteenth-century novel *A Coral Island*. It could even be a perception of the products of the British educational system in the 1950s. At a deeper level, however, it conveys a pessimism, characteristic of twentieth-century Britain, about the durability of civilised behaviour. The book could be seen as a modern parable on the theme of the nineteenth-century historian, Lecky, that 'civilisation is a veneer: scratch it and anything can happen'. It might even be interpreted as an updated version of *Leviathan*, written by the seventeenth-century political theorist, Thomas Hobbes. The latter constructed a political system based on the premise that, without proper constraints, humanity would return to a state of nature in which life would be 'solitary, poor, nasty, brutish and short'. *Lord of the Flies* shows just such a descent. Aldous Huxley (1894–1963) displays similar pessimism in *Brave New World* (1932), which provides the historian with an insight into a typical modern utopia – with its underlying assumption that scientific progress may actually contribute to a deterioration in the quality of human life. The whole concept of progress therefore becomes inverted, again a view held by a growing number of twentieth-century pessimists.

Perhaps the greatest British exponent of the multi-layered novel was George Orwell (1903–50). *Animal Farm* (1945) can be read either as a simple tale, or as an allegory of the high ideals and practical shortcomings of those aiming to create a modern utopia or, for the historically aware, an almost exact replica of the events in the Soviet Union under Stalin. This is indicative of the growing disillusionment in Britain in the late 1940s in the face of the same Soviet system which had been extolled during the 1930s by George Bernard Shaw. Orwell's *Nineteen Eighty-Four* (1949) is another example. Generally seen as a vivid portrayal of dictatorship, again within the context of an inverted utopia, it can also be read as a warning about the encroaching power of the Soviet system which, in 1948, took political control of much of eastern Europe. The two dates are obviously linked and, for a generation of Britons, came to symbolise the source and destination of the Communist threat. Despite his historical consciousness, however, Orwell took a number of liberties that for an historian would cross the bounds of acceptability. For example, in *Animal Farm*, he picked the wrong pig to call Napoleon: it was Trotsky, not Stalin, who was seen at the time as a Bonapartist, a perception which may well have led most Bolsheviks to support Stalin. Even so, he succeeded in capturing two paradoxes which symbolise the modern British hatred of totalitarian systems: 'War is Peace, Freedom is Slavery, Ignorance is Strength' and 'All animals are equal, but some are more equal than others'.

CONCLUSION

The late twentieth century has seen a remarkable increase in the number of secondary works published. The reason for this is an interaction between different levels of historical activity, but the catalyst is the increased significance attached to the primary source and a never-ending quest to see it in a new light.

The impetus comes from the enormous quantity of detailed research, usually connected with, or as the follow-up to, a doctoral thesis. This may unearth new sources or reinterpret existing ones or focus on documents which have previously been ignored or marginalised. The result is the development of an increasingly elaborate patchwork of detailed studies which have two important functions. One is to bring obscure primary sources within the range of any serious student of history. The other is to regenerate historical debate on a wide variety of issues, partly through the sources themselves, partly through the interpretation attached to them within the thesis or monograph. Other secondary works follow, representing a wide range of viewpoints. These, in turn, attract the 'synthesisers', who aim to provide a more composite interpretation covering a wider period.

This overall pattern becomes more problematic when applied to the history of the past decade or so. For one thing, the availability of many primary sources is circumscribed by the Official Secrets Act. As the thirty-year restrictions on government documents expire there is a scramble to reassess topics in the light of new evidence. This means that reinterpretations of contemporary history appear to occur in waves. Hence the Suez Crisis came under renewed scrutiny in the late 1980s and Britain's first application to join the EEC in the early 1990s. Unless current restrictions are lifted, the year 2004 should bring a new analysis of the industrial conflict experienced by the Heath government, while 2012 will refocus attention on the Falklands War. Never before have future debates about past issues been so predictable.

Yet in the intervening period, between the inadequately documented present and the opening of the floodgates in the future, the historian can only make incomplete assessments and explanations. In common with the political analyst, the historian therefore has to go in for a fair amount of creative writing. There is, however, a fundamental difference. The political analyst makes a virtue of this unresourced area, moving on to fresh issues as a matter of course. The historian, by contrast, presents a *provisional* interpretation – quite possibly based on political analysis. The ultimate aim is always to return to the period or issue once further primary resources are released. By the time these are available, a longer-term perspective will also have emerged, probably changing some of the conclusions already tentatively offered.

Some would argue that historical analysis of the present should not even be attempted. Politicians in Britain, many of whom are themselves historians, have imposed a double constraint. One is the longstanding control over the release of sources. The other, and more recent, example is the influence of the government after 1988 on the shaping of the type of history to be taught, under the National Curriculum, in secondary schools. The original proposals were adjusted, through government intervention, to increase the weighting of knowledge in relation to skills; even more interesting, it argued that the past should not be studied up to the present day. This, it is believed, allows a proper perspective to emerge; presumably it also removes history pupils from the influence of politics and sociology and, at the same time, frees current governments from detailed scrutiny. For how wide an audience was Nikita Khrushchev speaking when he said: 'Historians are dangerous people; they can upset everything'?

NOTES

1 INTRODUCTION

1 In J. Gardiner (ed.) *What is History Today?* (Atlantic Highlands, NJ 1988), pp. 19–20.
2 Ibid., p. 21.
3 Ibid., p. 22.

2 THE FIRST WORLD WAR AND ITS IMPACT

1 See S.J. Lee *Aspects of British Political History 1815–1914* (London 1994), ch. 19.
2 A.J.P. Taylor *English History 1914–1945* (Oxford 1965), p. 61.
3 *The Times*, April 1915.
4 Quoted in R. Pearce *Britain: Domestic Politics 1918–39* (London 1992), p. 31.
5 *The Daily Herald*, 20 August 1914.
6 *Hansard*, House of Lords, vol. 18, col. 238, 6 January 1915.
7 Pearce, op. cit. (London 1993), p. 42.
8 A.S. Milward *The Economic Effects of the Two World Wars on Britain* (London 1970), p. 45.

3 THE DECLINE OF THE LIBERAL PARTY 1914–40

1 G. Dangerfield *The Strange Death of Liberal England* (London 1966), p. 75.
2 C. Cook *A Short History of the Liberal Party 1900–92* (London 1993), ch. 5.
3 P. Adelman *The Decline of the Liberal Party 1910–1931* (Harlow 1981), ch. 1.
4 Ibid., ch. 1.
5 Quoted in ibid., ch. 1.
6 T. Wilson *The Downfall of the Liberal Party, 1914–1935* (London 1966), p. 18.

7 A.J.P. Taylor *England 1914–1945* (Oxford 1965), ch. 2.
8 M. Swartz *The Democratic Control in British Politics during the First World War* (Oxford 1971), p. 131.
9 Ibid., ch. 5.
10 A.R. Ball *British Political Parties: The Emergence of a Modern Party System* (London 1987), p. 120.
11 Adelman, op. cit., p. 55.
12 Quoted in A. Thorpe *Britain in the 1930s: The Deceptive Decade* (Oxford 1992), p. 40.
13 Ibid., p. 34.

4 THE 1924 LABOUR GOVERNMENT

1 For the history of Labour before 1914 see S.J. Lee *Aspects of British Political History 1815–1914* (London 1994), ch. 18.
2 H.A. Clegg *A History of British Trade Unions since 1889: Vol. II: 1911–1933* (Oxford 1985), p. 353.
3 C.L. Mowat *Britain between the Wars 1918–1940* (London 1955; 1964 edition), p. 169.
4 Quoted in R. Rhodes James *The British Revolution: British Politics 1880–1939* (London 1978), p. 469.
5 Quoted in ibid., p. 468.
6 M. Beloff *Wars and Welfare: Britain 1914–1945* (London 1984), p. 126.
7 A.J.P. Taylor *English History 1914–1945* (Oxford 1965), p. 201.
8 Clegg, op. cit., p. 368.
9 C.F. Brand *The British Labour Party* (Stanford, Calif. 1974), p. 98.
10 Mowat, op. cit., p. 174.
11 Clegg, op. cit., p. 368.
12 Brand, op. cit., p. 98.
13 Quoted in E. Estorick *Stafford Cripps* (London 1949), p. 70.
14 D. Marquand *Ramsay MacDonald* (London 1977), p. 328.
15 G. Phillips *The Rise of the Labour Party 1893–1931* (London 1992), p. 47.
16 B. Webb *Diaries, Vol. II*; p. 4.
17 Rhodes James, op. cit., p. 471.
18 Quoted in Taylor, op. cit., p. 214.
19 Ibid., p. 215.
20 W.N. Medlicott *Contemporary England 1914–1964* (London 1967, 1978 edition), p. 198.
21 Mowat, op. cit., p. 180.
22 Lord Parmoor *Retrospect* (London 1936), p. 188.
23 Quoted in Taylor, op. cit., p. 218.
24 L.C.B. Seaman *Post-Victorian Britain 1902–1951* (London 1966), p. 171.
25 Quoted in Mowat, op. cit., p. 189.
26 See Beloff, op. cit., footnote on pp. 140–1.
27 P. Snowden *Autobiography* (London 1934), Vol. II, p. 716.
28 R.W. Lyman *The First Labour Government 1924* (New York 1957), pp. 269–70.
29 Beloff, op. cit., p. 139.

NOTES

5 BALDWIN AND THE CONSERVATIVE ASCENDANCY BETWEEN THE WARS

1 S. Ball 'The Conservative Dominance 1918–40', in P. Catterall (ed.) *Britain 1918–1951* (London 1994) p. 34.
2 Quoted in R. Rhodes James *The British Revolution: British Politics 1880–1939* (London 1978), p. 461.
3 K. Young *Stanley Baldwin* (London 1976), p. 188.
4 Quoted in Rhodes James, op. cit., p. 460.
5 H. Macmillan *Winds of Change* (London 1966), p. 313.
6 C.L. Mowat *Britain Between the Wars* (London 1955), p. 164.
7 Quoted in Rhodes James, op. cit., p. 462.
8 Ibid., p.162.
9 L.C.B. Seaman *Post-Victorian Britain 1902–1951* (London 1966), p.168.
10 Mowat, op. cit., p. 164.
11 A.J.P. Taylor *English History 1914–1945* (Oxford 1965), ch. 6.
12 Ibid., ch. 7.
13 Seaman, op. cit., p. 183.
14 Ibid.
15 R. Pearce *Britain: Domestic Politics 1918–39* (London 1992), p. 85.
16 Rhodes James, op. cit., p. 524.

6 THE GENERAL STRIKE

1 P. Gregg *A Social and Economic History of Britain, 1760–1972* (London 1950; 1973 edition), p. 439.
2 Ibid., p. 441.
3 H.A. Clegg *A History of British Trade Unions since 1889: Vol. II: 1911–1933* (Oxford 1985), p. 424.
4 L.C.B. Seaman *Post-Victorian Britain 1902–1951* (London 1966), p. 195.
5 G. Phillips *The Rise of the Labour Party 1893–1931* (London 1992), p. 133.
6 G. McDonald 'The Defeat of the General Strike', in G. Peele and C. Cook (eds) *The Politics of Reappraisal 1918–1939* (London 1975), p. 69.
7 Quoted in C.L. Mowat *Britain between the Wars 1918–1940* (London 1955, 1964 edition), p. 310.
8 Quoted in R.A. Leeson *Strike: a Live History* (London 1973), p. 88.
9 Ibid., p. 89.
10 Quoted in W.H. Crook *General Strike* (London 1931), p. 323.
11 Quoted in R.H. Haigh, D.S. Morris and A.R. Peters *The Guardian Book of the General Strike* (Aldershot 1988), p. xix.
12 Sir Philip Gibbs *The Pageant of the Years* (London 1946), p. 354.
13 Quoted in McDonald, op. cit., p. 77.
14 Quoted in Mowat, op. cit., p. 321.
15 Quoted in J. Simkin *Contemporary Accounts of the General Strike* (Brighton 1985), p. 16.
16 *Hansard*, 6 May 1926, col. 585.
17 Crook, op. cit., p. 473.

395

18 *Yale Law Journal* 36, Feb. 1927, pp. 464–85.
19 Quoted in S. Nearing *British General Strike* (New York 1926), p. 73.
20 Mowat, op. cit., p. 313.
21 S. Pollard *The Development of the British Economy 1914–1967* (London 1969), p. 276.
22 Phillips, op. cit., p. 156.
23 Quoted in Mowat, op. cit., p. 319.
24 Gregg, op. cit., p. 443.
25 Quoted in W. Milne-Bailey *Trade Unions and the State* p. 71.
26 Reported in *The Times*, 10 May 1926.
27 McDonald, op. cit., p. 84.
28 Clegg, op. cit., p. 423.
29 A.J.P. Taylor *English History 1914–1945* (Oxford 1965), p. 230.
30 Seaman, op. cit., p. 202.

7 THE FIRST CRISIS OF LABOUR 1929–39

1 P. Adelman *The Rise of the Labour Party 1880–1945* (London 1972, 2nd edition 1986), p. 68.
2 H. Pelling *A Short History of the Labour Party* (London 1961, 1982 edition), p. 66.
3 Quoted in L.C.B. Seaman *Post-Victorian Britain 1902–1951* (London 1966), p. 206.
4 G.D.H. Cole and R. Postgate *The Common People 1746–1946* (London 1938, 1961 edition), p. 593.
5 Quoted in A.J.P. Taylor *English History 1914–1945* (Oxford 1965).
6 W. Ashworth *An Economic History of England 1870–1939* (London 1960), p. 399.
7 A. Morgan *J. Ramsay MacDonald* (Manchester 1987), p. 200.
8 Adelman, op. cit., Document 66.
9 Ibid., Document 73.
10 Ibid., Document 74.
11 Morgan, op. cit., p. 239.
12 Adelman, op. cit., Document 76.
13 Morgan, op. cit., p. 205.
14 S.R. Ward *James Ramsay MacDonald: Low Born Among the High Brows* (New York 1990), p. 287.
15 C.F. Brand *The British Labour Party* (Stanford, Calif. 1974), p. 161.
16 H. Dalton *The Fateful Years: Memoirs 1931–1945* (London 1947), p. 88.
17 J. Stevenson and C. Cook *The Slump* (London 1979) p. 116.
18 Quoted in R.M. Martin *TUC: The Growth of a Pressure Group 1868–1976* (Oxford 1980), p. 228.
19 G. Phillips *The Rise of the Labour Party 1893–1931* (London 1992), p. 61.

8 THE ECONOMY AND UNEMPLOYMENT BETWEEN THE WARS

1 D.H. Aldcroft 'The Locust Years? Britain's inter-war economy', in P. Catterall (ed.) *Britain 1918–1951* (Oxford 1994), p. 39.

2 R. Pearce *Britain: Industrial Relations and the Economy 1900–1939* (London 1993), p. 49.

3 S.N. Broadberry *The British Economy between the Wars: A Macroeconomic Survey* (Oxford 1986), p. 5.

4 Aldcroft, op. cit., p. 40.

5 Pearce, op. cit., p. 51.

6 Adapted from Pearce, op. cit., p. 57.

7 D.H. Aldcroft *The Inter-War Economy: Britain 1919–1939* (London 1973), p. 148.

8 Ibid., p. 160.

9 Economic Advisory Council *Report of the Committee on the Cotton Industry* (1930): Cmd 3615.

10 Aldcroft *The Inter-War Economy*, p. 163.

11 Liberal Party *The Liberal Industrial Enquiry, Britain's Industrial Future* (London 1928).

12 *The Times*, 2 November 1927.

13 G.C. Allen *The Structure of Industry in Britain* (London 1966), p. 9.

14 Aldcroft *The Inter-War Economy*, p. 187.

15 S. Pollard *The Development of the British Economy 1914–1967* (London 1969), p. 99.

16 D.H. Aldcroft *Full Employment: The Elusive Goal* (London 1984), pp. 14–15.

17 D. Powell *British Politics and the Labour Question, 1868–1990* (London 1992), p. 199.

18 See Aldcroft 'The Locust Years?'.

19 Quoted in T. Hatton 'Unemployment and the labour market in inter-war Britain', in R. Floud and D. McCloskey (eds) *The Economic History of Britain since 1700: vol. 2: 1860–1939* (Cambridge 1994), p. 363.

20 Hatton, op. cit., pp. 363–4.

21 H. Loebl *Government Factories and the Origins of British Regional Policy 1934–1948* (Aldershot 1988), Introduction.

22 See B.W.E. Alford *Depression and Recovery? British Economic Growth 1918–1939* (London 1972).

23 Pearce, op. cit., p. 117.

24 Loebl, op. cit., Introduction.

25 Aldcroft *The Inter-War Economy*, p. 155.

26 For an analysis of this debate, see R. Middleton *Towards the Managed Economy: Keynes, the Treasury and the Fiscal Policy Debate of the 1930s* (London 1985), pp. 7–9.

27 Pearce, op. cit., p. 120.

28 Loebl, op. cit., Introduction.

29 See A. Booth *British Economic Policy, 1931–49: Was There a Keynesian Revolution?* (Hemel Hempstead 1989).

30 Alford, op. cit., p. 81.

31 See G.A. Phillips and R.T. Maddock *The Growth of the British Economy 1918–1968* (London 1973), p. 22.
32 A.J.P. Taylor *English History 1914–1945* (Oxford 1965), p. 317.
33 S. Constantine *Social Conditions in Britain 1918–1939* (London 1983), p. 24.
34 Walter Greenwood *Love on the Dole* (London 1933), pp. 224–5.
35 J.B. Priestley *English Journey* (London 1934).
36 A. Hutt *The Condition of the Working Class in Britain* (London 1933), p. 153.
37 Pilgrim Trust *Men Without Work* (Cambridge 1938), p. 137.
38 P. Kingsford *The Hunger Marches in Britain 1920–1939* (London 1982), p. 235.
39 *Yorkshire Post*, June 1934.

9 VERSAILLES, FOREIGN POLICY AND COLLECTIVE SECURITY 1918–33

1 Quoted in M.D. Dockrill and J.D. Gould *Peace without Promise: Britain and the Peace Conferences, 1919–23* (London 1981), p. 19.
2 Ibid.
3 Ibid., p. 33.
4 Ibid., p. 255.
5 E. Goldstein *Winning the Peace: British Diplomatic Strategy, Peace Planning, and the Paris Peace Conference, 1916–1920* (Oxford 1991), p. 5.
6 Ibid., p. 279.
7 Dockrill and Gould, op. cit.
8 M. Trachtenberg *Reparation in World Politics: France and European Economic Diplomacy, 1916–1923* (New York 1980), p. 46.
9 Ibid., p. 48.
10 H. Nicolson *Peacemaking 1919* (London 1934), p. 186.
11 Ibid., p. 186.
12 Ibid., p. 187.
13 A. Headlam-Morley, R. Bryant and A. Cienciala (eds) *Sir James Headlam Morley: A Memoir of the Paris Peace Conference 1919* (London 1972), p. 161.
14 Ibid., p. 162.
15 Ibid., p. 162.
16 Quoted in S.J. Lee *Aspects of European History 1789–1980* (London 1982), p. 186.
17 W.H. Dawson *Germany under the Treaty* (London 1933), ch. XIII.
18 W. Carr *A History of Germany 1815–1945* (London 1969).
19 J. Néré *The Foreign Policy of France from 1914–1945* (trans. London 1975).
20 S. Marks *The Illusion of Peace* (London 1976).
21 See F. Fischer *Germany's Aims in the First World War* (New York 1967).
22 M. Trachtenberg 'Reparation at the Paris Peace Conference', *Journal of Modern History* (1979). Also M. Trachtenberg *Reparation in World Politics: France and European Economic Diplomacy, 1916–1923* (New York 1980).

Also W.A. McDougall 'Political Economy vs National Sovereignty: French Structures for German Economic Integration after Versailles', *Journal of Modern History*, 1979.

23 A. Lentin *Guilt at Versailles* (London 1985), ch. 6.
24 J.R. Ferris 'The Greatest Power on Earth: Great Britain in the 1920s', *The International History Review*, vol. XIII, 1991.
25 Ibid.
26 Ibid.
27 Hitler *Mein Kampf* (trans. R. Mannheim, New York 1971), p. 664.
28 J.A.S. Grenville (ed.) *The Major International Treaties 1914–1973* (London 1974), p. 105.
29 *The League of Nations Official Journal, Special Supplement* no. 44, p. 51, no. 22 (1926).
30 Grenville, op. cit., p. 108.
31 Quoted in A. Farmer *Britain: Foreign and Imperial Affairs 1919–39* (London 1992), p. 40.
32 Ibid.
33 Quoted in J.C.G. Rohl *From Bismarck to Hitler* (Harlow 1970), Ch. 5, Document 1.
34 Ibid.
35 A. Lentin *Lloyd George, Woodrow Wilson and the Guilt of Germany* (Leicester 1984), p. x.
36 Quoted in ibid., p. xii.
37 W.N. Medlicott *Contemporary England 1914–1964* (London 1967), p. 149.
38 C.L. Mowat *Britain between the Wars 1918–1940* (London 1955), p. 114.

10 FOREIGN POLICY AND APPEASEMENT 1933–9

1 Quoted in R. Blake *The Unknown Prime Minister. The Life and Times of Andrew Bonar Law* (London 1955), p. 448.
2 B. Morris *The Roots of Appeasement: The British Weekly Press and Nazi Germany during the 1930s* (London 1991).
3 Ibid., p. 4.
4 Ibid., p. 6.
5 *Week-End Review*, 8 July 1933.
6 R.A.C. Parker in W.J. Mommsen and L. Kettenacker (eds) *The Fascist Challenge and the Policy of Appeasement* (London 1983), p. 22.
7 W.N. Medlicott and D. Dakin (eds) *Documents on British Foreign Policy*, second series, Vol. XII, no. 694.
8 Quoted by Parker in Mommsen and Kettenacker, op. cit., p. 24.
9 Ibid., p. 26.
10 Ibid., p. 3.
11 Ibid., p. 38.
12 Ibid., p. 8.
13 D.A. Puzzo *Spain and the Great Powers 1936–1941* (New York 1962), Conclusions.
14 Quoted in Telford Taylor *Munich: the Price of Peace* (London 1979), p. xiv.

15 A.J.P. Taylor *The Origins of the Second World War* (Harmondsworth 1963), p. 26.
16 See A.J.P. Taylor, op. cit., ch. XII.
17 R.P. Shay in Mommsen and Kettenacker, op. cit., p. 96.
18 Quoted in G. Schmidt in Mommsen and Kettenacker, op. cit., p. 108.
19 Quoted in Telford Taylor, op. cit., p. 985.
21 Quoted in R. Douglas in Mommsen and Kettenacker, op. cit., p. 83.
21 Quoted in H. Noguères *Munich: The Phoney Peace* (London 1965), p. 359.
22 Quoted in R.A.C. Parker *Chamberlain and Appeasement: British Policy and the Coming of the Second World War* (London 1993), p. 10.
23 Ibid., p. 10.
24 Telford Taylor, op. cit., xiii.
25 Ibid., p. xiv.
26 Ibid., p. 978.
27 Quoted in Noguères, op. cit., p. 375.
28 Ibid., p. 375.
29 Ibid., p. 379.
30 Ibid., p. 387.
31 A.J.P. Taylor, op. cit., p. 437, note.
32 T. Taylor, op. cit., p. xv.
33 Ibid., p. 987.
34 Parker, op. cit., p. 347.
35 Ibid.
36 Douglas in Mommsen and Kettenacker, op. cit., p. 87.
37 See W.N. Medlicott *The Coming of War in 1939* (London 1963).
38 See S. Newman *March 1939: The British Guarantee to Poland* (Oxford 1976).
39 S. Newman, op. cit., p. 218.
40 Quoted in M. Gilbert and R. Gott *The Appeasers* (London 1963), p. 290.
41 Ibid., p. 323.
42 Ibid., p. 316.
43 Quoted in ibid., p. 316.
44 Quoted in ibid., p. 346.

11 THE SECOND WORLD WAR AND ITS IMPACT

1 R. Lamb *Churchill as War Leader* (London 1993), p. 340.
2 See K. Hildebrand *The Foreign Policy of the Third Reich* (London 1973), Ch. 5.
3 A.J.P. Taylor *The Second World War* (London 1975), p. 85.
4 Lamb, op. cit., p. 348.
5 Quoted in A. Farmer *Britain: Foreign and Imperial Affairs 1939–64* (London 1994), p. 16.
6 Lamb, op. cit., p. 339.
7 Quoted in Farmer, op. cit, p. 13.
8 Quoted in T.O. Lloyd, *Empire to Welfare State: English History 1906–1976* (Oxford 1979), pp. 217–18.

9 W.S. Churchill, *The Second World War*, Vol. 1 (London 1948), p. 597.
10 Quoted in S.J. Lee *Crime, Punishment and Protest, 1450 to the Present Day* (London 1994), p. 97.
11 Ibid.
12 Quoted in R. Pope *War and Society in Britain 1899–1948* (London 1991), p. 40.
13 Quoted in P. Adelman *Britain: Domestic Politics 1939–64* (London 1994), p. 15.
14 A.R. Ball *British Political Parties: The Emergence of a Modern Party System* (London 1981), p. 138.
15 A.S. Milward *The Economic Effects of the Two World Wars on Britain* (London 1970), p. 48.
16 S. Pollard *The Development of the British Economy 1914–1967* (London 1969), p. 308.
17 Milward, op. cit., p. 26.
18 F. Clark and R.W. Toms *Evacuation–Failure or Reform?* (London 1940), p. 2.
19 H.G. Wells *The New World Order* (London 1940).
20 A. Marwick 'Two World Wars: Their Impact on Britain', *Modern History Review*, September 1990. See also A. Marwick *Britain in the Century of Total War* (London 1968), p. 125.
21 M. Bruce *The Coming of the Welfare State* (London 1961), p. 326.
22 See P. Addison *The Road to 1945* (London 1975).
23 See R.M. Titmuss *Problems of Social Policy* (London 1950).
24 See C. Barnett *The Audit of War* (London 1986).

12 THE LABOUR GOVERNMENT 1945–51

1 Quoted in L.C.B. Seaman *Post-Victorian Britain 1902–1951* (London 1966), p. 421.
2 Quoted in D. Childs *Britain Since 1945: A Political History* (London 1992), p. 45.
3 Seaman, op. cit., p. 423.
4 P. Adelman *The Rise of the Labour Party 1880–1945* (London 1986), p. 8.
5 A. Calder *The People's War: Britain 1939–1945* (London 1969), p. 577.
6 D. Dutton *British Politics Since 1945: The Rise and Fall of Consensus* (Oxford 1991), p. 16.
7 D. Howell *British Social Democracy* (London 1980), p. 159.
8 A. Shonfield *Modern Capitalism* (Oxford 1965), p. 88.
9 P. Adelman *Britain: Domestic Politics 1939–64* (London 1994), p. 34.
10 Childs, op. cit., p. 25.
11 Quoted in Sir N. Chester *The Nationalisation of British Industry 1945–51* (London 1975), p. 39.
12 *Hansard*, vol. 418, col. 738 (1946).
13 Quoted in A. Horne *Macmillan 1894–1956* (London 1988), p. 258.
14 K. Morgan *Labour in Power 1945–51* (Oxford 1984), p. 123.
15 E.J. Hobsbawm *Industry and Empire* (Harmondsworth 1969), p. 247.
16 Childs, op. cit., p. 32.

17 Quoted in P. Adelman *Britain: Domestic Politics 1939–64* (London 1994), p. 38.
18 Seaman, op. cit., p. 441.
19 Childs, op. cit., p. 31.
20 *British Medical Journal,* 1943.
21 C.J. Bartlett *A History of Postwar Britain 1945–74* (London 1977), p. 88.
22 T.O. Lloyd *Empire to Welfare State: English History 1906–1976* (Oxford 1979), p. 308.

13 THE CONSERVATIVE DECADE: DOMESTIC POLICIES 1951–64

1 Quoted in A.R. Ball *British Political Parties: The Emergence of a Modern Party System* (London 1981), p. 152.
2 Quoted in R. Garner and R. Kelly *British Political Parties Today* (Manchester 1993), p. 81.
3 Ibid., p. 82.
4 Quoted in D. Dutton *British Politics Since 1945: The Rise and Fall of Consensus* (Oxford 1991), p. 41.
5 Quoted in C.J. Bartlett *A History of Postwar Britain 1945–74* (London 1977), p. 157.
6 A. Horne *Macmillan 1957–1986* (London 1989), p. 17.
7 Quoted in P. Adelman *Britain: Domestic Politics 1939–64* (London 1994), p. 82.
8 Ibid., p. 86.
9 Quoted in W. Thompson *The Long Death of British Labourism* (London 1993), p. 65.
10 H. Macmillan *Pointing the Way 1959–61* (London 1972), p. 23.
11 T.O. Lloyd *Empire to Welfare State: English History 1906–1976* (Oxford 1979), p. 381.
12 Ibid., p. 383.
13 *Keesings Contemporary Archives* (1962), p. 22246, section A.
14 Quoted in D. Childs *Britain Since 1945: A Political History* (London 1992), p. 142.
15 Adelman, op. cit., p. 107.
16 Bartlett, op. cit., p. 210.
17 Quoted in R. Garner and R. Kelly *British Political Parties Today* (London 1993), p. 145.
18 Quoted in A. Seldon *Churchill's Indian Summer: The Conservative Government 1951–55* (London 1981), pp. 244–5.
19 M. Hill *The Welfare State in Britain* (Aldershot 1993), p. 49.
20 Ibid., p. 57.
21 Quoted in Adelman, op. cit., p. 106.
22 A. Shonfield *British Economic Policy since the War* (London 1958), quoted in Childs, op. cit., p. 101.
23 S. Brittan *The Treasury under the Tories 1951–1964* (Harmondsworth 1965), p. 136.

14 YEARS OF REFORM AND CRISIS 1964–79

1 F. Stacey *British Government 1966 to 1975: Years of Reform* (Oxford 1975), p. 1.
2 D. Childs *Britain since 1945: A Political History* (London 1992), p. 212.
3 C.A.R. Crosland *Socialism Now* (London 1974), p. 26.
4 I. Budge and D. McKay *The Changing British Political System: Into the 1990s* (London 1988), p. 10.
5 H. Wilson *The Labour Government 1964–70: A Personal Record* (London 1971), p. 5.
6 Budge and McKay, op. cit., p. 10.
7 D. Powell *British Politics and the Labour Question, 1868–1990* (London 1992), p. 125.
8 Quoted in R. Taylor 'The trade union "problem" since 1960', in B. Pimlott and C. Cook (eds) *Trade Unions in British Politics* (London 1982), p. 188.
9 D. Dutton *British Politics Since 1945: The Rise and Fall of Consensus* (Oxford 1991), p. 65.
10 Quoted in R. Rhodes James *Ambitions and Realities: British Politics 1964–70* (London 1972), p. 214.
11 Quoted in L. Tivey and A. Wright (eds) *Party Ideology in Britain* (London 1989), p. 60.
12 K. Joseph *Reversing the Trend* (London 1975), p. 4.
13 Quoted in A. King 'Politics, Economics and Trade Unions', in H.R. Penniman (ed.) *Britain at the Polls, 1979: A Study of the General Election* (Washington DC and London 1981), p. 63.
14 Dutton, op. cit., p. 70.
15 D. Coates *Labour in Power? A Study of the Labour Government 1974–1979* (London 1980), p. 2.
16 Quoted in Tivey and Wright (eds), op. cit., p. 40.
17 W. Thompson *The Long Death of British Labourism* (London 1993), p. 102.
18 I. Crewe 'Why the Conservatives won' in Penniman (ed.), op. cit., p. 264.
19 Thompson, op. cit., p. 112.
20 Crewe, op. cit., p. 282.
21 Ibid., p. 284.

15 THATCHERISM AND AFTER, 1979–95

1 D. Kavanagh and P. Morris *Consensus Politics from Attlee to Thatcher* (Oxford 1989), p. 119.
2 M. Thatcher: Answer to a comment from a member of the audience in a television programme during the 1983 general election campaign.
3 W. Thompson *The Long Death of British Labourism* (London 1993), p. 144.
4 Quoted in H. Stephenson *Mrs Thatcher's First Year* (London 1980), p. 7.
5 Quoted in M. Holmes *The First Thatcher Government 1979–1983* (Boulder, Colorado 1985), p. 199.

6 Ibid., p. 200.
7 T. Dalyell, MP *Misrule: How Mrs Thatcher Has Misled Parliament from the Sinking of the Belgrano to the Wright Affair* (London 1987), p. xviii.
8 Ibid., p. xxii.
9 Quoted in Holmes, op. cit., p. 211.
10 *The Observer*, 9 January 1983.
11 See P. Jackson 'Policy Implementation and Monetarism: Two Primers', in P. Jackson (ed.) *Implementing Government Policy Initiatives: The Thatcher Administration 1979–83* (London 1985).
12 Ibid., p. 27.
13 Ibid., p. 29.
14 Holmes, op. cit., p. 212.
15 B. Coxall and L. Robins *Contemporary British Politics* (London 1994), p. 479.
16 Quoted in J. Foreman-Peck 'The Privatization of Industry in Historical Perspective', in A. Gamble and C. Wells (eds) *Thatcher's Law* (Oxford 1989), p. 142.
17 Ibid.
18 M. Pirie *Privatisation* (Adam Smith Institute, London 1985), p. 21.
19 Coxall and Robins, op. cit, p. 479.
20 Foreman-Peck, op. cit., p. 141.
21 *Politics Today. Education: Moving into the New Era* (Conservative Research Department, July 1990), p. 260.
22 B. Pimlott 'The Audit of Thatcherism', *Contemporary Record*, Autumn 1989.
23 Ibid.
24 Ibid.
25 Thompson, op. cit., p. 155.
26 M. Durham 'Major and Morals: Back to Basics and the Crisis of Conservatism', *Talking Politics*, Autumn 1994.
27 A. McConnell 'The Crisis of Conservative Party Funding', *Talking Politics*, Vol. 7, No. 1, Autumn 1994.
28 *Labour Party, Home Affairs Committee: Political Funding Enquiry* Labour Party Submission (London 1993), Table 4.
29 Figures from F. Conley: 'The Local Elections 1995', *Talking Politics*, Vol. 8, No. 1, Autumn 1995.

16 THE SECOND CRISIS OF LABOUR 1979–92

1 Quoted in D. Childs *Britain since 1945: A Political History* (London 1992), p. 307.
2 J. Callaghan *British Trotskyism: Theory and Practice* (Oxford 1984), p. 166.
3 Quoted in ibid., p. 168.
4 Ibid., p. 171.
5 Quoted in A. Mitchell *Four Years in the Death of the Labour Party* (London 1983), p. 32.
6 D. Kavanagh *Thatcherism and British Politics: The End of Consensus?* (Oxford 1987), p. 312.

7 W. Thompson, *The Long Death of British Labourism* (London 1993), p. 116.
8 Kavanagh, op. cit., p. 169.
9 B. Gould *A Future for Socialism* (London 1989), p. 133.
10 B. Jones 'Clause Four and Blair's Brilliant Campaign', *Talking Politics*, Vol. 8, No. 1, Autumn 1995.
11 Ibid.
12 B. Bivati 'Clause for Thought', in October 1993.
13 Ivor Crewe in the *Guardian*, 17 April 1993, quoted in S. Ingle 'Is Britain a One-Party State?', *Talking Politics*, Vol. 7, Number 1, Autumn 1994.
14 Thompson, op. cit., p. 158.
15 M. Moran 'Britain: A One-Party State?', *Talking Politics*, Vol. 7, Number 1, Autumn 1994.

17 FOREIGN POLICY AND DEFENCE 1945–70

1 F.S. Northedge *Descent from Power: British Foreign Policy, 1945–1973* (London 1974), p. 357.
2 J. Frankel *British Foreign Policy 1945–1973* (London 1975), p. 1.
3 *The Times*, 6 March 1946.
4 V. Rothwell 'Britain and the First Cold War', in R. Crockatt and S. Smith (eds) *The Cold War Past and Present* (London 1987), p. 60.
5 For a detailed analysis of this and other views see S. Croft *The End of Superpower: British Foreign Office Conceptions of a Changing World, 1945–51* (Aldershot 1994).
6 G. Ross (ed.) *The Foreign Office and the Kremlin, 1941–1945: British Documents on Anglo-Soviet Relations, 1941–1945* (Cambridge 1984), p. 251.
7 A. Bullock *Ernest Bevin: Foreign Secretary, 1945–1951* (London 1983), p. 422.
8 D. Reynolds *The Origins of the Cold War in Europe: International Perspectives* (New Haven 1994), p. 79.
9 See A. Shlaim 'Britain, the Berlin Blockade and the Cold War', *International Affairs*, 60, p. 984; and Reynolds, op. cit., Ch 3.
10 Quoted in Reynolds, op. cit., p. 87.
11 Quoted in D. Carlton *Anthony Eden: A Biography* (London 1981), pp. 332–3.
12 Ibid.
13 See C.J. Bartlett *The Long Retreat: A Short History of British Defence Policy, 1945–70* (London 1972), p. 121.
14 D. Carlton *Britain and the Suez Crisis* (London 1988), p. 100.
15 S. Ambrose *Eisenhower: The President 1952–1969* (London 1984), p. 382.
16 D.R. Devereux *The Formulation of British Defence Policy towards the Middle East, 1948–56* (London 1990), p. 185.
17 See D. Carlton *Anthony Eden: A Biography* (London 1981), p. 478.
18 Selwyn Lloyd *Suez 1956: A Personal Account* (London 1978), p. 259.
19 See *Report on Defence: Britain's Contribution to Peace and Security* (London, HMSO 1958).
20 *Report on Defence: Britain's Contribution to Peace and Security.*

18 FOREIGN POLICY AND DEFENCE 1970–1995

1 M. Dockrill *British Defence since 1945* (Oxford 1988), p. 104.
2 The Central Policy Review Staff *Review of Overseas Representation* (London HMSO 1977), p. ix.
3 Quoted in P. Riddell *The Thatcher Era and its Legacy* (Oxford 1991), p. 184.
4 W. Wallace 'Foreign Policy', in D. Kavanagh and D. Seldon *The Major Factor* (London 1994), p. 286.
5 L. Freedman, in Kavanagh and Seldon, op cit., p. 269.
6 B. Jones, A. Gray, D. Kavanagh, M. Moran, P. Norton and A. Seldon *Politics UK* (Hemel Hempstead 1991), p. 587.
7 Wallace, op. cit., p. 299.

19 BRITAIN AND EUROPE SINCE 1945

1 For an analysis of this process see S.J. Lee *Aspects of European History 1789–1980* (London 1982), ch. 32.
2 S. Greenwood *Britain and European Cooperation since 1945* (Oxford 1992), p. 8.
3 Quoted in A. Bullock *Ernest Bevin: Foreign Secretary* (London 1983), p. 520.
4 Greenwood, op. cit., p. 27.
5 Quoted in S. George *Britain and European Integration since 1945* (Oxford 1991), p. 5.
6 Quoted in A. Farmer *Britain: Foreign and Imperial Affairs 1939–64* (London 1994), p. 91.
7 Quoted in M.J. Hogan *The Marshall Plan: America, Britain and the Reconstruction of Western Europe, 1947–52* (Cambridge 1989), p. 369.
8 George, op. cit., p. 42.
9 Quoted in R.C. Mowat *Creating the European Community* (London 1973), p. 148.
10 R. Lamb *The Failure of the Eden Government* (London 1987), p. 92.
11 A.S. Milward *The Reconstruction of Western Europe 1945–51* (London 1987), p. 361.
12 *Keesings Contemporary Archives*, 22246A.
13 Greenwood, op. cit., p. 73.
14 Quoted in Lee, op. cit., p. 303.
15 Quoted in S. Holt 'British Attitudes to Membership', in G. Ionescu (ed.) *The New Politics of European Integration* (London 1972).
16 George, op. cit., p. 45.
17 Quoted in M. Camps *Britain and the European Community: 1955–63* (London 1964), p. 336.
18 A. Horne *Macmillan 1957–86* (London 1989), p. 446.
19 See A. King *Britain Says Yes: The 1975 Referendum on the Common Market* (Washington DC 1977).
20 R. Jenkins *A Life at the Centre* (London 1991), p. 495.
21 A. Geddes *Britain in the European Community* (Manchester 1993), p. 91.

22 B. Hill *The European Community* (London 1991), p. 84.
23 Geddes, op. cit, p. 92.

20 THE BRITISH EMPIRE AND COMMONWEALTH IN THE TWENTIETH CENTURY

1 J.R. Ferris 'The Greatest Power on Earth: Great Britain in the 1920s', *The International History Review*, vol. XIII, 1991.
2 A. Farmer *Britain: Foreign and Imperial Affairs 1919–39* (London 1992), p. 47.
3 The Report of the Inter-Imperial Relations Committee, Imperial Conference, 1926, in A.B. Keith (ed.) *Speeches and Documents on the British Dominions 1918–1931* (Oxford 1966), p. 161.
4 The Statute of Westminster, quoted in Keith, op.cit., pp. 30–5.
5 J. Darwin *The End of the British Empire: The Historical Debate* (Oxford 1991), pp. 10–11.
6 See C. Barnett *The Collapse of British Power* (London 1972).
7 See S.J. Lee *Aspects of British Political History 1815–1914* (London 1994), Chapter 15.
8 See A.P. Thornton *The Imperial Idea and its Enemies* (London 1959).
9 See G. Wasserman *The Politics of Decolonization* (Cambridge 1976).
10 See B. Lapping *The End of Empire* (London 1986).
11 See R. Holland *European Decolonization 1918–81: An Introductory Survey* (London 1985).
12 M. Lipton and J. Firn *The Erosion of a Relationship: Britain and India since 1960* (London 1975), appendix.
13 Darwin, op. cit., p. 70.
14 W.D. McIntyre *Colonies into Commonwealth* (London 1968), p. 9.
15 A.J.R. Groom 'The Commonwealth as an International Organisation', in A.J.R. Groom and P. Taylor (eds) *The Commonwealth in the 1980s: Challenges and Opportunities* (London 1984), p. 293.

21 THE IRISH ISSUE 1914–96

1 J. O'Leary *Recollections of Fenians and Fenianism* (1896), vol. 1, p. 121.
2 *Parliamentary Debates*, 5th series, vol. 36, col. 1445.
3 I. Colvin *The Life of Lord Carson* (London 1934), vol. 2, p. 79.
4 E. Norman *A History of Modern Ireland* (London 1971), ch. 2.
5 P. Arthur and K. Jeffrey *Northern Ireland since 1968* (London 1988), p. 5.
6 *Irish News*, 7 November 1932.
7 E. McCann *War and an Irish Town* (1974).
8 D. Quinn *Understanding Northern Ireland* (Manchester 1993), p. 22.
9 Cmd 532: *Disturbances in Northern Ireland*, September 1969.
10 Quoted in Quinn, op. cit., p. 68.
11 *Irish Times*, 7 July 1975.
12 Rev. M.W. Dewar *Why Orangeism?* (London 1959).
13 S. Wichert *Northern Ireland since 1945* (London 1991), p. 69.

14 Quoted in P. Neville 'The IRA: Origins and Recent History', in *Contemporary Record*, February 1991.
15 M. Cunningham 'British Policy in Northern Ireland', in *Politics Review*, September 1992.
16 *The Economist*, 25 February–3 March 1995, p. 27.
17 Ibid., p. 27.
18 D. Spring 'The Balance of Equal Rights', in *NI Brief – A Parliamentary Brief Commentary on Northern Ireland*, London 1995, p. 7.
19 Rev. Ian Paisley 'A One-Way Street To The Republic', in *NI Brief – A Parliamentary Brief Commentary on Northern Ireland*, London 1995, p. 50.

22 EQUAL OPPORTUNITIES AND WOMEN'S RIGHTS IN TWENTIETH-CENTURY BRITAIN

1 *Parliamentary Debates*, Fifth Series, 26 March–27 April 1917.
2 S. Lewenhak *Women and Work* (London 1980), p. 193.
3 Ibid., p. 193.
4 Ibid., p. 194.
5 Quoted in E.M. Meehan *Women's Rights at Work: Campaigns and Policy in Britain and the United States* (London 1985), p. 64.
6 A. Marwick *War and Social Change in the Twentieth Century* (London 1974), p. 16.
7 H. Smith 'The effect of the war on the status of women', in H. Smith (ed.) *War and Social Change: British Society in the Second World War* (Manchester 1986).
8 A. Carter *The Politics of Women's Rights* (London 1988), p. 10.
9 C. White *Women's Magazines: 1963–1968* (London 1970), p. 142.
10 Carter, op. cit., p. 27.
11 Carter, op. cit., p. 47.
12 Carter, op. cit., p. 38.
13 G. Greer *The Female Eunuch* (London 1971).
14 Carter, op. cit., pp. 84–5.
15 See S. Pennington and B. Westover *A Hidden Workforce: Homeworkers in England, 1850–1985* (London 1989), p. 155.
16 S. Dex and L.B. Shaw (eds) *British and American Women at Work* (London 1986), p. 124.
17 N. Folbre *Who Pays for the Kids? Gender and the Structures of Constraint* (London and New York 1994), p. 258.
18 IEA Health and Welfare Unit *Equal Opportunities: A Feminist Fallacy* (London 1992), Introduction (by Caroline Quest), p. 2.

23 IMMIGRATION, RACE RELATIONS AND THE PLURAL SOCIETY

1 T.E. Smith *Commonwealth Migration: Flows and Policies* (London 1981), p. 91.
2 Z. Layton-Henry *The Politics of Immigration* (Oxford 1992), p. 8.

3 Ibid., p. 31.
4 S. Saggar *Race and Politics in Britain* (Hemel Hempstead 1992), p. 121.
5 E. Powell *No Easy Answers* (London 1974), pp. 98–9.
6 See Layton-Henry, op. cit.
7 *Independent*, 9 October 1990.
8 A. Carter *The Politics of Women's Rights* (London 1988), p. 91.
9 Ibid., p. 107.
10 S. Pennington and B. Westover *A Hidden Workforce: Homeworkers in England, 1850–1985* (London 1989), p. 161.

24 PRIMARY SOURCES FOR BRITISH POLITICAL HISTORY 1914–95

1 M. Cole (ed) *Beatrice Webb's Diaries 1912–24* (London 1952).
2 *Lord Riddell's War Diary* (London 1933), p. 4.
3 Harold Nicolson *Peacemaking 1919* (London 1933).
4 D. Lloyd George *War Memoirs* (London 1934), p. 539.
5 Earl of Oxford and Asquith *Memories and Reflections* (London 1928).
6 L.S. Amery *My Political Life*, Vol. II, p. 483.
7 H. Macmillan *Winds of Change, 1914–39* (London 1966), p. 285.
8 M. Thatcher *The Downing Street Years* (London 1993), p. 860.
9 Siegfried Sassoon *Memoirs of an Infantry Officer* (London 1932), p. 192.
10 Quoted in S. Constantine *Unemployment Between the Wars* (London 1980), Document 21, p. 100.
11 G. Wilkinson 'Sources: Newspapers', *Modern History Review*, November 1991.

SELECT BIBLIOGRAPHY

This section is intended to make a selection from the works used in compiling this book to introduce the reader to further study. It is not in any way intended as an exhaustive bibliography of books available on twentieth-century Britain.

GENERAL WORKS

1914–45

The best overall work is still A.J.P. Taylor *English History 1914–1945* (Oxford 1965). Also most lucid are L.C.B. Seaman *Post-Victorian Britain 1902–1951* (London 1966) and W.N. Medlicott *Contemporary England 1914–1964* (London 1967, 1978 edition). More recent is M. Beloff *Wars and Welfare: Britain 1914–1945* (London 1984). With roots firmly in the earlier period, but not entirely justifying the promise of its title is R. Rhodes James *The British Revolution: British politics 1880–1939* (London 1978). There are several excellent detailed studies of the inter-war period. The classic account is provided in C.L. Mowat *Britain between the Wars 1918–1940* (London 1955, 1964 edition). More recent – and interpretative – are G. Peele and C. Cook (eds) *The Politics of Reappraisal 1918–1939* (London 1975); A. Thorpe *Britain in the 1930s: The Deceptive Decade* (Oxford 1992); and R. Pearce *Britain: Domestic politics 1918–39* (London 1992).

1945–95

There are fewer general books on the period since 1945. Among the most informative are C.J. Bartlett *A History of Postwar Britain 1945–74* (London 1977); D. Childs *Britain Since 1945: A political history* (London 1992); and P. Adelman *Britain: Domestic Politics 1939–64* (London 1994). The theme of consensus politics since 1945 is covered in D. Dutton *British Politics Since 1945: The Rise and Fall of Consensus* (Oxford 1991) and D. Kavanagh and P. Morris *Consensus Politics from Attlee to Thatcher* (Oxford 1989). More detailed

410

periods are covered by F. Stacey *British Government 1966 to 1975: Years of Reform* (Oxford 1975); R. Rhodes James *Ambitions and Realities: British Politics 1964–70* (London 1977); I. Budge and D. McKay *The Changing British Political System: Into the 1990s* (London 1988); and B. Coxall and L. Robins *Contemporary British Politics* (London 1994). The last of these is the best of a large number of general titles on current British politics.

POLITICAL PARTIES

General works on the development of parties include A. Beattie *English Party Politics, Vol. II* (London 1970) and A.R. Ball *British Political Parties: The Emergence of a Modern Party System* (London 1981, 1987 edition). A more recent perspective is provided in R. Garner and R. Kelly *British Political Parties Today* (Manchester 1993), while a more theoretical approach can be seen in L. Tivey and A. Wright (eds) *Party Ideology in Britain* (London 1989).

The original classic on the Labour party is H. Pelling *A Short History of the Labour Party* (London 1961, 1982 edition). More recent publications are: C.F. Brand *The British Labour Party* (Stanford, California 1974); P. Adelman *The Rise of the Labour Party 1880–1945* (London 1972, 2nd edn 1986); and G. Phillips *The Rise of the Labour Party 1893–1931* (London 1992). More detailed analysis can be found in R.W. Lyman *The First Labour Government 1924* (New York 1957); K. Morgan *Labour in Power 1945–51* (Oxford 1984); and D. Coates *Labour in Power? A Study of the Labour Government 1974–1979* (London 1980). The Labour crisis is dealt with effectively in W. Thompson *The Long Death of British Labourism* (London 1993).

Good overall surveys of the Liberal party are C. Cook *A Short History of the Liberal Party 1900–92* (London 1993) and P. Adelman *The Decline of the Liberal Party 1910–1931* (Harlow 1981). Two classics in interpretation are G. Dangerfield *The Strange Death of Liberal England* (London 1966) and T. Wilson *The Downfall of the Liberal Party 1914–35* (London 1966). Ideas are covered in M. Bentley *The Liberal Mind, 1914–1929* (Cambridge 1977) and the period of the First World War is dealt with in M. Swartz *The Democratic Control in British Politics during the First World War* (Oxford 1971).

The best overall study of the Conservative party is still R. Blake *The Conservative Party from Peel to Thatcher* (London 1985). Other titles include: H. Stephenson *Mrs Thatcher's First Year* (London 1980); M. Holmes *The First Thatcher Government 1979–1983* (Boulder, Colorado, 1985); A. Gamble and C. Wells (eds) *Thatcher's Law* (Oxford 1989); P. Riddell *The Thatcher Era and its Legacy* (Oxford 1991); and D. Kavanagh and D. Seldon *The Major Factor* (London 1994).

LEADING POLITICAL FIGURES

Considerable insight can be gained from a number of contemporary sources, including B. Webb *Diaries, Vol. II* (London 1952); H. Dalton *The Fateful Years: Memoirs 1931–1945* (London 1947); P. Snowden *Autobiography Vol. II* (London 1934); H. Macmillan *Pointing the Way 1959–61* (London 1972); H.

411

Wilson *The Labour Government 1964–70: A Personal Record* (London 1971); and R. Jenkins *A Life at the Centre* (London 1991). Biographies include D. Marquand *Ramsay MacDonald* (London 1977); A. Morgan *J. Ramsay MacDonald* (Manchester 1987); S.R. Ward *James Ramsay MacDonald: Low Born Among the High Brows* (New York 1990); K. Young *Stanley Baldwin* (London 1976); R. Lamb *Churchill as War Leader* (London 1993); A. Bullock *Ernest Bevin: Foreign Secretary* (London 1983); E. Estorick *Stafford Cripps* (London 1949); D. Carlton *Anthony Eden: A Biography* (London 1981); and A. Horne *Macmillan 1894–1956* (London 1988).

ECONOMIC AND SOCIAL DEVELOPMENTS

Introductory books on the economy are W. Ashworth *An Economic History of England 1870–1939* (London 1960) and E.J. Hobsbawm: *Industry and Empire* (Harmondsworth 1969), the latter integrating economic and political developments. The best overall coverage of the twentieth-century economy is in S. Pollard *The Development of the British Economy 1914–1967* (London 1969); G.A. Phillips and R.T. Maddock *The Growth of the British Economy 1918–1968* (London 1973); and R. Floud and D. McCloskey (eds) *The Economic History of Britain since 1700, vols 2 and 3* (Cambridge 1994). The period 1918–39 is lucidly analysed in D.H. Aldcroft *The British Economy between the Wars* (London 1983) and D.H. Aldcroft *The Inter-War Economy: Britain 1919–1939* (London 1973); a more detailed and complex analysis is provided in S.N. Broadberry *The British Economy between the Wars: A Macroeconomic Survey* (Oxford 1986). The best explanations of the impact of total war are in A.S. Milward *The Economic Effects of the Two World Wars on Britain* (London 1970); C. Barnett *The Audit of War* (London 1986); and A. Marwick *Britain in the Century of Total War* (London 1968). Social aspects of World War II are covered in R. Pope *War and Society in Britain 1899–1948* (London 1991) and A. Calder *The People's War: Britain 1939–1945* (London 1969).

Industrial problems are dealt with in G.C. Allen *The Structure of Industry in Britain* (London 1966), while the debate behind government management of the economy can be found in R. Middleton *Towards the Managed Economy: Keynes, the Treasury and the Fiscal Policy Debate of the 1930s* (London 1985) and A. Booth *British Economic Policy, 1931–49: Was there a Keynesian Revolution?* (Hemel Hempstead 1989). Unemployment and social problems are covered in D.H. Aldcroft *Full Employment: The Elusive Goal* (London 1984); S. Constantine *Social Conditions in Britain 1918–1939* (London 1983); B.W.E. Alford *Depression and Recovery? British Economic Growth 1918–1939* (London 1972); and P. Kingsford *The Hunger Marches in Britain 1920–1939* (London 1982). There is much valuable material in A. Hutt *The Condition of the Working Class in Britain* (London 1933).

TRADE UNIONS AND INDUSTRIAL RELATIONS

The original classic was G.D.H. Cole and R. Postgate *The Common People 1746–1946* (London 1938, 1961 edition). More recent publications include B. Pimlott and C. Cook (eds) *Trade Unions in British Politics* (London 1982); H.A. Clegg *A History of British Trade Unions since 1889, Vol. II 1911–1933* (Oxford 1985); R. Pearce *Britain: Industrial Relations and the Economy 1900–1939* (London 1993); R. Martin *TUC: The Growth of a Pressure Group 1868–1976* (Oxford 1980); J. Lovell *British Trade Unions 1875–1933* (London 1977); A. Briggs and J. Saville (eds) *Essays in Labour History* (London 1960); and D. Powell *British Politics and the Labour Question, 1868–1990* (London 1992).

Among the numerous books on the General Strike, I found the most useful to be: W.H. Crook *General Strike* (London 1931); R.A. Leeson *Strike: a Live History* (London 1973); R.H. Haigh, D.S. Morris and A.R. Peters *The Guardian Book of the General Strike* (Aldershot 1988); S. Nearing *British General Strike* (New York 1926); J. Symons *The General Strike* (London 1957), and G. Phillips *The General Strike* (London 1976).

EXTERNAL RELATIONS

The most concise compilation of primary sources is J.A.S. Grenville (ed.) *The Major International Treaties 1914–1973* (London 1974). All the general works mentioned in the first section cover foreign policy as a matter of course. Two titles, however, focus specifically on this area and provide an excellent introduction: A. Farmer *Britain: Foreign and Imperial Affairs 1919–39* (London 1992), and A. Farmer *Britain: Foreign and Imperial Affairs 1939–64* (London 1994).

The post-war settlement is covered in M.D. Dockrill and J.D. Gould *Peace without Promise. Britain and the Peace Conferences, 1919–23* (London 1981); E. Goldstein *Winning the Peace: British Diplomatic Strategy, Peace Planning, and the Paris Peace Conference, 1916–1920*; and A. Lentin *Lloyd George, Woodrow Wilson and the Guilt of Germany* (Leicester 1984). More controversial is M. Trachtenberg *Reparation in World Politics: France and European Economic Diplomacy, 1916–1923* (New York 1980). Primary sources worth locating are H. Nicolson *Peacemaking 1919* (London 1934), and A. Headlam-Morley, R. Bryant and A. Cienciala (eds) *Sir James Headlam Morley: A Memoir of the Paris Peace Conference 1919* (London 1972).

The transition from collective security to appeasement is dealt with in S. Marks *The Illusion of Peace* (London 1976). More detailed areas are covered in B. Morris *The Roots of Appeasement. The British Weekly Press and Nazi Germany during the 1930s* (London 1991) and J. Edwards *The British Government and the Spanish Civil War, 1936–1939* (London 1979). The controversy relating to Chamberlain's policy is covered in detail in Telford Taylor *Munich: the Price of Peace* (London 1979); A.J.P. Taylor *The Origins of the Second World War* (Harmondsworth 1963); and R.A.C. Parker: *Chamberlain and Appeasement: British Policy and the Coming of the Second World War* (London 1993); while the descent into war is the focus of W.N. Medlicott *The Coming of War in 1939* (London 1963) and S. Newman *March 1939: The British Guarantee to*

Poland (Oxford 1976). A lucid overall survey of the period is M. Gilbert and R. Gott *The Appeasers* (London 1963).

British foreign policy after World War II is dealt with in F.S. Northedge *Descent from Power: British Foreign Policy, 1945–1973* (London 1974) and J. Frankel *British Foreign Policy 1945–1973* (London 1975). A more detailed analysis is provided in S. Croft *The End of Superpower: British Foreign Office Conceptions of a Changing World, 1945–51* (Aldershot 1994) and G. Ross (ed.) *The Foreign Office and the Kremlin, 1941–1945: British Documents on Anglo-Soviet Relations, 1941–1945* (Cambridge 1984). An excellent analysis of Britain's changing priorities is provided in M. Dockrill *British Defence since 1945* (Oxford 1988); an earlier survey was C.J. Bartlett *The Long Retreat: A Short History of British Defence Policy, 1945–70* (London 1972). The best single work on the 1956 crisis is D. Carlton *Britain and the Suez Crisis* (London 1988); more detailed is D.R. Devereux *The Formulation of British Defence Policy towards the Middle East, 1948–56* (London 1990, p. 185).

There are four lucid general accounts of Britain's relations with Europe. These are: S. Greenwood *Britain and European Cooperation since 1945* (Oxford 1992); S. George *Britain and European Integration since 1945* (Oxford 1991); A. Geddes *Britain in the European Community* (Manchester 1993); and B. Hill *The European Community* (London 1991). More detailed studies of earlier periods are M.J. Hogan *The Marshall Plan: America, Britain and the Reconstruction of Western Europe, 1947–52* (Cambridge 1989); R.C. Mowat *Creating the European Community* (London 1973); and A.S. Milward *The Reconstruction of Western Europe 1945–51* (London 1987).

By far the best recent work on the British Empire is J. Darwin *The End of the British Empire: The Historical Debate* (Oxford 1991). Specific areas of debate and interpretation are covered in C. Barnett *The Collapse of British Power* (London 1972); G. Wasserman *The Politics of Decolonization* (Cambridge 1976); B. Lapping *The End of Empire* (London 1986); R. Holland *European Decolonization 1918–81: An introductory survey* (London 1985); and M. Lipton and J. Firn *The Erosion of a Relationship: Britain and India since 1960* (London 1975). The modern Commonwealth is the focus of A.J.R. Groom and P. Taylor (eds) *The Commonwealth in the 1980s: Challenges and Opportunities* (London 1984).

Finally, three books can be recommended for an overview of twentieth-century Ireland: E. Norman *A History of Modern Ireland* (London 1971); P. Arthur and K. Jeffrey *Northern Ireland Since 1968* (London 1988); and D. Quinn *Understanding Northern Ireland* (Manchester 1993).

INDEX

abdication, Edward VIII 80
Abortion Act (1967) 215, 345
Abse, Leo 215
Abyssinia, Italian invasion 143,
    147–50
Acheson, Dean 13, 202
Act of Union (1800) 10
Adams, Gerry 285, 331
Addison, P. 178, 401
Adelman, P. 41, 52, 98, 393, 396
aerial warfare: First World War 25;
    Second World War 167–9, 171;
    Spanish Civil War 152
affluence, inter-war years 126
Africa, British Empire 304, 306, 308
Agricultural Marketing Act 98
agriculture: minimum wage 176;
    reforms 50
aircraft production, post-Munich 154,
    161
Aldcroft, D.H. 109, 113, 116, 118,
    122–3, 397
Alford, B.W.E. 121, 124
Aliens Act (1905) 351
Aliens Restriction Act (1914) 351
Aliens Restrictions Act (1919) 351
'all-Ireland' policy 334–7
Allenby, Viscount 24
Alliance, SDP/Liberal 248–9, 255
Amin, Idi 351
Amritsar massacre (1919) 309
Anglo-German Naval Agreement
    (1935) 152
Anglo-Irish Agreement (1985) 334
Anglo-Irish Treaty (1921) 326–7
Anglo-Soviet Treaty (1921) 141
Anschluss (1938) 152, 163

appeasement policy (1933–9) 81, 137,
    139, 144–65
Arab–Israeli War, third 220
Argentina, Falklands War 280
arms reductions, MacDonald 97–8
Ashworth, W. 102, 396
Asian minorities, immigration 351
Asquith, H.H. 41–3, 44, 48, 50–2,
    55, 57; First World War 21,
    26–8, 46; General Strike 89; Ireland
    32, 322, 323; women's suffrage 36,
    339
Astor, Lady 340
Atkins Committee 341
Atkins, Humphrey 334
Atlantic Alliance 264
Attlee, Clement 72, 107–8, 183, **184**,
    193; 1950 general election 192;
    administration 7, 18, 261; post-war
    government 176; Second World
    War 171–2, 174
Australia, tariffs 79
Austria, Credit Anstalt collapse 100
autobiographies, primary sources
    362–4

'back to basics' campaign (1993) 244
Baghdad Pact (1955) 267
balance of payments 35, 208
Baldwin, Stanley 52, 54, 55, **71**, 103,
    104; administration 138;
    appeasement 144–5, 147, 151–3;
    Conservative ascendancy 68–81; free
    trade 50; General Strike 4, 82, 85–7,
    92–3, 95; gold standard 121; Lloyd
    George 29; moderation 128; Soviet
    Union 142; Spanish Civil War 151;

speeches 367, 369; women's suffrage 340
Balfour, Arthur James 60
Balfour Declaration (1917) 310
Balfour Declaration (1926) 307
ballots, trade unions 237
Bank of England, 1931 crisis 100, 104
Barnett, C. 178, 312, 401, 407
Bartlett, C.J. 193, 402
Basildon, new Toryism 227
Battle of Britain 154, 167–8, 172
BBC 75, 91, 93
Beaverbrook, Lord 26
Belgium 21, 145
Beloff, M. 57, 66, 394
Benn, Tony (Anthony Wedgwood) 224–5, 250, 253, 284, 313
Berchtesgaden agreement 157
Berlin Wall 202
Bevan, Aneurin 189–91, 193, 200
Beveridge Report (1942) 6, 177–8, 180, 182, 190
Beveridge, William 175
Bevin, Ernest 61, 87, 183, 193, 289, 290; General Strike 86, 87, 94–5; NATO 264; prescription charges 192; Second World War 171, 174
Birkenhead, Lord 88
Bivati, B. 257, 405
black women, double disadvantage 358–9
Blair, Tony 8, 239, 256–7, 259, 369
Blake, George, spy conviction 203
'Bloody Sunday' 223
Boards, nationalised enterprises 187–8
Boards of Guardians, local government 77
Bohemia, Nazi invasion 162
Bolsheviks 61, 63–4, 140–1, 150
bombing: Second World War 167–9, 171; Spanish Civil War 152
Bonar Law see Law, Andrew Bonar
Bonham, F.R. 73
Booth, A. 124
Boothby, Robert 77
Bosnia 285
Bow Group 196
Bramley, F. 87
Brand, C.F. 58, 394
Brandt, Willie 295
Briand, Aristide 286

British Broadcasting Company/Corporation see BBC
British Communist party 66
British Empire 10, 12, 14, 304–19
British Expeditionary Force 22
British Federation of Business and Professional Women 345
British Iron and Steel Federation 122
British Medical Association (BMA) 190–1
British Overseas Airways Corporation (BOAC) 81
British Rail 236
British Shipping (Assistance) Act (1935) 122
British Union of Fascists 127, 351, 355
Brittan, S. 208, 403
broadcasting, primary sources 368
Brockway, Fenner 313
Bruce, M. 177–8, 401
Brussels Treaty (1948) 286–7, 289, 291
Budge, I. 219, 403
budget, EEC 298
Bullock, A. 262, 405
Butler, R.A. 60, 181, 197–8, 203, 207
'Butskellism' 16
Butt, Isaac 322

cabinets, Second World War 172–3
Calder, A. 182
Callaghan, James 7–9, 18, **219**, 248, 251; administration 214, 222–3; devaluation 218; EEC membership 298; leadership 226; monetarism 234; nuclear defence 278; premiership 211; 'Winter of Discontent' 233
Cameron Commission (1968) 328
Campaign for Nuclear Disarmament (CND) 200, 251
Campbell case 64–5
Campbell, J.R. 64
Canada, tariffs 79
Carr, W. 135
Carter, Jimmy (James Earl) 285
cartoons, primary sources 369–83, **372–83**
Catholic discrimination, Stormont government 328–9
Catholicism, Northern Ireland 332–3

Cavell, Edith 26
censorship 173, 215
Central Electricity Board 75, 122–3
central government, Thatcher
    administration 239–41
Central Powers: defeat 22; First World
    War 25
Chamberlain, Austen 63, 75, 129,
    137–9, 143, 156
Chamberlain, Joseph 55, 74, 79, 262,
    316
Chamberlain, Neville 56, 75–6, 78–9,
    81, 121; appeasement 137, 144,
    147, 150, 149, 161–4; collective
    security 139; General Strike 86;
    Munich policy (1938) 6, 153–64;
    Second World War 27, 167, 171–3;
    Soviet Russia 142–3
Chanak crisis, Ottoman Empire 29,
    55, 307
Chichester-Clark, James 329–30, 333
child allowances 76
Childs, D. 190, 401
Christian churches, General Strike
    89–90
Church of England, abdication crisis
    80
Churchill, Winston 6, 16, 28, 138,
    170, 401; 1945 election 179–82,
    183; administration 261;
    anti-appeasement 157–60, 165;
    Baldwin 72–3; Britain's post-war
    role 262, 264; European integration
    290; French army 166–7; General
    Strike 86, 88, 91; gold standard 75,
    110; immigration 351; India 78,
    309; 'Iron Curtain' speech 263;
    premiership 195, 209; Russian
    Revolution 141; social services 206;
    speeches 165, 172, 263, 368–9;
    Suez Crisis 266; war leadership 169,
    171–4; welfare state 197
Citrine, W.M. 87
civil defence, Second World War 173
civil rights, Northern Ireland 329–30
Civil Service: reforms 212, 214;
    Thatcher administration 238,
    239–40; women 347
civil war, Ireland 326
Clause Four, removal 256–7
Clegg, H.A. 58, 85, 94, 394, 395

Clemenceau, Georges 130, 133, 136
Clinton, President Bill 285
Clynes, J.R. 56–7
coal industry 81–5, 88–9, 94, 98, 122,
    216; decline 114, 118; exports 83–4;
    nationalisation 188
Coal Mines Act (1930) 98, 122
Coal Mines Act (1938) 81
Coalition governments 27, 58, 68
coalition politics, First World War
    26–7
Coates, D. 225, 403
Cold War 9–10, 202, 263, 265, 276,
    313, 314; end 284; Suez Crisis 270
Cole, G.D.H. 30, 102, 396
collective security 135–40, 144–5,
    147–8, 155
Colonial Laws Validity Act (1865) 307
Colonial Office 308
Committee for European Economic
    Co-operation (CEEC) 290
Committee for Imperial Defence
    (CID) 154
Common Agricultural Policy (CAP)
    297
Common Market 292–3, 296; see also
    European integration
Commonwealth 10, 14, 19, 304–19,
    317; EEC membership 289–90,
    294–8; immigration 216, 350, 352,
    358
Commonwealth Immigrants Act
    (1962) 352
Commonwealth Immigrants Act
    (1968) 216, 358
Communism 64, 65, 108, 151, 284
competition, British inter-war industry
    113
Conciliation and Arbitration Service
    (ACAS) 220
conscientious objection, Second World
    War 173
conscription: First World War 22, 26,
    27, 43; Ireland 325; Second World
    War 173
consensus: break-up 223–5, 228, 240;
    immigration 353–4; political 14–19;
    revival 229; social 19–20
Conservatism, moderate 70
Conservative governments: domestic
    policies (1951–64) 195–210;

European integration 287; General Strike 82; missed opportunities 77; policies (1951–64) 205–9; women 347

Conservative party 2, 4, 7–8, 28–9, 32, 55; 1931 crisis 104–5; 1945 election 181–3; 1951 revival 193–4; ascendancy 68–81, 195–200, 211; consensus politics 15–19; decline 201–5; EEC membership 296; Falklands War 255; First World War 31, 46; foreign policy (1970s) 277; immigration 351–2; membership decline (1990s) 244; nationalisation 188; protectionism 51; right wing 246; scandals 243; Second World War 174–5; state education 60; strength (1980s) 253; women's support 348

controls, immigration 351–3
Cook, A.J. 88
Cook, C. 41, 393
Corn Laws 74; repeal 55, 104, 108
Cosgrave, W.T. 326–7
Costello, John 327
Cotton Industry (Reorganisation) Acts (1936, 1939) 122
cotton textiles industry, collapse 114, 118
Council of Europe (1949) 286
council house sales 241, 252, 254
counties, local government 77
Craig, James 326
Credit Anstalt, collapse 100
Crewe, I. 227, 403
Cripps, Stafford 106, 185–6, 193
crises years (1964–79) 218–28
Crosland, C.A.R. 218, 403
Crowe, Sir Eyre 130
Cuba Missiles Crisis (1962) 202, 274
Curtis, Lionel 316
Curzon, Lord 28, 31, 43, 129
Czechoslovakia 131, 145, 153–5, 157

Dail Eireann 325
Daily Express 384
Daily Herald 384
Daily Mail 384
Daily Mail printers' strike 86–7
Daily Mirror 384
Daily Telegraph 384

Dalton, Hugh 106, 108, 183, 185, 263
Dangerfield, G. 42, 393
Dardanelles campaign 24
Darwin, J. 311, 314, 407
Davies, Clement 188
Dawes Plan (1924) 62, 84
Dawson Report (1920) 191
Dawson, W.H. 135
De Gaulle, Charles 202, 275, 295–7, 311
de Valera, Eamon 325, 327
death penalty, abolition 215
decolonisation 10–11, 14, 311–15
defence (1945–70) 261–75
defence (1970–95) 276–85
Defence of the Realm Act (1914) 26, 28, 46
Delors, Jacques 299
demobilisation, First World War 36, 37
Democratic Labour Party 58
Democratic Unionist Party (DUP) 331–2, 335
Depression (1930s) see Great Depression
devaluation, (1931) 104
devaluation (1967) 218
Devereux, D.R. 270, 405
Devlin, Bernadette 330
devolution 214
diaries, primary sources 361–4
disarmament 61
discrimination: racial 355–6, 358–9; sexual 343; Stormont government 328–9
disease, inter-war years 127
Disraeli, Benjamin 312
Disraeli conservatism 78
divorce law, reform 215–16
Divorce Reform Act (1969) 345–6
Dockrill, M.D. 130, 133
Dockrill, M.L. 129
dole 79, 126
dollar, world dominance 110
Dominions 80, 306–7, 310
Douglas-Home, Alec, premiership 195, 203, **204**, 209
Dunkirk Treaty 289
Dunkirk withdrawal 161, 166–7, 171
duties, import 79
Dutton, D. 182, 224–5, 401, 403

Easter Uprising, Ireland 32, 324, 325
eastern Europe, Locarno Pact 139
Economic Advisory Council (1930) 99
economy: British decline 12–14;
   changes (1919–39) 109–13;
   Conservative policies (1951–64)
   205–9; downturn (1960–2) 201;
   EEC membership 300; First World
   War 33–5; infrastructure changes
   (1919–39) 113–18; inter-war
   109–28; Labour policies (1945–51)
   183, 185–7; post-Second World
   War 176, 185–7, 199, 207;
   post-war decline 292–4; Second
   World War 175–8
Eden, Anthony: appeasement 152;
   European integration 287, 291;
   premiership 195, 197, **198**, 209;
   Second World War 172; Suez Crisis
   266–70
education 189, 192, 206, 237, 343–4
Education Act (1870) 60
Education Act (1902) 60
Education Act (1918) 29, 35
Education Act (1944) 60, 189, 192,
   206
Edward VIII, abdication 80
Edwardian Liberalism 39
Egypt, Suez 267–8, 310
Eisenhower, Dwight D. 266, 274, 285
El Alamein, German defeat 169
elections 65–7, 227; *see also* general
   elections
electrical manufacturing industry
   117–18
Electricity Supply Act (1926) 75
Elizabeth II 318
Elton, G.R. 1
Emergency Powers Act (1920) 61, 85,
   93
Emergency Powers (Defence) Act 173
Empire 73, 79; collective security 146;
   European integration 290, 292, 294;
   Treaty of Versailles 136
employment, women 339, 343
Employment Act (1980) 237
Employment Act (1982) 237
Employment Act (1988) 237
Employment Act (1990) 237
enfranchisement, women 20, 36, 39,
   41, 75–6, 338–9

equal opportunities 216, 338–49,
   358–9
Equal Opportunities Commission
   (1975) 216, 346, 358
equal pay 341, 343, 345–6
Equal Pay Act (1979) 346
ethnic minorities 350
ethnicity: consensus 19; traditions 357
Europe between the wars (map) **132**
European Atomic Energy Community
   (Euratom) 286–7, 291
European Coal and Steel Community
   290
European Coal and Steel Community
   (ECSC) 286–7, 291, 295, 312
European Community (EC) 248, 251,
   254, 287, **288**
European Economic Community,
   French veto 270–1
European Economic Community
   (EEC) 286–7, 289, 292, 295–6,
   312; Britain's entry 277; British
   membership 9–10, 18, 202, 220,
   274, 294, 296–303; economic and
   monetary union 299; referendum
   215; two-track Europe 303
European elections (1995) 245
European Free Trade Association
   (EFTA) 287, 292, 294, 296
European integration 286–303
European Regional Development Fund
   (ERDF) 298
European Union 242, 284, 349
evacuation, Second World War 173,
   177
Exchange Rate Mechanism (ERM)
   244, 300–2

fascism, British policy 150
Factory Act (1937) 81
Falklands War: Commonwealth 316;
   defence cuts 276
Falklands War (1982) 8–9, 13, 232,
   279–82, 392
Family Allowances Act (1945) 189,
   342
Family Planning Act (1967) 215
Faulkner, Brian 330
Fawcett Society 344
feminism 20, 345
Fenians 322

Ferris, J.R. 136, 304, 407
Fianna Fail party 327
fighter production, Battle of Britain 167
finance: First World War 34–5; women's rights 343–4
Fine Gael party 327
First World War 2, 3–6, 21–37; Britain's post-war position 135–6; consensus 15; economic change 78; Empire 305–6; Irish question 325; Labour breakthrough 54; Liberal party decline 42–9; map *23*; mines 85; peace settlement 109, 129; social changes 69; social impacts 35–7; women's employment 339
Fischer, F. 135
Fitzgerald, Garret 334
Fontainebleau Summit (1984) 299
Foot, Michael 8, 18, 225–6, 282; Labour party leadership 248, 251–4; leadership 253–4; speeches 369
foreign affairs, Cold War 202
foreign policy 5–6, 8–10; appeasement (1933–9) 144–65; MacDonald administration 97, 99; Nazi 139
foreign policy (1918–33) 129–43
foreign policy (1945–70) 261–75
foreign policy (1970–95) 276–85
Foreman-Peck, J. 235, 236, 404
Forster, William Edward 60
France: Anglo-French *Entente* 21; decolonisation 311–12, 315; Depression 79; EEC membership 296–7, 301, 303; Empire 305; European integration 286–7, 289–91, 295; fall of 166, 168; First World War 22; frontier security 145; inter-war alliances 136–7, 140, 142; Ruhr occupation 62–3, 64, 84; Spanish Civil War 151; Suez Crisis 270–1; Treaty of Versailles 131
Franco-Czechoslovak Treaty (1925) 158
Franco-Soviet Pact (1935) 142
Frankel, J. 261, 405
free enterprise 224
free trade 50, 55
Free Trade Area (FTA) 291–2, 294, 300

Freeman, John, prescription charges 192
French, Sir John 22
French Resistance 171
French Union 316
Friedman, Milton 224, 233
fuel, VAT imposition 244
Fulton Report (1968) 212–14

Gaitskell, Hugh 7, 8, 16, 18, 205, 257; economic policy 185–6; EEC membership 293, 296; immigration 352; leadership 200; NHS 193; nuclear deterrent 274; premiership 197–8
Galtieri, Leopaldo 232, 233, 241, 279–80
Gandhi, Mahatma 309
Geddes Axe (1922) 29, 60
gender 19–20, 216, 314, 338–49, 358–9
general elections: 1906–10 31, 38, **40**, 48; 1910 31; 1918 27, 32, 38, 46, **48**, 48–9, 48, 53; 1922–9 38, 50–1, 55, **56**, 97, 99; 1931–5 38, 50–1, 80, **101**, 105; 1945 38, 128, 179–83, **180**; 1950–1 192–4; 1955–64 **196**, 209–10, 211, 222, 274; 1966–74 **212**, 221–2; 1979–92 211, 222, 225–8, **230**, 245–7, 254; 1995 245; suspension 31
General Strike (1926) 4, 15, 29, 82–96, 110, 121; Amery 363; Baldwin 72; causes 83–7; effects 94–6; failure 4, 75, 91–3; Government measures 76, 92–3
Geneva Protocol (1924) 63, 145
George, S. 291, 406
George V 103, 361
Germany 12; British appeasement 146, 148, 152; colonies 305; declaration of war (1939) 162–4; Depression 79; eastern frontiers 145; economy (1924) 62; EEC membership 303; European integration 293–5; fighter production 167; First World War 2, 5, 22; inter-war rehabilitation 137–8; invasion of Belgium 21; production techniques 83; rearmament 147;

reparations 62–4, 97, 131–4; reunification 301, 336; revisionism 137, 139, 145; rise of Hitler 98; Second World War defeats 169; Soviet Union 142; Spanish Civil War 151–2; stock market speculation (1929–31) 111; Treaty of Versailles 131, 138–9; Weimar Republic 32

gerrymandering, Stormont government 328, 329

Gibbs, Sir Philip 89

Gilbert, M. 164, 400

Gilmour, Ian 232

Gladstone, Herbert 54

Gladstone, William Ewart 104–5, 322–3

Goering, Hermann 167

gold reserves, First World War 35

gold standard 75, 79, 83, 103, 110

Goldstein, E. 130–1

Gordon-Walker, Patrick 352

Gorman, Teresa 244

Gorst, J.E. 73

Gott, R. 164, 400

Gould, Brian 254–5

Gould, J.D. 129, 130, 133

Government of India Act (1919) 309

Government of Ireland Act (1920) 326

government policy, inter-war 109–28

government powers, First World War 25–6

Great Depression 79, 115, 147, 363; British recovery 111, 113; Liberal party 53; political instability 106, 146

Greater London Council (GLC) 240

Greece, fall of 169

Greenwood, Arthur 98, 174

Greenwood, S. 289, 294, 406

Greenwood, Walter 126

Greer, Germaine 344–5, 408

Grenada, US invasion 282

Grey, Sir Edward 21

Griffith, Arthur 324, 326

Griffiths, James 190

Groom, A.J.R. 316, 407

gross domestic product (GDP) 14, 124–5, 207, 279, 301

gross national product (GNP) 292

The Guardian 384, 385

Guernica, German bombing 159

Gulf War (1991) 242, 256, 283

Hadow Committee 60

Hailsham, Lord 198, 203

Haldane, Viscount 57, 61

Halifax, Lord 144, 164

Hansard 367

Harare Declaration (1991) 318

Hattersley, Roy 226

Hatton, T. 119, 397

Hayek, F.A. 224, 233

Healey, Denis 220, 225, 234, 251–3, 274

health services, nationalisation 189

Heath, Edward 7–9, 16, 18, 198, **217**; administration 214, 216, 219–20; consensus 224–5; EEC membership 202, 277, 287, 295–8, 302; immigration 353, 354–5; Ireland 333; miners' strike 233; premiership 211; trade unions 216

Henderson, Arthur 57, 97, 129, 164

Herriot, Edouard 62–3

Heseltine, Michael 242, 246, 283

Hitler, Adolf 6, 80, 106, 131, 139, 146; British appeasement 152, 164; Chamberlain 156; *Mein Kampf* 136; Munich (1938) 153; Nazi invasions 161–4; rise to power 142–3; U-boat campaign 168; war strategy 167

Hoare, Samuel 144, 148, 151

Hoare–Laval Pact (1935) 81, 148–9

Hobsbawm, E.J. 190

Hodgkinson, George 87

Holland, R. 313, 407

Holmes, M. 234, 404

Home, Lord *see* Douglas-Home, Alec

Home Rule, Ireland 10–11, 104–5, 108, 322–6

Home Rule Bill (1912) 32

homosexuality 215

honours: Conservative party 245; sale of 55

House of Lords 39, 41, 76, 187, 215

Housing Act (1919) 36

Housing Act (1924) 58

Housing Act (1930) 98

Housing Acts, 1923 74

Howard, Michael 244

Howarth, Alan 246

Howe, Geoffrey 242, 299
Huddleston, Trevor 354
Hume, John 331
hunger marches 127
Hurd, Douglas 242
Hurricane fighter 167
Hussein, Saddam 283
Hutt, Allen 126

immigration 11, 20, 350–9
Immigration Act (1971) 216
imperial tariff barrier 79
Imperial War Cabinet, German
    reparations 133
Import Duties Act (1932) 79, 121–2
In Place of Strife White Paper (1969)
    221
Incitement to Mutiny Act 64
income tax 234
independence, Ireland 320–33
The Independent 385
Independent Labour Party (ILP) 108
India: colonisation 304, 306, 309;
    immigrants 350; independence 309,
    312, 319
India Bill 78
industrial economy 50
industrial relations 29, 36, 52, 94–5,
    221, 223
Industrial Relations Act (1971) 216,
    221
Industrial Revolution 83, 113
industry: British decline 113–14;
    economic infrastructure 109; First
    World War 33–4; inefficiency 83,
    113; modernisation lack 208–9; new
    115–17, 119; post-Second World
    War 176, 186–7; production
    (1919–21) 109–10; Second World
    War damage 176
inflation 220, 222, 234
integration: European 286–9;
    immigrants 354–8
international diplomacy, MacDonald
    government 62
International Monetary Fund (IMF)
    220
invasion force (1944) 169
Invergordon Mutiny 121
investments, First World War 35
Ireland: Act of Union (1800) 320;

all-Ireland solution 334; civil war
    326; Commonwealth 318–19;
    consensus politics 19; Home Rule
    10–11, 32, 39, 41, 104–5, 108,
    322–6; Liberal Governments 30;
    nationalism 322–3; republicanism
    322, 324–7, 330–7; resolution
    attempts 333–6; secession 69;
    twentieth century **321**
Irish Free State 308, 320, 326
Irish National Liberation Army (INLA)
    331
Irish Nationalists 11, 47, 69, 322–3,
    324, 325
Irish Republican Army (IRA) 32, 322,
    324–7, 330–7
Israel: Suez Crisis 270; US support 272
Italian campaign, Second World War
    169
Italy: Abyssinia invasion 143, 147,
    148–50; fascist regime 32; Spanish
    Civil War 150–1

Jackson, P. 239, 404
Japan: Manchuria invasion 147, 148;
    Second World War 171, 306;
    shipbuilding restrictions 97–8
Jarrow: hunger marches 127;
    unemployment 126
Jenkins, Roy: chancellorship 218–19;
    EEC membership 299; race
    relations 355; Whitehouse
    declaration 248
Jewish immigrants 350, 351
Jewish persecution, Nazis 162
Joseph, Keith 224–5, 235, 348, 403
Joynson-Hicks, William 76, 86, 88,
    340

Kamenev, Lev Borisovich 141
Kavanagh, D. 250, 405
Kellogg–Briand Pact (1928) 138, 145
Kennedy, John F. 202, 274
Kennedy, Joseph 164
Kent, J. 263
Kenya, Asian expulsions 352–3, 355
Kenyatta, Jomo 351
Keynes, J.M. 100, 104; gold standard
    75; industrial reconstruction 51,
    120; May Committee 102; Treaty of
    Versailles 130, 134, 146

Keynesian economics 79, 120, 123–4, 176, 233–4
Kilbrandon Commission 214
Kinnock, Neil 8, 18–19, 252, 254–6, 260
Kitchener, Lord 22
Korean War (1951) 193, 207, 264, 271
Krushchev, Nikita 202, 392

Labour governments: 1924 54–67, 71; 1929–31 97; 1945–51 75, 179–94; European integration 287
Labour party 3–8, 32; 1930s electoral revival 106–8; 1945 election 181–3; 1951 defeat 193–4; anti-racism 357; between the wars 68–9; consensus politics 15–19; crises 97–108, 247–60; defence expenditure (1974) 277; economic policies (1945–51) 183, 185–7; EEC membership 296, 298; finances 106; First World War 30–1, 46–7; General Strike 88, 89, 95–6; growth 39, 41–2, 48–9, 51; immigration 352–3; internal divisions 199–200, 252; left wing 224–5, 248–50, 254; long-term prospects 257–60; revival 203, 205, 242, 253; rise 54, 67; Second World War 174; Stanley Baldwin 73; state education 60; women's movement 346; Zinoviev Letter 141
Labour Party Conference (1979) 250
Labour Party Conference (1980) 248
Lamb, R. 166, 169, 172, 400
Lamont, Norman 244
Lansbury, George 105, 108
Lapping, B. 313, 407
Law, Andrew Bonar 28, 43, 46, 55, 70–1, 74; appeasement 145–6; protectionism 50; Versailles Treaty 130
law and order 227
Lawrence, T.E. 24
Lawson, Nigel 232
Layton-Henry, Z. 351
League of Nations 63, 97, 137; collective security 137–8, 144, 148–50; Disarmament Conference (1933) 147; Treaty of Versailles 131
Lebensraum 143

legal profession, General Strike 90
legislation, EEC 302
lend-lease, Second World War 175–6
Lenin, Vladimir Ilyich 141
Lentin, A. 135, 139
Lewenhak, S. 339–40, 408
Liberal Democrat party 19
Liberal governments 29–32; First World War 26–7
Liberal party 15–16, 18, 20, 55–7; Alliance 248; anti-racism 357; decline 2–4, 38–53, 67, 70, 107, 194; EEC membership 296; General Strike 89; nationalisation 188; proportional representation 222; Second World War 175; state education 60; welfare state 76–7, 190
Liberal Unionist party 49
Liberal–SDP Alliance 248–9, 255
Lilley, Peter 244
living standards 205–6
Lloyd George, David 26–31, 45, 73–4, 100, 108, 129–33; Chanak crisis 55, 307; Coalition government 15, 57, 68, 106, 179; economic policy 120–1; First World War 43; General Strike 89; Ireland 324, 326; Liberal decline 48–53; memoirs 362; Russian Revolution 140–1; Versailles Treaty 129–33; women's suffrage 338
Lloyd, T.O. 201–2, 402
local government 214, 240, 245, 302
Local Government Act (1929) 77
Local Government Act (1972) 214
Locarno Pact (1925) 63, 137–9, 142, 145, 147, 148
Loebl, H. 124, 397
Lomé Convention (1975) 298
London Conference (1924) 62
London Transport 61
Lords Reform, White Paper (1968) 215
Luftwaffe 159, 167
Lusitania, sinking 24
Luxembourg Agreement (1966) 295
Lyman, R.W. 66, 394

Maastricht Treaty 299–302, 303
McCann, Eamonn 330

McDonald, G. 93, 395
MacDonald, Ramsay 15, 41, 52, 74, 80, 96; 1929–39 Labour crisis 97–108; 1931 crisis 121; appeasement 144–5, 147; British foreign policy 129; collective security 146–7; expulsion from Labour party 103; First World War 30, 362; General Strike 86, 88, 89; moderation 128; National government 71, 78, 111; premiership 54, 57–8, 59, 60–5, 67; Soviet Union 141–2
McDougall, W.A. 135
McKay, D. 219, 403
Mackenzie King, William 306–7
Macleod, Iain 198, 313
Macmillan, Harold 7, 16–18, 72, 77, 402; Cuba Missiles Crisis 274; economic policies 207–8; EEC membership 292–4, 296; memoirs 363; premiership 195, 197–9, 198, 200–3, 209, 231; speeches 369
Maginot Line 158, 166
Maitland, Sir Arthur Steel 88
Major, John 17, 19, 243; all-Ireland policy 334; Civil Service 240; EEC membership 299–300; foreign policy 283–5; government 259; leadership 242–4, 256; Margaret Thatcher's memoirs 363; Post Office privatisation 236; premiership 229, 245
Manchuria, Japanese invasion 147, 148
manpower reductions, Thatcher administration 237
market forces, Keynesian economics 120
marketing boards, establishment 98
Marks, S. 135
Marquand, D. 61–2, 394
Married Women's Property Act (1882) 338
Marshall Plan (1948) 185, 263, 264, 286, 290
Marwick, A. 177, 178, 342, 401, 408
Marxism 247, 249–51
Mason, Roy 333
Matrimonial Proceedings and Property Act (1970) 346
Maudling, Reginald 198, 207–8, 333

Maxwell, Robert 384
May Committee (1931) 5, 100, 102–4
Mayer, Anthony 242
means test, introduction 123
media, General Strike 91
Medicott, W.N. 63, 163
memoirs, primary sources 362–4
Mendès-France, Pierre 311
Mental Health Act (1959) 206
Messina Conference (1955) 291
Middle East 266, 310; see also Suez Crisis
Militant Tendency 240, 249–50, 254
Milward, A.S. 35, 175, 293, 401, 406
miners: General Strike 82–5, 88, 89, 94; strikes 216, 220–1, 232–3, 238
minimum wage 26, 176
mining industry see coal industry
monarchy, abdication crisis 80
monetarism 17, 233–4, 236, 237, 238
monetary union 301
Monnet, Jean 290–1
Montgomery, Bernard Law 169
morality debate, Conservative party 244
Moran, M. 259, 405
Morgan, A. 103, 396
Morgan, K. 188, 401
Morley, Headlam 130
Morrison, Herbert 174, 183, 193
Mosley, Oswald 100, 127, 351, 355
motor industry 116–19, 186–7
Mowatt, C.L. 58, 63, 74, 91, 394
Munich Conference (1938) 6, 167
Murdoch, Rupert 384
Mussolini, Benito 32, 81, 150

Napoleonic War 168
Nasser, Gamel 13, 267
National Assistance Act (1948) 189
National Economic Development Council (NEDC) 201
National Executive, Labour party 107
National Front 20, 356–8
National governments 4–5, 15–16, 71–2, 79, 105–7; 1931 crisis 100–4, 121, 147; 1935 80; democratic threat 128
national grid 75
National Health Insurance 76
National Health Service (NHS) 6, 16,

36, 190–1, 209, 214; immigrant labour 350–1; Thatcher administration 237–8
National Health Service Reorganisation Act (1973) 214
National Health Service White Paper (1944) 182
National Health Services Act (1946) 189
National Incomes Commission (NIC) 201
National Insurance Acts 123, 190–1
National Insurance Industrial Injuries Act (1946) 189
National Service Act (1939) 173
National Unemployed Workers Movement (NUWM) 127
National Unemployment Assistance Board 123
National Union of Mineworkers (NUM) 221
National Union of Railwaymen (NUR) 88
nationalisation 6, 61, 248, 251; Clause Four 256–7; health service 190; Labour government (1945–51) 187–9; Labour party 200; mines 84; reversal 236–7
nationalism, growth of 314–15
Nationality Act (1981) 353–4
NATO see North Atlantic Treaty Organisation
naval warfare, First World War 24–5
Nazi Germany 9; anti-Jewish pogroms 162; appeasement 146; foreign policy 139; Jewish refugees 351; Soviet Union 142
Nazi–Soviet Non-Aggression Pact (1939) 143, 160
neo-Keynesianism 17, 185, 224
Nere, J. 135
Netherlands, decolonisation 311–12, 315
New Deal, United States 80
new industries, inter-war 115–17, 119
New Towns Act (1946) 189
Newman, S. 163, 400
News of the World 384
Newsom Report 344
newspapers, primary sources 383–5
Nicholson, Emma 246

Nicolson, Harold 130, 133, 146; memoirs 362
Nixon, Richard 278
non-interventionism 80
Norman, E. 325, 407
North African campaign, Second World War 168–9
North America, colonisation 304
North Atlantic Treaty Organisation (NATO) 10, 200, 262, 264, 273, 284; 1974 Defence Review 278; Bevan 200; Falklands War 281; France 271, 295; inception 286–7, 289–91
North–South harmony 313
Northedge, F.S. 261, 405
Northern Ireland 223–4, 320, **321**, 326–33
Northern Ireland Civil Rights Association (NICRA) 329
Norway, fall of 169
Nott, John 233
novels, primary sources 387
nuclear defence 251, 278
nuclear disarmament 248, 254
nuclear power 13

Obscene Publications Act (1959) 388
O'Connell, Daniel 320
Office of Gas Supply (OFGAS) 236
Office of Water (OFWAT) 236
official documents, primary sources 364–6
Official Secrets Act (1911) 214; primary sources 364, 365, 391
Official Unionist Party (OUP) 331–2, 335
OFGAS see Office of Gas Supply
OFWAT see Office of Water
Oil Petroleum Exporting Countries (OPEC) 220
Old Age Pensions Act (1908) 76
Ombudsman, introduction 214
O'Neill, Terence 329–30, 332
OPEC, Yom Kippur War 277
'Operation Sealion' 167
Organisation of European Economic Co-operation (OEEC) 286–7, 290
Orwell, George 126, 174, 390–1
Ottawa Conference (1932) 79
Ottoman Empire 2; Chanak crisis 29

Owen, David 226, 248, 255
Oxford University, degrees for women 341

Pacific: British Empire 304, 306, 308; Second World War 171
pacifism 46, 97
Paisley, Ian 331–2, 335, 408
Palestine 310, 312, 319
Pankhurst, Sylvia 339
Parker, R.A.C. 146, 148
Parliament Act (1911) 323
Parliament Act (1949) 187
Parmoor, Lord 57, 61
Parnell, Charles Stewart 322
party system, suspension of 100–3
peace settlement, Versailles 1919–20 129–35, 146
Pearce, R. 124, 397
Pearl Harbor, Second World War 161, 171
Pearse, Padraic 324
Peel, Robert 55, 104–5, 260
Pelling, H. 98, 396
Pensions Act (1925) 76
The People 384–5
Philby, Kim, defection 203
Phillips, G. 62, 86, 394, 395
Phipps, Sir Eric 147
Pimlott, B. 241, 404
Pirie, M. 235, 404
pluralism 350–9
pogroms, anti-Jewish 162
Poincaré, Raymond Nicolas Landry 62–3
Poland: 1939 invasion 143; frontier security 145, 162–3, 164; German non-aggression pact 155; Nazi invasion 162, 164; Treaty of Versailles 131
Polaris nuclear weapons 13, 297
Polish immigrants 350
politics, women 347
poll tax 242
Pollard, S. 91, 117
polls, public opinion 245, 256
Pompidou, Georges 297
Poor Law 60
Portillo, Michael 246
Portland spy scandal 203
Portugal, Salazar regime 151

Post Office, privatisation failure 236
Postgate, R. 102, 396
potato famine, Ireland 320
poverty: inter-war years 126–7; Thatcher administration 237
Powell, D. 221, 403
Powell, Enoch 224, 331, 353–4, 369
power, operation of 1–2
power-sharing, Northern Ireland 333–4
Prayer Book, revisions 76
Presbyterian Central Assembly, General Strike 90
Price Commission and Pay Board (1973) 216
Priestley, J.B. 126
primary sources, British political history 360–92
Prime Ministers 1908–95 3
Prior, James 232, 334
Private Eye 205
privatisation 17, 254; coal mines 29; Thatcher administration 234–6, 238
professions, women 340
Profumo affair 203
propaganda: General Strike 93; Second World War 174
proportional representation 222, 247
protectionism 50–2, 55, 74, 121–2
Protestantism, Northern Ireland 332–3
Provisional Sinn Fein 331
Public Order Act (1937) 128
public sector, efficiency 238
public sector borrowing requirement (PSBR) 236
Pugh, Arthur 87
Punch, cartoons 372–3, 377, 379–82
Pym, Francis 232

Quinn, D. 330, 408
quotas, immigration 351

race relations 11, 20, 350–9
Race Relations Act (1965) 352, 355
Race Relations Act (1968) 356
Race Relations Act (1976) 216, 356
Race Relations Board 355, 356
Rackmanism 202–3
radio, 1924 election campaign 65, 75
rating system 214
Reagan, Ronald 283

rearmament 81, 113, 153–4, 162
Redcliffe-Maud Report 214, 240
Redmond, John 322
Redwood, John 244, 246
Rees, Merlyn 226, 333
referendum, EEC membership 298
reforms, Thatcherite 233
reforms (1964–79) 211–28
Reith, John 91
religious intolerance, Ulster 328–9, 332
rent strikes 58
reparations, Germany 131–4
Representation of the People Act (1918) 4, 31, 32, 47–9, 69, 338
Representation of the People Act (1928) 76, 78, 340
Representation of the People Act (1948) 193, 194
Representation of the People Act (1969) 215
republicanism, Ireland 322, 324, 331
reserves, First World War 35
revisionism, Germany 137, 139
revolution, Ireland 320–33
Reynolds, D. 264, 405
Rhineland: demilitarisation 131; occupation 97; remilitarisation 143, 152
Rhodes James, R. 62, 80, 394
Riddel, Lord, diaries 361–2
riots: inner cities 232, 357–8; race 355
Ripon, Geoffrey, EEC membership 295
Robbins Committee Report 206
Rodgers, William 226; Whitehouse declaration 248
Romania, frontier security 163
Rome–Berlin Axis (1936) 152
Rommel, Field Marshall Erwin 169
Roosevelt, Franklin Delano: Second World War 171–2; Yalta 263
Royal Air Force (RAF) 154, 161, 167
Royal Commission on National Health Insurance (1926) 191
Royal Navy: Defence Review (1981) 279–80; numerical superiority 136, 167–8; post-Munich consolidation 161
Royal Ulster Constabulary 329
Russia: Dardanelles campaign 24; First

World War 5; Nazi invasion 171; Second World War 168, 172; Spanish Civil War 150–1; see also Soviet Union
Russian Revolution 32, 143, 144–1

St John Stevas, Norman 232
Salisbury, Lord 312–13
Samuel Commission, General Strike 82, 85, 87, 92
Samuel, Herbert Louis 88
Sandys White Paper (1957) 9, 13, 275
Sankey Report (1919) 85
Sassoon, Siefried, memoirs 363–4
Scargill, Arthur 233, 238, 246
Schlieffen Plan 22
Schonfield, A. 185, 401
Schuman Plan 291
Scotland, devolution 214, 223
Scottish National Party (SNP) 223
Scouller, R.E. 88
Seaman, L.C.B. 73, 76, 77, 86
seapower, British 24
second front, Europe 169
Second World War 6, 10, 14, 25, 26; British successes 168; consensus 16; declaration 162–4; economic impacts 185–6; European unity 286; Irish neutrality 327; outbreak 142; political impacts 172–5; social impacts 175–8; women's rights 342
Seear, Baroness 345
Selwyn Lloyd, economic policies 207–8
Sevres Protocol, Suez Crisis 270
sex discrimination 216, 341, 343, 346
Sex Discrimination Act (1975) 216, 346
Sex Disqualification (Removal) Act (1919) 341
Sexual Offences Act (1967) 215
Shay, R.P. 154
Shinwell, Emmanuel 186, 188, 197
shipbuilding industry, decline 115, 118
Shonfield, A. 208, 402
sickness benefit 76
Silverman 215
Simon, Viscount 89, 144
Singapore, fall of 169
Sinn Fein 11, 47, 69, 322–7, 331–4, 336–7; ceasefire 335–7; Easter

Uprising 32; Gerry Adams 285;
   Westminster representation 325
slum clearance 58, 98
slum dwellings, inter-war years 127
slump (1931) 98
Smith, Adam 234
Smith, H. 342, 408
Smith, John 8, 256
Snowden, Philip 57, 60, 66, 79, 100,
   121
social class, consensus 19–20
Social Democratic Federation 58
Social Democratic and Labour Party
   (SDLP) 331, 332, 334
Social Democratic Party (SDP) 8,
   248–9, 253, 255
social legislation, EEC 302
social policies, Conservative
   administration (1951–64) 205–9
social reforms (1945–51) 189–92
social reforms (1964–79) 215
social security legislation 76, 346
Social Security Pensions Act (1975)
   346
social welfare cuts, Thatcher
   administration 237
socialism 199–200, 247, 250–1, 255
Socialist Workers' Party (SWP) 357
Soviet Union 9, 13, 64, 66, 305;
   British antagonism 263; British
   inter-war relations 129, 140–3; Cold
   War 202; French détente 295; Nazi
   invasion 161, 168; superpower
   status 313–14
sovereignty, EEC membership 302
Spanish Civil War (1936–9) 147, 148,
   150–2
Special Areas Act (1934) 79, 122
Special Areas (Amendment) Act (1937)
   122
speeches: Churchill 165, 172, 263,
   368–9; primary sources 366–9
Spitfire fighter 167
Spring, Dick 335
spy scandals (1960s) 203
Stacey, F. 212, 403
Stalin, Joseph 142–3, 171
Stalingrad, German defeat 169
Stanley, Oliver 77
starvation, inter-war years 127
state education 60

state pensions 76
statistics, primary sources 385
Statute of Westminster (1931) 10, 307
Steel, David 215
steel industry: inter-war years 115, 118;
   nationalisation 187, 188
Stephens, James 322
stereotypes, women 348
sterling, decline 110
Stockholm Convention (1959) 292
Stopes, Dr Marie 126
Stormont assembly 223, 320, 328
Strandmann, P. von 135
Strasbourg Summit (1979) 299
Stresemann, Gustav 137, 137–9, 145
strikes 61, 227; General Strike (1926)
   82–96; legislation 76, 216; miners
   (1973) 220–1, 232–3, 238; seamen
   218; Thatcher administration 235
strikes (1924) 61
submarine warfare, First World War
   24–5
Sudeten crisis (1938) 152–3, 154–6,
   159
Suez Canal Company, nationalisation
   267
Suez Crisis (1956) 9, 13, 16, 197–9,
   209, 261, 391; British decline
   295–6, 314; criticism 18; impact
   266–72
suffrage 75, 338–9; see also
   enfranchisement; women's suffrage
suffragettes 39, 41, 339, 345
The Sun 384
Swartz, M. 46, 47

tariffs 74, 79, 316
taxation, indirect 234
Taylor, A.J.P. 74, 76, 394; Asquith 43;
   Chamberlain 153; Depression 125;
   General Strike 95; MacDonald 58;
   Second World War 169, 400;
   Versailles Treaty 129, 139
Taylor, Teddy 244
Taylor, Telford 157, 159
Thatcher, Margaret 8, 9, 17, **243**,
   255–6, 403; administration 226;
   Civil Service 214; EEC
   membership 287, 289, 299, 302–3;
   Falklands War 13; immigration
   353–4; Ireland 334; memoirs 363;

new radicalism 224–5, 228; premiership 211, 229–46, 252–3, 276, 279–83; speeches 369; unpopularity 242; women's opportunities 347–8
Thatcherism 229–46, 246, 250, 258, 259
Theatres Act (1968) 215
Third World 14, 298
Thomas, J.H. 88
Thompson, W. 225, 231, 251, 403, 404, 405
Thorneycroft, Peter, economic policies 207–8
Thornton, A.P. 312, 407
three-day week (1973) 221
The Times 27, 72, 384–5
Today 384, 385
Trachtenberg, M. 133, 135
trade 34–5, 109; EEC membership 300
Trade Disputes Act (1906) 90
Trade Disputes Act (1927) 76, 94–5
Trade Union Act (1984) 237
trade unions 39, 54, 65, 76, 220–1, 248–9; EEC social legislation 302; First World War 47; General Strike 94–6; legislation 76, 216; Liberal Governments 30; reform 253, 255; rights 251; Social Contract 220; Thatcher administration 235, 237–9, 255; women workers 339–40, 342, 343
Trades Union Congress (TUC) 4; General Strike 82, 84–9, 91–3
Trades Union Council (TUC) 100, 108, 221–2
transport, economic infrastructure 109
Transport and General Workers' Union (TGWU) 61
treaties, primary sources 366
Treaties of Rome (1957) 286–7, 291
Treaty of Brussels 290
Treaty of Locarno 155
Treaty of London (1839) 21
Treaty of Maastricht (1992) 287
Treaty of Versailles 5, 25, 129–36, 143, 305; collective security 138–9; German reparations 133–5; justice of 146
Trevelyan, C.P. 57, 60

Trimble, David 335
Trotsky, Leon 141, 249
Trotskyism 249–50, 254
Truman, Harry S. 266
Turkey, First World War 24, 25
'two nations', inter-war years 125–7
two-party system 211

U-boats, Second World War 168
Ulster 320, 323, 324–8, 330; Westminster rule 330
Ulster Defence Force (UDF) 332
Ulster Unionists 323–32, 334–5
unemployment 51, 52, 60, 77, 222, 227; inter-war years 112, 118–28; MacDonald administration 98–101; post-First World War 36–7; Thatcher administration 237, 238
Unemployment Act (1934) 80, 123
unemployment benefit 76, 79
Unemployment Insurance Act (1920) 36
Unemployment Insurance Act (1927) 77
Unemployment Insurance Act (1930) 123
Unemployment Insurance Acts (1924) 60
Union of Democratic Control (UDC) 46–7, 144
United Nations 267–8, 281, 315
United States 9, 10, 12, 263; Britain's post-war role 266; Cold War 202; competitive strength 136; Depression 79; European integration 296; First World War 24; foreign policy 278; French relations 295, 297; Korean War 264, 271; New Deal 79; Pearl Harbor 161; production techniques 83; Second World War 168, 169, 171–2; stock market speculation (1929–31) 111; Suez Crisis 267; superpower status 313–14; Treaty of Versailles 129–31; Wall Street crash 99, 110, 147

Versailles Treaty *see* Treaty of Versailles
Vichy France 169
Victorian values, Thatcher 230–1

wages 82, 86, 248
Wales, devolution 214, 223
Wall Street Crash 4, 99, 110, 147
Wallace, W. 283
Walters, Alan 232
war debts, First World War 35
Wasserman, G. 313, 407
Water Act (1973) 214
water privatization 236
Watergate Crisis 278
Webb, Beatrice 62, 361
Weimar Republic 32, 139, 142
welfare state 6–7, 16, 76–7, 209, 312;
    Conservative government 197;
    development 124, 176–8, 189–92;
    Northern Ireland 329; Thatcher
    administration 16, 18, 236–7
Wells, H.G. 177, 401
West Indies 306, 308, 350
Westland affair 232
Wheatley, J. 57–8
Whigs 2–3, 104–5, 260
Whitehouse declaration (1981) 248
Whitelaw, William 333
Widows, Orphans and Old Age
    Contributory Pensions Act (1925)
    76
Williams, Shirley 226, 248
Wilson, Harold 7–9, **213**, 248, 257,

403; administration 214–16, 218;
    EEC membership 287, 296, 298;
    foreign policy 274; immigration
    352–3, 354; Labour leadership 203,
    209–10; leadership 205; premiership
    211; prescription charges 192;
    speeches 369; trade unions 221–2
Wilson, Thomas Woodrow 130
'Winter of Discontent' 222, 226, 233
women: employment 339–40; equal
    rights 338–49; equality 11; House
    of Commons 340; Members of
    Parliament 340–1; suffrage 20, 30,
    36, 39, 41, 75–6, 338–9
women's liberation 344–5
Women's Social and Political Union
    (WSPU) 36
working class: Conservative swing
    (1979) 226; depoliticisation 106;
    embourgeoisement 252, 258
working hours regulation 61

Yalta 263
Yom Kippur War (1973) 277
Young, George 244
Young Plan (1929) 97

Zinoviev, Grigoriy 141
Zinoviev Letter 15, 51, 65–6, 141